Psychology
and Christianity

Psychology and Christianity:

Integrative Readings

Editors

J. Roland Fleck
and **John D. Carter**

Abingdon
Nashville

PSYCHOLOGY AND CHRISTIANITY: INTEGRATIVE READINGS

Copyright © 1981 by Abingdon

Library of Congress Cataloging in Publication Data
Main entry under title:
Psychology and Christianity.
  Bibliography: p.
  Includes index.
  1. Christianity—Psychology—Addresses, essays,
lectures.   I. Carter, John D.   II. Fleck, J. Roland,
1942- .
BR110.P78   261.5'15   81-7911   AACR2

ISBN 0-687-34740-8

MANUFACTURED BY THE PARTHENON PRESS AT
NASHVILLE, TENNESSEE, UNITED STATES OF AMERICA

C O N T E N T S

List of Contributors... 9
Introduction... 15

SECTION ONE
Introduction to Integration............................... 24

Chapter 1. Perspectives on the Integration of Psychology
and Theology.. 27
S. Bruce Narramore

Chapter 2. The Pulpit and the Couch.....................................46
Gary R. Collins

Chapter 3. The Task Ahead: Six Levels of Integration of
Christianity and Psychology...............................54
Robert E. Larzelere

Chapter 4. Dimensions of Personal Religion:
A Trichotomous View.....................................66
J. Roland Fleck

SECTION TWO
Models of Integration...................................... 81

Chapter 5. Secular and Sacred Models of Psychology
and Religion...83
John D. Carter

Chapter 6. The Nature and Scope of Integration: A Proposal..... 97
John D. Carter and Richard J. Mohline

Chapter 7. Behavior Modification of the Spirit........................ 112
Paul W. Clement

SECTION THREE
Maturity: Christian and Psychological................ 121

Chapter 8. Sin and Maturity... 124
David J. A. Clines

Chapter 9. Holiness and Health: An Examination of the
            Relationship Between Christian Holiness
            and Mental Health...140
            Eric J. Cohen
Chapter 10. Personality and Christian Maturity: A Process
            Congruity Model.. 148
            John D. Carter
Chapter 11. Self-Actualization and Sanctification.......................161
            James A. Oakland
Chapter 12. Intimacy and Spiritual Growth............................. 171
            Clark Barshinger

SECTION FOUR
            Religious Understanding and Thought................178

Chapter 13. The Development of Religious Concepts and Maturity:
            A Three-Stage Model..................................... 180
            J. Roland Fleck, Stanley N. Ballard, and
            J. Wesley Reilly
Chapter 14. The Teaching of Religious Concepts:
            A Three-Stage Model..................................... 190
            Stanley N. Ballard and J. Roland Fleck
Chapter 15. The Teachings of Jesus and Piaget's Concept
            of Mature Moral Judgment.............................200
            Bonnidell Clouse
Chapter 16. Kohlberg's Theory of Moral Development
            and the Christian Faith....................................211
            Dan Motet
Chapter 17. Conversion Experience, Belief System, and
            Personal and Ethical Attitudes...........................216
            Raymond F. Paloutzian, Steven L. Jackson,
            and James E. Crandall

SECTION FIVE
            Counseling and Therapy.................................. 228

Chapter 18. Jesus' Style of Relating: The Search for a Biblical
            View of Counseling.......................................231
            David E. Carlson
Chapter 19. Guilt: Three Models of Therapy...........................247
            S. Bruce Narramore
Chapter 20. Cognitive Theory/Therapy and Sanctification:
            A Study in Integration....................................254
            David Pecheur
Chapter 21. The Therapist and Christian Client in Relationship.. 275
            Anonymous

SECTION SIX

Human Sexuality...281

Chapter 22. Psychosexuality: A Three-Dimensional Model..........284
John H. Court and O. Raymond Johnston

Chapter 23. Homosexuality: Christian Ethics and Psychological
Research...295
Ted D. Evans

Chapter 24. Understanding Homosexual Behavior and
Life-Styles Clinically and Religiously...................301
John M. Vayhinger

Chapter 25. Christian Perspectives on the Treatment of
Sexual Dysfunction...317
James R. David and Francis C. Duda

SECTION SEVEN

Christianity and Psychological Theories.............324

Chapter 26. The Value of Freud's Illusion..............................327
Floyd Westendorp

Chapter 27. On the Place of Religion in the Thought
of Viktor Frankl...337
John J. Shea

Chapter 28. A Christian Client Considers Carl Rogers...............348
Joan L. Jacobs

Chapter 29. God and Behavior Mod: Some Thoughts Concerning
the Relationships Between Biblical Principles
and Behavior Modification...............................356
Rodger K. Bufford

Chapter 30. The Origins of Religion in the Child......................368
David Elkind

SECTION EIGHT

Popular Christian Psychologies..........................377

Chapter 31. Popular Christian Psychologies: Some Reflections.....379
Gary R. Collins

Chapter 32. Adams' Theory of Nouthetic Counseling................386
John D. Carter

Chapter 33. The Psychology of Gothard and Basic Youth
Conflicts Seminar..402
John D. Carter

Chapter 34. Biblical Counseling: A Basic View.......................414
Lawrence J. Crabb, Jr.

Index..427

LIST OF CONTRIBUTORS

BALLARD, STANLEY N. *Title:* Professor and chairman, department of psychology, Cedarville College, Cedarville, Ohio. *Degrees:* Diploma, Moody Bible Institute; Th.B. Baptist Theological Seminary; Th.M. Dallas Theological Seminary; M.S., Ph.D. North Texas State University. *Specializations:* Counseling psychology; integration of psychology and theology.

BARSHINGER, CLARK. *Title:* Associate professor, Trinity College, Deerfield, Illinois, and co-director, Barrington Counseling Associates, Barrington, Illinois. *Degrees:* B.A. The King's College, Briarcliff Manor, New York; M.Div. McCormick Theological Seminary; M.A. DePaul University; Ph.D. Northwestern University. *Specialization:* Counseling psychology.

BUFFORD, RODGER K. *Title:* Associate professor and director of counseling service and training, Psychological Studies Institute, Atlanta, Georgia. *Degrees:* B.A. The King's College, Briarcliff Manor, New York; M.A., Ph.D. University of Illinois. *Specializations:* Clinical psychology; behavioral psychology.

CARLSON, DAVID E. *Title:* Associate professor and chairman, department of sociology, Trinity College, Deerfield, Illinois and co-director, Barrington Counseling Associates, Barrington, Illinois. *Degrees:* M.A. Northern Illinois University; M.Div. Trinity Evangelical Divinity School; M.S.W. University of Chicago. *Specializations:* Psychotherapy; integration of psychology and theology.

CARTER, JOHN D. *Title:* Professor of psychology, Rosemead Graduate School of Professional Psychology, La Mirada, California. *Degrees:* A.B. Wayne State University; B.D. Conservative Baptist Theological Seminary; M.A., Ph.D. Graduate Faculty New School for Social Research. *Specializations:* Personality theory; research in schizophrenia; integration of psychology and theology.

CLEMENT, PAUL W. *Title:* Professor of psychology and director of The Psychological Center, Fuller Theological Seminary Graduate School of Psychology. *Degrees:* B.S., B.A. University of Washington; M.A. Pepperdine College; Ph.D. University of Utah. *Specializations:* Clinical psychology; behavioral psychology.

CLINES, DAVID, J. A. *Title:* Reader in biblical studies, The University, Sheffield, England. *Degrees:* B.A. Sydney, Australia; M.A. Cambridge. *Specialization:* Old Testament studies.

CLOUSE, BONNIDELL. *Title:* Professor of educational psychology, Indiana State University, Terre Haute, Indiana. *Degrees:* B.A. Wheaton College; M.A. Boston University; Ph.D. Indiana University. *Specializations:* Human development; moral development; educational psychology.

COHEN, ERIC J. *Title:* Clinical psychologist, Western Washington University Counseling Center. *Degrees:* B.A. Willamette University; M.A., Ph.D. Fuller Theological Seminary Graduate School of Psychology. *Specializations:* Marriage and family therapy; strategic therapies.

COLLINS, GARY R. *Title:* Professor of psychology, Trinity Evangelical Divinity School, Deerfield, Illinois. *Degrees:* B.A. McMaster University; M.A. University of Toronto; Ph.D. Purdue University. *Specialization:* Psychology.

COURT, JOHN H. *Title:* Associate professor and director of the psychology clinic, registered clinical psychologist, School of Social Sciences, The Flinders University of South Australia. *Degrees:* B.A. Reading; Ph.D. Adelaid. *Specializations:* Media and behavior; sexual behavior; behavior therapy.

CRABB, LAWRENCE J., JR. *Title:* Clinical psychologist and director, Institute for Biblical Counseling, Boca Raton, Florida. *Degrees:* B.A. Ursinus College; M.A., Ph.D. University of Illinois. *Specializations:* Clinical psychology; biblical counseling.

CRANDALL, JAMES E. *Title:* Professor of psychology, University of Idaho. *Degrees:* B.A., M.P.S. University of Colorado; Ph.D. University of Oregon. *Specializations:* Personality; human motivation; Adlerian psychology.

DAVID, JAMES R. *Title:* Acting chief, social work service, Walter Reed Army Medical Center, Washington, D.C. *Degrees:* B.A. St. Norbert College, West DePere, Wisconsin; Ph.D. candidate, Florida State

University; M.S.W. Worden School of Social Service, Our Lady of the Lake University. *Specializations:* Marital and family therapy.

DUDA, FRANCIS C. *Title:* Community Mental Health Activity, Fort Ord, California. *Degrees:* B.A. Barromeo College; M.S.W. Florida State University. *Specializations:* Marriage and family therapy.

ELKIND, DAVID. *Title:* Professor and chairman, Eliot-Pearson department of child study, Tufts University. *Degrees:* B.A., Ph.D. University of California, Los Angeles. *Specializations:* Child development; Piagetian theory and research.

EVANS, TED D. *Title:* Assistant clinical professor, Neuropsychiatric Institute, UCLA Center for the Health Sciences. *Degrees:* B.A. University of Southern California; Ph.D. Fuller Theological Seminary Graduate School of Psychology. *Specialization:* Clinical psychology.

FLECK, J. ROLAND. *Title:* Associate professor of psychology and editor, *Journal of Psychology and Theology,* Rosemead Graduate School of Professional Psychology, La Mirada, California. *Degrees:* B.A. Bryan College; M.Ed., Ed.D. University of Georgia. *Specializations:* Developmental psychology; counseling psychology; psychology of religion.

JACKSON, STEVEN L. *Title:* Doctoral candidate, University of Utah. *Degrees:* B.A. Baylor University, M.S. University of Idaho. *Specialization:* Clinical psychology.

JACOBS, JOAN L. *Degrees:* B.A. University of California, Berkeley; graduate study at the Biblical Seminary, New York, and Fuller Theological Seminary. *Specializations:* The mother of five children and the wife of a pastor in Altadena, California; author of the book *Feelings* and recently published articles in *Christianity Today* and *Eternity.*

JOHNSTON, O. RAYMOND. *Title:* Director, Nationwide Festival of Light, London. *Degrees:* M.A. Oxford; postgraduate qualifications in education and theology, University of London. *Specialization:* Relationship of Christian theology to social morality in the spheres of law, media, and education.

LARZELERE, ROBERT E. *Title:* Assistant professor, Western Conservative Baptist Seminary. *Degrees:* B.A. Wabash College; M.S. Georgia Institute of Technology; Ph.D. Pennsylvania State University. *Specializations:* Research methodology; integration of psychology and theology; family studies; social psychology; social development.

MOHLINE, RICHARD J. *Title:* Associate dean for administration, Rosemead Graduate School of Professional Psychology, La Mirada, California. *Degrees:* M.Div. Gordon Divinity School; M.Ed., Loyola University. *Specializations:* Theology; integration of psychology and theology.

MOTET, DAN. *Title:* Associate professor of psychology, Seattle Pacific University. *Degrees:* B.S. University of Bucharest, Romania; Ph.D. University of Washington. *Specialization:* Counseling psychology.

NARRAMORE, S. BRUCE. *Title:* Academic vice president, Rosemead Graduate School of Psychology, Rosemead, California. *Degrees:* B.A. Westmont College; M.A. Pepperdine University; Ph.D. University of Kentucky. *Specializations:* Psychopathology; psychotherapy; integration of psychology and theology.

OAKLAND, JAMES A. *Title:* Psychologist in private practice, Pasadena, California. *Degrees:* B.A. Seattle Pacific College; Ph.D. University of Washington. *Specializations:* Clinical psychology; psychoanalysis.

PALOUTZIAN, RAYMOND F. *Title:* Associate professor, Westmont College. *Degrees:* B.A. California State University at Los Angeles; M.A., Ph.D. Claremont Graduate School. *Specializations:* Social psychology; psychology of religion.

PECHEUR, DAVID. *Title:* Day treatment therapist, San Antonio Community Hospital, Upland, California. *Degrees:* B.A. Fairleigh Dickinson University; M.A., Ph.D. Rosemead Graduate School of Professional Psychology. *Specializations:* Cognitive behavior modification; cognitive therapy of depression.

REILLY, J. WESLEY. *Title:* Psychologist, Yellowstone Boys Ranch, Billings, Montana. *Degrees:* B.A. Cedarville College; M.A., Ph.D. Rosemead Graduate School of Professional Psychology. *Specializations:* Counseling psychology.

SHEA, JOHN J. *Title:* Assistant professor, Graduate School of Religion and Religious Education, Fordham University. *Degrees:* B.A. Villanova University; M.A. Catholic University; M.P.S. St. Paul University; Ph.D. University of Ottawa. *Specializations:* Psychology of religion; pastoral counseling.

VAYHINGER, JOHN M. *Title:* Professor and chairman, department of psychology and pastoral care, Anderson School of Theology, Anderson, Indiana. *Degrees:* A.B. Taylor University; B.D. Drew Theological

Seminary; M.A. Drew University; M.A., Ph.D. Columbia University. *Specializations:* Clinical psychology; pastoral counseling.

WESTENDORP, FLOYD. *Title:* Associate professor and acting chairman, department of psychiatry, Michigan State University. *Degrees:* A.B. Calvin College; M.D. University of Michigan. *Specializations:* Graduate psychiatric education; integration of Christianity and psychiatry.

INTRODUCTION

Integration of psychology and Christianity is a very new concept. Yet relating Christianity to the thought forms and intellectual understandings of a society and culture is not new at all. As early as the second and third century, the Christian apologists and philosophers were integrating Christianity with Greek philosophy and thought and interpreting it to the intellectual world in which Christianity was born. This integration was especially well developed in Alexandria, where a Christian university was founded by the early fourth century of the Christian era. By the fifth century, Augustine in *The City of God* had worked out an integrative schema of Christianity and Platonic thought, which became the dominant understanding through medieval times. In the thirteenth century, Thomas Aquinas worked out an even more complete integration of Christianity and Aristotelian thought. Since Aquinas' *Summa Theologica* there have been numerous less complete attempts. Recently, the Dutch philosopher Herman Dooyeweerd (1967) attempted to work out a complete integration between the liberal arts and sciences and Christianity. Whether any or all of these attempts has been successful, the principle has been established. Christians have been attempting to integrate their Christian faith with dominant thought forms of their culture for many centuries. Thus, integration, in principle, is not new.

On the other hand, the integration of Christianity and psychology is very new. In fact, it is almost totally post–World War II, with most of the substantive work done in the last fifteen years. One reason for the newness of integration with psychology is obviously that psychology itself is still quite young as a science, its birth customarily dated from the founding of a laboratory by Wundt in 1879. Since there were few psychologists or psychiatrists in the early days, psychology was slow in developing, and there could be little integration before there was a substantive body of psychology.

In addition, there was an antireligious bias on the part of some significant early psychological thinkers. The most prominent were Sigmund Freud, the founder of psychoanalysis, who viewed much, if not all, organized religion as an expression of neurotic tendencies, and J. B. Watson, the founder of behaviorism, who viewed the concept of mind, soul, and spirit

15

as unscientific. This bias inhibited the development of an integrative perspective because many Christians felt the field of psychology was itself anti-Christian, and therefore to be avoided.

Integration: The Meaning of the Term

The term "integration" has been used up to this point to describe the relationship of psychology and Christianity. There is nothing particularly important or significant about this term. In fact, it is quite arbitrary in itself. Some authors find the term unsatisfactory because it implies to them that psychology and Christianity are equals and that the term "integration" means they are being fused into some new third type of discipline (Ellen, 1980). Other psychologists have proposed terms such as "synthesis" or "psychotheology" in place of integration (McLemore, 1976), but these terms have not been accepted in general usage.

The term "integration," or its cognates as used in this chapter, implies nothing about the disciplines of psychology and Christianity (or theology as some writers prefer). Rather, the term is used in a descriptive sense as it is used by the majority of the authors of the various articles in this volume. It is used to describe the relationship between some aspect of Christianity and psychology. In addition, Carter (chapter 5) and Larzelere (chapter 3) use the term to refer to a model, i.e., a conceptual structure behind both psychology and Christianity that is common to both. Carter and Larzelere are not in conflict with the other authors; rather, they are addressing a different facet of the integrative process.

From the preceding discussion there are certain implications. Integration does not mean the fusion of psychology and Christianity into a third discipline. Nor is it the reduction of Christianity to psychology, creating psychologized Christianity or the reverse, Christianized psychology. In addition, integration is not lining up psychological and Christian concepts or experience, such as the id and original sin or unconditional positive regard and love, and calling the result "integration." All these approaches can be found somewhere in the history of the psychology of religion, but none of these approaches is integrative.

Finally, integration is not relating a theory with Christianity. At first, this statement may appear to be in conflict with an entire section of this book, section 7; but a close examination reveals it is not. Theory is part of psychology. It is an attempt to organize the data or parts of psychology into a coherent system. Thus, as part of psychology, these theories need to be examined and related to Christianity as part of the integrative task.

Before we proceed to discuss what integration is in a positive sense, a brief review of the conflict between psychology and Christianity is needed. Any student of psychology who is also a Christian is aware of psychologists and their theories which appear to be in conflict with Christianity. Also, there are many Christian thinkers or preachers who are antagonistic to psychology. How can the attitudes of these two classes of thinkers be understood in a book on the integration of Christianity and psychology? The following figure may help in understanding the aspects of conflict and nonconflict between Christianity and psychology.

CHRISTIANITY

		Systematic Theology	Data or Facts of Theology (Scripture)
	Theories of Psychology	Possible Conflict	Possible Conflict
PSYCHOLOGY			
	Data or Facts of Psychology	Possible Conflict	No Conflict

FIGURE 1: PSYCHOLOGY AND CHRISTIANITY:
Theories and Facts

In examining figure 1, both psychology and Christianity have been described in terms of two levels, theories and facts (data-Scripture), except that for Christianity the theories-level is called systematic theology, such as Calvinism, Arminianism, and dispensationalism. In each case theories or theologies are a human product. That is, theories or theologies are a product of human effort in organizing the facts into a conceptual system. Therefore, by their very nature, they are an elaboration and an interpretation of the facts, and subject to bias and error. For the present brief discussion we will ignore the idea that some so-called facts may be generated by particular theories since Larzelere (chapter 3) discusses this issue and its implication for integration.

In contrast to the theories-level is the facts-level. For psychology, the facts-level means genuine facts that are free of bias or error and are thus true in fact or reality. For Christianity, the facts-level means the data or facts of Scripture or of Christian experience that are genuine and/or real. As can be observed from figure 1, there may be conflict between various psychological theories and Christian theology, as well as between the facts of psychology or Christianity and the theories of the two. However, since God is the creator of the world and the author of Christianity, there can be no conflict between the facts of psychology and the facts of Christianity. This statement is the key assumption of integration and will be elaborated in detail shortly.

Thus, the implications of figure 1 for the individual interested in the integration of psychology and Christianity are twofold: one, there may be much apparent conflict between the theoretical aspects of psychology or Christianity and their facts or theories; and, two, there is no genuine conflict between the facts of psychology and the facts of Christianity. In concluding this section, it should be noted that the second implication means that the data or facts of some particular experiments may be interpreted as in conflict with Christianity; but more adequate methodology, sampling, or replication will show the genuine facts not to be in conflict with Christianity.

Integration as a Model

The integration of psychology and Christianity begins with the summary statement drawn from figure 1 above. The facts of psychology are not in conflict with the facts of Christianity; rather, the facts of each are part of a larger whole called "truth." This truth forms a unity, i.e., it is integral. While there may be different ways to discuss this presupposition, perhaps the simplest is to say that all truth is God's truth.

Since God is the creator of the universe, all principles and laws have their origin in him. What is often called "nature" in science or philosophy is in reality God's creation. As his creation, nature and its laws reveal the Creator. Hence, theologians have referred to the picture of God in nature as general revelation because nature reveals God as a powerful and orderly creator. On the other hand, God is revealed in the Scripture and in Jesus Christ in a special way, i.e., special or particular details about God's person, nature, and his plan for human life and its relationship with him are revealed in Scripture. Hence, theologians refer to Scripture as special revelation. Christianity is largely based on the Scripture and on Jesus Christ, who occupies a large place in the Scripture.

For many there appears to be a conflict or rift between Christianity and psychology, since Christianity is based on the Scripture and psychology is based on the observation of human beings as natural entities, i.e., as products of environment and heredity. Furthermore, the tendency has been to heighten the apparent rift and difference by the use of different methods of study in each discipline. Scientists, including psychologists, use the method of empirical observation and experimentation to study human nature. Thus, psychology is a product of scientific natural observation. Christianity and Christian theology were developed by the use of the human mind to study the Scripture and to formulate doctrine. This method is rational rather than empirical. The difference is still further heightened by the terminology theologians have used to describe the realm of science (in this case, psychology) and the realm of Christianity. Such terms as nature and grace, reason and faith, secular and sacred, or, as already indicated, general and special revelation—all suggest a dichotomy between truth in God's creation and his truth as revealed in the Christian scripture.

The integrationist believes this dichotomy is artificial. The integrationist believes that God created psychology when he created man in his own image (Gen. 1:26-27), i.e., he created all the principles, laws, and facts concerning human nature which psychology as a science has or will discover. God has also revealed many things about human nature in the Scripture. Hence, as the products of one creator, psychology and Christianity cannot be disjunctive or incongruent; rather, they are part of a fundamental integral unity which is truth or reality.

A second and corollary assumption for integration as a model is that psychology and Christianity are equally emphasized. Since they are neither fused nor reduced to each other and they are not lined up, an equal emphasis means that the data, principles, or concepts in psychology have a dynamic counterpart in Christianity or Christian theology. The reverse is also true. The data, principles, or concepts of Christianity have a dynamic counterpart in psychology. More will be said on this matter shortly, but first a figure which illustrates the three aspects of integration as a model will be presented.

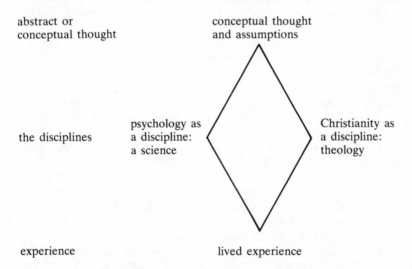

FIGURE 2: The three aspects of integration as a model

The three aspects of integration as a model can be seen in figure 2. First, integration is a way of thinking. Second, it is relating two disciplines. Third, it is a way of living.

As a way of thinking, integration is the search for the underlying conceptual framework which is common to both psychology and Christianity. Much of sections 1 and 2 deals with this aspect of integration in a formal way, but many other articles also focus on this aspect. This aspect of integration might be viewed as philosophical, theological, or theoretical by most psychologists.

The key assumption of this first aspect of integration is the unity of truth. Philosophically, this is expressed in the notion that truth is one, i.e., it is *not* fragmented scraps, isolated pieces, or logically contradictory or contrary truths. Rather, truth is whole and congruent. Theologically, this assumption is expressed as all truth is God's truth. Since God is one and the author of truth, this truth is unified and whole, i.e., its components are congruent or integrative. Theoretically, this assumption is expressed in the notion that any constructs that validly reflect or represent any data must be congruent with other constructs representing different data. The science-of-science movement as represented by the *International Encyclopedia of Unified Science* (1962) most clearly expresses at a theoretical level the unity-of-truth idea, though most proponents of this movement attempted to build that unity around physics. The unity of truth assumption exists at what Larzelere (chapter 3) would call the world-view level.

Clearly, this first aspect of integration involves abstract and theoretical thinking about the concept of reality that underlies psychology and Christianity. Hence, it involves relating the entire range of psychology and Christianity, and illustrates why integration means more than any particular theory in psychology.

The second aspect of integration as a model deals with the disciplines. As the figure of a diamond illustrates, the disciplines of psychology and Christian theology are separate disciplines. Each has its respective method of study, its data to be analyzed, and its resulting content. Hence, the disciplines are not fused or reduced to one another. Rather, at this level in thinking psychologically about human nature, the integrationist thinks psychologically about Christianity. The reverse is also true; the integrationist also thinks Christianly about psychology.

Other specific examples of this process of dialogical interaction occur in section 3 (Maturity: Christian and Psychological); section 4 (Religious Understanding and Thought); section 5 (Counseling and Therapy); and section 6 (Human Sexuality). In each of these sections specific concepts (i.e., maturity, moral development, therapy [healing], and sexuality) which occur in both the discipline of psychology and the discipline of Christianity are discussed. In most cases, the authors present concepts from either psychology or Christianity and then try to think dialogically or dynamically about the implication of a particular aspect in and for the other discipline.

While the integrity of the disciplines is maintained, the results of the dialogical interacting of thinking Christianly about psychology, and psychologically about Christianity, often lead the integrationist either upward in the diamond figure toward an abstract conceptual level or downward in the diamond figure to experience. The Carter and Mohline article (chapter 6) illustrates the upward movement. They begin with concepts from both disciplines and move upward toward a common conceptual framework behind psychology and Christianity. On the other hand, Barshinger (chapter 12) begins with the concept of intimacy from psychology and spirituality from Christianity, and then moves down the diamond toward their common integration point in experience, toward the third aspect of integration. The implication of this last point is simply that different authors tend to migrate to that aspect of integration with which they are most comfortable.

The third aspect of integration as a model is lived experience. While psychology and Christian theology may be conceived of as separate disciplines, psychology as the study of human nature and functioning, and Christianity as the study of Christian life and experience, they both converge as lived experience. Every person, whether Christian or non-Christian, lives an experience which involves values, goals, guilt, joy, hope, pain, and death—all of which are not only psychological and Christian concepts, but psychological and Christian experiences. This is true because for both psychology and Christianity experience is primary data.

Another way of describing this third aspect of integration is to recognize that the psychologist, Christian, and integrationist are persons. As such they learn, grow, think, feel, believe, change, and relate to God, self, and others. These human processes and the multitude of related experiences may be embraced, ignored, or denied, but they are, in fact, experienced. Both psychology and Christianity focus on personal human process and experience as primary whether those processes and experiences are reflected or unreflected, though often different aspects of these experiences are examined by each. In addition, since values, guilt, joy, hope, pain, and death are both psychological and Christian concepts, being an integrationist means experiencing these as both psychological and Christian.

Finally, the three aspects of integration are not isolated, but form a gestalt or dynamic whole. Obviously, if one does not think about psychology and Christianity, no integration is possible. Again, if one knows only psychology or only Christianity or neither, no integration is possible. In the third place, if an individual is defensive and denying some aspect of his experience, either psychologically and/or Christianly, he will not be able to see the implication of that experience in the respective discipline, let alone its integrative implication. Thus, all three aspects of the integrative model are necessary and form a functional whole.

Content and Levels of Integration

In addition to what has already been said about its nature, integration can be thought of as having content in the same way that psychology and

Christianity have content. The content of psychology includes the facts, laws, and theories from the various specialized areas of study such as abnormal, developmental, personality, and social psychology. Christianity also has a content such as God, the nature of man, the nature of Christ and his atoning work, and the church. Since most of the thinking on integration has been done by psychologists, efforts at developing integration have tended to follow the general content areas in psychology. In fact, most of the sections of this book are organized around some specific content area in psychology.

Carter and Mohline (chapter 6) specifically survey the entire connection between the content of psychology and Christian theology and propose a scheme for integrating the content areas from these two disciplines. Whether their proposal is correct or not, in the final analysis, they do raise many of the issues relevant to the content areas of psychology and theology.

Thus, much, if not all, of the second aspect of the diamond model of integration (i.e., the disciplines) can be considered the content of integration. And, most of the work by integrationists has begun with some specific content area in psychology and sought to find its dynamic counterpart in Christianity.

In addition, the content of integration exists at different levels of abstraction because psychology exists at different levels. The most abstract level is called by Larzelere (chapter 3) the world-view level. At this level, behaviorism, psychoanalysis, and other systems of psychology exist as interpretations of the entire field of psychology. Systematic theologies also exist at this level. The least abstract level Larzelere calls the data level, and it relates to the facts of experimental data or the facts in the Scripture or the facts of Christian experience. Since Larzelere discusses these two levels as well as the intermediate ones in detail, little more will be said about the various levels as such. However, it seems important to note that Christianity appears to be focused at the most and at the least abstract levels, while psychology seems to have a heavy concentration at the intermediate levels.

Hence, the Scripture states certain facts about God, man, the world, and then addresses the relationship among them from a world-view, i.e., eternal perspective. For example, "Train up a child in the way he should go, and when he is old he will not depart from it" (Prov. 22:6). This verse recognizes the fact that child-training influences children developmentally and requires the parents to train the child according to the divine perspective, "the way he should go." But little is said about the mechanism of training or learning in the Scripture other than that reward and punishment (reinforcement) influence behavior, and modeling by the parents is important. Psychology, on the other hand, has a great deal to say about the mechanisms of learning and how children acquire information and behavioral responses.

Many other examples could be discussed such as "Honor your father and your mother . . . that your days may be prolonged" (Deut. 5:16), "A soft answer turns away wrath" (Prov. 15:1), or "The man who commits adultery . . . destroys his own soul" (Prov. 6:32 LB). This difference in focus between psychology and Christianity needs to be attended to in doing and thinking about integration. Hence, scriptural data or facts often may need to be explained or interpreted by psychology and psychological facts, and theories need to be integrated with the world view of Christianity.

Summary

While the integration of psychology and Christianity is new in detail, it is not new in principle in that Christians have repeatedly over the centuries related their faith to the current thought forms. The term integration, though it is perhaps not ideal, is currently being used by psychologists to describe both the process and the resulting content of relating psychology and Christianity. Integration does not mean fusing psychology or Christianity to each other; nor does it mean relating Christianity to a particular psychological theory. Integration can be understood as having three aspects illustrated in figure 2: first, it is discovering the common ideas and conceptual structure behind both psychology and Christianity; second, it is thinking psychologically about Christianity and Christianly about psychology while preserving the respective methods and content of psychology and Christian theology; and, finally, it is a lived experience in which an individual is open to the experiential quality of both psychology and Christianity. In addition, integration has content—the laws, concepts, and facts of psychology as they relate to the laws, concepts, and facts of Christianity—and levels of abstraction; psychology and Christianity exist at both the facts and the theories-level.

References

Aquinas, Thomas. *Summa Theologiae.* 3 vols. ed. C. Herman. Westminster, Md.: Christian Classics, 1962.

Augustine. *City of God.* Garden City, N.Y.: Doubleday, 1959.

Dooyeweerd, H. *New Critique of Theoretical Thought.* 4 vols. Phillipsburg, N.J.: Presbyterian and Reformed, 1967.

Ellen, J. H. "Biblical Themes in Psychological Theory and Practice." *The CAPS Bulletin,* 1980, *6*, 2-6.

McLemore, C. W. "The Nature of Psychotheology: Varieties of Conceptual Integration." *Journal of Psychology and Theology,* 1976 *4*, 217-20.

Neurath, O., Carnap, R., and Morris, C. *International Encyclopedia of Unified Science.* Chicago: University of Chicago Press, 1962.

SECTION
ONE

INTRODUCTION TO INTEGRATION

The integration of psychology and Christianity is in its infancy, and much of the writing to date lacks both an adequate psychological and theological foundation. The newness of the area allows the developing integrationist to follow his natural interests and carve out an area of study. The four articles in this first section of the book introduce the reader to current thinking concerning approaches to and problems in the integration of psychology and Christianity. Narramore and Collins deal with broad issues while Larzelere focuses in on a specific six-level model, or strategy, of integration. Finally, Fleck approaches integration at the empirical research level and provides support for an integrated model of religious maturity.

Narramore in the 1973 inaugural issue of the *Journal of Psychology and Theology* presented the most comprehensive evaluation to that date of the status of efforts to integrate biblical and psychological truth. He noted that nearly all past efforts at a comprehensive integration by either psychologists or theologians have suffered from the same four deficiencies: (1) they lack objective, scientific data; (2) they lack clearly defined theological and philosophical underpinnings; (3) they lack a general theory of behavior; and (4) they lack a well-thought-out theory of personality. In addition, Narramore has cited several barriers thrown up by both the Christian community and the psychological community that hinder effective integration and the development of a distinctly Christian psychology.

Theoretical, research, and applied areas of study are enumerated as representative of the issues that need exploration before a comprehensive and meaningful Christian viewpoint on psychology can be delineated. Finally, Narramore specified four basic personal attitudes, or attributes, that must characterize the developing integrationist.

Whereas Narramore seemed to be writing to the broader Christian psychological and theological professional community, Collins has approached the integration of psychology and theology from the viewpoint of pastoral psychology and counseling. From a historical perspective he first divided pastoral psychology and counseling into five overlapping categories: (1) the mainstream; (2) evangelical pastoral counselors; (3) Christian professionals; (4) theoretician-researchers; and (5) popularizers.

He then looked into the future and stated that efforts in pastoral psychology and counseling should focus on five major areas in the next few years: (1) Christian counseling; (2) training and education; (3) preventive psychology; (4) theory and psychological apologetics; and (5) research.

While Collins is writing on a more practical level to a less sophisticated reader, he and Narramore are suggesting very similar problems in and approaches to the integration of psychology and theology. First, both state that the developing integrationist must be thoroughly familiar with psychology and theology. Second, they recognize the fear of psychology in the Christian community as a major barrier to integration. Finally, both authors stress that the integration of psychology and theology must be pursued on at least three levels: theory, research, and application.

Noting that most of the integrative efforts since Narramore's 1973 article have been at a theoretical, rather than a research or application, level, Larzelere has presented a model designed to illustrate and clarify the place and importance of research to the integration of psychology and Christianity. This model specifies six levels of psychological inquiry moving from a world-view (presuppositional) level through theoretical levels to an empirical-data level. These six levels are viewed as providing an overview of the areas that need to be dealt with in research integrating Christianity with psychology, and Larzelere suggested specific examples of integration tasks for each level. The model provides guidelines for future integrative efforts at the research level. In addition, with slight modification, the six-level model can probably be generalized and extended to the area of clinical application.

The article by Fleck is a good example of the type of research that Larzelere's model can potentially stimulate. Fleck has proposed and empirically tested a three-dimensional model of personal religious orientation or style: (1) intrinsic-committed religion—a personal and authentic commitment to religious values that are the master motive in life; (2) consensual religion—identification with religion for personality support; and (3) extrinsic religion—a self-serving, utilitarian use of one's religion.

This psychology-of-religion model parallels theorizing in the fields of sociology, social psychology, and education on types of people, levels of attitude change, and levels of valuing; it also integrates well with biblical concepts of maturity. In fact, it is probably the most sophisticated attempt to date at measuring the biblical concept of spiritual maturity.

The four articles in this section serve as an advanced organizer, raising general issues that are dealt with in more detail in later sections of the book. For example, section 2 (Models of Integration) and section 7 (Christianity and Psychological Theories) address in a more specific manner issues that both Narramore and Collins pointed out as significant. In addition, sections 5 (Counseling and Therapy) and 8 (Popular Christian Psychologies) elaborate additional areas focused on by Collins. The articles by Fleck (section 1) and Paloutzian, Jackson, and Crandall (section 4) are examples of research efforts consistent with Larzelere's model. Also, the other articles in section 4 (Religious Understanding and Thought) address potential empirical research areas. Finally, the articles in section 3 (Maturity: Christian and Psychological) are the theoretical counterpart to Fleck's empirical investigation of religious maturity.

PERSPECTIVES ON THE INTEGRATION OF PSYCHOLOGY AND THEOLOGY

S. Bruce Narramore

Recent years have seen a proliferation of new data, theories, and methods in psychology. At many points the concepts and data of this developing psychological science are impinging on areas traditionally dealt with by the church. In many quarters the whole process of "curing sick souls" is moving from the church to the doorsteps of psychologists and other mental health professionals. Increasingly, our society is looking to psychology to shed new light on the basic issues of human existence. Questions on the nature of man, society, and the universe are being directed more to the secular psychological community than to the church.

Most of us view this trend with mixed emotions. On the one hand we sense the great potential in a scientific study of man. We know that objective data and well-constructed theories may deepen our understanding of man, God's most complex creation. We are also aware that the church has sometimes failed to minister to the emotional needs of its constituents; and we realize the church has often failed to speak clearly to vital psychological issues. Undoubtedly the new insights of psychology can help us in these areas.

On the other hand, the rapid growth of the psychological sciences and professions may also be viewed as an encroachment on the ministry of the church. We sense a veiled threat (or sometimes obvious) to the authority of the Scriptures, the reality of the supernatural, and the role of the Christian ministry.

These mixed feelings touch a wide range of concerned Christians. The man on the street, for example, sees in psychology new insights that may provide relief from personal discomfort and despair. He gains new hope for "victory" through the application of psychological concepts or techniques. At the same time, he may also sense a slight feeling of guilt at turning outside the church for professional help. He may have been told his problems are entirely spiritual and that what he really needs is more faith or a deeper commitment, not psychotherapy.

Ministers, too, are caught up in this conflict. Confronted by a variety of deep emotional entanglements of parishioners they sense the need for a deeper understanding of the human personality. At the same time they feel the Bible should contain all answers to man's dilemma. If they look toward psychology they may feel a sense of disloyalty to the Scriptures.

Christian psychologists and related professional workers also have mixed feelings. They know their disciplines hold much truth; and they hope to apply this truth in the framework of their Christian faith. Yet, at the same time, they are aware of many barriers to this application. They face some clear differences of opinion with their secular community, and their Christian brothers are sometimes extremely resistant to any attempts to relate psychological principles to the Christian life.

But the minister and psychologist are not the only ones caught up in this conflict. The theologian, the physician, and the student of psychology and Scripture all share concerns for the whole man. They know they cannot minister effectively if they neglect the contributions of related disciplines.

But how do we go about this integration? In what way can the psychologist, minister, physician, or theologian effectively relate his Christian view of life to the secular study of psychology? And in what ways can the Christian church draw on the insights of psychology to build a more effective ministry?

The Present Status of Integrative Efforts Between Psychology and Christianity

There is a need to put our current thinking in an historical perspective. Why is it that nearly one hundred years after the founding of modern psychology we have only scattered attempts at integrating our Christian faith with psychological theory and data?

Over the past forty years we have an increasing number of Christians who are psychologists. We have also had a large number of ministers and theologians with interests in psychology. Many of these men have been productive. Some have initiated psychology majors in our Christian colleges. Others have entered private practice and started psychological clinics. Still others have written helpful books and articles on psychology from a Christian perspective. Through these efforts the role of a "Christian psychologist" has gained a certain respectability within the Christian community. From the evangelical community men like Collins (1964), Hyder (1971), C. Narramore (1960), Nelson (1960), and Tournier (1962) have written books directed to the Christian layman or pastor. These men combined some aspects of biblical and psychological truth to offer insight and guidance to Christians looking for help in personal living.

On a somewhat different level other authors have tried to find parallels between biblical truth and various schools of psychological thinking. Tweedie (1961), for example, did this with Frankl's Logotherapy. Pfister

(1948) and Barkman (1965) have attempted the same thing with psychoanalytic theory. And more recently Drakeford (1967) has taken a similar approach with a more directive "Reality Therapy" orientation.

From the theological or ministerial side of the fence men like Adams (1970), Hiltner (1949), Hulme (1956, 1970), LaHaye (1966), Oates (1962), and Roberts (1950) have offered similar publications. Although varying greatly in both their biblical positions and their psychological sophistication, all of these have played a part in bringing psychology to the attention of the church. To focus briefly on their contributions, we summarize as follows. All of these men have contributed to (1) gradually reducing the church's fear of psychology, (2) making some distinctions between spiritual and emotional maladjustments, (3) removing the stigma of seeking professional help for personal problems, (4) giving the layman increased insights into human behavior, (5) encouraging ministers and theologians to give attention to the whole person (including the emotional side of life), and (6) encouraging younger Christians to view the discipline of psychology as a potential field for Christian service. From the extreme defensiveness and isolation of the forties, men like this have helped the church come a long way.

But we still have far to go. Nearly all of our past efforts suffer from the same four deficiencies: (1) They lack objective, scientific data, (2) they lack clearly defined theological and philosophical underpinnings, (3) they lack a general theory of behavior, and (4) they lack a well thought out theory of personality. One of the few exceptions to this is the book *What, Then, Is Man,* authored by a group of Lutheran psychologists and theologians (Meehl et al., 1958). This book makes a good start on promoting a healthy dialogue on some basic issues of integration.

Without an explicit philosophical position, objective data, and a general behavior theory it is impossible to have a system of psychology. Since we lack these basic elements, we cannot accurately say there is such a thing as "Christian psychology." There are many Christian psychologists, but until we gain further data and refine our theoretical thinking it will be impossible to have a systematic Christian view of psychology. Even at this I suspect we may not have one generally accepted psychology for the Christian. Instead, we might expect several well-thought-out views of man in accordance with biblical truth and current psychological knowledge.

But let's back up a bit. Why is it that centuries after the Reformation and nearly one hundred years after the founding of modern psychology the Christian church still has not gathered any significant bank of psychological data? Why have we failed to carefully examine the underlying philosophical positions of secular psychology and suggest some biblical alternatives? And why have we not developed either a definitive Christian theory of personality or a general theory of behavior? In fact, why is it that in many corners of the evangelical church there remains considerable suspicion and distrust of psychological theory and data? And to look at the other side of the coin, why do many secular psychologists have serious quarrels with religion in general and evangelical Christianity in particular? Why is it that such mutual fear and skepticism exist?

If we are to have a meaningful interdisciplinary dialogue we must go beyond our past fears, prejudices, and misunderstandings. We must clearly see the issues at hand and begin to attack them one by one. To date the Christian has been generally fearful of psychology. At the same time the average secular psychologist has had his share of bad attitudes toward religion.

In discussing the mutual anxieties of psychologists and theologians when in each other's presence, Paul Barkman (1965) gives an interesting description. He writes:

> Rather typically, if a psychologist (of psychoanalytic orientation) were to listen to a theologian (of Calvanist orientation) discuss theology, the psychologist might be quite puzzled to find himself described as "an unregenerate soul who resists the Holy Spirit with worldly wisdom because of a depraved nature and an impenitent spirit." (Unless, of course, the psychologist were a minister's son—which many of them are.) To this he might reply that the theologian has "a paranoic personality trait disturbance with an unresolved oedipal complex, who is engaging in projection or repressed hostility toward a castrating father figure." The theologian might return home proud of his testimony, puzzled and a little shaken, and say to his wife, "Today I met a psychoanalyst!" The psychologist might well go home to his wife proud of his educative function, somewhat anxious and perplexed, and using his wife as a therapist say, "Today I met a preacher!" (pp. 9-10)

Barkman here picks up an attitude that has hindered integration. I would like to go further and suggest several reasons for our past failure to establish a distinctively Christian psychology. The first few of these reasons arise out of the twentieth century historical development of the Christian church, especially the effect of the liberal-conservative splits of the 1920s. These reasons include: (1) The Christian's fear of the naturalistic explanation of psychology; (2) the Christian's fear of the deterministic emphasis of psychology; (3) the Christian's difference with secular psychology's view of man; (4) the Christian's differences with a secular view of sex and some bad experiences with psychology; and (5) the Christian's fear of emotions, especially sex, aggression, and intimacy. The other barriers lie more at the feet of the non-Christian community. Among these are (1) the psychologist's superficial understanding of Christianity, (2) the psychologist's identity problem and his overconcern with objective scientism, (3) the psychologist's blindness to spiritual truth and his unconscious fear of spiritual issues like death and hell, and (4) realities of time. Let's consider each of these barriers.

The Historical Development of the Christian Church

During the great theological divisions of the twenties most denominations split into "liberal" and "conservative" elements. Each group went its own way. On the one hand the evangelical wing of the church focused on concepts like personal salvation, scriptural inerrancy, heaven and hell, and human depravity. On the other hand, the liberal church chose to minister to the social needs of man. Both wings were concerned for the individual. For the fundamentalist the concern was primarily for salvation. For the liberal the emphasis was a social gospel. In reacting to what they felt was the fundamentalist's negative emphases on hell, depravity, personal salvation, and inerrancy of Scripture, the liberal wing of the church began to focus more on human potential and social action. They rebelled against the fundamentalists' "pessimistic" view of man and began to hold out hope that through human effort workable solutions to man's dilemmas would be found. As this segment of the church moved further from a focus on biblical theology and personal salvation it turned increasingly to sociology, psychology, and politics as alternate means of ministering to the needs of man.

At the same time the "conservative" wing of the church reaffirmed its commitment to the authority of Scripture and renewed its focus on personal salvation through the redemptive work of Christ. In doing so this wing of the church largely disassociated itself from areas of political or social concern exhibited by the "liberals." The conservative church had a great deal of social outreach but they limited it largely in terms of medical health services, help for the down-and-outers, and assistance to members of local congregations.

In the 1920s a significant movement was unknowingly begun in the Christian church. A man by the name of Anton Boisen (1926) published an article challenging the church to become involved in the emotional ills of man. In issuing this challenge Boisen said:

We have therefore this truly remarkable situation—a church which has always been interested in the care of the sick, confining her efforts to the types of cases (physical) in which religion has least concern and least to contribute, while in those types in which it is impossible to tell where the domain of the medical worker leaves off and that of the religious worker begins (mental problems), there the church is doing nothing. (p. 9)

Boisen soon became a spokesman for those encouraging the church to minister to the emotional needs of society. By 1930 this new emphasis gained so much ground The Council for Clinical Pastoral Training was formed. This organization functioned to stimulate and coordinate new efforts at training ministers to cope with the personal problems of parishioners. Soon many seminaries were asking students to take short-term internships in mental hospitals as a means of becoming sensitive to the psychological needs of people.

To all this the liberal church reacted favorably. Here was a way to minister to the inner needs of man. Psychology offered hope for the present world, not a "pie in the sky" brand of Christian faith. In the thirties and forties, liberal pastoral counseling was strongly influenced by the therapeutic teachings of Sigmund Freud. A distinct emphasis began to move throughout the pastoral counseling movement.

Rather than being viewed as sinful, people with problems were seen as sick. Feelings of guilt and remorse were no longer seen as Christian virtues. Instead, they were the results of inhibited upbringings which resulted in overly strict superegos (consciences). The goal of the pastor-counselor was no longer viewed as leading parishioners to accept God's forgiveness of their sins. Instead, the goal was to relax the strictness of this harsh superego so the person could be freed to enjoy his life. Well-known liberal theologians like Harry Emerson Fosdick (1943) took up the banner of this new view of man. In his book *On Being a Real Person* Fosdick endorsed the psychoanalytic view that neuroses arose not from a lack of responsibility but from an overly strict conscience. He wrote:

Indiscriminate praise of conscientiousness is psychologically dangerous. Many people worry themselves into complete disintegration over mere trifles and others have consciences so obtuse that they can get away with anything. (p. 133)

This thinking fit well with the liberal doctrine of man. A person with emotional problems was not necessarily a depraved sinner. Instead, he was a victim of his environment. The solution to his ailments did not necessarily lie in a spiritual new birth and consequent growth. Instead, it lay in an anthropocentric growth process which needn't be concerned with supernatural phenomena.

During the 1940s a new influence came into American psychology and was soon heartily endorsed by the liberal pastoral counseling movement. This was the "non-directive" or "client-centered counseling" of Carl Rogers (1942). Raised in what he describes as a "strict religious environment" Rogers later attended Union Theological Seminary. His writings reflect a strong rejection of the idea that man is basically sinful. Instead he focuses on the innate tendency toward growth and actualization. Given a healthy environment man will throw off his negative reactions and develop into a healthy, fully functioning person. Based on these underlying presuppositions Rogers' therapeutic method centered on providing the client a warm, accepting, non-judgmental atmosphere. Rather than giving directive advice to a person in need of outside guidance, Rogers' "client-centered therapy" encouraged the client to seek his own solutions. The counselor was no longer an expert or a guide. Instead he was an accepting friend who listened empathetically to the struggles of another human being. This counseling method had great appeal to the liberal church. Once again, it fit in with a positive view of the nature of man and his potential.

But neither psychoanalytic nor client-centered therapy had much room for biblical insight or directive counsel. As the pastoral counselor began to rely largely on these secular theories, the idea that man was a spiritual being in need of salvation and spiritual counsel gradually slipped into the background. As a matter of fact, a counseling approach that gave much attention to specific biblical teaching seemed somehow suspect and unscientific. In the minds of the intellectual liberals, any strong reliance on scriptural teaching smacked of authoritarianism and the "fundamentalist mentality." Liberal theology was believed to have progressed beyond this narrow view!

In recent years one final force has pressed into the mental health picture of the liberal church. This is the influence of existential philosophy and psychology. After two world wars many continental theologians began to rethink their views on the goodness and potentials of man as well as God's revelation to man. Søren Kierkegaard (1944) began to focus on existential encounters as sources of true meaning in life. Later existentialists developed this thinking and propounded the idea that man had to struggle to find personal meaning and identity in the midst of a confusing and meaningless world. This thinking is now playing a significant role in the personal ministry of the liberal and neo-orthodox wings of the church.

To bring us up to date, let's briefly summarize these main psychological influences on the liberal church. In the twenties there was a needed awareness of the inner emotional needs of man prompted first by the influence of Anton Boisen. Since this wing of the church was in the process of rejecting the traditional theological view of man it was immediately receptive to the influence of psychoanalytic writings which portrayed man as a sick individual needing psychological help rather than a sinner needing grace. After twenty years of this influence the client-centered therapy of Carl Rogers came on the scene and was heartily endorsed. Finally, in recent years the influence of the existentialists has brought a focus on the need to find subjective, personal meaning out of an existential crisis encounter.

Each of these influences, the psychoanalytic, the Rogerian, and existentialist, has one thing in common: They have very little room for a theology which focuses on sin, personal salvation, and biblical absolutes. In other words, the focus on personal adjustment and mental hygiene has been largely divorced from the teachings of the Bible and placed within the framework of a secular psychology. This is the great weakness of the liberal church. They have no hope of developing a biblically sound perspective of psychology since they have forsaken the authoritative teachings of the Scriptures. While discussing this development and the fact that many professional psychologists are now dissatisfied with their traditional psychotherapeutic approaches, Hobart Mowrer (1961) asks, "Has evangelical religion sold its birthright for a mess of psychological pottage?" In other words, Mowrer, a secular psychologist, is aware that much of the church has lost its potentially helpful contributions to psychology. Instead of standing on the Scriptures and offering some alternative perspectives, many Christians have merely jumped indiscriminately on the current psychological bandwagon.

While the liberal church was busy adopting a basically secular approach to personal adjustment and psychology, the evangelical church took a different tact. It steered clear of psychology. The pastoral counseling of the typical conservative minister was often limited. And when he did counsel it was usually following a conversion or in periods of death, grief, or special hardship. While many evangelical ministers were sensitive and supportive, the bulk of their ministry was of a directive, Bible-teaching nature that failed to cope with many of the hidden wishes and frustrations of emotional living. The typical conservative minister was twenty or thirty years behind his liberal churchman in being aware of the contributions of psychology to the understanding of men.

The Fear of Naturalistic Explanations

A primary reason for the evangelical's failure to encounter psychological science concerned the influence of the *supernatural*. Psychology, of course, was deeply committed to naturalistic explanations. If it were to build a science of behavior, it would have to have a set of laws. It would have to be able to accurately predict behavior given all the influential variables. This left no room for supernatural influences.

This stance brought threat and apprehension to the evangelical. If psychology could explain and modify human behavior without reference to spiritual principles, the whole concept of the supernatural was in question. This is the very turn the liberal church took in adopting the naturalistic views of a secular psychology. Although few would voice this fear it seems clear that part of the uneasy anxiety suffered by evangelical Christians in the presence of psychology is traceable to his fear of losing the influence of the supernatural.

The Fear of Determinism and Irresponsibility

Another conservative fear was that when people understood the causes of behavior man would no longer feel responsible for his actions. Psychotherapy, especially psychoanalytically oriented therapy, was seen as an attempt to set men free of their inhibitions and turn them into impulsive, irresponsible sinners. Although this attitude is a gross misrepresentation of most psychological theory, it has persisted even until today. In a criticism common to the anti-psychological stance of many Christian writers Jay Adams (1970) states:

The idea of sickness as the cause of personal problems vitiates all notions of human responsibility. This is the crux of the matter. People no longer consider themselves responsible for what they do wrong. Instead they blame society—"ours is a sick society," they say. Others specifically blame grandmother, mother, the church, a school teacher, or some other particular individual for their actions. Freudian psychoanalysis itself turns out to be an archeological expedition back into the past in which a search is made for others on whom to pin the blame for our behavior. The fundamental idea is to find out how others have wronged us. It should not be difficult to see how irresponsibility is the upshot of such an emphasis and how many of the domestic and world wide problems we face in our time are directly related to it. (pp. 5-6)

While many practicing psychologists certainly have been guilty of allowing clients to avoid responsibility, this is due more to their personal therapeutic deficiencies than to the falsity of most psychological theory. Take psychoanalytic theory, for example. It has been most severely criticized as promoting irresponsible acting out and immediate gratification of all desires. In contrast to this, Waelder (1960), a well-respected analyst, writes:

A psychoanalytic approach to education, finally, does not mean that children should get what they want when they want it. Rather it means an attempt to find for each situation the proper balance between satisfaction and frustration, in the light of the general principle that we have to search for the optimal ingredients of healthy development, viz., love and discipline; how to love without pampering and how to discipline without traumatizing. (p. 254)

Suffice it to say, psychology's emphasis on determinism and the Christian's fear that psychological explanations will lead to irresponsibility have been major barriers to attempts at integration.

The Fear of Humanistic Views of Man

The influence of Rogers and similar theoreticians was also rejected by the evangelicals. This was apparently due both to his emphasis on the nature of man and to his therapeutic method. To a doctrinally oriented, Bible-teaching movement, the idea of sitting quietly and empathizing with the needs of parishioners was difficult enough to swallow. Add to this the view that man is essentially good and you can see how out of line with the traditional evangelical approach Rogers' views would be. They were entirely out of keeping with the counseling approach that had a ready verse for every human need. The evangelical church was not yet ready for a deep look at the inner emotional needs of man. In discussing the church's frequent failure to apply its theology to human experience William Hulme (1956) writes:

The successors of the great churchmen of the past have too often communicated the doctrines of the church in a legalistic fashion that had little relation to the dynamics of the human personality. The result is an overintellectualized religion that is unable to reach the deep emotional conflicts of life. Such a religion plays into the hands of those who would rather rationalize than resolve these conflicts. (p. 8)

The Fear of Sex

The centrality of sexual impulses to Freudian theory was a red flag to conservative churchmen. They feared that therapeutic approaches emphasizing the inhibitions of sexual feelings as basic to neuroses would lead to a lowering of standards and a movement from a biblical position. This was a sign that psychology was "of the devil" and had nothing to offer a biblical Christian. Without going into depth, it is obvious that this view had some truth. On the other hand, it may have been overdone. The high view of sexuality endorsed in Scripture has certainly not been accepted by an unsaved world. At the same time, it is equally apparent that many Christians have been guilty of promoting a repressive, unrealistic view of sex. This conflict served to place almost insurmountable barriers between some Christians and the discipline of psychology.

The Christian's Fear of Feelings

Feelings can be frightening. Intense love, moods of depression, outbursts of anger, and needs for support are carefully avoided by many people. For Christians especially, there is the fear that love will turn to lust or discouragement to despair. In earnestly desiring to live the Christian life, everyone builds facades to hide their inner selves. Christians are told they should be happy, so they smile (even though they hurt inside). They are told Christians should be loving so they try to love (even though they feel quite differently). And they are told Christians should be saintly so they put on an outward show of piety.

From the day of their conversion Christians begin learning the rules of their Christian subculture. They are taught how to act, think, and feel in order to live the "victorious life." In one group or denomination the "key" is found in an external set of legalistic actions. In another culture the sign of spiritual maturity is to be found in an aggressive witness. If a person is really "filled with the Spirit" he will show it by his soul-winning efforts. For other groups the sign of spiritual success is the "baptism of the Spirit." Speaking in tongues becomes a sure indication of spiritual blessing or maturity.

These and other emphases in various Christian cultures lead the Christian follower to try to mold his life style in accordance with the standards and ideals of his unique subculture. In doing this, many are forced to put on the expected external trappings at the expense of an honest encounter with their true emotions.

An example of this negation of emotion is found in the prevalent parallel between a railroad train and the Christian life. We are told the engine is fact (the Bible), the next car is faith (trust in God's Word), and the caboose is feeling. The train of the Christian life must obviously be pulled by fact and followed by faith. The train (Christian experience) will run with or without the caboose (feeling).

In fact, major decisions in life should be based on the Word of God. But this simple analogy tends to picture feelings as kind of a nuisance factor in the Christian life. The impression is sometimes given that we would be better off without emotions. They just lead to subjective, feeling-oriented decisions which muddy the waters of consistent Christian living.

Another common manifestation of this fear of feelings and intimacy is found in one of our favorite hymns. We are told, "Are you weary, are you heavy hearted? Tell it to Jesus alone." In other words, don't share your problems with another person. Instead, hold it in, hide your needs, and "tell it to Jesus alone." What a contrast this isolationistic view of the Christian life is to the following passages:

Bear ye one another's burdens and so fulfill the law of Christ. (Gal. 6:2)

Confess your faults one to another, and pray one for another, that ye may be healed. The effectual fervent prayer of a righteous man availeth much. (James 5:16)

Wherefore comfort yourselves together and edify one another, even as also ye do. (1 Thess. 5:11)

This fearful avoidance of feelings in the Christian life has encouraged many to erect or maintain rigid barriers against deep involvement and has caused others to approach Christian service as an obligation rather than the natural result of living a fulfilling life. In the area of psychology, it has caused many to anxiously steer clear of any involvement for fear of contaminating a pure, "objective," intellectualized theology with the "subjective" content of inner human nature.

Summary of the Christian Fears

We can now see why the church has largely failed to make distinctive contributions to psychology. Instead of ministering to the inner emotional needs, the evangelical church has focused primarily on the need for personal salvation, doctrinal orthodoxy, and moral purity. Its social emphasis was largely in the realm of physical medicine. A series of important conflicts with psychology have held the evangelical back from the potential contributions of psychology.

The liberals have failed because they moved from their biblical moorings and adopted an essentially secular psychology. Neither group is actively applying the vast resources of scriptural teachings to the daily personal needs of the average man or to the academic study of psychology.

Psychology's Failure to Participate in Integrative Efforts

But we cannot lay the failure to develop a sufficiently integrated view of man entirely at the feet of the Christian community. Psychologists, too, have played their part in isolationism. Let's look at some reasons for the hesitancy of psychologists to join with Christians in an effort to gain a broadened view of man.

Superficial Understanding of the Christian Faith

As a starter, few psychologists theorizing about the nature of man are actively religious. Many have had only superficial contact with biblical Christianity, while others have had very negative encounters. Take the psychotherapist who has counseled a number of Christian patients, each suffering from a deep sense of worthlessness and guilt. These clients naturally relate these feelings to their Christian experience. They think their guilt and condemnation come directly from the Lord. And what is the therapist to conclude? His natural response is that religion is a destructive force that causes people to feel worthless and guilty. Add to this a brief encounter with the term "total depravity" and our psychologist is sure that religious faith attempts to sabotage positive mental health by instilling deep feelings of guilt and fear.

The Psychologist's Identity Problem

But there are other reasons for psychological skepticism about a theological encounter. As a discipline, psychology still is rather young. In contrast to the natural sciences, psychology has had a hard time finding its niche. The inner workings of the mind have a tint of the subjective, an alien word to experimental scientists. As a matter of fact, even now some people argue that psychology is still somewhat less than science. To overcome its identity problem psychology has had to make determined efforts to establish itself in the mainstream of the scientific world. To do this it had to emphasize major tenets and methods of objective science. These, of course, included a rigid adherence to the scientific method and to naturalistic assumptions about the universe.

Based on this philosophy, graduate training programs ignore the possibility of supernatural phenomena. Trained in these types of programs, a prospective scientist cannot easily escape adopting a similar attitude toward supernatural phenomena. The religious devotee is seen as either naive, dependent, unscientific, and possibly as all three! Otto Fenichel (1945), a staunch supporter of orthodox psychoanalysis, says:

Scientific psychology explains mental phenomena as a result of the interplay of primitive physical needs—rooted in the biological history—and the influences of the environment on these needs. There is no place for any third factor. (p. 5)

Unclear Perceptions

Still another difficulty is the fact that certain perceptions on truth and reality are not open to the unbeliever. The apostle Paul writes:

Even so the things of God knoweth no man, but the Spirit of God. Now we have received, not the spirit of the world, but the Spirit who is of God; that we might know the things that are freely given to us of God. Which things also we speak, not in the words which man's wisdom teacheth, but which the Holy Spirit teacheth, comparing spiritual things with spiritual. But the natural man receiveth not the things of the Spirit of God; for they are foolishness unto him, neither can he know them, because they are spiritually discerned. But he that is spiritual judgeth all things, yet he himself is judge of no man. For who hath known the mind of the Lord, that he may instruct him? But we have the mind of Christ. (1 Cor. 2:11-16)

Paul makes the clear point that there is a wisdom which the person who does not possess a personal relationship with Christ cannot possess. It is impossible for the unregenerate person to comprehend some aspects of the truth. In spite of great personal sensitivity and insight, the non-Christian psychologist has a limited vision on the condition of man. Some conflict in views of the nature of man and his functioning are clearly due to this lack of perception of the non-Christian person. At this point we should add a word of caution. Some Christians have a way of writing off every difference of opinion with a non-Christian to his "lack of spiritual discernment." While this is often true, sometimes the misunderstanding is as much our fault as it is our unsaved friend's. We tend to clutter up the Christian message with our own brand of Christian subculture and cloud over a clear picture of biblical truth. In these cases we need to help our non-Christian colleague cut through these externals to the core ideas of Bible truth.

Realities of Time

But these factors alone do not account for the hesitancy of psychologists to join in an integrative encounter. The practical realities of time and competence make it difficult for the average man to master his chosen discipline effectively, let alone take the time to really see the viewpoints and teaching of a related profession. Even well meaning, open-minded men are limited in their ability to dialogue intelligently with colleagues in other disciplines.

The Unique Challenge for Christian Psychology

This concludes our survey of some of the barriers to effective integration. But where do we go from here? If we are going to push ahead for a comprehensive understanding of the human part of God's creation, we must have a group of committed Christian professionals who are willing to invest their time and efforts in furthering the integration of psychology and scripture. To do this effectively will require both the delineation of areas for study and a certain set of personal attributes and attitudes. We must begin by identifying the potential contributions of a psychological study from a Christian point of view. Without attempting to be comprehensive, let me suggest a number of areas that need to be explored. These issues must be dealt with if we are to develop a meaningful Christian viewpoint on psychology and its applications.

The Challenge of Theory

Consider first the theoretical issues. Several of these have traditionally divided psychologists and theologians. Determinism and personal responsibility are key examples. Any acceptable Christian view of man will have to include a satisfactory resolution of arguments centering around determinism, choice, and responsibility. All respectable scientists acknowledge the lawfulness of behavior and most adhere to some form of determinism. The theologian, on the other hand, in spite of some theoretical debates on election and predestination, is essentially committed to a view of human responsibility. How are we to reconcile these seemingly conflicting views?

Of no less concern is the mind-body question. Can man and his mental functions be reduced entirely to the physiological? Or do we reject the assumptions of this materialistic monism? Similarly, how are we to view conversion? Can we accede to a psychological explanation of this phenomenon? Or can we move closer to clarifying the interrelations of divine intervention, conditioning processes, and inner attitudes? And what about the guilt problem? Are we to view guilt as a "divinely given rebuke or conscience warning light"? Or is it merely an "introjected parent" or "conditioned response"?

And what about miracles and faith healing? The Bible clearly reports these occurrences. Psychologists explain them away as psychological phenomena, a kind of spontaneous remission based upon an infantile belief in magic. Some theologians likewise try to dismiss these present-day events by dispensationalizing them out of existence. But does this really resolve the problem? Can't we come to some more definitive thinking on these issues?

After surveying a number of pastors and psychologists Meehl et al. (1958, p. 5) conclude, "We are prepared to state firmly that he who does not come to terms with such theoretical problems as determinism, guilt, original sin, materialist monism, conscience and conversion cannot even begin to work out a cognitive reapproachment between Christian theology and the secular sciences of behavior." After nearly fifteen years these still appear to be among the most basic issues facing us today.

The Challenge of Data

Now let's turn to the area of objective data. What are some areas that need more careful study? Certainly we need to study the effects of spiritual conversion. We know the process of regeneration makes important inner changes. But shouldn't we expect to find them manifested in demonstrable overt behavior? And what about the sanctification (growth) process? Are believers, in fact, evidencing superior adjustment to their non-Christian counterparts? Or is the sole effect of the Christian life an insurance policy for eternity?

The influences of different variables in the development of morality should be a prime area of study. Mature morality is a major goal of Christian training. Yet we are all aware of gross failures in this area and the large percentage of dropouts among second generation Christians. What accounts for these successes and failures? Can we really write this off as solely a matter of spiritual dedication?

The attitudes and belief systems of Christians are also a rich potential field of study. The present state of research here is very inconclusive. Sanua (1969) writes:

A number of empirical studies, which do not support the general belief that religion is the fountainhead of all moral tenets of our society, have been reviewed in this paper. According to Allport (3) religious instruction seems to include a contradictory set of beliefs. He stated that "most religious persons tend to internalize the divisive role of religion, whereas only a small minority are able to accept the unifying bond, moral and ethical principles underlying religion." Thus, on the one hand, religious leaders advocate love of all mankind and the equality of men as being children of God, while, on the other hand, certain religious teachings hold that only those who possess the "truth" may be saved.

As a result, religious education as it is being taught today does not seem to ensure healthier attitudes, despite its emphasis on ethical behavior. This should raise a major point of discussion among religious leaders to determine whether possibilities exist to remedy this failure to communicate the ethical aspects of religion rather than its ritual. (p. 1211)

Can we go beyond this view and design carefully controlled studies of various religious groupings to come to a clearer understanding of the results of Christian life and training? Although these studies pose some difficult methodological problems, they seem essential to clarifying certain distorted images people hold of Christians and finding out to what extent they differ from their unsaved counterparts.

Outcome studies on "Christian psychotherapy" also are important. The many variables of this interpersonal process and the general finding that the therapist's theoretical orientation is less important than the process variables raise serious questions about the ability to come to definitive conclusions. Yet if we are claiming some sort of superiority for "Christian counseling," it's about time we stopped to see if claims are backed by solid data.

Another area for study is the effectiveness of various forms of Christian ministries. What personal, organizational, and strategic variables account for our failures and successes? Studies could be done in local churches, missionary organizations, educational institutions, and a wide variety of other settings. In relationship to this we need longitudinal studies of vocational fulfillment and success in different Christian ministries. Some mission boards have nearly a 50 percent drop-out rate over the first two terms of service. Can we devise more effective screening processes through objective research? Or does our reliance on the Holy Spirit rule out this approach to personnel selection?

The Challenge of Application

And what about pragmatics? Out of our research and theorizing can we find effective ways of ministering to a world in need? Can we offer suggestions for maximizing the effectiveness of worship services? Is the new "Body Life" emphasis producing more mature believers? Can we improve our Christian education system? Can we train our Christian workers more efficiently? Can we improve our counseling skills? And can we devise educational or counseling programs that will make a sizable dent in the problem of the disintegrating American family?

These and other questions come to our attention. We could double or triple this list with little effort. Some of the problems are large and some are small. Some are largely abstract and theoretical while others have an immediate relevance to Christian living. But all are within the domain of the Christian psychologist and concerned minister or theologian. They are issues that have not been satisfactorily resolved for most of the Christian world, let alone the secular professional. Perhaps here, in these areas, we have a portion of the unique calling of the Christian psychologist. I am convinced that God has some specific plans for Christians in the field of psychology. These plans must fit into his overall ministry in the world. If we fail to address these issues, the church will continue to limit its effectiveness in some very vital areas.

The Personal Challenge

But it is not enough to merely delineate specific problem areas. If we are to be most effective we must pursue our task with a basic set of personal and professional attitudes. The human factor will be a major determinant of the success of our endeavors. As Christians, we must recognize that it is impossible to segment our lives into the sacred and the secular. The very vocations we select, the problems we choose to tackle, and the theoretical framework of our efforts are all influenced by our personal lives in general and our relationships to God in particular.

The first essential attitude for effective integration is a respect for the complete inspiration and authority of the Scriptures. Without using the Bible in a narrow-minded, prejudicial way, we must acknowledge it as God's objective, accurate revelation to man. When our human views (contaminated by our limited perceptions) come into conflict with the Bible we must place our allegiance in the Scripture. This does not mean we naively close our eyes to apparent conflicts. There are times we may need to re-evaluate our theological positions. If we are honest we must all admit there is a good bit of cultural dogmatism in all of our beliefs. We must be willing to get beyond this and make clear studies of seeming conflict areas. Once we are sure of a biblical teaching we must refuse to try to twist and distort clear teachings of the Scriptures to fit our human thinking or our psychological theories. As psychologists we should be most alert to the universal tendency to project our own needs, conflicts, and biases onto our scriptural interpretations. We should also be aware of the fact that our distinctive is our credence in God's inerrant Word. If we fail to base our work on this we are building on an inadequate foundation and will have a psychology essentially no different from the secular psychologist.

Secondly, we must have an attitude of commitment to the scientific method and rigorous academic study. We must not allow ourselves to be second-rate professionals because of our Christian stand. For too long Christians have copped out on rigorous study and research by claiming all the truth they need to know is contained within the Bible. While all the truth necessary to understand salvation and God's basic dealings in the universe is there, there is certainly much more truth we need to know. If we are to develop a significant body of integrative truth, we must hold out high standards for our professional endeavors.

Thirdly, we need a personal commitment to Jesus Christ. If we are to be motivated to pursue an in-depth study of the nature of man, we must see a spiritual purpose in our work. We must see ourselves as servants of God called to understand the workings of creation. In many unique ways those of us ministering in the various areas of psychology have the opportunity of leading others into deeper spiritual truth. Unless we keep a vision of God's plan of salvation for the human race we will reverse our priorities and our professional endeavors will become sterile intellectual exercises that actually serve to defend against inner spiritual and emotional needs instead of becoming part of the redemptive plan of God. This is probably one of the most common pitfalls of the evangelical. In working for academic and professional respectability we minimize our personal spiritual lives and short-circuit God's total involvement in our lives.

Finally, we need an attitude of respect for both the Christian and the secular community. As Christians we will lose our effectiveness if we develop a superior or paranoid attitude toward the world. If we degrade the data of our science and set ourselves outside the scientific method we are doomed to failure. An isolationistic attitude may maintain our doctrinal purity but it will cause us to fail to grab hold of a large portion of God's general revelation.

Likewise, if we as psychologists set ourselves against our theologians we handicap our studies. We must get beyond our personal vocational interests, our personal spiritual experiences, and our personal prejudices to avail ourselves of rounded truth. Even within the evangelical community we continue to have divisions. Theologians often see psychology as an inferior source of truth when compared to the Bible (which I believe we must acknowledge if we're honest). But with this attitude often comes a certain sense of superiority and disdain for psychological endeavors. On the other hand, we psychologists like to think of ourselves as more broad minded, open, and scientific (which I think many theologians must admit if they are honest). But with this we adopt a certain sense of superiority at not being so "narrow minded" as the theologian. Similarly, the scholar and academician tends to look with disdain on his applied brethren. They are viewed as less rigorous and scientific. At the same time the practitioner (be he ministerial, medical, or psychological) often has a certain bias toward his academic colleague. He may accuse him of being impractical and insensitive to human need.

If we can lay aside our personal prejudices (way of defending against our unconscious feelings of inferiority) and develop a truly cooperative attitude we will soon be a long way along the road of integration.

Summary

The evangelical church has a great opportunity to combine the special revelation of God's Word with the general revelation studied by the psychological sciences and professions. The end result of this integration can be a broader (and deeper) view of human life. Historically we have failed to have sufficient dialogue and interaction. Currently we are in a position to gather relevant objective data, seek well-constructed theoretical views, and find improved techniques for applying our biblical and psychological data. To do this we need a group of committed professional people who can mix a personal piety with a commitment to the authority of the Word of God and to high quality professional endeavors.

References

Adams, J. *Competent to Counsel*. New Jersey: Presbyterian and Reformed Publishing Company, 1970.

Barkman, P. *Man in Conflict*. Grand Rapids: Zondervan Publishing House, 1965.

Boisen, A. "Challenge to Our Seminaries." *Christian Work*, 1926, 120.

Collins, G. *Search for Reality*. Wheaton: Key Publishers, 1964.

Drakeford, J. *Integrity Therapy*. Nashville: Broadman Press, 1967.

Fenichel, O. *The Psychoanalytic Theory of Neurosis*. New York: W. W. Norton & Co., 1945.

Fosdick H. *On Being a Real Person*. New York: Harper & Row, 1943.

Hiltner, S. *Pastoral Counseling*. New York: Abingdon Press, 1949.

Hulme, W. *Counseling and Theology*. Philadelphia: Fortress Press, 1956.

Hyder, O. *The Christian's Handbook of Psychiatry*. Old Tappan, N.J.: Fleming H. Revell, 1971.

Kierkegaard, S. *Concept of Dread*. Princeton: Princeton University Press, 1944.

LaHaye, T. *Spirit Controlled Temperament*. Wheaton: Tyndale House Publishers, 1966.

Meehl, P., Klann, R., Schmieding, A., Breimeier, K., and Schroeder-Slomann, S. *What, Then, Is Man?* St. Louis: Concordia Publishing House, 1958.

Miller, K. *A Second Touch*. Waco: Word Books, 1967.

Mowrer, H. *The Crisis in Psychiatry and Religion*. Princeton: Van Nostrand, 1961.

Narramore, C. *The Psychology of Counseling*. Grand Rapids: Zondervan Publishing House, 1960.

Nelson, M. *Why Christians Crack Up*. Chicago: Moody Bible Institute, 1960.

Oates, W. *Protestant Pastoral Counseling*. Philadelphia: The Westminster Press, 1962.

Pfister, O. *Christianity and Fear: A Study in History and in the Psychology and Hygiene of Religion.* London: George Allen & Unwin Ltd., 1948.

Roberts, D. *Psychotherapy and a Christian View of Man.* New York: Charles Scribner's Sons, 1950.

Rogers, C. *Counseling and Psychotherapy: New Concepts in Practice.* Boston: Houghton Mifflin, 1942.

Sanua, V. "Religion, Mental Health and Personality: A Review of Empirical Studies." *American Journal of Psychiatry,* 1969, 125, 9.

Tournier, P. *Guilt and Grace.* New York: Harper & Row, 1962.

Tweedie, D. *Logotherapy and the Christian Faith.* Grand Rapids: Baker Book House, 1961.

Waelder, R. *Basic Theory of Psychoanalysis.* New York: International Universities Press, 1960.

THE PULPIT AND THE COUCH

Gary R. Collins

When people had personal problems, only 28 percent went to professional counselors or clinics; 29 percent consulted their family physician, and 42 percent sought help from a clergyman. These were some of the findings of a survey made in the late fifties by the Joint Commission on Mental Illness and Health. Although the figures are now out of date, it still is accurate to conclude that pastors are called upon to do much of the counseling that is done in this country. A second conclusion follows from this: the theological seminary has the duty of equipping pastors for this important part of their ministry.

In one sense, pastoral counseling has been with us for centuries. The Old Testament is filled with accounts of godly men and women who were used by the Holy Spirit to encourage, guide, support, confront, advise, and in other ways help those in need. Jesus was described as a "Wonderful Counselor," and his followers were appointed not only to preach but to deal with the people's spiritual and psychological needs (Matt. 10:7-8). Later, the New Testament epistles gave great insight into the counseling techniques of their inspired writers. Throughout the Christian era church leaders have engaged in what have been called the four pastoral functions: healing, sustaining, guiding, and reconciling.

What we now know as the pastoral counseling movement, however, was begun by some pastors and physicians about fifty years ago. Perhaps the best known of the founding fathers was Anton T. Boisen, a minister and writer, who during the first sixty years of his long life experienced a number of psychotic breakdowns, three of which led to confinement in mental institutions. Boisen became convinced of the need to train seminary students for work with the mentally ill. Beginning with only a few students, he began a loosely organized training program for seminarians at Worcester State Hospital in Massachusetts.

From this simple beginning, "Clinical Pastoral Education" (CPE) has developed into a highly organized movement. Much of its work has been admirable: providing standards for the training of pastoral counselors; convincing hospital personnel of the importance of involving pastors in treatment of the physically and mentally ill; investigating ways in which theology and the psychological sciences can be related; showing the importance of training in counseling for seminarians; demonstrating that the personal and spiritual development of the seminarian is at least as important as his intellectual training for the ministry.

In the thirties and forties, when many seminaries were adding clinical pastoral training to their curricula, theologically conservative schools were skeptical. CPE appeared to be a theologically liberal movement, and this, coupled with a general distrust of psychology, undoubtedly caused evangelicals to stay apart.

While in no way endorsing CPE theology, Christian psychologists Clyde Narramore and Henry Brandt showed that a biblical approach to counseling was possible, and some evangelicals began to see the relevance of psychology to theological education. Now most conservative seminaries and Bible schools have courses in pastoral counseling, and some even have highly developed departments of pastoral psychology and counseling. Evangelical contact with the CPE movement remains minimal, however, and evangelicals have no clearly delineated or widely accepted biblical approaches to the counseling process.

Pastoral psychology and counseling can be divided into five overlapping categories that might be labeled the mainstream, the evangelical pastoral counselors, the Christian professionals, the theoretician-researchers, and the popularizers.

1. The mainstream. Most of the current training takes place within the guidelines of the CPE movement. Numerous hospitals have CPE training programs with carefully planned curricula and certified instructors. Many seminaries make one quarter of CPE training a requirement for graduation. People in the field follow with interest CPE-oriented publications, such as the *Journal of Pastoral Care.* Supervised counselor training and exposure to hospital settings can be a valuable experience, which CPE clearly provides, but the training raises several problems for theologically conservative people. First, following the leadership of Princeton's Seward Hiltner, CPE tends to consider personal experience rather than Scripture the foundation of training. Thomas Oden describes the method this way:

The overwhelming weight of authority for theological knowledge is given to experience, and in this sense the American pastoral care movement belongs essentially to the tradition of a liberalizing, pragmatizing pietism. One first does certain things and experiences certain relationships, like shepherding the flock, and only then draws valid theological conclusions. (*Contemporary Theology and Psychotherapy,* Westminster, 1967, p. 89)

Oden, who makes no claim to be an evangelical, makes this perceptive comment:

Although we hardly wish to challenge the validity of interview analysis in pastoral care, we seriously question whether this alone is adequate as a vantage point for drawing theological conclusions without the theological equilibrium that comes from the sustained study of Scripture and tradition and the struggle for rational and systematic self-consistency. (p. 90)

A second problem is that the CPE movement tends to borrow uncritically from humanistic secular psychology. In a book on the clinical training of ministers Hiltner says:

In terms of basic attitude, approach, and method pastoral counseling does not differ from effective counseling by other types of counselors. It differs in terms of the setting in which counseling is done, the religious resources which are drawn upon, and the dimension at which the pastor must view all human growth and human problems. (*The Counselor in Counseling,* Abingdon, 1950, p. 11)

The "religious resources" and "dimension" about which Hiltner speaks are not very well defined, but one gets the impression in another of his books *Pastoral Counseling* that prayer, Bible reading, and references to Christian doctrine are merely a part of the pastoral counselor's collection of techniques.

Third, people in the CPE movement appear to have little tolerance for conservative theological positions. Certainly in the past and perhaps in the present, evangelicals have tended to be directive, authoritarian counselors, insensitive to the needs and feelings of counselees. CPE leaders have resisted this approach and have been quick to notice the rigidities and insecurites that are often found among conservative Christians. Evangelicals also present a biblically based theology that to many critics appears to be narrow-minded and inflexible. As a result of these observations and the failure of evangelicals to show that a theologically conservative approach to counseling is more effective than the work done by CPE-trained counselors, theologically liberal counselors have tended to develop an inflexibility of their own in which they fail to take conservatives seriously.

Of course, pastoral counselors, like theologians, cover a broad theological spectrum. Some of the most familiar persons in the mainstream movement—William Hulme, Wayne Oates, John Drakeford, Carroll Wise, and John Sutherland Bonnell, for example—while probably not evangelicals, nevertheless take a more sympathetic view of conservative theology than would others like Seward Hiltner, Ernest Bruder, Edward Thornton, Russell Dicks, and, perhaps, Howard Clinebell.

2. Evangelical pastoral counselors. Currently the most outspoken and lucid opponent of the CPE mainstream is Jay E. Adams, professor of practical theology at Westminster Seminary. In several controversial but widely influential volumes, Adams ruthlessly criticizes counseling that is not based on Scripture and proposes a directive approach that he calls "nouthetic counseling."

Adams is clearly familiar with the contemporary psychological literature. Many of his criticisms of the mainstream are well founded, and more than anyone else he has attempted to develop an approach to counseling that is consistent with the truths of Scripture. Regrettably, however, Adams's lack of formal training in psychology leads him to oversimplify and reject too quickly the arguments of his opposition. His confrontational approach to counseling is clearly based on Scripture, but he appears to overlook other Bible passages that show the equal importance of supportive, referral, and insight counseling. Adams also has a tendency to attack psychological writers—Christian and non-Christian alike—in an unkind, name-calling manner. This undermines some of his arguments; what he says might be taken more seriously if it were presented more graciously.

Less influential than Adams are several other evangelical pastors-turned-counselors. William E. Crane, Maurice Wagner, and Paul D. Morris, for example, have written books on pastoral counseling from an evangelical perspective. In addition to pastoral training each of these men has had formal training in psychology. Their writing does not have the abrasive character of Adams's writing, but as yet none has published an approach as well developed as nouthetic counseling.

3. *The Christian professionals.* As might be expected, evangelicals who have formal training in psychology, psychiatry, and related areas have done most of the biblically oriented writing in pastoral psychology and counseling. Some of these professionals, like Donald Tweedie, James Dobson, Bruce Narramore, Quentin Hyder, James Mallory, and Anthony Florio, have directed their writings primarily to lay readers; but others, such as Clyde Narramore and I, have in addition written books and papers that deal with counseling from a pastoral perspective.

The quality and theological sophistication of these various works varies, of course. Most of the writers in the area risk ostracism from their professional colleagues for even daring to take religion seriously. It is not surprising that they proceed somewhat cautiously in their criticisms of psychology and in their attempts to combine psychology and theology. More than the others, however, these people understand the professional literature and the intricacies of the counseling process. It is from them, and others like them, that the most creative work in this field must come.

Observations at professional meetings suggest that many unknown evangelicals are working in counseling. Most of them do not write and hence are not widely known, but in their day-to-day work they are attempting to integrate biblical teachings with counseling techniques and concepts. The recently founded *Journal of Psychology and Theology* has given many of these counselors a forum for expressing their ideas.

4. *The theoretician-researchers.* One involved in a pastoral counseling ministry might easily conclude that research and theory are of minor importance. On the contrary, these areas are crucial. First, they add professional and intellectual support to the conclusions of Christian counselors, and, second, they provide an apologetic for facing the anti-Christian challenges constantly being raised in university psychology classes.

Many years ago Freud dismissed religion as an illusion, a "universal obsessional neurosis" that by serving as a narcotic helps potentially troubled people maintain their stability. B. F. Skinner's behaviorism, Ellis's rational-emotive therapy, Rogers's humanistic approach to counseling, Maslow's third-force psychology—all attack the very basis of Christianity and present the church with what may be one of its greatest current intellectual challenges.

Evangelicals for the most part have avoided this battleground, and psychology has cut the theological moorings of numerous students and psychologists in training. Vernon Grounds wrote a series of articles in this area published in *His* in 1963, and Bruce Narramore outlined some of the problems in an article in the *Journal of Psychology and Theology* (January, 1973). Among the writers who have attempted to discuss psychology and religion from a biblical perspective are Paul Tournier, R. O. Ferm, P. F. Barkman, H. W. Darling, and, in a joint work, Bruce Narramore and B. Counts. Perhaps the two most widely consulted volumes are *What, Then, Is Man?* by Meehl and his Lutheran colleagues and my own *Search for Reality*. Regrettably, the first is very difficult to read and the second is probably too elementary.

5. *The evangelical popularizers.* This survey would be incomplete without some reference to the popular speakers who crisscross the country dispensing practical advice on daily living. The best known of these is Bill Gothard with his "Institute of Basic Youth Conflicts." Others are Keith Miller, Bruce Larson, Tim LaHaye, Howard Hendricks, Norman Wright, and the men who work for Family Life Seminars. Some, like Bill Gothard, are best known as speakers; others, like Paul Tournier, Keith Miller, Charlie Shedd, and Marabel Morgan, are best known through their books; and Tim LaHaye and others are known as both lecturers and writers.

Professional psychologists and social observers view these people with amazement. They seem to have come on the scene suddenly, they attract large followings, and in most cases they have little or no training in psychology. They appear to have several characteristics in common. All deal with down-to-earth subjects, give simple explanations for problems, provide workable formulas for success and problem-solving, communicate effectively without psychological jargon, have attractive personalities, are at least somewhat biblically oriented, and say something that is in some way unique. In an age of economic and political instability, declining morals, and increasing crime, these popularizers proclaim a measure of hope, stability, and the promise of success. People follow them like sheep looking for a shepherd.

Professional counselors complain that the popularizers are overly simplistic and might do harm by their "self-help" formulas for psychological stability and principles for spiritual growth. Yet without doubt many people are helped by these popular Christian psychologies. Perhaps this shows again the truth of Paul's words in First Corinthians

1:27-29: "God chose what is foolish in the world to shame the wise, God chose what is weak to shame the strong, God chose what is low and despised in the world, even things that are not, to bring to nothing things that are, so that no human being might boast in the presence of God."

Compared with the less conservative segments of the Church, evangelicals have been slow to enter pastoral psychology and counseling. There are still pockets of mistrust of psychology and acceptance of the naïve view that commitment to Christ automatically eliminates all problems.

But progress is evident. Christian graduate schools of psychology at Fuller, Rosemead, and Georgia State; advanced degree programs in pastoral psychology and counseling at Trinity, Conservative Baptist, and Fuller; commendable undergraduate psychology programs at colleges like Gordon and Bethel; the emergence of Christian counseling centers in Atlanta, Grand Rapids, southern California, and other places; the sudden expansion of the Christian Association for Psychological Studies (6850 Division Avenue South, Grand Rapids, Michigan 49508); the appearance of the evangelically oriented *Journal of Psychology and Theology* (13800 Biola Avenue, La Mirada, California 90639); the influence of the popularizers; the willingness of evangelical mission boards to have psychologists help them select and counsel missionaries; the psychological research on religious experience conducted by William Wilson and his evangelical colleagues at Duke University—developments like these signify an explosion of interest. There is no one geographical or academic center for this activity, and as yet there are few established leaders, though several are emerging.

As we move into the last quarter of this century it seems to me that our efforts should focus on five major areas:

1. Christian counseling. Is it simply a Rogerian, Freudian, or behavioristic approach with occasional prayer and references to the Bible, or is counseling based on biblical assumptions in some way unique? Counseling techniques depend largely on the personality of the counselor and the nature of the counselee's problems. We are unlikely to arrive at one biblical approach to counseling, any more than we have discovered one biblical approach to missions, evangelism, or preaching. Still, we should try to uncover the various techniques and approaches that arise out of or are clearly consistent with the teachings of Scripture. Then we should try out these techniques, testing their effectiveness not by subjective feelings about whether or not we are "really helping people" but by carefully controlled assessment techniques.

2. Training and education. How do we train people to be effective counselors? This problem has concerned secular psychologists and mainstream pastoral counselors for several years. Only now are researchers learning how to select sensitive people and mold them into perceptive counselors. Much of this work can be applied to training

Christian counselors, but in addition we must be alert to the spiritual qualifications for counselors that are mentioned in Galatians 6:1 and elsewhere.

The training of Christian counselors must take place on three fronts. The first is the training of professionals. This usually occurs in graduate schools of psychology and in counseling centers where students get practical experience. Second, evangelicals must give special attention to training pastors and other church leaders to counsel. This is the major responsibility of the seminaries; their task is not only to train students but to give continuing education to missionaries, ministers, and other Christian workers.

A third area of training is sure to be of increasing importance in the coming decade: the training of laymen for "peer counseling." Nobody knows how many people turn to relatives, neighbors, friends, or fellow church members when they are in psychological and spiritual need, but it may be that this is where most counseling takes place. Some creative work in this area is being done at the Link-Care Foundation in Fresno, California. Other training centers must join in considering such questions as how we select and train lay counselors, how they should be supervised, what kinds of problems they can handle best, how they can be trained to make referrals and to whom, and even whether such people should be doing counseling at all. It is possible that a little counseling knowledge can be a dangerous thing, but no knowledge might be worse.

3. Preventive psychology. The well-known proverb that an ounce of prevention is worth a pound of cure has only recently been applied to the field of counseling. In the secular world, Caplan's *Principles of Preventive Psychiatry,* published in 1964, did much to alert counselors to the importance of helping people avoid problems or stop existing ones from getting worse. Two books by Clinebell and one by Glenn Whitlock have pointed to the need for preventive pastoral psychology, but these books take no real biblical stance. Premarital counseling is a form of prevention that has been widely used by Christians and non-Christians alike, and the books and speeches by the popularizers help many people to avoid problems; but apart from these two areas very little has been done in preventive psychology. It is a wide open field for those who believe that being committed to Christ can influence how one copes with life's problems.

4. Theory and psychological apologetics. This area presents two overlapping concerns for evangelicals. First, we must help Christian students and psychologists see that despite the analyses of Freud, Skinner, and others, Christianity and psychology need not be antithetical. Christians in psychology are in a unique position to study matters like the meaning of life, the effect of belief on psychological functioning, and the ways in which psychological science and Christian faith can be integrated to bring a fuller understanding of human behavior. They must not abandon the field of personality theory, philosophy of science, or the psychology of religion. In these fields evangelicals can make a special contribution, and young Christians in psychology must be helped to see this. They must also be helped to see that psychological analyses of faith healing, conversion, Christian behavior, persuasion techniques, beliefs, attitudes, and religious experience need not undercut the Christian's belief system. There are good answers and counterarguments to the challenges that come to Christianity from psychology.

Closely related to this should be a clear, concise outreach to nonbelievers within the psychological disciplines and to laymen who are sophisticated psychologically. The non-Christian may, while criticizing and rejecting the concept of religious presuppositions, uncritically and religiously accept a whole group of philosophical assumptions as a basis for his own psychological conclusions. This inconsistency should be pointed out. In addition, the relevance and intellectual bases of Christianity need to be presented to people who are discovering that psychology, while powerful, does not have all the answers to human problems. Like the young student, the professional who offers anti-Christian psychological analyses needs to be shown his errors and faulty conclusions.

This theoretical and apologetical emphasis is one of the most difficult. Psychologists are remarkably resistant to anything philosophical or theological, and their students are easily swayed by psychological analyses. To do work in this area one must be thoroughly familiar with both theology and psychology, skilled in communicating, and astute in observing the changing psychological scene.

5. Research. Good research is hard, sometimes frustrating, costly in time and often in money. Christian professors are often too busy with course work to engage in extensive research. The universities do not encourage research into religious experience, and money for such projects is difficult to raise. Furthermore, variables such as Christian maturity, faith in God, or counseling effectiveness are very hard to investigate empirically. Perhaps these obstacles have dissuaded many from entering psychological research, but this work must be done if we are to counsel, train, prevent, and theorize efficiently.

Psychology and counseling present the evangelical with an exciting and potentially rewarding challenge. It is a relatively new field and needs creative thinkers who are willing to be pioneers. But creativity and interest are not enough; the pioneers must be products of solid psychological and theological training, and they must be deeply committed to the authority of Scripture, to the importance of natural revelation, and to the lordship of Jesus Christ.

THE TASK AHEAD: SIX LEVELS OF INTEGRATION OF CHRISTIANITY AND PSYCHOLOGY

Robert E. Larzelere

Notable strides have been made in recent years in the integration of Christianity and psychology. **The growth of organizations such as the** Christian Association for Psychological Studies indicates the increasing interest in this topic. New books are appearing more frequently which integrate a Christian perspective with psychology in general (e.g., Collins, 1977; Myers, 1978) or with specific psychological topics (e.g., Dobson, 1974; Gorsuch and Malony, 1976; Meier, 1977; Narramore and Counts, 1974). Sufficient integration has been done to warrant categorization of various types of approaches to the integration task (Carter, 1977; Crabb, 1977; McLemore, 1976).

Progress has been somewhat uneven, however. The *Journal of Psychology and Theology* has seen a substantial increase in theoretical papers submitted but relatively little increase either in research papers or in clinical application papers that are relevant to integration.[1]

This article attempts to address the first of these shortcomings by developing a model designed to show the potential contribution of research to integration. This model also illustrates the interrelationships among a variety of integration tasks. Previous overviews of integration have generally clarified the distinctions among different types of approaches to integration. In contrast, this model attempts to suggest ways that different integration strategies could complement one another.

Briefly, the model specifies six levels of scientific inquiry, varying from a World View (presuppositional) level through theoretical levels to a Data level. A growing number of psychologists are becoming more aware of the interrelationships among world views, psychological theories, and psychological research. This seems to be largely due to a growth in the prestige of non-behavioristic perspectives, particularly in developmental psychology. Until the late 1960s behaviorism was clearly the dominant

This article was earlier read as a paper presentation at the 1979 convention of the Christian Association for Psychological Studies, Minneapolis, Minnesota. John D. Carter and Robert M. Nuermberger are gratefully acknowledged for their extensive and helpful critiques of earlier versions of this article.

[1]J. R. Fleck, personal communication, April 3, 1979.

model in experimental psychology. Consequently, its presuppositions remained unexpressed and unquestioned and its propositions were largely unchallenged. After behaviorism competed with nonbehaviorist theorists such as Piaget for some time, it became obvious to some developmental psychologists that differences in world views and presuppositions were basic to many differences in theoretical propositions, data interpretations, and research questions (Overton and Reese, 1973; Reese and Overton, 1970). Other psychologists (e.g., Marx and Hillix, 1979) are also becoming aware of such issues, due largely to the influence of Kuhn's (1970) book on paradigms in science.

This is encouraging to Christian social scientists for several reasons. First, such discussions of world views make the area of major differences between Christianity and secular psychology more explicit. Previously, Christians were aware that some of their values and presuppositions conflicted with some conclusions made in the name of psychology. However, the general stance of psychologists was either to accept their own presuppositions uncritically or to deny the existence of any distinctive presuppositions of their own by claiming that their social science was value free. It can be argued that apparent differences between Christianity and secular psychology reflect a clash between world views similar to the clash between the behaviorist (or mechanistic) and organismic world views. This is not to say that the clash between mechanistic and organismic presuppositions is as basic as the differences between Christian and secular presuppositions.

Second, because of competing world views in experimental psychology, a Christian psychologist is often not alone in criticizing a position that is inconsistent with a Christian world view. For example, Collins (1977) uses mostly criticism from within secular psychology in discussing the shortcomings of each of the three major forces in contemporary psychology.

But another implication is of major importance for this article. Reese and Overton (1973), Kuhn (1970), and others emphasize the importance of the interrelationships among world views, theoretical propositions, and empirical research. This leads fairly directly to the model of six levels of scientific inquiry to be developed in this article. This model, in turn, can serve as a guide for the various integration tasks that need to be emphasized in coming years. An overview of the six-levels model will be presented first. Then each of the six levels will be discussed in turn, along with some potential tasks that could be done at that level to further the integration of Christianity and experimental psychology.

Six Levels of Scientific Inquiry

Table 1 outlines six levels of scientific inquiry, modified from Clore and Byrne (1974). Note that the levels vary from abstract (World View) to concrete (Data) and from theoretical to empirical. Movement down the table involves deduction; movement upward represents induction. As Clore and Byrne note, the meaning of confirmation or disconfirmation differs from level to level and confirmation or disconfirmation at one level affects neighboring levels the most and distant levels the least.

The World View level is in many ways the most basic and yet the most difficult to conceptualize. The central component of this level would be the world view adhered to. The major world views used in psychology today are mechanism (i.e., behaviorism) and organicism (e.g., Piaget, Kohlberg, Gestalt psychology). They are considered by many to be incompatible, with their incompatibilities reflected throughout all six levels (Collins, 1977; Overton, 1973; Overton and Reese, 1973; Pepper, 1942; Reese and Overton, 1970). A psychologist uses a particular world view, explicitly or implicitly, as a guide and rationale for his or her theoretical and empirical work. World views determine the appropriateness of theoretical formulations, of types of questions, and of methods of gathering and analyzing data. Scientific procedures at each lower level must be consistent with the World View level. Consequently, the empirical evidence generated by psychologists generally supports the world view they adhere to (Overton, 1973; Overton and Reese, 1973).

TABLE 1
Levels of Scientific Inquiry

Level	Description	Meaning of Repeated Disconfirmations
World View	Basic assumptions and values	Impossible, directly
General Proposition	General models and theories	Impossible, directly
Linkage	Induction and deduction	Need better linkages or unity of overall conceptual framework becomes questionable
Specific Proposition	Specific models and empirical laws	Modify proposition or reinterpret data
Hypothesis	Deriving hypotheses and generalizing from data	Incorrect hypothesis
Data	Admissible elements of information	Original data not replicable or of limited generalizability

Adapted from Clore and Byrne (1974).

The intermediate levels consist of two classifications of propositions (General and Specific) and two types of connections (Linkage and Hypothesis). Psychological theories and propositions cannot really be neatly dichotomized into two categories. Instead there is a continuum from general, inclusive propositions to specific, limited propositions. The dichotomy is useful, however, to simplify the discussion and yet highlight some important differences between general and specific psychological propositions.

Similarly, the connective levels are not neat dichotomies, but hypotheses can be generated more readily from specific propositions than general ones. Logical reasoning is usually the primary linkage between general and specific propositions, whether moving inductively (generalization) or deductively. Inductive generalization also links data to specific propositions, but hypotheses are the preferred way to linking those levels deductively.

No psychological issue at any level can be considered adequately without also dealing with related issues at other levels. All the levels are interdependent with each other. Clore and Byrne (1974) give examples of representative publications at each level pertinent to their research program on interpersonal attraction. At the Data level, they cite Byrne's (1961) early finding that the more similar two strangers' attitudes are, the more attracted they tend to become toward each other. Byrne and Clore's (1970) statement of the reinforcement-affect model of attraction was cited as an example of related work at the General Proposition level. They noted, in turn, that this was related to assumptions of determinism, hedonism, and neobehaviorism (World View level).

Keeping in mind the interdependencies among the different levels of psychological inquiry, let us turn to a consideration of the tasks involved in integrating Christianity and experimental psychology at each of the six levels.

World View Level

The major task at this level is to clarify the presuppositions of world views used in secular psychology and to compare them with presuppositions appropriate for a Christian world view. Collins (1977) has done an excellent job of comparing Christian and behaviorist presuppositions, which are summarized in table 2.

TABLE 2
Basic Presuppositions of Behaviorism and Christian Psychology

Behaviorism	*Christian Psychology*
empiricism	expanded empiricism
determinism	determinism and free will
relativism	biblical absolutism
reductionism	modified reductionism
naturalism	Christian supernaturalism

Adapted from Collins, 1977.

For example, behaviorists assume that empirical data are the preferred if not the only sources of data. The expanded empiricism presupposition of Christian psychology indicates that the sources of data include the Bible, intuition, and logical thinking as well as empirical observation. This is the major presuppositional distinction affecting the task of integrating Christianity and psychology at the Data level. The major distinction between secular and Christian psychology at the Data level is that Christian psychology recognizes the Bible as data whereas secular psychology does not. As will be shown, this distinction affects the integration task at all the intermediate levels.

General Proposition Level

Most overt conflict between secular and Christian psychology occurs at this level. For example, the apparent conflict over evolution is not basically over the special theory of evolution, but over the philosophical development of evolutionism and over the general theory of evolution (Bube, 1968). Also, the conflict over Skinner's behaviorism is not over the empirical findings of behaviorists, but over such generalizations as Skinner's (1971) *Beyond Freedom and Dignity.*

Most Christians have limited their responses to the General Proposition level, stating that such and such a position is wrong because it is inconsistent with the Bible. As noted in table 1, however, it is virtually impossible to disconfirm any general proposition directly. Instead, an argument for modifying or rejecting some general psychological proposition must focus substantially on other levels of scientific inquiry.

Thus, one integration task at this level would be to clarify the assumptions (World View) behind the general proposition in question. Collins (1977) does a good job of this in regard to the often-accepted conclusion of secular clinicians "that religion is archaic, inhibiting, immature, and often harmful" (p. 100). He points out that such a conclusion is based on two assumptions: (1) that whatever cannot be observed satisfactorily by the scientific method does not exist, and (2) that the religious beliefs of the emotionally disturbed provide an accurate indication of religion itself.

As is evident from table 1, such an argument cannot disconfirm a general proposition (e.g., that religion is harmful, etc.). It does make clear, however, that the proposition of interest is based substantially on some questionable assumptions and not on hard data alone.

It also opens the door to alternative general propositions which explain similar data but which are consistent with alternative presuppositions. Indeed, this is a second integration task at the General Proposition level: to develop alternative general propositions which are consistent with the other levels of Christian psychology. This will often involve reinterpretation of specific psychological propositions and data, which will be discussed at the appropriate levels.

A closely related third integration task is to integrate existing knowledge. This is one of the two major purposes of psychological theories (Koteskey, 1975). The other purpose, to predict new findings, is more directly relevant to the Specific Proposition and Hypothesis levels. Christian psychologists need to develop alternative general propositions that integrate existing psychological knowledge. For example, Koteskey (1975, 1978) has shown how Christian psychology could integrate behavioristic and humanistic propositions by recognizing that behaviorism is most relevant to the finite aspects of humans and humanistic psychology is most pertinent for the personhood aspects.

Another integration task at this level is to reinterpret the importance of psychological propositions. World views often influence which propositions psychologists focus on. For example, Lewis and Spanier (1979) identify seventy-four specific propositions relating independent variables to marital quality and stability. By induction they derived thirteen more general propositions and three most general propositions. Each of the thirteen intermediate propositions summarized between two and eleven specific propositions. Yet four independent variables indicating religiosity and seven independent variables reflecting a common lifestyle of evangelical Christians were nowhere revealed in the thirteen intermediate propositions. Thus, religiosity and an evangelical lifestyle were regarded as of minor significance even though the actual data support their importance for marital adjustment at least as much as many of the intermediate propositions. (In contrast, Stephens, 1978, concludes that religiosity is one of the six most clearly supported predictors of marital adjustment.)

In sum, the integration tasks at the General Proposition level include clarifying the presuppositions of general psychological propositions, proposing alternate propositions if necessary, developing general propositions to integrate existing knowledge, and reinterpreting the importance of some propositions. Integration at this level must necessarily involve other levels as well, since disconfirmation or modification of general propositions is impossible directly. Therefore, let us turn our attention to other levels.

Linkage Level

This level involves connections between general propositions and specific ones, linkages that are crucial for the unity of an overall conceptual framework and are necessary for indirect evidences for or against general propositions. The opinion that a given general proposition is inconsistent with Scripture is only a starting place. Then, Christian psychologists need to identify relevant scriptural passages and relevant empirical data and develop generalizations for more theoretical levels from both kinds of data. At the Linkage level, this will involve generalizations from more specific propositions. It would be preferable, as Bannister and Wichern (1978) have suggested, to have Christian psychologists and theologians cooperate in such an endeavor. Better yet, if possible, is McQuilkin's (1977) recommendation to have both areas of expertise residing in the same person. The objective of either approach would be to achieve the proper balance between special and general revelation, in this particular case, in the task of making generalizations. Such generalizations should yield general propositions that are more consistent than existing ones with Scripture and with empirical data. For example, Myers (1978) uses both psychological and theological data to support his holistic position on the mind-body problem.

Once some alternate general propositions are made, the Linkage level is again important for deducing specific propositions which can be tested empirically. With or without alternate general propositions, Christian psychologists could derive specific propositions from secular psychological propositions which seem questionable. If these, in turn, were not supported empirically, the general proposition in question would need to be modified.

Thus, at the Linkage level, the integration tasks include induction and deduction, both with the goals of developing alternative general propositions when necessary and of pointing out the limitations of accepted general propositions.

Specific Proposition Level

At this level, a Christian psychologist may find fewer apparent conflicts with a secular psychology than at the General Proposition level. The major type of integration task at this level involves reinterpretation (Koteskey, 1975). We need to consider reinterpreting psychological conclusions if scriptural data sheds more light on it. Again several integration tasks are especially relevant at this level.

First, Christian psychologists may often need to reinterpret labels. While a research participant's responses to a questionnaire or to an experimental procedure may fit quite nicely into a Christian psychological perspective, the labels put on sets of those responses reflect the researcher's (or test designer's) presuppositions and biases. Consequently, a Christian psychologist should question whether the label actually describes the corresponding set of responses. For example, Glock and Stark (1966) concluded that American anti-Semitism was rooted in conservative Christian beliefs. One crucial link in their argument was the hostile attitude of Christians toward the contemporary Jewish religion. But this was indicated by agreement with such items as "The Jews can never be forgiven for what they did to Jesus until they accept him as the true Saviour." If someone strongly disagreed because he believed that Jesus never existed or that the crucifixion never occurred, he would be given a score indicative of low anti-Semitism. Thus, Christian beliefs themselves were confounded with Glock and Stark's items.

This labeling problem is obvious in other areas of research as well. One study (Murrell and Stachowiak, 1967) predicted that authoritarianism would be lower in families with well-adjusted children than in families in which at least one child was seeking psychological counseling. When their findings indicated that the two groups differed in the opposite direction, they changed the label of authoritarianism to cooperation and effectiveness of leadership. Similarly Price (1973) had different explanations for the low proportion of individuals who changed their opinion after new relevant information was given. The group high in self-actualization was thought to have a realistic perspective and high awareness of the situation. In contrast, the group low in self-actualization was considered rigid and unwilling to assimilate new information. The data were quite similar for both groups (a middle group was much more flexible than either extreme), but widely contrasting labels were used depending on the level of self-actualization.

Christian psychologists need to be sensitive to the fact that labels reflect expectations and presuppositions as well as the actual data. Therefore, reinterpretation may involve searching for new labels which reflect the data fairly and also are consistent with a Christian world view.

Second, Christian psychologists need to reinterpret the importance of findings. Many psychologists seem to be expert at selectively attending to findings that support their own positions. Two examples relevant to Christians are the issues of the advisability of premarital sex and of spanking. In both cases, the general social scientific view is the opposite of the traditional Christian position. The data support the Christian stand on premarital sex and the social scientific position on spanking. Yet the data relating premarital sex to subsequent marital satisfaction are either ignored or pushed aside as a minor finding full of methodological problems. In contrast, Sears, Maccoby, and Levin's (1957) finding that severity of punishment is associated with hostile aggressiveness in children is cited as a major basis for the elimination of corporal punishment (e.g., Steinmetz and Straus, 1974) with little or no mention of the size of the relationship ($r = .16$), methodological shortcomings, or the possibility that children's aggressiveness may influence parental discipline (Bell, 1968).

These examples also suggest a third related area of reinterpretation at the Specific Proposition level: the reinterpretation of the importance of methodological shortcomings. Psychologists are quick to search for methodological shortcomings of findings that do not fit their own viewpoint, but slow to criticize supportive findings. This situation is not necessarily bad as long as psychologists in different camps are subjecting each other's findings to the same amount of methodological scrutiny. The danger comes when the search for methodological shortcomings favors one group over another, as has been the case when so few Christian psychologists have asked such questions publicly.

Hypothesis Level

This brings us to the Hypothesis level, which links empirical data to specific propositions. One purpose of theoretical propositions is to predict new findings. Christians can find a wealth of ideas for new hypotheses as a byproduct of reinterpreting specific psychological propositions. Alternative labels, a broader picture of relevant research, and awareness of methodological shortcomings often lead quite naturally to research hypotheses. For example, it would be interesting to discover whether Glock and Stark's (1966) findings would be replicated if an alternative measure of hostility against the Jewish religion was used which was not confounded with basic Christian beliefs.

Such hypothesis testing is theoretically of crucial importance for increasing the prestige of a Christian psychology among non-Christian experimental psychologists. In reality, Bem (1979, p. 541) is probably right when he says that convenience of the vocabulary, current interests of psychologists, and relevance of a theory to those current interests affect the prestige of a theory more than do hypothesis tests. But that merely says once again that presuppositions and values influence how readily various theories will be accepted.

Although the name of this level emphasizes the deductive linkage between the Specific Theory level and the Data level, the inductive linkage (generalization) is just as important. The major integration task here, as at the Linkage level, is the appropriate interrelating of scriptural and empirical data.

Data Level

At this level there should be little problem with integrating psychological data into a Christian psychology. If all truth is God's truth, then reliable empirical data should fit into a Christian world view. However, two possible problems should be noted. The first is that the sample may be inadvertently biased by the researcher's presuppositions. This is a common criticism, for example, of Maslow's study of self-actualized persons (Koteskey, 1975). Another example is Leathers (1970), who eliminated a subject because he was a "religious fanatic." According to his research design, a confederate was to be supportive of his comments for the first half of a discussion period but then become very unsupportive for the second half. He was interested in discovering the effect of trust destruction on the communication process. Perhaps he discovered an important behavioral distinction of certain committed Christians, but, if so, it apparently did not fit his expectations or world view.

A second possible problem is that Christian psychologists may be much more familiar with empirical data than with biblical data in their areas of psychological expertise. A closer balance could be achieved by collaboration with theologians or by the development of biblical exegesis tools by psychologists.

Conclusions

These six levels of scientific inquiry provide an overview of the areas that need to be dealt with in integrating Christianity with secular psychology. Some specific integration tasks at each level have been suggested. Certainly the suggestions here can be refined and additional integration tasks can be added.

There seems to have been relatively little integration done at the intermediate levels. Most integration of Christianity and psychology has focused on broad issues, such as finding the proper balance between psychology and theology. More books are needed, such as Myers' (1978), which evidence good psychological scholarship as well as good understanding of relevant Scriptures. An apparent conflict between a psychological conclusion and a traditional Christian position could often be an excellent starting point for specialized integration work. One approach would be to identify the related integration tasks at each level of scientific inquiry. Then the integration tasks that seem to have the most potential fruitfulness could be worked on.

A secondary purpose of the six-levels model is to improve understanding among people interested in a Christian perspective of psychology. All too often, a specific proposition or application is rejected as unbiblical by Christians because an associated general proposition of presupposition contradicts Scripture (e.g., Vos, 1978). Hopefully, a better understanding of the interrelationships among world views, theories, and research findings will reduce this tendency to "throw out the baby with the bathwater."

Perhaps an analogous six levels could be developed for psychological applications in general, and psychological counseling in particular. The most obvious difference would be the substitution of practical application levels for specific research levels, yielding modified versions of the Hypothesis and Data levels. Some good initial attempts to relate presupposition and world views to counseling theory and practice are already available (Amundson and Willson, 1973; Collins, 1977).

The major thrust of the six-level model, however, involves research. Relatively little research has been done that relates directly to the integration of Christianity with secular psychology. Hopefully, the six levels clarify the place and importance of research for integration. If so, we should see a substantial increase in the quantity and quality of integration research and in the impact of Christian psychologists on our secular colleagues in the years to come.

References

Amundson, N. E., and Willson, S. "The Effect of Different Reality Perspectives on Psychotherapy." *Journal of Psychology and Theology*, 1973, *I* (3), 22-27.

Bannister, R. S., and Wichern, F. G. "A Theological Research Design Towards a Biblical Psychology." *Christian Association for Psychological Studies Bulletin,* 1978, *4* (1), 11-14.

Bell, R. Q. "A Reinterpretation of the Direction of Effects in Studies of Socialization." *Psychological Review,* 1968, *75,* 81-95.

Bem, D. J. "Social Psychology." In E. R. Hilgard, R. L. Atkinson, and R. C. Atkinson (eds.), *Introduction to Psychology* (7th ed.). New York: Harcourt Brace Jovanovich, 1979.

Bube, R. H. "Biblical Revelation." In R. J. Bube (ed.), *The Encounter Between Christianity and Science.* Grand Rapids: Eerdmans, 1968.

Byrne, D. "Interpersonal Attraction and Attitude Similarity." *Journal of Abnormal and Social Psychology,* 1961, *62,* 713-15.

Byrne, D., and Clore, G. L. "A Reinforcement Model of Evaluative Responses." *Personality: An International Journal,* 1970, *1,* 103-28.

Carter, J. D. "Secular and Sacred Models of Psychology and Religion." *Journal of Psychology and Theology,* 1977, *5* (3), 197-208.

Clore, G. L., and Byrne, D. "A Reinforcement-Affect Model of Learning." In T. L. Huston (ed.), *Foundations of Interpersonal Attraction.* New York: Academic Press, 1974.

Collins, G. R. *The Rebuilding of Psychology.* Wheaton, Ill.: Tyndale House Publishers, 1977.

Crabb, L. J., Jr. *Effective Biblical Counseling.* Grand Rapids: Zondervan Publishing House, 1977.

Dobson, J. *Hide or Seek.* Old Tappan, N.J.: Fleming H. Revell, 1974.

Glock, C. Y., and Stark R. *Christian Beliefs and Anti-Semitism.* New York: Harper & Row, 1966.

Gorsuch, R. L., and Malony, H. N. *The Nature of Man: A Social Psychological Perspective.* Springfield, Ill.: Charles C. Thomas, 1976.

Koteskey, R. L. "Toward the Development of a Christian Psychology: Man." *Journal of Psychology and Theology,* 1975, *3* (4), 298-306.

————. "Toward the Development of a Christian Psychology: Learning and Cognitive Processes." *Journal of Psychology and Theology,* 1978, *6* (4), 254-65.

Kuhn, T. S. *The Structure of Scientific Revolutions* (2nd ed.). Chicago: University of Chicago, 1970.

Leathers, D. G. "The Process Effects of Trust-Destroying Behavior in the Small Group." *Speech Monographs,* 1970, *37,* 180-87.

Lewis, R. A., and Spanier, G. B. "Theorizing about the Quality and Success of Marriage." In W. R. Burr, R. Gill, F. I. Nye, and I. L. Reiss (eds.), *Contemporary Theories about the Family* (Vol. 1). New York: Free Press, 1979.

Marx, M. H., and Hillix, W. A. *Systems and Theories in Psychology* (3rd ed.). New York: McGraw-Hill Book Co., 1979.

McLemore, C. W. "The Nature of Psychotheology: Varieties of Conceptual Integration." *Journal of Psychology and Theology,* 1976, *4* (3), 217-20.

McQuilkin, J. R. "The Behavioral Sciences under the Authority of Scripture." *Journal of the Evangelical Theological Society,* 1977, *20,* 31-43.

Meier, P. D. *Christian Child Rearing and Personality Development.* Grand Rapids: Baker Book House, 1977.

Murrell, S. A., and Stachowiak, J. G. "Consistency, Rigidity, and Power in the Interaction Patterns of Clinic and Non-Clinic Families." *Journal of Abnormal Psychology,* 1967, *72,* 165-272.

Myers, D. G. *The Human Puzzle.* New York: Harper & Row, 1978.

Narramore, B., and Counts, B. *Guilt and Freedom.* Irvine, Calif.: Harvest House, 1974.

Overton. W. F. "On the Assumptive Base of the Nature-Nurture Controversy: Additive Versus Interactive Conceptions." *Human Development,* 1973, *16,* 74-89.

Overton, W. F., and Reese, H. W. "Models of Development: Methodological Implications." In J. R. Nesselroade and H. W. Reese (eds.), *Life-Span Developmental Psychology: Methodological Issues.* New York: Academic Press, 1973.

Pepper, S. C. *World Hypotheses: A Study in Evidence.* Berkeley: University of California Press, 1942.

Price, D. A. "Relationship of Decision Styles and Self-Actualization." *Home Economics Research Journal,* 1973, *2,* 12-20.

Reese, H. W., and Overton, W. F. "Models of Development and Theories of Development." In L. R. Gouley and P. B. Baltes (eds.), *Life-Span Developmental Psychology: Research and Theory.* New York: Academic Press, 1970.

Sears, R. R., Maccoby, E. E., and Levin, H. *Patterns of Child-Rearing.* Evanston, Ill.: Row, Peterson, 1957.

Skinner, B. F. *Beyond Freedom and Dignity.* New York: Alfred A. Knopf, 1971.

Steinmetz, S. K., and Straus, M. A. (eds.). *Violence in the Family.* New York: Dodd, Mead, 1974.

Stephens, W. "Predictors of Marital Adjustment." In T. F. Hoult, L. F. Henze, and J. W. Hudson (eds.), *Courtship and Marriage in America.* Boston: Little, Brown, 1978.

Vos, A. "A Response to 'God and Behavior Mod.'" *Journal of Psychology and Theology,* 1978, *6* (3), 210-14.

DIMENSIONS OF PERSONAL RELIGION: A TRICHOTOMOUS VIEW

J. Roland Fleck

Theoretical Development

Two-Dimensional Theories of Religiosity

Allport conceptualized the intrinsic-extrinsic personal religion dichotomy as unidimensional and bipolar, referring to a difference in motivational characteristics. According to Allport, extrinsically motivated persons subordinate religious practices and beliefs to the satisfaction of personal needs and motives, while intrinsically motivated individuals subordinate their personal motives and practices to the precepts of their religion. Intrinsic religious orientation is seen by Allport to be mature religious sentiment, whereas extrinsic orientation is seen to be immature. The former, more mature religious sentiment as defined by Allport (1950) has six attributes which represent the religious concommitants of Allport's general characteristics of psychological maturity.

Allport (1950) states the religiously mature person is conscious of the complexity of his religion and is involved in a continuous examination and reorganization of his religion. Though critical of his faith he is also articulate about it. The religiously mature person's faith may have its beginnings in simple and earlier drives, but it has undergone a transformation until it has itself become a master motive. As a result the religiously mature person's moral life is consistently directed by his religion.

The religiously mature individual's religion is comprehensive, raising the main and crucial questions of life and at the same time making the answers to these questions functional. Tolerance is a natural characteristic of this comprehensiveness. Thus the religiously mature person's religion is harmonious with the greater context of life in general. Religion is not departmentalized or isolated from other aspects of the world. Finally, the religiously mature individual has the ability to hold a belief in suspension until it is confirmed or modified, knowing that commitment is possible without complete certainty.

Used by permission of the author. Paper presented at the 1977 Annual Meeting of the Society for the Scientific Study of Religion, Chicago, Illinois, October 28. The author is indebted to Dr. Bernard Spilka of the University of Denver for his encouragement of this study and his assistance in the statistical analysis.

Feagin (1964) operationalized the intrinsic-extrinsic concept and used an "Intrinsic/Extrinsic Scale" of twenty-one items developed by Allport (1954). Feagin's factor analysis produced separate intrinsic and extrinsic factors which suggest separate intrinsic and extrinsic dimensions. In a comprehensive evaluation of the intrinsic-extrinsic literature, Hunt and King (1971) concluded that intrinsic and extrinsic orientations may be separate dimensions, not bipoles of one dimension as Allport suggests.

Spilka conceptualized committed and consensual religious orientation as separate dimensions representing broad differences in cognitive style and expression (Allen, 1965; Allen and Spilka, 1967). According to Allen (1965): "The committed style involves a personal . . . commitment to religious values wherein the full creed . . . is internalized. . . . The consensual style involves a conformity or acquiescence to religious values wherein the full creed is not meaningfully internalized . . ." (p. 13).

Allen and Spilka (1967) differentiate between committed and consensual religious orientation in terms of five structural components: content, clarity, complexity, flexibility, and importance. In terms of these five structural components,

the committed orientation . . . reflects an emphasis on the abstract relational qualities of religious belief which tend to be nonambiguous, well differentiated . . . and diversity-tolerant. It also involves a personal, devotional commitment to religious values which suffuse daily activities. The consensual orientation . . . reflects an emphasis on the concrete, literal qualities of religious belief which tend to be vague . . . non-differentiated . . . relatively restrictive and diversity-intolerant. It also involves a detached . . . , possibly vestigial commitment to religious values. (Allen, 1965, p. 14)

Both the theoretical conceptualization of the committed-consensual dichotomy (Allen, 1965; Allen and Spilka, 1967) and the more recent research findings by Spilka and his associates (Allen and Spilka, 1967; Raschke, 1973; Spilka and Minton, 1975; Minton and Spilka, 1976; Spilka and Mullin, 1977) indicate that committed religious motivation is more mature than consensual religious motivation. There is also great similarity between Spilka's conceptualization of the five structural components of committed religious orientation and Allport's six attributes of mature religious sentiment explicated earlier.

Spilka and Minton (1975) hypothesized that these two major approaches to defining personal religion, the intrinsic-extrinsic dichotomy and the committed-consensual dichotomy, are not examining personal belief from two different vantage points, but are actually dealing with the same phenomena. However, the research evidence to date indicates greater overlap between the intrinsic and committed dimensions than the extrinsic and consensual dimensions. This lack of overlap between consensual and extrinsic in comparison to committed and intrinsic is indicated in a study by Spilka and Minton (1975). The intrinsic and committed dimensions were highly correlated (r > .80), but the correlations between the consensual and extrinsic dimensions were much lower (r = .39 and r = −.12). Therefore, the consensual scale would seem to be measuring a substantially different dimension than the extrinsic scale. They also note that ". . . the intrinsic-extrinsic scales appear to be measuring opposing tendencies," whereas ". . . the committed-consensual measures are . . . independent of each other" (p. 8).

A Three-Dimensional Theory of Religiosity

The present author believes personal religion may be better accounted for by a trichotomous model, rather than the dichotomous models of Allport and Spilka. This thinking is due in part to the research findings that demonstrate very little overlap between the extrinsic and consensual dimensions. In addition, theory and research in the fields of sociology, social psychology, and education, presenting models for three types of people, three levels of attitude change, and three levels of valuing independently stimulated this effort to look for this same three-level phenomenon in the area of personal religion.

Building upon the theoretical conceptualizations of Reisman (1961), Kelman (1961), and Krathwohl et al. (1964), and the research findings of Brown (1964), and Hoge (1972), this article proposes a three-dimensional model of personal religion. The three dimensions include an intrinsic-committed religious orientation similar to Spilka's committed and Allport's intrinsic dimension, a consensual religious orientation in which religion supports personal comfort and relief, and an extrinsic religious orientation in which religious membership and participation are used in a self-serving, utilitarian manner for social purposes, such as gaining social standing and acceptance in the community. This latter dimension is similar to Allport's extrinsic dimension.

The sociologist David Reisman (1961) describes three different social character types: other-directed, tradition-directed, and inner-directed. Although Reisman's primary thrust concerns the difference in social character between people of different regions, eras, and groups, his other-directed, tradition-directed, and inner-directed social types seem to parallel the characteristics of the extrinsic, consensual, and intrinsic-committed dimensions of personal religion proposed in this article.

Reisman defines the other-directed person as one whose "contemporaries are the source of direction—either those known to him or those with whom he is indirectly acquainted. . . . The goals toward which (he) . . . strives shift with that guidance . . ." (p. 21).

The tradition-directed person lives a pattern of conventional conformity which reflects "his membership in a particular . . . clan . . . ; he learns to understand . . . patterns which have endured for centuries, and are modified but slightly . . . The important relationships of life may be controlled by . . . rigid etiquette . . . Moreover, the culture provides religion to occupy and to orient everyone" (p. 11).

In describing the inner-directed person, Reisman notes that the source of direction for this individual is internalized. "As the control of the primary group is loosened . . . a new psychological mechanism is invented. . . . This instrument . . . keeps the inner directed person on course even when tradition no longer dictates his moves. The inner-directed person becomes capable of maintaining a delicate balance between his life goal and the buffetings of his external environment" (p. 16).

Herbert Kelman (1961) proposed a three-process theory of attitude change, which included compliance, identification, and internalization. These three processes correspond to the proposed extrinsic, consensual, and intrinsic-committed religious styles, respectively.

According to Kelman, "Compliance can be said to occur when an individual accepts influence from another person or from a group because he hopes to achieve a favorable reaction from the other" (p. 62). Here the expression of opinion, even though the person may privately disagree with what he is expressing, is instrumental in the production of a satisfying social effect. The behavior tends to be related to a person's values only in an instrumental rather than an intrinsic way.

"Identification occurs when an individual adopts behavior derived from another person or a group because this behavior is associated with a satisfying self-defining relationship to this person or group" (p. 63). Identification maintains the individual's relation to a group in which his self-definition is anchored. To maintain his self-definition as a group member an individual has to model his behavior along particular lines and has to meet the expectations of his fellow members. Identification, like compliance, does not occur because the behavior or attitude itself is intrinsically satisfying to the individual. It occurs because of the satisfying relation to another person or group, and it requires the activation of the relation in order for it to occur. However unlike the compliance situation, the individual actually believes in the attitudes and actions that he adopts as a result of identification. Attitudes adopted through identification do remain tied to the external source and dependent on social support. They are not integrated with the individual's value system, but rather tend to be isolated from the rest of his values.

"Internalization can be said to occur when an individual accepts influence because the induced behavior is congruent with his value system" (p. 65). Here the content of the induced attitude or behavior is intrinsically rewarding. The attitude or behavior helps to solve a problem or is demanded by the values of the individual. He perceives it as inherently conducive to the maximization of his values.

In attempting to classify educational objectives which emphasize a feeling tone, an emotion, or a degree of acceptance or rejection, Krathwohl et al. (1964) recognized that people hold attitudes and values at different levels. They present a classification system in which values are considered to be affective states internalized at three levels of importance —acceptance level, preference level, and commitment level. These three levels form an internalization continuum very similar to Kelman's three processes of attitude change and appear to parallel in many respects the proposed extrinsic, consensual, and intrinsic-committed religion dimensions.

The lowest level of valuing, the acceptance level, is described as the level at which the individual is merely willing to be identified with the value or valued object and very little more. One cannot infer any motivation at this level of valuing.

At the preference level of valuing the individual actively begins to seek out the value or valued object. It is an intermediate level of involvement and the first level at which one can infer any kind of motivation in relation to the value.

The highest level of valuing, the commitment level, is described as the level at which the individual is clearly perceived as holding the value. The individual "acts to further the thing valued in some way, to extend the possibility of his developing it, to deepen his involvement with it and with the things representing it" (Krathwohl et al., 1964, p. 149). There is a real motivation to act out the behavior. "In some instances this may border on faith, in the sense of it being a firm emotional acceptance of a belief upon admittedly nonrational grounds" (Krathwohl et al., 1964, p. 149).

The three dimensions of personal religion proposed in this article are characterized as moving from compliance to religion for personal gain (extrinsic religious orientation), to identification with religion for support (consensual religious orientation) to internalization of religion for its own intrinsic value (intrinsic-committed religious orientation).

Extrinsic religion is conceptualized as being very similar to Allport's extrinsic religious orientation. Religious membership and participation are used in a self-serving, utilitarian manner for social purposes, such as meeting the right people, gaining acceptance and social standing in the community, realizing economic gain in one's business, etc.

Consensual religion is conceptualized in this article as a separate dimension from extrinsic religion. Religious authority, beliefs, ceremony, membership, participation, practices, ritual, and the religious group itself are used as personality supports or a haven for personal comfort, relief, and strength. Consensual religionists are characterized by a shallow and restrictive mode of thinking resulting in a simple conformist orientation to life, including steady, routine, and regular participation in institutionalized religious beliefs and practices.

Intrinsic-committed religion is conceptualized as being essentially the same as Spilka's committed religious orientation and Allport's intrinsic religious orientation. It involves a personal and authentic commitment to religious values which become the master motive in life and suffuse daily activities. Committed religionists display a high sense of perspective combined with an open, flexible, many-valued approach to faith and life.

Intrinsic-committed religion is mature religion—mature psychologically and religiously (Fleck, Ballard, and Reilly, 1975). Consensual religion and extrinsic religion are immature both psychologically and religiously, but in different ways.

Empirical Support for the Three-Dimensional Model of Religiosity

There are at least two research studies whose findings tend to support the proposed three-dimensional model of personal religion. Brown (1964), using Allport's definitions of intrinsic and extrinsic religious orientation to classify the answers to incomplete sentences about the role of religion in one's life, found that some subdivision of the two categories was necessary. He divided the responses into seven categories: intrinsic, borderline (between intrinsic and extrinsic), extrinsic (self-serving), extrinsic (conventional acceptance), little bearing, irrelevant (extrinsic disbelief), and antagonistic (intrinsic disbelief). Disregarding the last three categories, which deal with disbelief, Brown's intrinsic category parallels the intrinsic-committed religion dimension in the proposed model. Extrinsic (conventional acceptance) is an institutionally based extrinsic orientation and seems to be very close in meaning to the consensual religion dimension in the proposed model that involves the use of religion as a personality support. Extrinsic (self-serving) would seem to parallel closely the extrinsic religion dimension in the proposed model, which is also self-serving and utilitarian.

Hoge (1972), in the construction of the ten-item Intrinsic Religious Motivation Scale factor, analyzed twenty-eight items (nineteen of the items used by Feagin to measure intrinsic and extrinsic religious orientation and nine new items). The first factor was very large, and the ten items in the Intrinsic Religious Motivation Scale loaded strongly on it. Factor 2 had several strong loadings on extrinsically stated items emphasizing religion as personal comfort and relief. Items loading on this factor include: "Church is important as a place to go for comfort and refuge from the trials and problems of life"; "What religion offers most is comfort when sorrow and misfortune strike"; and "The primary purpose of prayer is to gain relief and protection." Factor 3 had loadings on extrinsically stated items emphasizing the relation of churchgoing to social status in the community, although this factor was not very stable. Items loading on this factor include: "One reason for my being a church member is that such membership helps to establish a person in the community"; "A primary reason for my interest in religion is that my church is a congenial social activity"; and "Occasionally I find it necessary to compromise my religious beliefs in order to protect my social and economic well-being." Factor 1 parallels the intrinsic-committed religion dimension in my proposed three-dimensional model; factor 2 parallels the consensual religion dimension; and factor 3 parallels the extrinsic religion dimension.

Method

Subjects. Participants in this study consisted of 569 undergraduate college students representing six colleges. Three hundred and two students came from five Christian colleges, while the remaining 267 came from a community junior college.

Instrumentation. An eighty-item Attitudes about Religion Scale was compiled by the author. This scale included Spilka's forty-five-item Religious Viewpoints Scale, ten additional extrinsic religious orientation items from the Allport-Feagin Scale, seven intrinsic and two extrinsic items constructed by Hoge, and sixteen additional consensual items constructed by the author and his students. A six-point Likert format was employed in seventy-four items with respondents indicating degree of agreement or disagreement with each item: 1 = strongly disagree; 6 = strongly agree. A four-alternative multiple-choice format was employed in the remaining six items.

Procedure. The Attitudes about Religion Scale was administered to each participant in this study. The eighty religious orientation items were subjected to factor analysis using the principal components approach with approximation to simple structure by varimax orthogonal rotation. The latent root-one criterion for stopping factor extraction was employed. Items were considered when they loaded .30 or above on the resulting factors. When agreement was reached regarding the composition of the meaningful and clearly established item configurations, scales were selected and K.R. 20 reliability coefficients were obtained.

Results

Stopping factor extraction utilizing the latent root-one criterion resulted in seventeen factors. Three, and possibly four, of the factors represent meaningful dimensions.

Factor 1 is by far the largest factor, accounting for 37 percent of the variance. It includes twenty-four items, all with factor loadings of .60 or above (see table 1). It is clearly an intrinsic-committed factor almost identical in description to Allport and Feagin's intrinsic, Spilka's committed, Hoge's intrinsic, and the intrinsic-committed dimension proposed in this article as one-third of the three-dimensional model of personal religion. The items loading on this intrinsic-committed factor describe a personal and authentic commitment to religious values that become the master motive in life and suffuse daily activities.

TABLE 1
Factor 1: Intrinsic-Committed

Item Number	Factor Loading	Item
28	.84	I try hard to carry my religion over into all my other dealings in life. (Spilka: Committed; Allport-Feagin: Intrinsic; Hoge: Intrinsic)
7	.84	Nothing is as important to me as serving God as best I know how. (Hoge: Intrinsic)
8	.83	My faith involves all of my life. (Hoge: Intrinsic)
14	.83	My ideas about religion are one of the most important parts of my philosophy of life. (Spilka: Committed)
13	.83	My religious beliefs are what really lie behind my whole approach to life. (Spilka: Committed; Allport-Feagin: Intrinsic; Hoge: Intrinsic)
38	.82	Prayer influences my dealings with other people. (Hoge: Intrinsic)
10	.79	One should seek God's guidance when making every important decision. (Hoge: Intrinsic)
79	.77	If not prevented by unavoidable circumstances, I attend church (a) more than once a week; (b) about once a week; (c) two or three times a month; (d) less than once a month. . (Spilka: Committed; Allport-Feagin: Intrinsic)
80	.75	How much time during the week would you say you spend reading the Bible and other religious literature? (a) more than two hours; (b) one to two hours; (c) less than one hour; (d) none. (Spilka: Committed)
71	.73	My interest in and real commitment to religion is greater now than when I first joined the church. (Spilka: Committed)
77	.73	How do you personally view the story of creation as recorded in Genesis? (a) literally true history; (b) probably true history; (c) a symbolic account which is no better than any other account of the beginning; (d) not a valid account of creation. (Spilka: Consensual)
55	.72	In my life I experience the presence of the Divine. (Hoge: Intrinsic)

Item Number	*Factor Loading*	*Item*
75	.72	I read literature about my faith or church: (a) frequently; (b) occasionally; (c) rarely; (d) never. (Spilka: Committed; Allport-Feagin: Intrinsic)
4	.71	Religion is especially important to me because it answers many questions about the meaning of life. (Spilka: Committed; Allport-Feagin: Intrinsic)
58	.70	I often think about matters relating to religion. (Spilka: Committed)
9	.67	Quite often I have been keenly aware of the presence of God or the Divine Being. (Spilka: Committed; Allport-Feagin: Intrinsic)
17	.66	If I have the opportunity to explain my beliefs to a non-Christian group I do it. (Hoge: Intrinsic)
74	-.66	Religion is a subject in which I am not particularly interested. (Spilka: Committed—reverse score)
64	.64	The Bible is perfect, without errors of any kind. (Spilka: Consensual)
57	.63	I try to obey the teachings of the Bible even when I don't feel like it because the right feeling will follow. (Fleck: Consensual)
65	-.62	It doesn't matter so much what I believe so long as I lead a moral life. (Allport-Feagin: Extrinsic; Hoge: Extrinsic)
11	.62	I like to go to church for I get something worthwhile to think about, and it keeps my mind filled with right thoughts. (Fleck: Consensual)
20	.62	Believing as I do about religion is very important to being the kind of person I want to be. (Spilka: Committed)
32	.60	I feel the church services give me inspiration and help me to live up to my best during the following week. (Fleck: Consensual)

Factor 2 accounts for 10 percent of the variance and includes nine items with factor loadings ranging from .73 to .35 (see table 2). This factor closely parallels Spilka's consensual religious orientation which emphasizes the concrete, literal qualities of religious belief (e.g., ritual, ceremony, order, etc.). This factor would appear to represent partially the consensual religion dimension proposed in this article, where religious authority, beliefs, ceremony, membership, participation, practices, ritual, and the religious group itself are used as personality supports or a haven for personal comfort, relief, and strength. The support and security derived from ritual, ceremony, and order seem clear in this factor, but the support function of religious authority, beliefs, and the religious group itself is absent. A sort of obsessive compulsive style is described by the items loading on factor 2.

TABLE 2
Factor 2: Consensual I—Ritual

Item Number	Factor Loading	Item
31	.73	The precision and orderliness with which religious ceremonies are performed is important. (Spilka: Consensual)
16	.67	I think that the placement and treatment of the various articles of worship is very important in a worship service. (Spilka: Consensual)
60	.66	One of the most important aspects of religion is the religious ceremonies. (Spilka: Consensual)
73	.64	The ritual of worship is a very important part of the religious ceremonies. (Spilka: Consensual)
69	.61	The more a religious service is ritualized the more it has meaning for me. (Spilka: Consensual)
45	.55	It is important to me that religious services be standardized. (Spilka: Consensual)
50	-.50	I do not think that the sequences of prayers, songs, etc., is very important in religious services. (Spilka: Consensual—reverse score)
41	.43	I like to think that people all over are going through nearly the same ritual in their religious worship. (Spilka: Consensual)
2	.35	The aim of missionaries should be to establish church buildings where religious services and ceremonies can be conducted. (Spilka: Consensual)

Factor 3 (actually the eighth factor extracted) accounts for 6 percent of the variance and includes seven items with factor loadings ranging from -.66 to -.33 (see table 3). It is clearly an extrinsic factor almost identical in description to Allport and Feagin's extrinsic religious orientation, and the extrinsic dimension proposed in this article. The items loading on this extrinsic factor describe a self-serving utilitarian style of religion.

TABLE 3
Factor 3: Extrinsic—Self-Serving

Item Number	Factor Loading	Item
59	-.66	The purpose of prayer is to secure a happy and peaceful life. (Spilka: Consensual; Allport-Feagin: Extrinsic)
72	-.66	The primary purpose of prayer is to gain relief and protection. (Allport-Feagin: Extrinsic)
62	-.56	What religion offers me most is comfort when sorrows and misfortune strike. (Allport-Feagin: Extrinsic)
66	-.49	I pray chiefly because I have been taught to pray. (Allport-Feagin: Extrinsic)
63	-.40	Brotherly love was the heart of the teaching of Jesus. (Spilka: Committed)
67	-.36	A primary reason for my interest in religion is that my church is a congenial social activity. (Allport-Feagin: Extrinsic)
70	-.33	Although I am a religious person I refuse to let religious considerations influence my everyday affairs. (Allport-Feagin: Extrinsic; Hoge: Extrinsic)

Factor 4 (actually the eleventh factor extracted) accounts for 4 percent of the variance and includes five items with factor loadings ranging from .67 to .30 (see table 4). It is the weakest and least clear of the four factors but appears to be another aspect of the consensual religion dimension proposed in this article. The support function of religious authority, belief closure, participation, and the religious group itself seems to be emphasized. If factor 2 describes obsessive-compulsive religion, then factor 4 describes a repressed, denying religious orientation.

TABLE 4
Factor 4: Consensual II—
Belief Closure and Group Dependency

Item Number	Factor Loading	Item
47	.67	I feel more confident when my pastor and church pray for a concern of mine than if I pray alone. (Fleck: Consensual)
68	.54	Doubting my religious beliefs reflects a lack of faith. (Fleck: Consensual)
48	.50	Obedience to my religious faith is more important than understanding the reason for obedience. (Fleck: Consensual)
46	.43	Religion is most real to me during my attendance at public church or religious services. (Spilka: Consensual)
44	.30	In matters of religion there is no compromise. (Fleck: Consensual)

The item combinations making up the four factors were then evaluated to see if reliable scales could be constructed. The K.R. 20 reliability coefficients ranged from .63 to .96, suggesting the utility of these instruments for the assessment of religious orientation. Using the twenty-four items loading on factor 1 as an intrinsic-committed scale yields a reliability of .96 (see table 1). By taking only the six highest loading items on factor 1 (i.e., items 28, 7, 8, 14, 13, and 38), the resulting intrinsic-committed scale (scale 1) loses very little reliability (K.R. 20 = .93) and highly correlates with the original twenty-four items scale (r = .96). Therefore, the six-item scale can be adequately substituted for the original twenty-four items.

Scale 2 parallels factor 2 (Consensual I: Ritual; see table 2) and has a reliability of .81. It is composed of eight items (i.e., items 31, 16, 60, 73, 69, 45, 41, and 2).

Scale 3 is identical to factor 3 (Extrinsic: Self-Serving; see table 3) and has a reliability of .73. It is composed of seven items (i.e., items 59, 72, 62, 66, 63, 67, and 70).

Scale 4 is identical to factor 4 (Consensual II: Belief Closure and Group Dependency; see table 4) and is the most unreliable of the four scales (K.R. = .63). It is composed of five items (i.e., items 47, 68, 48, 46, and 44).

Discussion

Table 5 contains the intercorrelations among the four scales, and in most instances the coefficients range from low to moderate in strength. The relationships among the Intrinsic-Committed scale (scale 1), Consensual I scale (scale 2), and Extrinsic scale (scale 3) are very similar to previous findings (Spilka and Minton, 1975; Minton and Spilka, 1976; Spilka, Stout, Minton, and Sizemore, 1977). The Intrinsic-Committed and Consensual I scales correlate .06 in the present study as compared to Committed-Consensual relationships of .19, -.05, and .31 in the three above-cited studies. The Intrinsic-Committed and Extrinsic scales correlate -.26 in the present study, as compared to Committed-Extrinsic relationships of -.41 and -.13 in two of the above-cited studies. The Consensual I and Extrinsic scales correlate .49 in the present study, as compared to Consensual-Extrinsic relationships of .39, .55, and .45 in the three above-cited studies.

TABLE 5

Intercorrelations among the Religious Orientation Scales
(N = 569)

		Scales	
Scales	2	3	4
1	06	-26*	37*
2		49*	41*
3			18*

*p>.001

Note: Code for scales is the same as designated in tables 1-4.
        Decimal points are omitted.

The Intrinsic-Committed and Extrinsic scales in the present study appear to be measuring somewhat opposing tendencies, whereas the Intrinsic-Committed and Consensual I scales are quite close to being independent of each other. The moderate relationship between Consensual I and Extrinsic in this study, as well as similar moderate relationships between Consensual and Extrinsic in previous, studies suggests that, even though something in common is present, the magnitude of the correlation coefficient is low enough to indicate that Consensual I and Extrinsic are dealing largely with different characteristics.

The Consensual II scale significantly correlates with the other three scales (Intrinsic-Committed, r = .37; Consensual I, r = .41; Extrinsic, r = .18). Because of the unreliability of this scale and no previous related research, only tentative comments can be made concerning these relationships. Although there is a moderate relationship between the Consensual I and Consensual II scales, they appear to be tapping largely different aspects of the proposed consensual dimension. Consensual II also appears to be a less extrinsic dimension than Consensual I, as indicated by its lower correlation with the Extrinsic scale (i.e., r = .18 versus r = .41).

Both Reilly (1978) and Constantini (1979) replicated the finding of intrinsic-committed, consensual, and extrinsic factors, which further validates the proposed trichotomous model of personal religious orientation. Wessel (1979) found differing personality concommitants for consensual and extrinsic religious individuals, substantiating the importance of distinguishing between these religious dimensions and not considering the two to be reflecting the same religious orientation.

The results of the factor analysis provide substantial support for the validity of the proposed three-dimensional model of personal religion. The Intrinsic-Committed factor parallels the proposed intrinsic-committed dimension and is essentially the same as Spilka's committed and Allport-Feagin's intrinsic. The Extrinsic factor parallels the proposed extrinsic dimension in which religion is used in a self-serving, utilitarian manner. This factor is essentially the same as Allport's extrinsic religious orientation. The Consensual I factor taps a substantial portion of the proposed consensual dimension. This factor is clearly the same as Spilka's consensual religious orientation which emphasizes the concrete, literal qualities of religion such as ritual, ceremony, order, etc. Missing from this factor is the proposed security, strength, and support derived by the consensual religionist from a closed belief system and identification with religious leaders and the religious group itself. The Consensual II factor seems to represent some of the aspects of the proposed consensual dimension that are absent in the Consensual I factor. The support function of belief closure and dependency upon religious leadership and the religious group itself is emphasized. The Consensual II factor is unstable and needs further study to ascertain whether it is solely an artifact of the present sample or a valid factor that needs further refining.

References

Allen, R. O. "Religion and Prejudice: An Attempt to Clarify the Patterns of Relationship." Doctoral dissertation, University of Denver, 1965.

Allen, R. O., and Spilka, B. "Committed and Consensual Religion: A Specification of Religion-Prejudice Relationships." *Journal for the Scientific Study of Religion*, 1967, *6*, 191-206.

Allport, G. W. *The Individual and His Religion*. New York: The Macmillan Co., 1950.

———. *The Nature of Prejudice*. Cambridge, Mass.: Addison-Wesley, 1954.

———. "Religion and Prejudice." *Crane Review*, 1959, *2*, 1-10.

———. *Personality and Social Encounter*. Boston: Beacon Press, 1960.

———. "The Religious Context of Prejudice." *Journal for the Scientific Study of Religion*, 1964, *4*, 91-99.

Allport, G. W., and Ross, J. M. "Personal Religious Orientation and Prejudice." *Journal of Personality and Social Psychology*, 1967, *5*, 432-43.

Brown, L. B. "Classifications of Religious Orientation." *Journal for the Scientific Study of Religion*, 1964, *4*, 91-99.

Constantini, T. L. "The Relationship of Birth Order and Sex to Religious Orientation and God Concept." Doctoral dissertation, Rosemead Graduate School of Professional Psychology, 1979.

Feagin, J. R. "Prejudice and Religious Types: A Focused Study of Southern Fundamentalists." *Journal for the Scientific Study of Religion,* 1964, *4,* 3-13.

Fleck, J. R., Ballard, S. N., and Reilly, J. W. "The Development of Religious Concepts and Maturity: A Three-Stage Model." *Journal of Psychology and Theology,* 1975, *3,* 156-63.

Hoge, D. R. "A Validated Intrinsic Religious Motivation Scale." *Journal for the Scientific Study of Religion,* 1972, *11,* 369-76.

Hunt, R. A., and King, M. B. "The Intrinsic/Extrinsic Concept: A Review and Evaluation." *Journal for the Scientific Study of Religion,* 1971, *10,* 339-56.

Kelman, H. C. "Processes of Opinion Change." *Public Opinion Quarterly,* 1961, *25,* 57-78.

Krathwohl, D. R., Bloom, B. S., and Masia, B. B. *Taxonomy of Educational Objectives: Handbook II: Affective Domain.* New York: David McKay Co., 1964.

Minton, B., and Spilka, B. "Perspectives on Death in Relation to Powerlessness and Form of Personal Religion." *Omega,* 1976, *7,* 261-68.

Raschke, V. "Dogmatism and Committed and Consensual Religiosity." *Journal for the Scientific Study of Religion,* 1973, *12,* 339-44.

Reilly, J. W. "Ego Identity Status and Religious Orientation." Doctoral dissertation, Rosemead Graduate School of Professional Psychology, 1978.

Reisman, D. *The Lonely Crowd.* New Haven, Conn.: Yale University Press, 1961.

Spilka, B., and Minton, B. A. "Defining Personal Religion: Psychometric, Cognitive, and Instrumental Dimensions." Paper presented at the 1975 convention of the Society for the Scientific Study of Religion, Milwaukee, Wisc., Oct. 24, 1975.

Spilka, B., and Mullin, M. "Personal Religion and Psychosocial Schemata: A Research Approach to a Theological Psychology of Religion." *Character Potential,* 1977, *8,* 57-66.

Spilka, B., Stout, L., Minton, B., and Sizemore, D. "Death and Personal Faith: A Psychometric Investigation." *Journal for the Scientific Study of Religion,* 1977, *16,* 169-78.

Wessel, S. J. "The Relationship of Psychosocial Maturity to Intrapersonal, Interpersonal, and Spiritual Functioning." Doctoral dissertation, Rosemead Graduate School of Professional Psychology, 1979.

SECTION
TWO

MODELS OF INTEGRATION

There has been an increasing volume of writing on various aspects of integration over the last ten years. The articles in this section represent three rather divergent attempts to provide a framework or model by which some of the diverse aspects of psychology and Christianity may be ordered. They all address some common elements, areas, or assumptions by which the two fields may be organized along some underlying dimension(s). Thus these models attempt to simplify the task of integration by providing a conceptual framework for it. In the first article, Carter has examined the four models, or approaches, which psychologists and Christians have each adopted in relating to one anothers' discipline. These approaches or models are called: Against, Of, Parallels, and Integrates. Carter maintains that individuals in each field have used one of these models in relating to or interpreting the two fields.

The implications of this article for students of psychology of religion are twofold. First, Carter has provided a classification scheme for understanding the various perspectives that authors have taken in discussing psychology and religion. Thus, it also becomes a view of a number of theoretical points of view. Second, the classification scheme by its very nature implies that there is *no* objective scientific perspective or absolute religious perspective which escapes *making* assumptions about the nature of the relationship between the two fields. Hence, the article has attempted to outline the various assumptions that are taken for granted by the proponents of each model as *the* truth. Carter is not denying objectivity in the approach to psychology and Christianity; rather he is examining and articulating the presuppositions various authors have already taken on the subject. Are Carter's four models explanatory? Are there other models? Are the various psychologists and Christian teachers correctly classified?

Carter and Mohline's article is titled: "A Proposal." Thus, by its nature, it is schematic and pragmatic. After outlining both psychology and Christian theology, or doctrine, they have combined these two outlines into a unified common conceptual outline. It is this unified common conceptual outline that constitutes their proposal for a full scope of integration. In addition, they have attempted to show at least some initial content for integration in each of the seven areas that form their integrative proposal.

This article has raised several issues that Carter and Mohline attempt to address. First, they have recognized that their unified or integrative outline is not the usual outline of either psychology or Christian theology. Second, they have recognized that psychology and theology have a different level of abstraction, i.e., psychology tends to be more methodological, and theology tends to be more metaphysical. Third, and finally, they have recognized the formative or preliminary nature of their proposal. It might be interesting for the reader to accept their invitation to modify or correct their initial proposal for an integrative framework of psychology and theology. Are there areas of psychology and theology that have been omitted? If so, can they be added without a change in the seven integrated areas? If not, does the whole framework need to be changed or can an area be added?

In the first part of his article with its intriguing title, "Behavior Modification of the Spirit," Clement has grappled with the issue of how psychology and theology can be related. He argues that the disciplines are clearly different and deal with different content and have different methods, yet psychology and theology come together in the individual person. Here is the issue and the dilemma: How can the disciplines be separate and yet integrated in each person? In many respects this article by Clement, at least its first half, is in conflict with the previous article by Carter and Mohline, who, while recognizing differences between psychology and theology as disciplines, argue for their inherent unity rather than for their diversity as does Clement.

In the second half of the article Clement has maintained that behavior modification in the form of operant and classical conditioning techniques can influence various aspects of the person; e.g., operant techniques tend to apply to the muscles and classical techniques to the glands and viscera. In a similar way, he has argued that behavior modification techniques can be applied to the central nervous system, and thus to the spirit. The implied equation of the central nervous system and the human spirit is an interesting idea, and the reader will be challenged by the thought of a behavioral approach to influencing spiritual aspects of persons. If the behavioral approach to influencing the human spirit seems incorrect, are there other ways to change it, such as psychoanalysis or Rogerian therapy? Or is the human spirit not susceptible to any psychological influence? The nature of the answers to these questions probably can be classified in one of the four models described by Carter in the first article in this section.

SECULAR AND SACRED MODELS OF PSYCHOLOGY AND RELIGION

John D. Carter

For the last fifteen to twenty years there has been a resurgence of interest in the psychology of religion as evidenced by such encyclopedic works as Strommen's *Research on Religious Development.* Psychology's interest in religion which was evident during the early decades of this century (James, Starbuck, and others) appears to have virtually died out during the 1930s and 1940s and early 1950s if the volume of publications is a criteria. Apparently, interest was rekindled at the 1959 APA convention symposium entitled: "The Role of the Concept of Sin in Psychotherapy." This renewed interest in psychology and religion by psychologists culminated two years ago in the APA's addition of Division 36—Psychologists Interested in Religious Issues.

A parallel interest in psychology's relationship to Christianity has developed in the evangelical Christian community. The growing number of books and articles and even evangelical psychological associations illustrates the evangelical psychologist's interest in psychology and Christianity (Collins, 1975). This interest seems to be part of what Bloesch (1973) has called the *Evangelical Renaissance.*

This article is an analysis of the four approaches or models by which psychologists have attempted to relate psychology to religion. It also analyzes a parallel version of these four models by which evangelical psychologists have attempted to relate to psychology and Christianity. These two analyses are called secular and sacred respectively; they constitute the bulk of this article. Since the parallel versions of the models have developed separately, there is some difference in terminology. Psychologists have been concerned with religious phenomena and so explore religion while evangelical psychologists have been concerned with Christianity and so explore psychology and Christianity rather than religion in general. The difference in terminology will be reflected in each analysis. A section comparing the two analyses or versions of the four models including the issues and a summary will conclude this paper. An

An earlier form of this article appeared at the Joint Conference of the Christian Association for Psychological Studies and the Western Association of Christians for Psychological Studies in Santa Barbara, California, June 25-29, 1976.

outline of the four secular and sacred models appears in tables 1 and 2 respectively. These tables must be studied in conjunction with the explanation in the text in order to fully appreciate the coherent nature of each model.

Secular Models

The four approaches psychologists have taken to psychology and religion are described as four models. Each model has its own character and pattern which have also been described in more detail and summarized in tables 1 and 2. These same four models also appear to parallel the four models that evangelical psychologists have used in their analysis of psychology and Christianity. Thus, it becomes apparent that sacred and secular versions of psychology and religion are two sides of the same model.

The first secular model is the psychology *Against* religion model. This approach holds that religion has or had a detrimental effect on mankind and on society because it is unscientific and, therefore, perpetrates myths. Hence, religion is viewed as exploiting individuals by its institutional character, i.e., by its ability to control and inhibit free expression of humans in society, particularly in the area of sexual functioning. Thus, religion is viewed as being aligned with the oppressive forces in society. Second, as an institution in the broader sense, religion is able to reach into the individual's family life and shape his conscience so that guilt is produced with all of its detrimental and pathological effects. Thus, religion is the creator of needless, personal, emotional pain. Third, religion is, at best, allowable for children and for primitive people who are not sophisticated enough to recognize its limiting function. At its worst, religion perpetuates immaturity in both a personal and intellectual sense: in the personal sense, religious views of personhood prevent autonomy and self-actualization in order to conform to the religious ideal; in an intellectual sense, religion perpetuates a view of the world and human nature which is intellectually and scientifically unacceptable. In summary, this model maintains that religion is essentially anti- or unscientific, i.e., mythological, while psychology (as defined by the holder's view) represents a scientifically acceptable view of man, his nature, and functioning. This model is thus based on naturalism and has an antisupernaturalistic stance. Freud (1957) and Ellis (1970) are examples of this approach.

The second model is the psychology *Of* religion model. Holders of this view, like their counterpart in the Christian approach, tend to assume a mysticism, humanism, or parenthesism (and sometimes a naturalism) rather than the antisupernaturalism of the *Against* model. Thus, man is a spiritual-moral being whose being needs to be free of oppressive forces whether societal, technological, or religious. Secondly, religion is good in general, i.e., it is viewed as ally, at best, and as benign, at worst. Thirdly, religious metaphors or concepts are accepted and integrated in a psychological manner. The pure religious nature or content of the religious concepts are excluded or overlooked (either explicitly or implicitly) and, in turn, the concepts are infused with or interpreted as having some psychological meaning derived from a particular psychological theory. The psychological benefits of religions and its functioning in healthy individuals are stressed, particularly in terms of the psychologized version of the religion(s). Jung (1962), Fromm (1966), and Mowrer (1961) are the clearest examples of this model.

The third model—Psychology *Parallels* religion—is harder to define in its secular form than in its sacred form. Holders of this view do not write specifically on their view. Rather, they are active in both spheres and may have written in both. Since the psychological community generally is unaware of the religious one and vice versa, there is little need to communicate or articulate any intellectual or rational connection of the two spheres of functioning. The view appears to be that quality functioning and productivity in both areas of endeavor are desirable, but no interaction is necessary: Psychology is scientific and religion is personal (and perhaps social also). A major example provides the best articulation of this model:

TABLE 1
Four Secular Models of Psychology and Religion

I. Psychology *Against* Religion
  1. Science or scientific method is the only valid means to truth.
  2. Truth claims other than science are destructive.
  3. Religion (as myth) rather than truth is destructive.
  4. Religion's destructiveness is its prohibitive or inhibitive effect on its members and society.
  5. "Scientific" (valid) psychology is the solution to individual problems.
  Examples: Ellis and Freud

II. Psychology *Of* Religion
  1. Man is a spiritual-moral being (at least in a humanistic sense).
  2. Religion, technology, science, or society which denies man's spirit, and thus his nature, creates pathology.
  3. Most or all religions have recognized the spiritual-human quality of man and thus have the right approach.
  4. The particular cultural-social-theological definition of man must be discarded in favor of a truly psychological definition of human functioning.
  5. Good psychology translates the valid insights of religion into psychology and uses them for human good.
  Examples: Fromm, Jung, and Mowrer

III. Psychology *Parallels* Religion
  1. Religion and psychology are not related.
  2. Each exists in its own sphere. One is scientific and the other is not.

3. Religion is a personal (and social) matter while psychology is intellectual and academic.
4. Both religion and psychology can be embraced. There is no conflict since they do not interact.
Example: Thorne

IV. Psychology *Integrates* Religion
1. A unifying or integrating view of truth in religion and psychology is both possible and desirable.
2. The truth or insights from psychology or religion will have some correspondence with the other discipline.
3. The truth or valid principles of religion and psychology are in harmony and form a unity.
4. Religion as socially manifested may be pathological but its intrinsic nature is not.
5. Valid religion and religious experiences are helpful in transcending the pains of existence or in assisting in the maturing process of growth.
Examples: Allport, Frankl, and Guntrip

Thorne (1950), for many years the editor of the *Journal of Clinical Psychology,* maintains that

. . . primary reliance should be placed on scientific methods when they are *validly* applicable, but that philosophy and religion also have their proper sphere of activities beyond the realm of science. (p. 471)
A distinction should be made between religion-oriented *spiritual counseling* and scientifically-oriented *personality counseling.* . . . It must be recognized in the beginning that the theoretical and philosophical foundations of spiritual and scientific approaches are basically different. (p. 481)

While Thorne goes on to discuss the place of religion in counseling, his position is clear. Counseling, as scientifically based and grounded, is separate and even at points in opposition to religiously oriented counseling, yet there is clearly a place for religion as part of knowledge and culture. Also, its influence on certain counselees must be recognized and addressed.

The psychology *Integrates* religion model recognizes the healthy aspects of religion. It basically assumes that man needs a unifying philosophy of life and that religion, in its healthy expression, can provide an understanding of life both existentially and metaphysically which is broader than psychology. As a corollary, it assumes that religion can provide a personally integrating function in one's life, both intraspherically and interpersonally. The model also recognizes that the human condition is less than ideal and that personal and religious maturity does not automatically occur. Thus, there is unhealthy religion as well as individual and social pathology (i.e., hostility and defensiveness can occur inside as well as outside religion). Finally, a healthy religion is viewed as assisting or aiding in the transcendence of, or liberation from, pathology. Allport (1950) and

Frankl (1975) are examples of this approach. Guntrip (1956, 1967) also appears to hold the *Integrates* assumptions, but articulation of these implications is not developed yet.

Sacred Models

Since the original presentation of the sacred models (Carter and Mohline, 1974), there have been two other attempts to define the models used in integrating psychology and Christianity (Crabb, 1975, and Farnsworth, 1976). The former briefly outlines essentially the same four sacred models, but labels them differently and describes them in a confrontive *(Against)* rhetoric. The latter even more briefly outlines five models, three of which are directly equivalent to the *Against, Of,* and *Integrates* models and the other two appear to be versions of the *Parallels* model.

As indicated above, evangelicals have used the same four models that secular psychologists have used to describe and interpret relationship between Christianity and psychology. It should be noted that though the structure of the models is the same, the content is different and was developed independently.

The first model is the Christianity *Against* psychology approach. This model affirms that there is a radical difference between what the Bible says about man and what psychologists say. Holders of this view are either implicitly or explicitly committed to a presuppositionalism in which the unbelieving psychologists can discover no significant truths about the nature or functioning of man, especially Christian man. Secondly, they place a radical emphasis on the redemptive aspects of the Bible with a heavy stress on the difference between the believer and the unbeliever, between the old man and the new man. Thus, prayer, Bible reading, "trusting Christ," and "relying on the Holy Spirit" or a combination of these are pursued as scriptural means for coping with life and its problems.

Thirdly, the discovery and application of God's laws from the Scriptures are stressed as solutions to all of life's problems. Thus, emotional problems or "nervous breakdowns" are a result of violation of divine laws. Therapy in this approach consists largely of telling or encouraging people to follow God's requirements. While salvation by grace alone is maintained by holders of this approach, solutions to emotional difficulties come from obedience to God's laws rather than accepting God's love and grace.

Psychologically, the approach of this school of thought can be summarized by the statement "All emotional problems are really spiritual problems." It should be noted that with few exceptions those who hold this view have no graduate training in psychology. Many evangelical psychologists would maintain that Adams' (1973) counseling techniques are representative of this approach.

The Christianity *Of* psychology model represents almost a direct antithesis of the first model discussed. This second approach also maintains that there is a difference between the Bible and the facts of science, experience, and reason, but in this case the latter is favored. The holders of this view tend to be committed to a naturalism, mysticism, or humanism rather than a supernaturalism. Also, they stress the universal aspects of the Bible rather than the redemptive aspects. The Christian is not viewed as essentially different from other men, but as all other men, he is in need of the therapeutic benefits which psychology offers.

A third characteristic of the Christianity *Of* psychology model is its attempt to interpret the tenets of various "schools" of psychology as truly redemptive and Christian. They *selectively* translate or interpret various passages or concepts from the Bible into their particular psychology, i.e., aspects of the Bible are mapped into the writings of some "school" of psychology which a particular psychologist holds. The founder of the school, be he Freud, Jung, or Rogers, becomes elevated so that what is acceptable in the Bible is what fits into the particular theory. Thus, the view to be propagated and used as a therapeutic tool is the Christianized version of some psychological theorist. Only a slightly different version of this "Christianizing" process occurs when it is not a theory but some particular principle, process, or experience which becomes the criteria, e.g., group experiences or interpersonal relations, as stressed by some who take this approach. Various biblical passages are then used to give biblical sanction for the concept already accepted as true.

In its theological form, the Christianity *Of* psychology approach has been the position of liberalism. However, there are some current evangelicals who tend to adopt this approach. These evangelicals become so involved with accepting the client and helping him to express his repressed emotions that they ignore or implicitly deny the existence of sinful actions and attitudes. To varying degrees they reject or ignore any passages of Scripture which speak of restraint, control, commitment, or mature *Christian* living. Other evangelicals so stress some experience, e.g., good interpersonal relations, that Christian experience tends to become synonymous with good interpersonal relations (Petersen and Broad, 1977).

The *Against* and *Of* models just discussed represent extremes. Each has a cookie cutter style. Onto the dough of Scripture and psychology each presses its cookie cutter. The dough inside the cutter is retained as the whole truth and what is on the outside is rejected as false. Hence, the *Against* and *Of* models must be rejected as an inadequate approach to a Christian psychology. The remaining two approaches attempt to steer a middle course.

The third model—Christianity *Parallels* psychology—emphasizes the importance of both the Scripture and psychology, but assumes either explicitly or implicitly that the two do not interact. There are two versions of this model. The first version can be called the *isolation* version. The holders of this version maintain that psychology and the Scripture or theology are separate and there is no overlap (Clement, 1974). That is, each is encapsulated, and there is no interaction because these methods and contents are different. However, since both are true, both must be affirmed but remain separate. The second version can be called the *correlation* version. Holders of this approach attempt to correlate, plug into, or line up certain psychological and scriptural concepts, e.g., superego is equivalent to the conscience, id is equivalent to original sin, and empathy is equivalent to love (agape). Holders of the correlation version often assume they are integrating when in actuality they are simply lining up concepts from different spheres. The basic difference between correlating and integrating (which will become clearer after the *Integrates* model is discussed) is that that correlating assumes there are two things which need to be lined up and thus ignores the system or configuration of concepts in each while integrating assumes there is ultimately only one set (configuration) of concepts, laws, or principles which operates in two disciplines. It is the discovery of the one configuration which constitutes integration, not the lining up in concepts. Note that Farnsworth treats the correlation version as a separate model.

Correlating can be clearly seen in *What, Then, Is Man?* Paul Meehl (1958), the general editor and author of several sections, outlines a solid theological view of salvation and then proceeds to discuss three psychological views of conversion and their implications for the orthodox biblical view he has just outlined. His theology never wavers, but it is as if his theology is on one side of a cliff and his psychology on the other and he is trying to build a bridge across but is not sure where to anchor the bridge on the psychological side.

Many Christian therapists either wittingly or unwittingly adopt this approach. Having been trained in the best institutions of the day, they practice the type of psychology they have learned. Being believers, they read their Bibles and attend church but there is little if any genuine meshing of their psychology and their Christianity. Bridge building is correlating not integrating.

The fourth model—Christianity *Integrates* psychology—basically assumes that God is the author of all truth, both the truth he has revealed in the Scripture and the truths discovered by psychology or any other scientific discipline. Hence, there is an expected congruence between Scripture and psychology because God has revealed himself in a special way in Scripture and in a general way in creation and also *via* his image in man (Gen. 1:26, 27). Man has fallen into sin and thus God's image in man has become marred, warped, or distorted. It is never lost, and it is being renewed through personal appropriation of salvation in Christ (Eph. 4:24; Col. 3:10). The holder of the Christianity *Integrates* psychology model never presumes that *all* the claims to discovered truths in psychology are genuine unless they are congruent and integratable with the Scripture, nor does he believe that certain traditional interpretations of Scripture are true either. God created psychology when he created man in his image. Man has become marred but yet he is redeemable, and thus psychology is congruent and integratable with Christianity. This approach emphasizes both the Scripture and psychology *because they are allies.* Psychology used in this model has a small *p*, i.e., it is the psychology that existed before the word was discovered, while psychology as used by the other three models has a capital *P* and refers to systems or theories. This is a critical difference.

There are many psychologists and pastoral counselors who are seeking to promote both understanding and growth in individuals. Hence, there is a vast popular literature on psychology and the Scripture available. However, it is often very difficult to distinguish between the correlation version of the *Parallels* model and genuine integration in this popular literature because its goal is to promote practical Christian living rather than conceptual understanding. Much of the technical work exploring the nature and the content of the integration of psychology and the Scripture appears in two periodicals, *The Journal of the American Scientific Affiliation* and the *Journal of Psychology and Theology.* Many of the members of the Christian Association for Psychological Studies and Western Association of Christians for Psychological Studies hold to the *Integrates* model. Crabb (1975), Hulme (1967), van Kaam (1968), and Wagner (1974) are examples of this model.

Evaluation of the Four Sacred or Christian Models

Since there is a plethora of literature currently being written on the integration of psychology and Christianity, a separate section is being given to the Christian or sacred models.

The four sacred or Christian models of psychology and Christianity just described, in reality, are only aspects of larger approaches to a Christian view of life which might be called Christianity and culture. Space does not allow for the expansion of this idea but if the reader will substitute the word "culture" (in its anthropological sense) for "psychology" in each model, he will be able to see how the four models to psychology grow out of four approaches to a Christian view of life.

Specifically, the Christianity *Against* psychology model assumes that there is no general revelation or common grace which God has revealed or given to man which can be discovered by a non-Christian psychologist.

Besides running counter to systematic theology and Christian apologetics, this assumption is peculiar for two reasons. First, man was created in God's image (Gen. 1:26, 27), and though marred, it has not been destroyed by the Fall (Eph. 4:24; Col. 3:10). Secondly, the similar assumption does not seem to be held for medicine, economics, or physics, i.e., truth which applies to Christians may be discovered by nonbelievers in these fields. Why not in psychology?

Though largely implicit, the Christianity *Against* psychology approach holds a surface view of sin and pathology. In practice, though not theologically, sin and pathology are reduced to symptoms. The counselee is doing, saying, or thinking the wrong things, and he is not doing, saying, or thinking the right things. Thus, therapy essentially becomes telling the counselee what the Bible says and how he or she should respond regardless of how little or much the counselor listens to the counselee. Therapy in this approach tends to become a symptoms removal or works sanctification depending upon whether it is viewed psychologically or theologically. At times, adherents to this approach sound remarkably similar to a parent lecturing an adolescent in their therapeutic techniques while the biblical emphasis on "out of the abundance of the heart the mouth speaks" (Matt. 12:34-35) or "truth in the inward parts" (Ps. 51:6) is bypassed in favor of behavioral compliance. Thus, the volume of scriptural quotation in "Christian" psychology books in no way guarantees its faithfulness to content or intent of Scripture. It is from this limited view of God's revelation in nature (man) and its limited view of sin and pathology that the Christianity *Against* psychology practitioner criticizes the committed Christian professionals who accept one of the latter two approaches, presuming they are taking the *Of* model approach. The adherents of the Christianity *Against* psychology approach appear to see only the scripturally invalid claims to psychological truth and thus essentially reject psychology. The adherents of the Christianity *Of* psychology approach appear to accept all claims to psychological truth (i.e., all claims they are committed to as valid) and thus essentially reject the integrity of Scripture.

TABLE 2
Four Sacred Models of the Scripture and Psychology

I. The Scripture *Against* Psychology
   1. Basic epistemological assumption: Revelation is against reason, i.e., the Scripture is contradictory to human thought both rationally and empirically.
   2. Soteriology and the Fall are stressed so as to eliminate and ignore creation and providence.
   3. Basic psychological assumption: The Scripture contains all the precepts of mental health.

    4. All emotional problems are spiritual problems because they result from disobedience.

    5. All problems can be solved by obedience to Scripture if the individual is confronted with a relevant passage of Scripture.

    Example: Adams

II. The Scripture *Of* Psychology

    1. Basic epistemological assumption: Human reason is more fundamental, comprehensive (technical), and contemporary than revelation.

    2. Creation and providence are stressed so as to ignore or eliminate soteriology and the Fall.

    3. Basic psychological assumption: Psychology has discovered the basic principles of emotional health, maturity, and good interpersonal functioning.

    4. Emotional problems can be solved by consulting a therapist or applying the principles of emotional maturity and good interpersonal relations.

    Example: Relational theology

III. The Scripture *Parallels* Psychology

    1. Basic epistemological assumption: Revelation can never be reduced to reason nor can reason be reduced to revelation.

    2. God requires obedience to both revelation and reason. Hence, there is an implicit tension existing in the approach.

    3. Both creation-providence and soteriology are stressed but they belong to different spheres.

    4. Spiritual problems should be dealt with by the pastor; emotional problems by a psychologist or psychiatrist.

    Examples: Clement (Isolation) and Meehl (Correlation)

IV. The Scripture *Integrates* Psychology

    1. Basic epistemological assumption: God is the author of both revelation and reason because all truth (and truths) are God's truth and thus ultimately a part of a unified or integrated whole.

    2. Creation-providence is stressed equally with soteriology.

    3. All problems are, in the principle, a result of the Fall but not, in fact, the result of immediate conscious acts.

    4. Since values are significant both for the Christian and for therapy, a genuine Christian therapy is necessary.

    5. *Paraklesis* is the pattern for this type of therapy.

    Examples: Crabb, Hulme, van Kaam, Wagner, Carter, and Mohline

However, since the propagators of the Christianity *Against* psychology approach have had almost exclusively theological rather than psychological training, they do have many helpful insights into Scripture. Their works can be read with profit (if their oppressive rhetoric can be ignored) by those professionals whose training has been exclusively psychological in nature. Furthermore, since many problems have a behavioral symptom component, the Christianity *Against* psychology approach helps to relieve the pressure of symptoms for many persons.

Little needs to be said concerning the Christianity *Of* psychology model. At best, in the opinion of those who hold this view, the Bible provides a convenient set of metaphors into which various psychological concepts can be translated. The evangelical, who operates from this approach, seems to be caught up with some psychological concepts or theoretical perspectives to such an extent that they are not able to see the larger implications of their approach. They tend to see only their favored concept or perspective in the Scripture. Thus, the totality of the biblical emphasis is limited. Ramm (1972) has described the weakness of such groups of evangelicals in a paper entitled "Is it safe to shift to 'interpersonal theology'?"

The greatest strength of the Christianity *Parallels* psychology is also its greatest weakness. It avoids the pitfalls of the *Against* and *Of* models, but it offers no positive constructive alternatives. Many professionals who operate from this approach (especially the isolation version) have had little or no theological or biblical training but are competent psychologists. The militancy of the proponents of the *Against* model often has the effect of inhibiting many of this group who are searching from some biblical insight into psychology. The parallelists are aware of their own competency and the general psychological naivité of the *Against* proponent and, therefore, tend to be very wary of any claims regarding the discovery of "the" biblical psychology. Other parallelists seem to arrive at their position because they believe that the laws and methods of psychology are separate from the laws and methods of theology, or economics, or any discipline for that matter. However, all disciplines are integratable in a grand Christian philosophical scheme though this integration has little to do with their therapeutic practice.

Many evangelical psychologists who are only correlating believe they are integrating. This is confusing and unfortunate. As was indicated, genuine integration involves the discovery and articulation of the common underlying principles of both psychology and the Scripture, i.e., how general grace and special grace are related in reference to psychology. In addition, there are many evangelical counselors and therapists who "believe in" integration but whose therapy in no appreciative way differs from their secular colleagues except for an occasional reference to God or the Bible. It is difficult to know in what sense this kind of therapy can be called integrative or Christian, except that both therapist and client are Christians. This observation is not intended to be a pejorative comment but a descriptive categorization.

The strength and weakness of the Christianity *Integrates* psychology model also rests on its basic assumption: that psychology is integratable with Christianity. This is an open assumption, and the burden of proof rests on the proponent of this mode. The practical proponents of this approach have proclaimed this assumption although they were not able singlehandedly to supply the details. The number of articles, not to mention books, appearing in the two scholarly journals mentioned, as well as in other periodicals, suggests that the more theoretically-oriented integrators are beginning to discover the details of integration. The process of integration takes time. The bulk of psychology as a discipline is less than fifty years old and much of it is less than thirty years old. Christians must study psychology and then study the Scripture to discover its psychology. Little biblical psychology will be discovered if one does not know any psychology.

The integrators tend to emphasize the inner or depth aspect of man, as the source of both problems and health, in keeping with the biblical emphasis on the heart as the motive source of actions (Matt. 15:18-19; Luke 6:45). Also, many integrators tend to approach therapy, however, implicitly from the biblical concept *paraklesis,* meaning support, comfort, consolation, or encouragement (exhortation). With its broad meaning, *paraklesis* could apply to any therapy from crisis intervention to long-term analysis. *Paraklesis* is a gift given to the church (Rom. 12:6-8), and the integrator presumes Christian counseling is part of the larger ministry of the church.

Thus, the *Integrates* model assumes a Christian view of man which includes God's special revelation in the Scripture and his general revelation in nature (Rom. 1:20; Ps. 19:1) and man (Gen. 1:27).

Table 2 lists five therapists who are examples of those following the *Integrates* model. Each has a different theoretical orientation and is attempting to move from that base to an integrative one with the Scripture. Thus, the differences in style and vocabulary, hopefully, will not obscure the genuine integration in each.

Evaluation: Christian and Secular Models

This section will begin with a comparison of the two versions of each model and conclude with a discussion of a broader base of the four models.

The four sacred and secular models of psychology and religion are clearly not equally similar. The greatest difference appears in the *Against* model. This difference occurs because either psychology or religion is rejected in the *Against* model but it is the opposite part in the sacred and secular versions. However, the difference in a content or orientation should not blind one to the striking equivalence in style and structure. However, the difference in content often leads the secular and sacred proponents of this model to dogmatic clashes. The difference in the *Of* model is much less noticeable. Both sacred and secular versions assume a humanistic-naturalistic or metaphysical view. The difference seems to be in the use of metaphors. The sacred approach predominately uses religious metaphors, but with understood psychological meaning, while the secular approach uses psychological metaphors in such a way as to incorporate religious meanings.

The sacred and secular *Parallels* model is perhaps the most similar, but it is also the least defined. It is most similar in that the central structures, religion and psychology, are separated in both versions. Because religion and/or Christianity and psychology are maintained separately, there is little definition to the model except the maintenance of the separate disciplines. However, the correlation version of the sacred *Parallels* model does attempt to line up the two disciplines.

There is a great deal of similarity between the secular and sacred *Integrates* model. There tends to be a broad philosophical or metaphysical orientation to this model. This seems to be a function of the nature of the *Integrates* model which calls for an awareness and integration of two distinct bodies of knowledge. The adherents of this model seem to focus on the underlying issues in both psychology and religion without a loss of technical mystery of some area of the field of psychology. Also, the adherents' interest in a religious understanding and the integration of it with psychology is a result of personal belief, experience, and commitment.

As indicated, there have been only four approaches to the relationship between psychology and religion. Two versions of these models, sacred and secular, have been described and compared. Each version of each model (see tables 1 and 2) is founded on a relatively coherent set of assumptions. In reading and discussing psychology and religion, it is important to bear in mind the model which is being assumed. Since individuals explicitly hold to one of these four models, misunderstanding often occurs when another individual holds to a different model. The misunderstandings often tend to degenerate into conflicts when the nature of implicit assumptions behind the models are not recognized. Also, there are psychologists who intellectually assume one model but who are affectively committed to another.

In conclusion, the four models may be viewed as a new interpretation of an old problem: relating the secular and the sacred. *Christ and Culture* (Niebuhr, 1951) describes five approaches Christians have taken in relating their religious faith to a secular world. The Christian, or religious version of the four models, represents an application or extension of four of these approaches to psychology. Thus, relating the Christian faith to psychology is really only part of the larger problem of relating the Christian faith to the world of life and thought.

Finally, the four models may be thought of as parallel to some of the proposed solutions to the mind-body problem. How can the mind and body, two different aspects of a person, be related in one individual? How can psychology, a scientific discipline, be related to religion or Christianity, a revealed and historical faith? While there have been a number of proposed solutions to the mind-body problem, Beloff (1962) maintains the mind-body problem may be reduced to four basic solutions. The four models presented in this article appear to parallel four of these solutions. The *Against* and *Of* models appear to parallel the materialism and idealism solution. Each model denies one aspect of the problem just as materialism and idealism deny one aspect of the mind-body problem. The *Parallels* model seems equivalent to psychophysical parallelism. The *Integrates* model appears to be similar to the double aspect solution of the mind-body problem. These mind-body problem parallels are not to be thought of as total or definitive, only suggestive. Any light this suggestion throws on the relationship between psychology and religion at this primitive stage of understanding will be helpful.

References

Adams, J. *The Christian Counselors Manual*. Grand Rapids, Mich.: Baker Book House, 1973.

Allport, G. W. *The Individual and His Religion*. New York: The Macmillan Co., 1950.

Beloff, J. *The Existence of Mind*. London: Macgibbon & Kee, 1962.

Bloesch, E. *The Evangelical Renaissance*. Grand Rapids: Eerdmans, 1973.

Carter, J. D., and Mohline, R. J. "A Model and Modes for the Integrative Process." A paper presented at the meeting of the *Christian Association for Psychological Studies*, Oklahoma City, Okla., April 12-14, 1974.

————., and Mohline, R. J. "The Nature and Scope of Integration: A Proposal." *Journal of Psychology and Theology*, 1976, *4* (1), 3-14.

Clement, P. "Behavior Modification of the Spirit." A paper presented at the *Convention of the Western Association of Christians for Psychological Studies*, Santa Barbara, May 24-25, 1974.

Collins, G. "The Pulpit and the Couch." *Christianity Today*, 1975, *19*, 1087-90.

Crabb, L. *Basic Principles of Biblical Counseling*. Grand Rapids: Zondervan Publishing House, 1975.

Ellis, A. *Reason and Emotion in Psychotherapy*. New York: Lyle Stewart, 1970.

Farnsworth, K. "Integration of Faith and Learning Utilizing a Phenomenological Existential Paradigm for Psychology." A paper presented at the *Christian Association for Psychological Studies*. Santa Barbara, June 25-29, 1976.

Frankl, V. *The Unconscious God*. New York: Simon & Schuster, 1975.

Freud, S. *The Future of an Illusion*. Garden City, N.Y.: Doubleday & Co., 1957.

Fromm, E. *You Shall Be as Gods*. New York: Fawcett, 1966.

Guntrip, H. *Psychotherapy and Religion*. New York: Harper & Row, 1956.

————. "Religion in Relationship to Personal Integration." *British Journal of Medical Psychology*, 1967, *62*, 423-33.

Hume, W. *Counseling and Theology*. Philadelphia: Fortress Press, 1967.

Jung, C. *Psychology and Religion*. New Haven, Conn.: Yale University Press, 1962.

Meehl, P. *What, Then, Is Man?* St. Louis: Concordia Publishing House, 1958.

Mowrer, O. H. *The Crisis in Psychiatry and Religion*. Princeton, N.J.: Van Nostrand, 1961.

Niebuhr, H. R. *Christ and Culture*. New York: Harper & Row, 1951.

Petersen, B., and Broad, S. "Unmasking: An Interview with Waldon Howard" (including comments). *Eternity*, July 1977, 21-22.

Ramm, B. "Is It Safe to Shift to an 'Interpersonal Theology'?" *Eternity*, 1972, 21-22.

Thorne, F. "Principles of Personality Counseling." Brandon, Vt.: *Journal of Clinical Psychology*, 1950.

van Kaam, A. *Religion and Personality*. Garden City, N.Y.: Doubleday, 1968.

Wagner, M. *Put It All Together*. Grand Rapids: Zondervan Publishing House, 1974.

THE NATURE AND SCOPE OF INTEGRATION: A PROPOSAL

John D. Carter and Richard J. Mohline

Integration can be thought of as three things: the relationship of Christian and secular concepts, the way a Christian functions spiritually and psychologically, and a way of thinking (i.e., synthetically). The primary purpose of this paper is to focus on the first meaning of integration, namely relating Christian and secular concepts so that a model can be developed. This obviously involves the second and third meaning of integration because ultimately integration cannot be separated from thinking and an emotional self-understanding. In a theological sense our model can be thought of as a model for integrating general revelation and special revelation.

Integration is both very new and very old. It is both very general and quite specific. Its oldest form is its most general. How does one live as a Christian in a secular world? H. R. Neibuhr (1951) calls this problem the problem of Christ and culture. The stance of the paper follows what Niebuhr would call the Christ-transforms-culture pattern or what elsewhere has been called the Scripture-integrates-psychology model (Carter, 1975). In the second century some specific works began to appear on the nature of man, his relationship to God, and the working of the spirit in the believer. Tertullian's (The Soul), Gregory of Nyssa's (On the Soul), and Augustine's (The Soul) are the best known and most thorough of these works. Little systematic and no biblical psychology appeared until the eighteenth century. Some of Luther's works and Melanchthon's are possible exceptions to this observation as are some specific shorter works by others. Delitzsch's *A System of Biblical Psychology* (1855/1966) summarizes and systematizes all that has been written on biblical psychology to that date. Conservative theology does not seem to have moved beyond Delitzsch until some very recent studies on the image of God in man (Clines, 1968; Berkouwer, 1962) and the nature of the soul (Howard, 1972; Jackson, 1975).

In spite of these significant works and the extensive devotional literature

Presented at a conference on "Research in Mental Health and Religious Behavior," Atlanta, Georgia, January 24-26, 1976.

© *Journal of Psychology and Theology*, 1976, *4*, 3-14. Used by permission of the authors.

in both Catholic and Protestant thought, integration is profoundly new for two reasons: (1) There was no organized body of psychological knowledge which could be considered a science in either a natural or social sense until the twentieth century; (2) the culture, therefore, never pressed a secular definition of man and his functioning in the Christian world until this century.

The recent emergence of psychology and its redefinition of man is evident to all students of psychology and contemporary history. However, the emergence of a secular definition of man poses a challenge to Christian thought which is new in detail but not in kind. Historically, doctrine has emerged from a secular or heretical challenge to the Christian church. The third to fifth centuries saw repeated challenge of the Christian church by Arianism, Apollinarianism, Nestorianism, and Eutychianism until the doctrine of Christ's two natures and one sustenance with the Father was fully articulated at the council of Chalcedon in 451 A.D. While the nature of the atonement and the nature of the church were debated during this period, there was never an outside challenge to sharpen and focus the issue except for the *lapsi* controversy in the third and fourth centuries over the sacraments and their functioning. It was not until the Reformation that there was a challenge which forced the redefinition of the church and its sacraments as well as the nature of its authority in the Scripture. Again, it is not until the ninteenth century when higher criticism and science began to challenge the Scripture and the Christian church's view of God (and the natural order) that a clarified view of the doctrine of the Scripture begins to emerge.

What is called integration in this paper represents a Christian response to the challenge of a secular definition of man and his intrapsychic and interpersonal self. A perusal of major systematic theology texts reveals that there are large sections on God, Christ, the church, and the atonement but the sections on man (anthropology) and the Holy Spirit's relationship to man are dwarfed by comparison. Integration is new then because it is an attempt to relate Christian thought to the challenge of contemporary culture's attempt to define man according to a secular psychology. This does not imply that psychology is wrong in principle but only that psychology must be integrated with a Christian view of man, his nature, and his destiny.

The primary purpose of this paper is to construct an integrated model of psychology and Christian theology which is intrinsic to each discipline and congruent with both. There are several assumptions (postulates) upon which the model is built: (1) All truth is God's truth, therefore, the truths of psychology (general revelation) are neither contradictory nor contrary to revealed truth (special revelation) but are integrative in a harmonious whole; (2) theology represents the distillation of God's revelation of himself to man in a linguistic, conceptual, and cultural media man can understand and which focuses primarily on man's nature and destiny in God's program; (3) psychology as a science is primarily concerned with the mechanisms by which man functions and the methods to assess that functioning. Nevertheless, the content of psychology as a science (including theory) provides a statement on the nature and functioning of man.

The Model

Building on the three assumptions just outlined, the methodological approach taken in forming the model to be outlined was as follows. Twelve systematic theological works were examined with the goal of determining a common content of theology. The same was done for sixty-five general psychology texts which commonly survey the entire field of psychology. After outlining the content of both fields, an attempt was made to determine a common intrinsic structure which is metaphysically inherent in both though it is not the usual outline of either. An outline of the scope of theology relevant to our model appears in table 1.

An outline of the scope of psychology relevant to our model appears in table 2. Combining these two outlines, the structure common to both appears in figure 1, which represents the *intrinsic common structure of both psychology and theology*. There may be many outlines which are meaningful to psychology or theology respectively but as far as we are able to determine there is only this one which appears inherently meaningful to both simultaneously. (Like a simple structure factor solution in factor analysis, it is arbitrary but nevertheless it is the most meaningful solution psychologically.)

TABLE 1
Scope of Theology

1. Theology Proper	Prolegomena	Nature, Necessity, Divisions
	Theism	Existence of God
	Bibliology	Revelation and Inspiration
	Theology	Nature of God, Father, Son, Holy Spirit, Essence, Attributes, Unity, Decrees, Works
2. Angelology	Origin	
	Nature	
	Works	
3. Christology	Incarnation	Impeccability of Christ
(Pneumatology)	Kenosis	Offices of Christ
	Nature of Christ	Propitiation
	Hypostatic Union	Reconciliation
		Atonement
4. Anthropology	Origin	
	Character	
	Unity	
	Constitution	

5. Hamartiology	Nature Universality Origin Imputation Consequences	
6. Soteriology	Election Calling Regeneration Conversion Repentance	Faith Justification Adoption Sanctification Perseverance
7. Ecclesiology	Meaning Nature Founding Organization	Mission Gifts Baptism and Lord's Supper
8. Eschatology	Second Coming Resurrections Judgments Millennium Final State	

Before an explanation of the basic common areas diagrammed in figure 1 can be made some general observations and qualifications on the meaning of the common areas are in order. First, the locus of explanation is different in theology and psychology: The locus of the former is generally historical and socio-cultural while the latter is descriptive (clinical), developmental, experimental. Second, the level of explanation is different in theology and psychology: The level of the former is metaphysical, and the latter is empirical or scientific. Third, theology's epistemology is revelational while psychology's epistemology is scientific.

We believe that in spite of these differences in focus, psychology and the theology are integrative. Since Scripture is metaphysical and revelational in character it makes theology more comprehensive than psychology in locus of explanation, level of explanation, and epistemology. Therefore, psychology is integrative into theology to the extent that psychology remains methodological rather than metaphysical.

TABLE 2
Scope of Psychology

1. Science of Psychology	Foundations of Psychology Definitions Philosophical Origins
2. Psychic Phenomena	Occult Extrasensory
3. Counselor	Preparation

	Modeling	
	Interpersonal Relations	
4. Personality	Theories of Personality	Structures
	Freud Adler	Self-concepts
	Jung (Many others)	Mind
	Skinner	Will
	Rogers	Emotions
	Maslow	Relationships
5. Psycho-	Anxiety and	
pathology-	Guilt Biophysical—Drugs	
	Neurosis Intrapsychic—Analysis	
Psycho-	Psychosis Phenomenological—Free patient	
therapy	Behavioral—Conditioning and Extinction	
	Sociocultural—Structure, Community	
6. Development	Stages—Child, Adolescent, Adult	
	Aspects—Heredity, Environment	
	Processes—Learning Remembering	
	Perception Thinking	
	Motivation Intelligence	
	Senses Emotions	
7. Social	Defining the Group	Status Phases
Psychology	Performance	Roles Process
	Commitment	Types Origins
	Norms	Goals Leadership
8. Psychology of	Goals	
Rewards	Expectations	
	Reinforcement	

In spite of the differences just discussed, there is a congruity of psychological content and principles in each common area with the exception of theology proper-science of psychology which deals with presuppositions and methodology in both disciplines. We are proposing that the common content and principles in each area constitute the scope of integration. The nature, character, and levels of the integratable material in each area varies, but we are asserting that basic principles and content of psychology are integratable into their equivalent theological area. In the Christ-Counselor and the Eschatology-Rewards areas there is obviously more extensive theological content which is not included in the integration. On the other hand, the psychological content or principles in each area are usually interpreted in their broadest or more complex form rather than in terms of basic process because of the difference in the locus and level of explanation in psychology. Also the flow or logical unfolding of the model will be indicated by the order in which the common areas are discussed.

The intention of the paper is to outline the nature and scope of integration. Therefore, we have not attempted to elaborate all aspects of each area for two reasons: There is not enough space in the paper and the

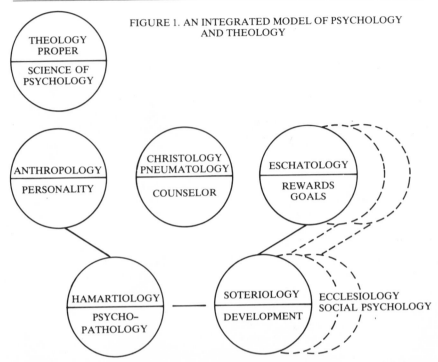

FIGURE 1. AN INTEGRATED MODEL OF PSYCHOLOGY AND THEOLOGY

full integration of each area has not been developed. There is much left to be developed. This paper is like the girder structure of a skyscraper. There is much filling in to be done before the building is complete. Finally, we believe our method of surveying many texts bypasses the theoretical quality of systematic theologies and allows for the determination of basic biblical doctrine.

Theology Proper-Psychology as Science

It is in this area that the differences in locus of explanation, level of explanation, and epistemology between theology and psychology are most evident. These differences could be called differences in presuppositions, i.e., theology and psychology have different starting points and are attempting to do different things. However, their communality is that both begin by describing their respective methodology, basic nature, and assumptions.

All Protestant theologies begin with a statement of theology proper which includes statements about the existence of God, his nature and attributes, the trinity, and God's self-disclosure, i.e., the nature of revelation and inspiration. Also included in this section is God's action in creating and maintaining the world. Thus theology proper encompasses God's nature and attributes, revelation, and creation including the natural and spiritual character of the real world.

There is no formal counterpart to much of theology proper in psychology as a science. It is this lack of equivalence which reveals the more comprehensive character of theology. However, all general or introductory psychology texts which survey the whole field begin with a systematic or historical statement on the discipline or science of psychology which includes a statement on the scientific method, the nature of experimentation, and the nature of empirical laws. Thus there is a formal similarity in that both theology proper and the science of psychology areas are methodological and propaedeutic to the rest of their discipline. When God created man as part of the natural order he set in motion the lawful, natural relationships which are studied as psychology. Hence, there is one aspect of theology which is integrative between theology proper and the science of psychology, namely the lawful relationship which exists in and between men. Thus, while there are similarities between these two disciplines the differences indicate that theology is more comprehensive and forms a backdrop into which psychology may be integrated. Angels and ESP phenomena are included in this area by definition.

Anthropology-Personality

Anthropology is the theological doctrine which deals with the creation and nature of man. The Bible describes man as created in the image of God (Gen. 1:27). Augustine in *The City of God* interpreted the image as understanding, memory, and will, while Luther (n.d./1955) made it innocence and original righteousness; Calvin (1559/1957) tried to synthesize these two views. More recently (Brunner, 1939) the image has been interpreted as the ability to have interpersonal relationships. Currently (Clines, 1968; Berkouwer, 1962) the image is being interpreted as man's God-given dominion over the earth with all the requisite abilities to carry out this task. Regardless of how the image has been interpreted, biblically it is clear that man is created in the image of God (Gen. 1:27) and that something happened to the image (in the Fall) since it is being renewed in salvation-sanctification (2 Cor. 3:17; Col. 3:10). Also, God predestined the renewal in eternity past (Rom. 8:29). Thus, the image is the fundamental structural concept of man's nature and is more fundamental than heart, soul, spirit, or mind which appear to be functioning subaspects of man though often are used to stand for the whole man.

Turning to personality theory (under which we are assuming the basic processes of learning, perception, memory, and motivation), it is beginning to become evident that every personality theory is an implicit statement of the nature of man. Maddi (1972) and Rychlak (1972) have organized personality theories into models. Rychlak describes behaviorally oriented theories as being Lockean in their underlying assumptions, phenomenological or existential theories as Kantian, and analytical theories as a mixture of the two. On the other hand, Maddi describes analytic theories as assuming a fundamental unresolved conflict (two conflicting tendencies) at the basis of personality. He describes phenomenological or existential theories as assuming only one principle, either fulfillment or consistency as the basis of personality. Maddi denies behavior theories as truly being personality theory, because they postulate no internal core tendency. Nevertheless, he recognizes the empty organism assumption of behavioral theories. Thus, it is evident that personality theories, however they differ in content, all make an implicit or explicit assumption about the nature of man and are therefore psychologically equivalent to biblical anthropology.

Sin (Hamartiology)—Psychopathology

The attempt to relate sin to psychopathology does not imply that all sin manifests itself as pathology or the reverse. Rather, the relationship is one of loss of potential, i.e., both sin and psychopathology are concepts which express lowered functioning, loss of potential, and/or inappropriate behavior. Theologically man's sin or fallen condition is described in terms of the effects of the fall or states of sin: (1) total depravity, (2) penalty or condemnation, (3) alienation, and (4) guilt. Though the vocabulary and number of effects described have varied with particular theologies, a pattern is clear. These states of sin mean that as a result of the fall each human being is totally fallen, is under sentence of death, is alienated from God, and is guilty for his specific sins. These four states appear to be, in our opinion, integratable with specific psychological experiences or feelings associated with psychopathology: *total depravity* with experiences of worthlessness or inferiority; *penalty, punishment,* or *condemnation* with experiences of fear and anxiety; *alienation* with experiences of loneliness or lack of belongingness (and dependency); and *guilt* with experiences of guilt. While all men are in the various states which result from mankind's fallen condition and all men experience these emotions and feelings from time to time, these experiences seem particularly evident in psychopathology. It is our opinion that hostility and anger which are also associated with pathology are defenses against the above four experienced feelings.

We hypothesize that the pathology associated with the psychoanalytic, behavioral, and phenomenological theories of personality discussed in the anthropology-personality section are related to the states which result from the Fall. The analytic emphasis on conflict and impulse life (occurring in personality and especially psychopathology) seems to relate to fear, anxiety, and threat of punishment. The behavioral emphasis on responses seems to relate to guilt which results from illegal action or behavior and threat from external stimuli. Phenomenological and existential psychology which stress worth and/or more interpersonal concepts, e.g., conditions of worth, seem to focus on the pathology associated with the states of depravity and alienation. The hypothesis that each of the basic theories of pathology have emphasized a specific aspect of the effects of the Fall is only a hypothesis. Thus it needs to be explored and investigated.

Soteriology-Developmental Process

After one has carefully integrated a theory of personality with a biblical anthropology and psychopathology with hamartiology, there arises the need to develop an adequate developmental theory integrated with the doctrine of salvation. The doctrine of soteriology (salvation) has traditionally been articulated in terms of the *order salutes* or the order of salvation. While soteriology could be related to child growth and development, we have chosen to limit our discussion to client growth or development in the therapeutic process. The subdoctrines in the order of salvation examined in this regard are election, calling, regeneration, conversion, repentance, faith, adoption, justification, sanctification, and perseverance.

This section will focus only on the primary dynamic found in each doctrine in the order of salvation and its potential for integration into the therapeutic process.

Election means that since God is who he says he is, and has really done all the things he says, and has chosen the believer, how else can he feel but worthwhile. Just as election is a starting point in the order of salvation, so dynamically a sense of worth in the client is a cornerstone in developing a healthy, therapeutic experience.

Calling conveys the idea of a body of truth being extended to potential listeners. The good news is presented to a world in need of the truth to redeem them from their plight. The dynamics of "truth" are available to each client. Either the client has the "truth" within him or it needs to be made known to him depending on one's therapeutic approach. The therapist will help to facilitate the knowledge of the "truth" in order to proceed in the therapeutic process.

Regeneration is that moment-in-time when the new birth takes place. When the moment is experienced, no one is absolutely certain. In a real sense, it is like conception, we know what precedes it, and we can observe the growth that follows it, but we are not absolutely certain when conception takes place. This is true of a client in therapy. We know that some knowledge or information is available to the client (either intrinsically or extrinsically) that precedes an insight which precipitates a decision and the subsequent growth. The dynamic in this doctrine which can be integrated into our therapeutic process is insight.

The doctrine of *conversion* is a change from one state to another, from the state of dissonance with God to a state of harmony with God. It is usually conceived to include two items: *repentance* and *faith*. Repentance is a turning from the state of dissonance, and faith is a turning toward God. In therapy, we cannot determine the moment-in-time that the client gains the insight, but we clearly observe the turning around, or the change in behavior, attitudes, or self-perception. Therefore, the therapist can observe the "conversion" experience in the therapeutic process which is based upon an insight into a truth that the client sees related to his worth as a person.

Justification is an act of God's free grace, wherein he pardons all of our sins and accepts us as righteous in his sight. In regeneration man receives a new life and a new nature, in justification he receives a new standing (just as though he never sinned). The dynamic that seems to be most relevant here is acceptance. In order for adequate therapeutic relations to be developed, the client must feel a measure of acceptance from his therapist. This acceptance is directly related to the client's own sense of worth as he relates to the therapist. Without a feeling of acceptance, there will be minimal disclosure, and the process of therapy will be thwarted.

The definition of *adoption* as indicated in the New Testament literally means "placing as a son." This means that the Christian has been placed as a son in the family of God in such a way as to receive all the benefits that Jesus the Son of God has at his disposal. As sons we are heirs of the Father and joint-he is with his Son. The dynamic that seems to be most prominent is the doctrine of the feeling of belonging. This dynamic can be translated into a therapeutic process. The client has the need to feel a sense of belonging and the therapist can communicate this by his acceptance of the client as he is.

Perseverance, if properly understood, can be a very comforting doctrine as well as a highly motivating one. The intent of perseverance in this paper is to emphasize the ongoing growth in the experience of the believer to the end. This is not an attempt to take an Arminian or Calvinist view. The dynamic that we are seeking to implement in the therapeutic process is motivation. It is not only the hope "out there" but the implementation of the truth working within the person producing the fulfillment of that hope. The same dynamic of motivation is applied to the client through the therapeutic process.

Sanctification, as elaborated in the New Testament, is both a state and a process whereby the individual is being set apart for the work of God in his life. Sanctification is spoken of as having happened when a person first believes, as a process that goes on throughout the Christian experience, and as a final condition that occurs at the return of Christ. Sanctification can be summarized as the potential of experiencing. The integrative dynamic found in the doctrine of sanctification is essentially the idea of growth or actualization. Growth is that ingredient of life operating in the client that includes the above-named dynamics producing a wholeness or fulfillment in a person.

Christology-Counselor

The person and work of Christ are found in the doctrine of Christology. Christ's work provides a divine model particularly of the dynamic truths to be embodied by the counselor in the therapeutic process. A thorough understanding of Christ's life also could provide the structure for developing an adequate model for anthropology-personality. There are essentially five areas of the person of Jesus Christ that we would like to consider in developing this model: (1) Jesus' concept of himself; (2) his relationships; (3) his volition—will; (4) his knowledge—mind; (5) his emotions—feelings. These five areas can be thought of as representatives of man's personality. Jesus came to transform all these areas in man's personality: (1) man needs to be realigned with the Father and thus gain a clear self-concept (Gen. 1:28; Col. 3:10); (2) man's relationship needs to be restored with other people; (3) man's will and motivation need to be redirected; (4) man's mind needs to be renewed; (5) man's emotional life needs to be reorganized.

Christology deals formally with the following basic doctrines: (1) incarnation—God becomes flesh; (2) kenosis—the humility of Christ; (3) the natures of Christ; (4) hypostatic union—the unity of the two natures as one; (5) impeccability—Jesus' inability to sin; (6) offices of Christ-prophet, priest, and king; (7) propitiation—covering for sin; (8) reconciliation—bringing God and man together; and (9) atonement—accomplishment at the cross to reconcile man to God. An exploration of each of the above doctrines provides insights into Jesus as counselor in his relationship to the believer as client. Space does not allow for the development of all these doctrines as they may relate to Christ as a model for counseling, but some suggestions will be made.

The *incarnation* implies truth (reality) becoming embodied. The therapist must become something, i.e., take on something that is not part of daily experience in order to help the client. The incarnation also suggests a coming to man. The therapist comes to the client in hearing and listening to his problems.

The *kenosis* suggests an identification with and reduction of the exercise of one's abilities. The therapist must reduce the full scope of his ability and knowledge, and focus on what the client is experiencing.

The *two natures of Christ and the hypostatic union* suggests the process of hearing or being empathic with the client without becoming identified with his problems, i.e., being present to, but distant from the client. Yet the therapist remains one person.

Christ's *impeccability* (regardless of one's theory) implies that the therapist needs to be impeccable in his therapeutic relationship to his clients.

The *offices of Christ* refer to specific aspects of Christ's role and functioning. These appear to relate to the various therapeutic styles or techniques the therapist may use. Christ's three offices suggest that the counselor needs to be in control of the counseling situation in terms of superintending the process (king); that he needs to accept, listen with empathy, and attend to the client (priest); and the counselor needs to interpret, give insight, or confront the client because he has knowledge or understanding of the therapy process (prophet). Carlson (1976) has focused an entire paper on prophetic and priestly aspects of Christ's style of counseling.

Propitiation, reconciliation, and *atonement* indicate that what Christ did regarding man's sin leads the believer to a new relationship to God (and to others). The complex dynamics of these doctrines suggest at least that what the therapist does in regard to the client's pathology ought to lead to a new or fuller relationship to God and to others.

Finally, much that the counselor does therapeutically will assist the client in his relation to others as well as God. This is especially true when the therapist is a Christian and can assist the client directly in this regard. These suggested dynamics represent only the beginning exploration into the implication of Christ's nature, person, and work for psychology and therapy. It is our opinion that specific theories of therapy have focused on different healing dynamics, as was suggested in the sin-pathology section, which are all present in Christ's person and work. Theories can be explored individually or in terms of the common denominators of therapeutic effectiveness (Frank, 1974).

Ecclesiology-Group Process

Ecclesiology is the biblical doctrine that develops the concepts that are embodied in the church. These concepts include the meaning of *ecclesia,* the membership, leadership, gifts, government, standard, mission, and ordinances of the church. This section of the paper will only concern itself with the body of Christ as a model that can integrate the principles and process of group therapy, though it is our opinion that these principles have a broader application into the whole field of social psychology.

The New Testament stresses three concepts that were pregnant with meaning in the early church: *ecclesia, koinonia,* and *agape.* Ecclesia emphasizes the idea of a called out people getting together koinonia emphasizes the idea of fellowship or sharing together, and finally, agape means love and acceptance for a person as he is. The dynamics of these three concepts provide a cornerstone in developing a healthy group therapeutic experience. Group therapy is essentially two or more people getting together to share their mutual feelings and problems in a context of concern for what each other is experiencing.

Group therapy has been successful to the extent that it allows or provides for these dynamics to operate. It should also be noted here that a careful study of group process such as was done by Ohlson (1970) and Rogers (1970) would indicate that all too often the body of Christ has eliminated its potential therapeutic effectiveness by not allowing the process to continue. A fear of intimacy and self-disclosure has generally been the cause of this failure.

The goals of the body of Christ are found in Ephesians 4:1-16 where particular emphasis is placed on *unity of the group, developing each person, growing up, and edifying the body of love.* An examination of these concepts indicates that they are not essentially different from those outlined by Ohlson and Rogers. These principles are common to all groups, but they are especially important in group therapy.

The body of Christ affords a deep and meaningful *acceptance* of each member one for another. There is the acceptance of people from all walks of life, all races, all colors, both sexes—whatever the person's background. This is the cornerstone of every effective group. When a group communicates acceptance to each of its members, it is saying that they are important to the group and are accepted just as they are. The member who feels this acceptance will find some of his own needs met and therefore will be willing to contribute and become involved in the goals and purposes of the group.

Just as the body of Christ requires *loyalty* and *commitment* by each member in order to grow, so each group, especially therapy groups, needs its members to be committed to the group to be effective.

The body of Christ has expectations! When individuals believe and join a church, most are confronted with certain expectations: sharing their faith with the unsaved, loving and ministering to other members of the church, helping to finance the work of the Lord, and promoting the welfare of the church. Every therapy group has expectations or norms which regulate group and member functioning.

The body of Christ also gives each believer the feeling of *belonging.* When a person comes into the body of Christ there is a good feeling within him that he belongs. God has built into man a need to belong which is fundamental. A group which can create this feeling in its members will be more effective and have higher member involvement in the group activities.

The body of Christ sets before each believer a very clear and direct program which becomes partially his *responsibility.* A person who is a member of a family or any other group has a sense of responsibility to the group and its task.

Finally, *security* is one of the cornerstones found in the body of Christ. It is important for each believer to feel secure in Jesus Christ and secure in the presence of other Christians. A sense of security provides a place in the present and a certainty for the future. Whenever a group fails to provide security and belongingness, members lose a sense of responsibility and the group becomes ineffective and may even dissolve.

Acceptance, belongingness, responsibilities, and security: These are just a few of the forces active in the body of Christ that have been studied in other group situations (Lindzey and Aronson, 1968; Yalom, 1970).

Eschatology-Reward, Expectations, and Goals

The difference between eschatology and the psychology of rewards, expectations, and goals seems obvious. Eschatology describes the final end of the last judgment, the second coming, and the final end time. In these events human history as we know it ends. However, the psychology of rewards, expectations, and goals describe final events which are less cosmic and more finite in nature. First, most of human living, whether individual or group, involves goal setting and goal seeking whether immediate or mediate. There is little behavior of action which is purposeless. While psychologists have not as a rule discussed purpose, the concept of motivation implies purpose in spite of drive theory's denial of purpose. Also actualization or self-actualization implies purpose as an end state. Thus a great deal of what the actualization theorists (e.g., Rogers, 1967; Maslow, 1968) have described as maturity, and/or a fully functioning person, becomes a goal or eschatology. Thus while human history moves to its final goal or end, so human behavior repeatedly moves toward specific goals. Second, the Bible describes the second coming as the blessed hope of the believer. Psychology also speaks of expectation or hope, though there have been only a few systematic investigations (Mowrer, 1960; Stotland, 1969; Tolman, 1959). On the other hand, psychology has extensively described fear which is the reverse of hope, i.e., negative expectations. Third, eschatology describes a coming last judgment. Judgment means rewards and punishment because there is responsibility. While psychologists have discussed rewards, punishment, and incentives, they have often combined them in the more general term, reinforcement. Various personality theories and therapies also discuss responsibility and choice. We are suggesting the psychology of goals, expectations, rewards, and responsibilities, whether of individuals and/or groups, parallel and are integrative with their cosmic eschatological equivalent.

Conclusion

We are committed to the assumption that all truth is God's truth. Thus the truths (principles, dynamics, and content) of psychology are integrative with the truths of the Scripture as they have been systematized by theology. We have surveyed the content of theology and psychology to determine a common model which is intrinsic to both. The model was diagrammed in figure 1 and then the integrated content of the common area was described. Since this is an initial proposal of an encompassing model, our assertions regarding the details of the content areas are exploratory at some points. Also, the depth and riches of the content areas were far from exhausted. Therefore, we welcome criticism and suggestions.

References

Berkouwer, C. G. *Man: The Image of God.* Grand Rapids: Eerdmanns, 1962.

Brunner, E. *Man in Revolt.* London: Lutterworth Press, 1939.

Calvin, J. *Institutes of the Christian Religion,* Vol. 1. H. Beveridge, trans. Grand Rapids: Eerdmanns, 1957. (Originally published, 1559).

Carlson, D. E. "Jesus' Style of Relating: The Search for a Biblical View of Counseling." A paper presented at the conference on Research in Mental Health and Religious Behavior, Atlanta, Georgia, January 24-26, 1976.

Carter, J. "Four Models of the Integration Process." A paper presented at the secod annual meeting of Western Association of Christians for Psychological Studies, Santa Barbara, California, May 30-31, 1975.

Clines, D. J. A. "The Image of God in Man." *Tyndale Bulletin,* 1968, *19,* 53-103.

Delitzsch, F. A. *System of Biblical Psychology.* Grand Rapids: Baker Book House, 1966. (Originally published, 1855).

Frank, J. *Persuasion and Healing* (rev. ed.). New York: Schocken, 1974.

Howard, J. K. "The Concept of the Soul in Psychology and Religion." *Journal of the American Scientific Affiliation,* 1972, *24,* 147-154

Jackson, B. "The *Psuche* in Psychology and Theology." *Journal of Psychology and Theology,* 1975, *3,* 3-10.

Lindzey, G., and Aronson, E. *The Handbook of Social Psychology,* Vol. IV. (2nd ed.). Reading, Mass.: Addison-Wesley, 1968.

Luther, M. *Luther's Works I.* (J. Pelikan and H. Lehmann, ed. and trans.). Philadelphia: Fortress Press, 1955.

Maddi, S. *Personality Theories* (rev. ed.). Homewood, Ill.: Dorsey Press, 1972.

Maslow, A. *Toward a Psychology of Being* (2nd ed.). Princeton, N.J.: Van Nostrand, 1968.

Mowrer, O. H. *Learning Theory and Behavior.* New York: John Wiley, 1960.

Niebuhr, H. R. *Christ and Culture.* New York: Harper & Row, 1951.

Ohlsen, M. M. *Group Counseling.* New York: Holt, Rinehart and Winston, 1970.

Rogers, C. *On Encounter Groups.* New York: Harper & Row, 1970.

————. *On Becoming a Person.* Boston: Houghton Mifflin, 1967.

Rychlak, J. F. *Introduction to Personality and Psychotherapy.* Boston: Houghton Mifflin, 1972.

Stotland, F. *Introduction to Personality and Hope.* San Francisco: Jossey-Bass, 1969.

Tolman, E. C. "Principles of Purposive Behavior." In S. Koch ed., *Psychology: A Study of a Science* (Vol. 2). New York: McGraw Hill Book Co., 1959.

Yalom, I. A. *The Theory and Practice of Group Psychotherapy.* New York: Basic Books, 1970.

BEHAVIOR MODIFICATION OF THE SPIRIT

Paul W. Clement

Concerning human behavior, the Bible tends to tell *what* and *why*, but it is weak on *how*. For example, the Scriptures say to spread the gospel, but they don't provide many details about how to do so. The Bible is not a technical manual for missionaries; it wasn't intended to be. Under the general leadership of Donald A. McGavran the church-growth movement has proposed that anthropology has something to say to missionaries about the technical aspects of spreading the gospel (McQuilkin, 1973). A new breed of missionary is applying the data and methods of contemporary anthropology to solve some of the problems of missions and church growth. Scientifically grounded technical manuals for missionaries are being written by members of the church-growth movement.

The basic proposition of the present paper is that psychology also has many useful things to say about how to spread the gospel and how to move toward personal, spiritual goals. Empirically oriented, experimentally based, psychology is not an enemy of spiritual growth and development; it is potentially a major ally.

Assumptions

Bumblebees Can Fly

Many people seem to believe that one can't be a Christian *and* be committed to scientific psychology (at least not to a "behavioral" brand). Such an assumption seems to lead to a second, i.e., there is no relationship between spiritual development and behavioral change. Having made these two assumptions, there is no need to search for ways of promoting spiritual birth and development through behavior modification strategies.

Individuals who hold to the above two assumptions are similar to the ignorant engineer who held, "According to the theory of aerodynamics, as may be readily demonstrated through wind tunnel experiments, the

This paper is based on the keynote address delivered by the writer at the First Annual Convention, Western Association of Christians for Psychological Studies, Westmont College, Santa Barbara, California, May 24, 1974. Used by permission of the author.

bumblebee is unable to fly. This is because the size, weight, and shape of his body in relation to the total wingspread make flying impossible" (Anonymous, 1974). If bumblebees were to take this engineer seriously, they would not try to fly. If Christians accept the idea that behavior modification is of no spiritual value, they won't try to use it.

For bumblebees the story has a happy ending: "The bumblebee, being ignorant of these scientific truths, goes ahead and flies anyway—and makes a little honey every day" (Anonymous, 1974). For man there can be a happy ending by ignoring the two negative assumptions presented above and accepting the proposition that behavior modification (as flight for the bumblebee) is possible.

"Truth" Is Dangerous

A second basic assumption of the present paper is that truth, as time, is relative. The tendency not to see truth as relative lies behind the destructive history of this particular concept. The concept of truth has probably been the source of more damage than any other concept yet invented by man. More wars have been fought, more family arguments have occurred, and more friendships have ended over the "truth" than over any other single concept. In contrast, looking at truth in relative terms is freeing and helpful.

Words and concepts are qualitatively different than the objects or events they represent. Also they are quantitatively different, capturing only a small fraction of the object or event being represented. Any description of an object or event is, of necessity, incomplete; however, the more perspectives used to describe an object or event, the more complete the description.

There are many perspectives which are usually used to decide what is true or false. Each perspective provides a reference point or set of reference points for truth statements. Rather than using a perspective to make truth statements, better orientation is to decide how *useful* a given perspective is for solving a given class of problems. Rather than asking, "Is the proposition true or false?" ask, "Does the proposition help me to solve a problem with which I am grappling?"

Dooyeweerd (1954), a Dutch Christian philosopher, has dealt extensively with the problem of perspectives. In the second volume of his four-volume work, he gave an elaborate exposition of fourteen philosophical perspectives; he calls them "cosmic modalities" or "law spheres." A student of Dooyeweerd, Spier (1953, pp. 31-33; 1954, pp. 31-122), has provided a much more concise account of these fourteen perspectives: (1) numerical, (2) spatial, (3) physical, (4) biotic, (5) psychical (feeling), (6) analytical (thought), (7) historical, (8) linguistic (symbolic meaning), (9) social, (10) economic, (11) aesthetic, (12) juridical, (13) ethical, and (14) pistical (faith). Spier (1953, pp. 34-35) concluded the following about the cosmic modalities:

This sovereignty in one's own law sphere really means that the various cosmic aspects are mutually irreducible. Each aspect is an original *meaning-phase* of life with its own unique *central idea* (meaning-nucleus), with its own significance, not to be reduced from the other aspects. Each of these aspects has received its own laws from God, which cannot be transferred from one sphere to the other. Physical laws cannot be applied to the psychological aspect of sensation. A sensation can neither be measured nor weighed. Nor can historical data be explained as psychological reactions. Though this may seem to work, yet, there always remains something which obstinately refuses to be psychologized. Still another example: the juridical, ethical, or faith life of men cannot be reduced to historical phenomena. Reality opposes this reduction of a class of things, characterized by a specific aspect from which it derives its meaning, to a differently qualified class of things. Whoever reduces faith to reason kills true faith and allows living religion to sink into barren reasoning.

Statistics Can Help

Students of inferential statistics learn a concept that is very useful is solving a fundamental problem in the integration of psychology and theology. It is the concept of orthogonal relationships. Two factors are orthogonally related, if they are independent or uncorrelated. For example, within the psychological dimension intelligence and extraversion are orthogonal. Knowing how bright or dull a person is in no way suggests how outgoing or withdrawn he may be. There are many orthogonal factors within psychology. Knowing where a person scores along each psychological factor provides information about the individual which could not be obtained from any other orthogonally related factor. Each orthogonal factor expands our knowledge of the person; the more orthogonal factors, the better.

Not only are there many orthogonal factors within psychology, there are many orthogonal relationships between psychology and other disciplines. Each philosophical perspective is represented by one or more disciplines. When two or more disciplines come out of the same philosophical perspective, they may be nonorthogonal, i.e., correlated or interdependent. When two disciplines come out of two different philosophical perspectives, they are necessarily orthogonal. Such is the case with psychology and theology.

As with all orthogonally related disciplines, psychology and theology are complementary. Both add to a more complete picture of man's experience. Logically they cannot contradict each other, since contradictions can only take place *within* a perspective. Clashes *between* perspectives can only produce pseudo contradictions.

What Language Are You Speaking?

Each discipline can be viewed as a language or family of languages. Within each language there are dialects. These dialects correspond to the theories found within a discipline. Perceived in this manner, asking, "Which discipline is true?" makes no more sense than asking, "Which is true, Chinese or Russian?" Questions of truth are not relevant, but questions of usefulness are very much in order. Languages vary in their suitability for dealing with different kinds of phenomena.

Within psychology and theology there are many dialects that make communication within each discipline very difficult and communication between the two disciplines sometimes almost impossible. An important step toward improved intra- and interdisciplinary communication is simply acknowledging the existence of the disciplinary languages and their dialects. Such an acknowledgment may then lead to learning some of the other languages and dialects so that meaningful communication can take place.

There Are No Split Personalities

Although there are many perspectives for viewing man and many related languages for describing him, each person remains a whole, unitary, indivisible, living being. Man, as any object of study, is always different than any perspective of him or than any description of him. A contrasting, faulty assumption that seems to occur is that individuals can somehow be disintegrated, be divided into components, or be dehumanized by being analyzed through some philosophical, psychological, or theological perspective. Fortunately, no matter what is said about a person, the person remains *in toto*.

Definitions

This section of the paper deals with the three key words of the title by providing definitions of each.

Behavior

There are six basic kinds of behavior with which a psychologist can deal. They are identified in table 1. These six behavioral categories result from the paired combinations of two types of environmental controlling events (antecedents and consequences) with three types of response systems in the human body. Behavior consists of a change in the tension level of muscles in comparison to a resisting state, a change in secretory activity of the glands, or a change in bioelectrical activity within the central nervous system.

TABLE 1
Six Basic Types of Behavior

Primary Controlling Stimuli	Response Systems		
	Striated Muscles	Smooth Muscles, Glands, Heart	Central Nervous System
Antecedents	Reflex	Emotional Reaction	Sensation/ Perception
Consequences	Action	?	Thought

Changes in the environment can produce (elicit) reactions in each of the response systems. Such reactions can be produced by unconditioned stimuli. Unconditioned stimuli are those events that can produce a reaction without the person having had prior learning experiences with the stimuli. Previously neutral stimuli may acquire the eliciting power of an unconditioned stimulus through the process known as classical, respondent, or Type S conditioning. Somatic reflexes, emotional reactions, and sensations are relatively discrete, stereotyped responses.

Each of the response systems is also capable of producing changes in the environment. Such behaviors produce or remove reinforcers. Positive reinforcers are stimuli that strengthen the behavior that produces them. Negative reinforcers are stimuli that strengthen the behavior that removes them. The person learns as his behavior changes his world through a process known as instrumental, operant, or Type R conditioning. Actions, those responses studied via biofeedback, and thoughts are relatively complex, patterned responses. At the present, no term has been coined to label the second type of consequence-controlled behavior; therefore, table 1 identifies that behavior with a question mark.

Very complex patterns of behavior occur based upon two facts: (1) Most responses produce external and internal stimuli; (2) these response-produced stimuli may function as elicitors or reinforcers for other behaviors. An infinite number of sequences is possible. Each person provides much of his own environment, which influences his behavior, which influences his environment, ad infinitum. One of the fascinating things about man is that at the same time he can be both observer and object, both experimenter and subject, both skinner and pigeon.

In summary, behavior consists of (1) somatic reflexes, (2) emotional reactions, (3) sensations/perceptions, (4) actions, (5) those responses studied via biofeedback, and (6) thoughts.

Modification

The second term of the title is "modification" which primarily means change. "Change" means to increase, strengthen, or add to a behavior, *or* to decrease, weaken, or subtract from a behavior. Under certain conditions "modification" can also mean to maintain a behavior that will change, if no intervention is applied. Various dimensions of a behavior may be modified including (1) frequency, (2) intensity, (3) topography, (4) complexity, and (5) time of occurrence.

Spirit

The third key term of the title is "spirit." According to Vine (1940) the word "spirit" or *pneuma* is used to mean eighteen different things in the New Testament. The present paper uses "spirit" to cover only some of the New Testament usages. Only those usages referring to man's spirit (in contrast to the Holy Spirit) are being used. The New Testament meanings include (1) the immaterial, invisible part of man; (2) the disembodied man; (3) the sentient element in man—that by which he perceives, reflects, feels, and desires; (4) the goals, aims, or purposes of a person; (5) character; (6) moral qualities; (7) "the inward man," i.e., believers; and (8) those who claim to be the depositories of the gifts of the Holy Spirit.

Vine (1940) stated, "The spirit may be recognized as the life principle bestowed on man by God" (p. 55). The spirit of man is not a *thing;* it is a *process,* series of events, or dynamic energy. Losing sight of the distinction between object and process leads to much confusion. Objects have mass; processes involve changes or transformaions in energy. Processes are recognized by observing changes in objects, including the human body. Since in man's experience processes are only viewed in conjunction with objects, each process is identified by a special kind of "object-process" noun intended to communicate an object in process. The "object-process" noun represents a high level of abstraction which does not match any observable object. Table 2 presents some representative concepts which illustrate the differences between objects, processes, and object-processes.

TABLE 2
Some Correlated and Contrasting Concepts

Object	Process	Object-Process
Muscle	Moves	Movement
Lung	Breathes	Breath
Heart	Beats	Heartbeat
Gland	Secretes	Secretion
Reticular formation	Activates	Arousal
Nerve	Conducts	Impulse
Brain	Thinks	Thought
Brain	Perceives	Perception
Brain	Thinks and Perceives	Mind
Body	Lives	Life, Spirit

"Spirit" is the highest level of object-process noun referring to man. "Spirit" seems to capture the distinctive qualities of man. The two most important of these qualities may be the ability (1) to develop self-awareness and (2) to become aware of God. Awareness consists of a complex set of perceptions and thoughts that are closely intertwined, one important element of awareness being the perception of a perception.

Three Classes of Man

In his book, *He That Is Spiritual,* Chafer (1918) described three classes of man: (1) the natural man, (2) the carnal man, and (3) the spiritual man.

The natural man is alive biologically and may have developed some degree of self-awareness, but he has not become aware of the basic elements of God.

The carnal man, however, has become aware of his creator. He has perceived the Father by having met his Son, Jesus Christ. He has gone through the greatest "ah ha" experience of all. The biblical metaphor used to label this event of becoming a carnal man is "being reborn" or "being born again." Of course, "to be born" means "to start living." Biologically birth is a prerequisite for normal psychological development. Without a birth there would be no life and no subsequent growth, learning, and maturity. Similarly without spiritual birth there can be no subsequent spiritual development. One of the great human tragedies is a baby who is born but who fails to develop along one or more important anatomical or psychological dimensions. Stunted spiritual growth is also possible, producing some of the anomalies and curiosities of the spiritual world.

The spiritual man is the person who has experienced the great "insight" regarding himself and God, and is in the process of expanding his awareness. He is in the process of growing, learning, and maturing. Being a spiritual man does not represent some end state; it is part of a lifelong process of development.

Problems

Although the Bible sets spiritual birth and growth as two major goals for man, the means for reaching these goals are not spelled out extensively. Many Christians would argue that these particular goals can only be reached through the work of the Holy Spirit; however, the Holy Spirit does not work in a vacuum. The Holy Spirit most often works through (by way of) people. If the Holy Spirit works through people, he must do so by way of their behavior. Once human behavior is perceived as a potential tool for the work of the Holy Spirit, psychology becomes relevant.

Unfortunately, empirical psychology has often been rejected as an ally of the church, but empirical psychology is of great potential benefit. For present purposes, "psychology" is defined as the science of behavior. That part of psychology that seems particularly relevant to spiritual issues is the psychology of behavior change.

The mistake made by clinical psychology and psychiatry for several decades was ignoring empirical research on the psychology of behavior change. Once psychotherapists turned to experimental psychology for help, the therapeutic approach known as behavior modification (or behavior therapy) began to develop. This particular orientation has produced several dozen different methods for producing therapeutic behavior changes. Therapeutic approaches developed prior to the behavioral one typically provided no more than a few discrete methods each. The relative precision and power of behavior modification techniques is being acknowledged by an increasingly large number of clinicians.

Clinical psychology and psychiatry did not start using experimental psychology to solve problems of living *until* a few leaders in these two fields accepted the proposition that scientific methods and data are relevant. Christian lay persons and clergy have not yet grasped the relevance of a scientific psychology of behavior change to reaching spiritual goals; therefore, the field of *behavior modification of the spirit* has not yet developed. The time, however, for putting experimental psychology to work in promoting spiritual growth has arrived.

A Psychological Perspective

Goldstein, Heller, and Sechrest (1966) captured the kind of set sketched out in the preceding section in their book *Psychotherapy and the Psychology of Behavior Change*. They stated, "It is our basic contention . . . that increased understanding and efficiency, as well as the development of new techniques for altering patient behavior, may most rapidly and effectively be brought about by having major recourse to research findings from investigations initially oriented toward the psychology of behavior change" (p. 4). Their book provides a good model for one that needs to be written (perhaps with the title *Spiritual Development and the Psychology of Behavior Change*).

They suggest many possibilities for promoting change. A few examples of these appear below with suggested applications to the spiritual realm. Although the focus of Goldstein, Heller, and Sechrest (1966) is on the "resistant" patient, the following translations of their suggestions are aimed at the resistant *believer* or the potential believer.

First, a task (that calls for a written statement of how and why the person might find himself more favorably predisposed toward the messages of the Bible) would render him more open to the leading of the Holy Spirit (cf. Goldstein, Heller, and Sechrest, 1966, p. 109). Second, preaching that encourages delayed compliance decreases the threat value of the message (cf. p. 178). Third, personal witnessing preceded by weak counterarguments against the gospel immunize the nonbeliever against other stronger arguments (cf. p. 183). Fourth, personal witnesses to Christ should be seen as powerful, rewarding, nurturant, and successful (cf. p. 198). Fifth, giving new believers prior information about the processes of spiritual growth, the basic ideas underlying it, and the techniques to be used will facilitate progress toward manifesting the fruits of the Holy Spirit (cf. p. 249).

I would not be surprised to find that among the statements made in the preceding pages there has been something offensive for everyone. Some readers may be asking, "By what right does one person engage in behavior modification on another person's spirit? Who sets the goals?" The fact remains that a behavioral technology is available and rapidly growing for modifying the spiritual dimensions of man. The church may turn its back on this particular reality and let the opponents of the New Testament message use this very behavioral technology to stifle the acceptance of Christ's good news.

There may be many readers who strongly believe in spreading the life-expanding news of Jesus, but who simply refuse, knowingly, to use "behavior modification" on another person. For such individuals the new field of behavioral approaches to self-regulation may provide a resolution (Goldfried and Merbaum, 1973; Mahoney and Thoresen, 1974; Miller, Barber, DiCara, Kamiya, Shapiro, and Stoyva, 1974; Thoresen and Mahoney, 1974; Watson and Tharp, 1972).

A basic theme running throughout these books is that there is something incredible about man. His behavior can be studied and modified much as Skinner could do with a rat or pigeon; but, unlike a rat or pigeon, a person can be *both* experimenter *and* subject within the same skin. If one buys the assumption that behavior is lawfully determined, as one begins to discover what some of the laws are, a person can begin to run experiments on himself. He can see how those laws come out in his own behavior. The ultimate, then, is achieved when the person joins forces with the Holy Spirit and uses self-administered behavioral strategies to modify his own spirit.

References

Anonymous. "The Theory of Aerodynamics." *Bits and Pieces,* 1974, 7 (May), 19.

Chafer, L. S. *He That Is Spiritual.* Findlay, Ohio: Dunham Publishing Co., 1918.

Dooyeweerd, H. (4 vols.; trans. by D. H. Freeman, and H. de Jongste). *A New Critique of Theoretical Thought.* Philadelphia: Presbyterian and Reformed Publishing Co., 1954.

Goldfried, M. R., and Merbaum, M. *Behavior Change Through Self-Control.* New York: Holt, Rinehart and Winston, 1973.

Goldstein, A. P., Heller, K., and Sechrest, L. B. *Psychotherapy and the Psychology of Behavior Change.* New York: John Wiley, 1966.

Mahoney, M. J., and Thoresen, C. E. *Self-Control: Power to the Person.* Monterey, Calif.: Brooks/Cole Publishing Co., 1974.

McQuilkin, J. R. *How Biblical Is the Church-Growth Movement?* Chicago: Moody Press, 1973.

Miller, N. E., Barber, T. X., DiCara, L. V., Kamiya, J. Shapiro, D., Stoyva, J. *Biofeedback and Self-Control: An Aldine Annual on the Regulation of Bodily Processes and Consciousness.* Chicago: Aldine Publishing Co., 1974.

Spier, J. M. (trans. by F. H. Klooster). *What Is Calvinistic Philosophy?* Grand Rapids: Eerdmans, 1953.

———. (trans. by D. H. Freeman). *An Introduction to Christian Philosophy.* Philadelphia: Presbyterian and Reformed Publishing Co., 1954.

Thoresen, C. E., Mahoney, M. J. *Behavioral Self-Control.* New York: Holt, Rinehart and Winston, 1974.

Vine, W. E. *An Expository Dictionary of New Testament Words with Their Precise Meanings for English Readers.* Vol. IV. London: Oliphants, 1940.

Watson, D., and Tharp, R. *Self-Directed Behavior: Self-Modification for Personal Adjustment.* Monterey, Calif.: Brooks/Cole Publishing Co., 1972.

SECTION
THREE

MATURITY:
CHRISTIAN AND PSYCHOLOGICAL

Maturity is a concept that has been described extensively by psychologists such as Jourard, Jung, Maslow, May, and Rogers. They have used terms such as self-disclosure, transcendent functioning, self-actualization, courage, growth, and being process. Christians also have extensively discussed spiritual maturity, but they use theological or biblical concepts such as holiness and sanctification. Is there a difference in terminology only, or is there a difference between psychological and spiritual maturity? If there is, does this difference apply to both Christian and non-Christian?

Sin is not usually associated with maturity; in fact, most Christian churches would probably associate maturity, and certainly Christian maturity, with the absence of sin. On the contrary, Clines has argued that innocence cannot be harmonized with Christian maturity. Thus, Clines would seem to be in agreement with Rollo May in his analysis of Billy Budd in *Power and Innocence*. Rather than innocence, Clines asserts that it is risk-taking that is the key to maturity. When risks are taken in the ethical or spiritual realm there are obviously uncertain outcomes, one of which is sin. Thus, it is through risk-taking that sin becomes associated with maturity.

Clines' article ranges widely across a multitude of issues including the relationship of ethics, creativity, and wholeness as they relate to psychological and Christian maturity. He noted that psychological theorists do not seem to agree on basic dimensions of motivation. He also discussed the dilemma of a choice between two evils, a situation in which the lesser evil becomes a good, and thus sin as the least undesirable alternative becomes the choice of the mature person.

Is the psychologically mature individual less sinful from a Christian perspective? Is the "saint" more psychologically mature than others? Is Clines right about sin's being a necessary concept for explaining Christian maturity? Whatever the reader's opinions on these issues, one cannot help but be challenged and stimulated by this engaging article.

"Holiness and Health" is the first of three articles (the other two being "Personality and Christian Maturity" and "Self-Actualization and Sanctification") in this section that explicitly address the similarity and difference between psychological and Christian maturity. In the previous article, Clines touched on the issue in passing by suggesting that psychological maturity is concerned with holiness while Christian maturity has an ethical concern. Cohen has explored the relationship of Christian and psychological maturities, or, as he terms them, holiness and health, by examining four possibilities: (1) The two are totally independent of each other; (2) they are the same; (3) they are different but correlated; and (4) there is causality involved in their relationship.

It appears that Cohen has addressed the four logically possible relationships between psychology and Christianity. Before you as reader reach a conclusion on this issue, you will probably find it informative to compare Cohen's conclusions with Oakland's discussion of self-actualization and sanctification, as they do not appear to agree in more than terminology. In addition, the conclusions reached on this issue of holiness and health are probably related to one of the four models of psychology and Christianity described by Carter (chapter 5).

The article "Personality and Christian Maturity" falls easily into three sections. The first one is an in-depth discussion of three personality theorists—Rogers, Gendlin, and Jung—which will probably be informative apart from any discussion of Christian maturity. Carter has argued that these three theorists, although using different terminology, postulate two underlying processes as definitive of personality and developmental maturity: wholeness and actualization.

In the second part of the article Carter argued that the New Testament describes Christian maturity, or sanctification, in terms of the same two processes which Rogers, Gendlin, and Jung view as characteristic of human personality although obviously the New Testament uses a different vocabulary. Carter's analysis of the biblical material focused on the fundamental concepts of salvation and sanctification rather than on isolated verses of Scripture.

In the final section Carter attempted to address the similarity-dissimilarity issue in the relationship between psychological and Christian maturity. He does this by introducing two distinctions: first, the distinction between the process of actualization and holiness, and the contents of those processes. The second distinction is between who is being actualized: the Christian or the non-Christian. It will be informative to compare his solution to that of the immediately preceding article ("Holiness and Health") and the following one ("Self-Actualization and Sanctification"), although differences in terminology must not be confused with differences in perspective.

Oakland has described psychological and Christian maturity in terms of self-actualization and sanctification. His discussion begins by reviewing the concept of sanctification in Reformed and Wesleyan theology. In addition, he weaves in biblical material on the topic. While recognizing that Adler, Goldstein, Horney, and Rogers—all postulate a self-actualizing concept, Oakland has developed his approach to psychological maturity around Maslow's concept of self-actualization. He does this because Maslow's analysis of self-actualization is more comprehensive and also because it is based on healthy individuals. The fifteen aspects or characteristics of actualizers, as described by Maslow, are analyzed very insightfully into three clusters: (1) being a relatively open person, (2) having a strong belief system or calling, and (3) having a balance between individuation and social relationships.

There appears to be little difference for Oakland between sanctification and self-actualization. This can be more easily observed if Christ's name is substituted at appropriate places in Maslow's discussion of self-actualizers. The issue of the similarity of Christian and psychological maturity is further developed by noting the similarity of eighteenth- to nineteenth-century religious groups and twentieth-century encounter groups. The increasingly religious character of humanistic and transpersonal psychology is also recognized. Oakland's perspective on the similarity-dissimilarity of psychological and Christian maturity should be compared to Cohen's and Carter's in the previous two articles, keeping in mind the difference in terminology.

Each of the immediately preceding three tended to use a different set of terms to describe psychological and Christian maturity. Cohen referred to health and holiness; Carter referred to personality and Christian maturity (sanctification); and Oakland referred to self-actualization and sanctification. Barshinger shifts the vocabulary of discussion to intimacy and spiritual growth, but Barshinger's shift is more than a shift in vocabulary. It is a shift from an objective discussion of the topic to a subjective or personal discussion. Barshinger has defined intimacy as "the ability to let yourself be known by others, God, or yourself." Intimacy is viewed as preceding personal-emotional growth. However, since intimacy is so tied to interpersonal (or psychological) relationships, personal-emotional growth, according to Barshinger, often precedes spiritual growth.

Barshinger has also made a distinction between religious spirituality and intuitive spirituality. This distinction is a reflection of Fleck's distinction between consensual and committed-intrinsic religion (chapter 4); however, again, Barshinger's discussion has a personal or subjective orientation, in contrast to Fleck's objective research analysis. Thus, Barshinger shows the reader that the personal or intimate side of maturity should not be lost in the intellectual analysis of this topic.

Is it possible to take this personal attitude to all psychology? To all Christianity? Or only to certain aspects of each? If the reader likes the personal approach, Jacobs (chapter 28) should be consulted.

SIN AND MATURITY

David J. A. Clines

This essay is concerned with the question. To what extent, if at all, is sin necessary to maturity? That is to say, is there a positive value in sin in the development of the human personality?

At first sight, these questions may seem pointless. If sin is what is damaging to the human personality, or if it is what is unnatural for man as created by God, how can sin promote human development or maturity? More briefly, can what is bad produce what is good? Yet, further reflection suggests that in our experience the most mature people frequently seem to have a far from unblemished record, while the innocent are often only the naive. The person who never made mistakes never made anything, we are inclined to say; that is to say, achievement is attained by being able to use one's errors constructively, not by being so timid as to avoid situations where errors can be made. Can this be true also in the moral and emotional sphere, in what way would we want to say that the development of human personality is achieved only at the cost of "sinning boldly" rather than by avoiding the temptation and by keeping as far from sin as possible?

That has seemed to me, on reflection, to be a serious question not to be shrugged off by conventional appeals to morality, Christian or otherwise, that would be somewhat scandalized by any suggestion that vice could be more rewarding than virtue. However it is answered, nevertheless, the question is something of a paradox since it becomes a question only to those who have a firm commitment to the value of virtue. For the amoralist, for whom there is no distinction between good and evil, there is no sin and, therefore, nothing that of itself stands in the way of human development; for the immoralist, for whom evil is good, sin is by definition the path to maturity; only for the moralist, who already believes that sin is damaging and harmful, can it be a serious question whether at times life is so simple as his values indicate.

My method in this paper is to examine under the first two headings, by way of clearing the ground, cases where sin apparently leads to maturity:

This is a revised version of a paper presented in a colloquium on "The Power of Positive Sinning?" under the auspices of *Care and Council*, 2 All Souls Place, London W1N 3DB.
© *Journal of Psychology and Theology*, 1977, *5*, 183-96. Used by permission of the author.

under the first heading cases where sin is only apparently sin, and under the second, cases where the sin is real enough, but where the alternative is worse, and where, therefore, the bad is comparatively "good." The third section deals with the main subject of the paper; there I suggest that it is not sin that leads to maturity but risk-taking, which exposes one to the possibility of sin (and hence brings about the apparent connection of sin with maturity). In the fourth section I deal with both the Christian ideals of innocence and maturity to all individuals. And in the fifth section I believe I have shown a way in which an affirmative answer can be given to our original question, Is sin necessary to maturity? by replying: Yes, in our world, but when it is the sin of *others,* that is, when it is *suffered.*

When "Sin" Is Not Sin

1. If we accept, for the time being, that sin is what other people who ought to know say that it is, it is not at all difficult to argue that maturity often comes about through sin, that is, the rejection of others' understanding of what constitutes sin. Such is a case where "sin" is not sin. Sin properly speaking is not what parental conditionings or social morals say it is; liberation from others' systems of values and the autonomous choice of one's own values are a process of maturation. That does not mean that the values one chooses as an alternative to one's parents' or one's society's values are necessarily better values; but the process of internalizing values by determining them for oneself is one of the tokens of maturation. The immature person either lacks values, or is dominated by a rigid set of values that threaten him, or perhaps fluctuates between these two poles; the mature person, on the other hand, has achieved his own personal autonomy from purely external sets of values by making values of his own (Carter, 1974). What one has been accustomed to thinking of as sin becomes merely "sin."

2. The maturation involved in gaining autonomy from ingrained notions of "sin" comes about, so it frequently appears in fits and starts, in "breakthrough" situations. One suddenly realizes that what one has been taught and has uncritically accepted from table manners or proper language or sexual behavior or permissible amusements is no longer valid, i.e., has value for oneself. Many people who have been brought up "strictly," that is to say, within a complex set of values in which the boundary between sin and non-sin is clearly defined, are well able to remember the *first* time they achieved the autonomous decision to break the taboo. They would say, and would often be well entitled to with a good Christian conscience I would think, that sin had suddenly become merely "sin" for them and at that moment they grew up.

For some every such act of autonomy is achieved only at great cost (Warlick, 1973). Paul Tillich writes in his autobiography:

I was able to reach intellectual and moral autonomy only after a severe struggle. My father's authority . . . which, because of his position in the church, I identified with the religious authority of revelation, made every attempt at autonomous thinking an act of religious daring and connected criticism of authority with a sense of guilt. The age-old experience of mankind, that new knowledge can be won only by breaking a taboo and that all autonomous thinking is accompanied by a consciousness of guilt, is a fundamental experience of my own life. (1967)

3. It is not difficult to find biblical illustrations of these points. On two occasions at least in the life of David we find him in breach of conventional taboos, as "sinning" against the mores of his society. In the first case (1 Sam. 21:1-6) David is on the run for his life from Saul; at Nob he needs food for his men, but all that is available is "holy" food, dedicated to God's use. David breaks through the taboo on holy food and persuades the priest to allow the holy food to be used for the sustenance of life. Whether David can be said to "mature" by his extension of the sphere of the holy to include all that preserves life cannot be said from the narrative, but here at least he is making an autonomous decision—against conventional morality—in favour of a "sin" which does not turn out to be sin, properly speaking. It is of the greatest significance that Jesus appeals to this story when his disciples are accused of "sin" against conventional interpretation of the law—that to pluck heads of grain on the sabbath constitutes work (Mark 2:23-28). And here at least the "sin" of Jesus' disciples *is* connected with the behavior of the mature person: The sabbath is made for man, so man is lord of the sabbath (v.27). That is to say, the "sin" in the grainfield marks the autonomy of the mature person who has exempted himself from external constraints by internalizing his values.

The second episode from David's life presents us with a strangely unconventional mode of behavior. In 2 Samuel 12:16-23 David faces the death of the illegitimate child Bathsheba has borne to him. While the child is dying, David mourns and fasts and resists the support of his household; but when the child dies, David puts off his mourning garments, eats, and becomes himself again. This behavior of David's is not cynicism or despair, but a buoyancy that refuses to be bound by the conventional view of right and wrong behavior, and a freedom to take life as it comes, not with callousness or indifference but with personal autonomy (Brueggemann, 1972). The dynamics of David's grief may be strange even to many of us, but his "sin" against conventionality in this respect can hardly be regarded as anything but a tremendous affirmation of the autonomy of the mature person.

4. By the standards of conventional respectability, Jesus also is a "sinner." Not only does he assert himself against the law (only apparently, of course), as for example in his freedom about sabbath observance (e.g., Luke 14:1-6) or his rejection of conventional mores ("You have heard it said . . . but I say unto you," Matt. 5:33-34.), but he makes himself notorious as a "friend" of "sinners" (Matt. 11:19), who eats and drinks

with them (Mark 2:16). In John 9:24 it is said directly by the religious establishment: "We know that this man is a sinner." I would suggest that it is in his mature freedom to choose his own values that Jesus incurs this charge.

5. As an example of a particular area where "sin" need not be sin, we may consider the emotion of anger. Here it is not a question of achievement or expression of maturity through personal autonomy but of the mature person's control of and expression of his or her feelings. It would be granted by most psychologists that while consistently hostile or aggressive behavior is a mark of immaturity, the inability to express the emotion of anger and the sense of need to repress all feelings of hostility is itself also a sign of immaturity. The mature adult has aggression available, which, however, normally serves constructive and productive ends rather than infantile, sadistic, or masochistic purposes (Saul, 1971).

Many moralists, on the other hand, have regarded anger as sinful, and many Christians believe that anger is bad or at least infantile. They have been hard pressed in that case to explain biblical references to the anger of God (somewhat disguised by the less normal term "wrath"), or episodes in which Jesus displayed anger, or the New Testament injunction, "Be angry and sin not" (Eph. 4:26). Theologians have at times attempted to ease the problem of God's anger by defining it not as an emotional attitude or volitional activity on God's part but as the inevitable and impersonal process of retribution in a moral universe (Dodd, 1932); some of our translations of the New Testament (the KJV in particular) have largely solved the problem of Jesus' anger by using less emotive words; and the saying in Ephesians has been regarded as a paradox, or as signifying "be angry—if you cannot help it—but do not sin, by prolonging your anger" (Masson, 1953).

Such an approach is, however, an evasion of the biblical evidence. To consider only examples of anger on the part of Jesus is enough for our purpose. In Mark 3:5 Jesus regards the Pharisees with anger *(orgē)* when they refuse to answer him whether it is lawful to heal on the sabbath. In John 11:33 Jesus approaches the tomb of Lazarus with anger (the verb *embrimaomai* is used), presumably at the "violent tyranny" of death (as Calvin puts it). Elsewhere, the same verb is used in Jesus' charge to the blind men who are healed (Matt. 9:30) and to the leper who is cleansed (Mark 1:43), without so simple a justification of Jesus' anger being evident. In addition, there are episodes in the life of Jesus in which anger is manifested, such as the cleansing of the temple (Mark 11:15-17.), though no explicit language of anger is used, and other occasions when the force of his language implicitly argues that he is angry (e.g., his reference to Herod as "that fox" [Luke 13:32], or his woes upon hypocrites, scribes, and Pharisees in Matthew 23) (Brouse, 1974; Cerling, 1974a, 1974b; Pedersen, 1974).

None of this is to say that anger is never sinful, and it is noteworthy that

Jesus expresses anger on comparatively few occasions. Nevertheless, the examples cited should be enough to show that anger is not necessarily sinful, and may at times be only a "sin."

6. It may further be questioned whether mechanical mistakes or errors should be regarded as sin. If sin is thought of as anything less than sheer perfection, errors in spelling or the multiplication tables, or bad judgment in driving or woodworking must be thought of as sin. It is preferable, however, to regard sin as a relational concept, to be used primarily of personal offences against God, and secondarily of offences against others. This is a more biblical view of the nature of sin, where sin is viewed less as the breaking of rules—though that outlook is not altogether absent—and more as acts of rebellion or personal despite against God (Clines, 1976a).

It may even be asked in this connection whether the sinlessness of Jesus or the innocence of Adam necessarily involves the kind of mechanical perfection here described. Are we to assume, for example, that Jesus as a boy never forgot a lesson, never spelled a Hebrew word incorrectly, or, if we could imagine his playing some ball game, never mishit a ball, and never failed to achieve perfection in every sphere? Such questions raise themselves when we are considering "sin" that is not sin.

7. In short, what we have been dealing with in this section are what Martin Luther referred to as "fictitious sins." The passage of his letter to Philip Melanchthon of August 3, 1521 is justly famous and deserves to be quoted:

If you are a preacher of grace, then preach a true and not a ficitious grace; if grace is true, you must bear a true and not a fictitious sin. God does not save people who are only fictitious sinners. Be a sinner and sin boldly, but believe and rejoice in Christ even more boldly, for he is victorious over sin, death, and the world. As long as we are here (in this world) we have to sin . . . It is enough that . . . we have come to know the Lamb that takes away the sin of the world. No sin will separate us from the Lamb, even though we commit fornication and murder a thousand times a day. (Krodel, 1963, pp. 370-72)

Luther is here far from advocating "the power of positive sinning." He is warning against overscrupulousness and charging the young Melanchthon to recognize that only genuine sins can be forgiven; he is making our very distinction between sin and "sin." His injunction, "sin boldly" or "strongly" *(pecca fortiter)* should not be taken out of its context as was done by his detractors and enemies, but should be seen as a plea to disregard mere "sins," and to seek forgiveness for the genuine sins we are bound to commit while we are in this world.

The psychological language of maturity is not being used by Luther, but he is nevertheless clearly urging Melanchthon to grow up and face the realities of genuine sin, repentance, and grace. In psychological terminology, we might say he is urging upon him a firm sense of reality, which many would describe as an important attribute of maturity (Saul, 1971).

8. To conclude, we can say that "sin" can promote maturity. This is not an unimportant conclusion to reach, for frequently "sin" of the kind I have been referring to is strongly resisted by the conscience, and a sensitive person can often find it as difficult to resist the promptings of his or her overscrupulous conscience against such trivial matters as to resist it on much more serious issues. I do not argue that "sin" against conventional morality inevitably leads to maturity, but only that it is possible for it to form part of the maturing process.

When Sin Is the Lesser of Two Evils

1. There is another type of sin which, I will argue, can promote maturity. Here I am considering actions which of themselves are in fact sinful (whatever the criteria used for defining sinfulness may be) but which are less sinful than the only possible alternatives. It might be claimed that the lesser of two evils is not in fact an evil since it is comparatively a good. I cannot refute that view, and it is probably true to say that the only reason why maturity can be achieved through the lesser of two evils is precisely because it is actually a good. I can only reply that most people are aware of the kind of situation that arises where one is compelled to choose between two lines of action, neither of which one would have voluntarily chosen to follow: In such situations the lesser of two evils can function as a good. No one would want to claim that a person matures through depravity, but I want to leave room for the kind of situation where "bad" behavior apparently has a positive outcome.

2. The concept of the lesser of two evils has a long history, confirming the enduring presence of this human problem. The idea is perhaps first met with in Homer where Menelaus faces the loss of both the body and the armor of Patroclus to the Trojans and decides for "the most preferable of evils" (*Iliad*, 17.105). The theme was taken up by Aristotle (*Nicomachean Ethics*, Book 9), to whom Cicero was no doubt referring when he commented: "Philosophers tell us that we should not only choose the least of all possible evils, but even extract from them what good we can" (*De officiis*, 3.1), thus making a virtue out of his exile from Rome. As "Tully's Offices," Cicero's work had a great influence on the moral education of the Middle Ages and beyond, so it is not surprising to find Criseyde, torn between honour and a life, saying in Chaucer's *Troilus and Criseyde*, "Of harmes two, the lesse is for to chese" (2,470), and Thomas à Kempis, of the 15th century, writing, "Of two evils the less is always to be chosen" (*Imitation of Christ*, 3, 12.2), referring to suffering in the present life in preference to suffering in hell.

3. A biblical example will serve to clarify the situation. We may take the case of Job who believes he is being unjustly afflicted by God. We, the readers of the book, cannot refuse Job our sympathy, for all the theology of

his time linked suffering with sin, as the friends amply testify, while the narrator has made it plain to us that Job *is* a righteous man and does not deserve to suffer. The only thing we know that Job does not know is that God is not the proximate cause of his suffering and that Satan is. But God seems to be ultimately responsible since he has given permission to Satan to afflict Job, and it is only to prove God in the right that he is being made to suffer at all. So although we can hardly call God unjust, as Job does, we can agree with Job that his suffering is undeserved and that it stems ultimately from God.

Under these circumstances, what is Job to do? Is he to bow to the inscrutable will of God and "not sin with his lips," as the picture of Job in the first two chapters has it, or is he to express the aggressions and hostility the poetic speeches of the book show him to be feeling? To put the matter crudely, is he to be polite or frank to God? That is, is he to dissimulate about his real feelings, or is he going to let his aggression out into the open?

No sympathizer with the book of Job can doubt that Job does the right thing. In fact, God himself enthusiastically praises Job for having said the right thing (42:7-8) even though Job has made the bitterest and most untruthful accusations against God, and even though Job has had to repent of his wild words (42:3, 6). In fact, by challenging God to show what he has against him and by demanding that the reason for his suffering be made plain (e.g., 31:35ff.), Job has given God the opportunity of revealing himself to him personally (chs. 38-41).

I would suggest that in blurting out his true feelings before God rather than attempting to cover them up, Job has chosen the lesser of two evils. Given that he felt as he did, he has done the best thing—which must also be said to be an evil since it involves blasphemy against God! This is a maturing process for Job, for he is learning how to handle his anger. According to Madow (1972), "the first step in dealing with anger is to recognize that you are angry and admit it to yourself"—an aspect of an accurate perception of reality and acceptance of oneself which Maslow (1954) lists as features of the mature personality. Job also takes Madow's second step in dealing with anger which is to "identify the source of the anger," a task which friends of Job attempt to frustrate by refusing to acknowledge that God can be the source of Job's anger. They are victims of the mechanism of displacement as Madow calls it: they attempt to make Job and Job's behavior the source of his anger. As Madow (1972) says:

The sources may be difficult to ferret out if the real instigator of the anger is someone who is powerful or who can harm us in some way and with whom, therefore, it is not prudent to be angry. We tend to handle such a situation by looking for another possible source on which to blame anger . . . and we usually do it unconsciously.

The friends are described excellently here, but Job pushes beyond them to insist that it is God with whom he must have dealings since it is God who is the source of his anger.

The maturing process in Job is seen also in his growing sense of autonomy—even over against God—and the consequent sense of his own identity. The climax of his speeches comes with the words of 31:35-37:

Oh, that I had one to hear me!
(Here is my signature! let the Almighty answer me!)
Oh, that I had the indictment written by my adversary!
Surely I would carry it on my shoulder;
I would bind it on me as a crown;
I would give him an account of all my steps; like a prince I would approach him.

Job has here broken the idol of God as the all-dominating father-figure and exults in his own identity as man ("like a prince"). It is true that by the end of the book Job adopts the properly humble attitude of the creature before his creator ("I have uttered what I did not understand, things too wonderful for me," 42:3), but this comes only after he has achieved a mature self understanding and self-acceptance. Once he has spoken to God "like a prince," he can never approach him as a worm, though he may despise himself for his unjust accusations against God and repent of them in dust and ashes (42:6).

Maturity and Sin

1. Up to this point, we have focused on the concept of sin, and I have been arguing that sin does not lead to maturity except in some cases where sin is wrongly defined ("fictitious sins") or where the sin is the lesser of two evils (and so a comparative "good"). It is time now that we examine the concept of maturity, to see whether there are ways in which it could be promoted by "genuine" sin.

2. It appears that every psychologist has his own definition of what constitutes maturity, and it is indeed no less difficult to determine what is mature behavior than to decide what is sinful behavior. There is, however, much common ground among psychologists, and I have allowed myself to be guided by the several accounts of maturity which I present here briefly.

The characteristics of a mature personality as established in a study by Barron (1954) of "soundness as a person" among graduate students were: effective organization of work toward goals, correct perception of reality, character and integrity in the ethical sense, interpersonal and intrapersonal adjustment.

According to Maslow (1954), the following are the chief attributes of the mature or "self-actualizing" personality: efficient perception of reality and comfortable relations with it; acceptance of self, others, nature; spontaneity; problem centering; detachment; independence of culture and environment; continued freshness of appreciation; limitless horizons;

social feeling; deep but selective social relationships; respect for other human beings; ethical certainty; unhostile sense of humor; creativeness.

Allport (1963) summarizes in his own way the criteria of maturity that he has reviewed as: extension of the sense of self (full participation in life); warm relating of self to others; emotional security (self-acceptance); realistic perception, skills, and assignments; self-objectification (insight and humor); a unifying philosophy of life.

For Saul (1960), the main characteristics of maturity are: capacity to live independently; capacity for responsibility and productivity; freedom from inferiority feelings, egotism, and competitiveness; socialization and domestication; sexual integration; absence of aggressiveness; a firm sense of reality; flexibility and adaptability.

According to Carter (1974), there are five basic dimensions to maturity: having a realistic view of oneself and others, accepting oneself and others, living in the present but having long-range goals, having values, developing one's interests and abilities and coping with the task of living.

3. What is remarkable about all these accounts of maturity is, first, that in no case is anything approaching what Christians term sin called for to enable an individual to mature; second, that in some cases, on the contrary, positive ethical standards are regarded as developing maturity; and third, that a great deal may be said about maturity without mentioning values at all, and hence that much of what is involved in maturity has no relation to sin or virtue. This last point is perhaps the most significant: While no one would recommend depravity as a means to maturity, no one recommends goodness either as the royal route to maturity. So the two concepts, maturity and sin, only overlap to a small extent; they are not concepts that belong to the same sphere. If sin or evil is mentioned in such psychological analyses it is thought of as the persistence of infantile traits and as the result of impaired emotional development (Saul, 1960); that is, it is defined in terms of lack of maturity.

4. The Christian theologian may be a little disappointed that his or her writ does not appear to run freely in the territory of psychology, but a similar situation exists with respect to physical health. There are *some* relationships between sin and goodness on the one hand and physical health on the other (depravity is often bad for one's health, and physical healing is at times related to Christian salvation); but on the whole, a person may be perfectly fit physically but be quite below average morally speaking.

5. If this is the case also in the realm of maturity, certain items that may at first sight seem necessary for our discussion lose their significance. So, for example, if we wished to discuss the maturity of Jesus, his sinlessness is only partly relevant to the subject. No doubt we should wish to affirm that Jesus was a mature person according to most of the criteria outlined above, but the evidences for his maturity come from episodes related in the Gospels and not from the broad principle of his sinlessness. Or, to take

another example, jut because sin and maturity are not entities of the same kind, we are unable to affirm that Adam and Eve in Eden were immature simply on the grounds of their not having sinned. In their case, we do not have enough knowledge about their behavior in paradise to either affirm or deny that they were mature.

6. To expand the last point a little: C. S. Lewis (1942) has rightly warned us against the presumption that the innocence of humanity before the Fall is the same thing as naivety. Milton, at any rate, pictured Adam as a fully developed man, lord of the human race, and—had he not fallen—still living in Paradise, whither all generations of men would come from the ends of the earth to pay him homage (*Paradise Lost*, 11, 342).

It is true, nevertheless, that the biblical account of the Fall contains some hints that it may be read as the story of a progress in maturity. Of course, the basic thrust of the story is that the succumbing to temptation is an act of rebellion against God for which Adam and Eve are punished by exclusion from the Garden. When, however, we observe that upon eating the fruit "their eyes were opened," and that God himself acknowledges that the human pair have "become like one of us, knowing good and evil" (Gen. 3:22), we begin to wonder whether this is not a story also of an advance in maturity—and all the more so when one discovers that the phrase "knowing good and evil" appears to be used in other Hebrew literature as signifying having reached the years of maturity (Buchanan, 1956). Man's decision to choose for himself what is good and evil, thus rejecting the authority of God, may perhaps be seen as an act of autonomy, leading to heightened maturity.

I do not, however, believe that these are necessary implications of Genesis 3. The knowledge Adam and Eve gain is indeed a deeper self-awareness, but not all self-awareness or acts of autonomy lead necessarily to greater maturity. Only by some doctrine of a "greater good" (corresponding to the "lesser evil" spoken of earlier) can anything positive be found in the Fall story. Only when it is viewed from a broader perspective, as initiating the history of salvation or as bringing into being a world where there can be not only guilt but also forgiveness, can the Fall be spoken of as *felix culpa* ("blessed sin").

7. The direction in which this section of the paper is moving is to suggest that we should speak of, and aim at, maturity without concerning ourselves too much about sin. It is not that in our maturing we do not sin or that out of our sin no good leading toward maturity can be brought by the grace of God, but that sin is somewhat beside the point when we are speaking of maturity. What is more to the point, and what is the reason why the question of sin and maturity is raised in the first place, is the connection of risk-taking with maturity. The one who takes a risk is bound to fail, or fall, more often than the person who will take no chances; but risk-taking is, I suggest, at the heart of development toward maturity. If maturity is understood as a dynamic balance (Saul, 1960) between various attitudes

(dependence and independence, giving and getting, autonomy and socialization, constructive and destructive aggression), the risk of leaning too far in one direction or the other is plain enough; or if maturity is viewed as openness to oneself and others, the risks attached to such openness are only too plain. "He who risks and fails can be forgiven. He who never risks and never fails is a failure in his own being" (Tillich).

8. It is very interesting in this connection to consider the interpretation of David as "the trusted man" that is offered by Brueggemann (1972). David, he suggests, blazes a new trail for maturity in ancient Israel in that he knows himself to have been taken on by God, i.e., accepted by God. He is trusted, and, therefore, can trust. Because he has been accepted, he knows that he is meant for life; he is committed to over-living, with all its risks, rather than under-living. David fails, of course, and with disastrous results; but the story of David does not dwell on the failure, for it is not suggested that an innately trustworthy man has failed. David has nothing to recommend him; it is only that God has set his love upon him.

9. It is here that Ecclesiastes, too, comes into his own. He is not the pessimist or cynic he has often been charged with being; he has a positive approach to life, epitomized by his injunction, "Whatever your hand finds to do, do it with all your might" (9:10). His "pessimism" stems from his sense that death negates all values in life, including those for which he as a wise man and teacher has labored, and including those, like happiness, which he as a normal human being has taken for granted. But his recognition of the significance of death for human values does not lead him to despise virtue, or wisdom, or happiness. His last word is: "Fear God and keep his commandments; for this is the whole duty of man" (12:13); and he positively encourages his readers to confident and happy living (9:7-9)—within the brackets, so it might be put, imposed by death. For him too, life is not meant to be a matter of overscrupulosity, forever worrying about sin and guilt ("Be not righteous overmuch," 7:16), but to be lived and enjoyed; within the broad limits of the duty of man—to keep the commandments—God has given men a wide freedom within which to move and live. Hence, Ecclesiastes can say characteristically: "Go, eat your bread with enjoyment, and drink your wine with a merry heart; for God has already approved what you do" (9:7). There is a risk of overindulgence and of self-indulgence in living life on Ecclesiastes' pattern, but it is the risk involved, as with David, of over-living rather than under-living. To worry all the time about infringements of an absolute morality is not going to lead to a mature outlook; but not to worry is to run the risk of infringements and even of "genuine" sins of which one will need repentence. But to live boldly rather than morbidly is Ecclesiastes' word of wisdom which relates directly to our topic.

10. Finally, under this heading we must consider the supreme risk-taker: Jesus. The most interesting thing about the temptation stories is not that Jesus does not succumb—that we would have expected from what

we have come to learn of Jesus in the Gospels—but that they are there at all, or rather, that they happened at all. For they mean that Jesus was not afraid to expose himself to temptation. To spend forty days alone in the desert after one's call to a work of suffering is to lay oneself open to doubts about the authenticity of that call, second thoughts about the direction of one's life. To allow oneself to be taken to a high mountain and shown the kingdoms of the world is simply exposing oneself to temptation. Jesus takes those risks, but does not fail. There's the question of Jesus' relationship to women. It was not the risk of scandal—for he ran that risk easily, and was no doubt blamed by many for too free an association by the standards of his time with Mary and Martha, the Mary from Magdala, the Samaritan woman. But what risk did he run to his own sinlessness by insisting on treating women as people and ministering to their needs for intimacy? Or, must we believe in the sexlessness as well as the sinlessness of Jesus? Or, what of the scene in Gethsemane? What a risk to expose to himself and to his Father the true feelings of his truly human nature that shrank from the thought of approaching death! How much better a Socratic or Stoic resignation would have served him if his object had been to prevent all possibility of his turning back at this critical moment, of his crying off of his destiny! But Jesus as a risk-taker opens the whole issue of his life's work up to doubt in the last hours of his life—in order that he may decide afresh in favour of God's call. Had he not risked anything in Gethsemane, his death could have been an act of fortitude, but never a decision, never a triumph.

Against Maturity: A Dissentient Report

1. We cannot leave the subject on that note, however, for there has been within Christianity a strong tradition that has seemed to value innocence or naivety highly, and that might, therefore, appear to dissent from the conclusion so far reached.

This attitude comes to the surface most notably in the monastic tradition. For Gerard Manley Hopkins, for example, "Nothing is so beautiful as spring," which is not merely an aesthetic judgment, but a religious statement, for the spring of natural year is "A strain of the earth's sweet being in the beginning / In Eden garden." Hopkins imagines that the Edenic innocence of youth can be captured and kept fresh through dedication to Christ, Christ can "have, get," "Innocent mind and Mayday in girl and boy, / Most, O maid's child, thy choice, and worthy the winning" (Hopkins, 1953).

2. This outlook has a long and honorable background. In the language of Jesus, the "innocent" or "under-aged" (Gk. *nēpios*) are those to whom the secrets of the kingdom have been revealed, in distinction to the "wise" and "learned" (Matt. 11:25; Luke 10:21). With Paul the term *nēpios* is used in a more negative sense, to refer to immature Christians (1 Cor. 3:1; Eph. 4:14). Nevertheless, he uses the verbs *nēpiazo,* "to act as a child,"

in the sense of being innocent or ignorant of wrongdoing (1 Cor. 14:20) and expresses the same attitude as Jesus through his use of the term *teleios* "perfect." While there are some in his churches who would think of themselves as *teleioi*, "perfect, mature" (1 Cor. 2:6; Phil. 3:15), he is at pains to point out that he does not regard himself as having yet become *teleios* (Phil. 3:12, using the verb *teleioō*). The "maturity" or "perfection" of Christian existence is something that may be prayed for (Col. 4:12), but not something that has been achieved (Schnackenburg, 1963).

3. These two points made above might persuade us that maturity is in some way opposed to innocence, simplicity, and single-mindedness. That is not the case, for as we have seen above in the allusion to Milton and C. S. Lewis, innocence is not equivalent to immaturity; nor is what Paul means by "maturity" quite the same thing that a psychologist means. For Paul "perfection" is essentially a moral concept of Christlikeness. While modern psychology would agree with Paul in regarding maturity as a goal rather than an already attained achievement, the two types of maturity are different; the psychological concept of maturity, while it may include some ethical content, is not itself an ethical concept, but expressive of the soundness or wholeness of personality.

4. It, therefore, follows that a person may be mature in a psychological sense without being a Christian. It also follows that a person may be ethically "mature," in Paul's sense, and display many of the characteristics of Christlikeness without being psychologically very mature. Of course, psychological maturity is a proper goal for a Christian (even more so perhaps than is physical health), and, of course, God is concerned with the psychological well-being of persons, and salvation can extend to the psychological aspects of a person as well as to one's physical well-being. But that is not the end of the matter.

5. We may go further and assert that psychological maturity is not the most important goal for everyone. Some people will never achieve anything like a normal adult maturity of the psychological kind because of irreparable damage done to them in childhood or by their present environment, but may lead useful and good Christian lives all the same. In the same way, many will never enjoy a day's good health physically, but are not thereby relegated to a second division in Christianity. This is a point rarely made it would seem by psychologists since their professional concern is to assist the development of human personalities. It is good to have seen in one author at least (Anderson, 1971) the recognition that "maturity is a dynamic process that is ever changing. Levels of maturity will be different for different people," just as levels of peformance at the piano will vary from individual to individual and will vary in one individual from one day to the next.

6. The foregoing point is borne out by studies in the creativity of artists, composers, and writers. The most creative people do not always seem to

have been among the most mature. If we take obsessional behavior as a characteristic of immaturity, it is interesting to observe, as Storr (1972) points out, that "many of the world's great creators have exhibited obsessional symptoms and traits of character. Dickens, Swift, Dr. Johnson, Ibsen, Stravinsky, Rossini, and Beethoven are amongst this distinguished company." Storr can also mention impressive examples of schizoid-like individuals, such as Kafka, who have been great creative geniuses, even though the schizoid personality plainly lacks some of the most essential characteristics of maturity, such as a correct perception of oneself and the world and the ability to relate warmly to others.

The world would be an incomparably poorer place without the legacy of immature personalities such as these. It is pointless to protest that their work would have been the greater had they not been so handicapped, for it is precisely in their lack of maturity that they speak so directly to the human condition. One might as well argue that Beethoven's last works would have been greater had he not become deaf, or that Milton would have been a better poet had he not lost his sight; for it is precisely in these disabilities that the greatness of their achievement lies. Psychologists, on the other hand, give the impression that maturity and development of the personality should be the overriding goal of everyone. I simply wonder whether this need be so, and even if it were so, whether it would be a good thing. Hence, the dissentient report against maturity which I think should be voiced alongside any enthusiasm for a life-affirming reaching after maturity.

More Sinned Against Than Sinning

1. Under this quotation from *King Lear* (3.2.57), I want to suggest that there is a way in which sin *can* lead to maturity: that is, when one is sinned against rather than commits sin. Here again, it is not necessarily the case that being sinned against leads to maturity; it may lead to revenge or withdrawal. But in a sinful world, it is one of the blessings that exists that wrongful suffering can develop one's capacities as a person.

2. As a slogan, and not as a proof text, for this view, I take the passage from Hebrews 5:8-9: "[Jesus] learned obedience through what he suffered; and being made perfect [the verb *teleioō*] he became the source of eternal salvation to all who obey him." Jesus' "perfection" or "maturity" comes about through what he suffers: "To suffer death for God's sake is itself described as the attainment of perfection" (Bruce, 1965). Though he was already the Son of God (Heb. 5:8), he was able to grow in obedience and maturity through being sinned against. The author to the Hebrews, like Paul, has in mind, of course, moral rather than psychological "maturity," so this passage can only be illustrative of the argument that is being developed here.

3. The theme of learning through suffering had already a long history when it was taken up and used by the author of Hebrews (Coste, 1955). In Greek literature the resemblance between the words *epathon* "I suffered" and *emathon* "I learnt" was often played upon. Thus Aristotle says of initiates into the mystery religions that "those being initiated [the verb *teleo*] must not learn *(mathein)* but experience, suffer *(pathein)*," while a proverb runs, "If you do not suffer *(pathēs),* you will not learn *(mathēs),*" and a fable of Aesop concludes: "The story shows that sufferings *(pathēmata)* become lessons *(mathēmata)* for men." Zeus, according to Aeschylus' *Agamemnon* (176ff.) "has shown men the way to understanding by giving them the law: learning through suffering."

4. In the Old Testament also suffering is often viewed as educative. In the wisdom books, of course, we find many sentences like "Yahweh corrects the one he loves, as a father the son in whom he delights" (Prov. 3:12), or "He who has not been tested knows little." (Ecclus. 34:10)—but in such cases the suffering is deliberately inflicted for the good of the sufferer.

Something much closer to the idea of undeserved suffering leading to maturity or wisdom appears in the book of Job, and above all in the figure of the righteous servant of the Lord of Isaiah 53 who is "humiliated by suffering" (53:3, cf. NEB) but through the suffering brought upon him by others (53:5, 7-9) gains wisdom (so "prosper" in 52:13 should probably be translated), and "by his knowledge" (alternatively, "by his humiliation") is shown to be innocent before the many (53:11, RSV "shall make many to be accounted righteous"). Here the servant of the Lord is the man who does nothing but lets everything happen to him (Clines, 1976*b*); by allowing himself to be sinned against he gains insight, relates to others, has long-range goals, enjoys a unifying philosophy of life, finds meaning in his work. Only perhaps in backhanded ways like this can sin lead to maturity.

Conclusion

Perhaps maturity can be achieved through simple innocence and unworldliness. But, it is more likely that those who seek ethical purity by withdrawal from the world and from exposure to temptation can attain that goal largely at the cost of developing a full human maturity. Involvement in the rough and tumble of the world, in which one can take risks, can be hurt, and can make mistakes, is for most people the means by which maturity is gained. Sin is not a route to maturity, but it is in a sinful world that development in maturity has to occur.

References

Allport, G. W. *Pattern and Growth in Personality*. London and New York: Holt, Rinehart, and Winston, 1963.

Anderson, G. C. "Maturing Religion." *Pastoral Psychology,* 1971, *22,* 17-22.

Barron, F. "Personal Soundness in University Graduate Students." In *Publications in Personality Assessment and Research* (No. 1). Berkeley: University of California Press, 1954.

Brouse, K. D. "Anger: A Biblical and Psychological Study." In R. K. Bower (ed.), *Biblical and Psychological Perspectives for Christian Counselors.* South Pasadena, Calif.: Publishers Services, 1974.

Bruce, F. F. *Commentary on the Epistle to the Hebrews.* London: Marshall, Morgan, & Scott, 1965.

Brueggemann, W. *In Man We Trust: The Neglected Side of Biblical Faith.* Richmond: John Knox Press, 1972.

Buchanan, G. W. "The Old Testament Meaning of the Knowledge of Good and Evil." *Journal of Biblical Literature,* 1956, *75,* 114-20.

Carter, J. D. "Maturity: Psychological and Biblical." *Journal of Psychology and Theology,* 1974, *2* (2), 89-96.

Cerling, C. E. "Anger: Musings of a Theologian/Psychiatrist." *Journal of Psychology and Theology,* 1974a, 2(1), 12-17.

――――. "Some Thoughts on a Biblical View of Anger: A Response." *Journal of Psychology and Theology,* 1974b, *2* (4), 266-68.

Clines, D. J. A. "A Biblical Doctrine of Man." *Christian Brethren Research Fellowship Journal,* 1976a, *28,* 9-38.

――――. "I, He, We, and They: A Literary Approach to Isaiah 53." *Journal for the Study of the Old Testament,* 1976b, Supplement Series, 1.

Coste, J. "Notion grecque et notion biblique de la ´souffrance éducatrice." *Recherches de Science Religieuse,* 1955, *43,* 481-523.

Dodd, C. H. *The Epistle to the Romans.* London: Hodder & Stoughton, 1932.

Hopkins, G. M. *Poems and Prose of Gerard Manley Hopkins.* (W. H. Gardner, ed.). Harmondworth: Penguin Books, 1953.

Krodel, G. E. (ed.). *Luther's Works (Letters 1)* (Vol. 48). Philadelphia: Fortress Press, 1963.

Lewis, C. S. *A Preface to Paradise Lost.* London: Oxford University Press, 1942.

Madow, L. *Anger.* New York: Charles Scribner & Sons, 1972.

Maslow, A. H. *Motivation and Personality.* New York: Harper & Row, 1954.

Masson, C. *L'epître Saint Paul aux Ephésiens.* Neuchâtel: Delachaux et Niestlé, 1953.

Pedersen, J. E. "Some Thoughts on a Biblical View of Anger." *Journal of Psychology and Theology,* 1974, *2* (3), 210-15.

Saul, L. J. *Emotional Maturity* (3rd ed.). Philadelphia: Lippincott, 1960.

Schnackenburg, R. "Christian Adulthood According to the Apostle Paul." *Catholic Biblical Quarterly,* 1963, *25,* 354-70.

Storr, A. *The Dynamics of Creation.* London: Secker & Warburg, 1972.

Tillich, P. *On the Boundary: An Autobiographical Sketch.* London: Collins, 1967.

Warlick, H. C. "Tillich's Consciousness of Guilt and Autonomous Thinking." *Foundations.* 1973, *16,* 25-40.

HOLINESS AND HEALTH: AN EXAMINATION OF THE RELATIONSHIP BETWEEN CHRISTIAN HOLINESS AND MENTAL HEALTH

Eric J. Cohen

I was standing today in the dark toolshed. The sun was shining outside and through the crack at the top of the door there came a sunbeam. From where I stood that beam of light, with the specks of dust floating in it, was the most striking thing in the place. Everything else was almost pitch black. I was seeing the beam, not seeing things by it.

Then I moved, so that the beam fell on my eyes. Instantly the whole previous picture vanished. I saw no toolshed, and (above all) no beam. Instead I saw framed in the irregular cranny at the top of the door, green leaves moving on the branches of a tree outside and beyond that, 90 odd million miles away, the sun. Looking along the beam, and looking at the beam are very different experiences. (Lewis, 1970, p. 212)

If we objectively stand back and "look at" theology and psychology, we see two academic disciplines; each employs methodologies aimed at the development of theoretical and conceptual, explanatory treatises concerning their respective subject areas. From this perspective, theology can be defined as "the study of the nature of God and religious truth" (*American Heritage Dictionary,* 1970) and psychology as "the study of human behavior and mental activity" (Hilgard, Atkinson, and Atkinson, 1953, p. 10). Such definitions are descriptive, but they are in no way adequate.

If we now move into a position that allows us to "look along" these two disciplines, so that our vision is fully influenced by them, the picture becomes quite different. We no longer are absorbed in trying to define theology and psychology proper because we are now in a position to look through them, that is, by means of them; the question of what they are is totally superseded by what they now direct our attention toward and allow us to see and experience. It is like the man who sees his spectacles lying on his desk. They sit as a detached object which he can observe and touch. When he puts them on, however, he no longer is aware of what they look or feel like. Any interest in the spectacles themselves is surrendered to the greater reality of what they now enable him to see and experience by virtue of his "looking through" them.

To look through Christian theology is to encounter God and his

©*Journal of Psychology and Theology*, 1977, 5, 285-91. Used by permssion of the author.

self-revelation. It is to come into an understanding of reality and history as revealed in the person of Jesus the Christ. The goal of Christian theology goes beyond simply determining truth, for theology's chief purpose is the progression of man toward godliness. To look through theology is to existentially move toward God. The promotion of holiness is the paramount concern.

To look through clinical psychology is to see man in terms of his inadequacies, his pathologies, and his potentials for growth and change. It is to venture beyond abstract, theoretical frameworks into personal encounter. The concern and goal of clinical psychology is ultimately the development, maintenance, and cultivation of emotional stability and well-being. The promotion of mental health is the paramount concern.

Functional integration between Christian theology and clinical psychology requires a perspective of "looking through" (along); it hinges upon an understanding of their purposes and goals. Quite simply, we need to recognize that the primary and ultimate business of theology is the promotion of holiness, while that of psychology is the promotion of mental health. Integration at a functional level centers upon the relationship between health and holiness, and it is the nature of this relationship which I wish to explore now. Consideration will first be given to a theological understanding of holiness and some contemporary conceptions of mental health. I will then progress to an examination of relationship in an effort to determine what holiness has to do with health (mental) and health to do with holiness.

A proper considerstion of holiness must begin with an explication of holiness as an attribute of God. The meaning of holiness is rooted in God, for God is a holy God by virtue of his transcendence, his pure moral integrity, and his righteousness. The transcendence, or "otherness" of God, separates him from all creation. Parsons (1974, pp. 27-28) writes:

He is utterly above and beyond all other "gods." "Who among the gods is like you, Yahweh? Who is your like, majestic in holiness?" (Exodus 15:11). He is completely different from man. "For I am God, not man: I am the Holy One in your midst" (Hosea 11:9). This "otherness" of God is basic to the idea of holiness. If a single word is demanded to describe it, that word must be "separation." God's holiness sets Him apart from all else.

In addition to God's transcendence, holiness is rooted in God's ethical purity and moral perfection. The moral character of God is unblemished, and this quality not only defines his holy nature, but also serves as a definitive parameter for holiness in man (1 Peter 1:15). Finally, God's holiness is based on his righteousness and goodness. He is consistent in himself of all that he requires of his people (Lev. 11:44), and his holy actions are a mediation of his justice and mercy (Ps. 25:8).

It is essential to understand the divine nature of holiness, for holiness has no existence or meaning apart from God. When we discuss holiness as it relates to man, we need to bear in mind that human holiness is inextricably bound to divine holiness. Theologically, man's holiness is only realized through God's "justification" and "sanctification" of him (Koberle, 1938). Holiness is, therefore, a condition attributed to man by virtue of his being justified "in Christ" (Rom. 3:24) as well as being a "progressive work" (Ryle, 1952) which God carries out in man. "Justification is an act of God as gracious judge, sanctification is a work of God as merciful physician" (p. 328). Human holiness is, therefore, experienced on two levels. It is a position in Christ which allows man to be seen in the light of divine holiness (justification), and it is a quality of life which he progresses toward as a member of the body of Christ, indwelt by the Holy Spirit (the Spirit who promotes holiness [sanctification]).

The quality of man's being holy is a reflection of God's holiness. Christians are called to be morally pure, righteous, and spiritually transcendent (John 17:14). Human holiness, however, is not primarily a function of individual holiness. Man's holiness is actualized as he participates as a member in the body of Christ. Christ's body constitutes the holy church (Parsons, 1974). Individual holiness is a result of participation in Christ's body, for it is here that divine holiness is mediated. Oscar Cullman goes as far as saying that holiness is "the fact of belonging to the saints" (Jones, 1961) which involves communion in the body of Christ.

It is impossible to comprehensively define holiness here, but the aspects we have examined are all essential. Most important is the fact that holiness is of God. Christian holiness in man can only come from being "in Christ" (2 Cor. 5:17), from being "indwelt" by Christ (Gal. 2:20), and from being made thereby a "habitation of God in the Spirit" (Eph. 2:22) (*Harper's Bible Dictionary,* 1952, p. 265). It is a divine quality of life which is attributed to man and which man progresses toward experientially as he participates as an individual member with the body of Christ.

If we turn now to a definitional consideration of the concept of mental health, we will discover a myriad of difficulties. The basic problem centers around the multiplicity of orientations within the field of psychology and the numerous proposals they embody concerning the nature of mental health and mental disorder. Only a general discussion of these views is possible here, and the reader is referred to the works of Millon (1973) and Oden (1960) for a more systematic and in-depth elaboration of the distinctions involved.

There are basically two definitional trends within psychology concerning mental health. First, there is the approach which views mental health solely in terms of the absence of pathology. In this negativistic vein, the focus is upon mental disorder, pathology, and abnormality. Health is simply a secondary category for that which is not unhealthy. The other definitional trend stresses the more optimistic notion of health being the realization and actualization of human potentiality. From this perspective, the goal of the mental health professional goes beyond simply alleviating or eradicating pathological symptoms. It involves more fundamentally the facilitation of human actualization at both an individual and interpersonal level. This second approach to defining mental health is not a negation but an extension of the first, and is, therefore, preferable. This approach is also important in that it has been a strong influence in contemporary Western society due to the awareness and concern over mental health it has brought to nonpathological ("normal") individuals. A detailed explication of this concept of mental health, however, must be left in abeyance so that we can move on to the more pertinent issue of the relationship between holiness and health as we now understand it.

In examining the relationship of holiness and health, I would like to explore four possibilities: (1) that they are totally independent of one another; (2) that they are one and the same; (3) that they are different from one another, but have a correlational relationship of some kind; and (4) that there is some causality involved in their relationship.

There are those who would claim that holiness and mental health are orthogonal qualities having no correspondence whatever to one another. The reasoning involved in such an approach stems from the differentiation between sin and mental illness (Connery, 1960). While sin involves moral responsibility, illness does not. As C. S. Lewis puts it, "bad psychological material is not a sin, but a disease, it does not need to be repented of, but to be cured" (1943, p. 85). Lewis, however, would not go so far as to say that holiness, therefore, would have no relationship to health. In this I would concur. It is one thing to say that they are not the same, but it is quite another to claim full independence.

The first clue to some form of relationship between holiness and health can be found in the very words themselves. O. R. Jones (1961) points out the etymological affinity between the words holiness, wholeness, and health. He writes:

It seems to me that "wholeness" understood in a special sense, could be used as a substitute for "holiness" in many contexts . . . . The ultimate root is "hal" from which the word "whole" itself derives, and it is worth remembering that the word "health" comes from the same root. We shall see in due course that "holiness" is also closely associated with "health" in the Old Testament as well as the New Testament. (p. 89)

It is reasonable then to assume that some form of relationship, besides an orthogonal one, exists between health and holiness. Ruling out the first possibility (total independence), the next consideration is the other extreme, namely that holiness and health are actually one and the same. This is by no means an uncommon perspective, and it is one which can be supported by both biblical data and a specific strand of psychological literature. The biblical roots for postulating a complete correspondence between health and holiness begin in the Old Testament where there existed the notion that a proper relationship to the Lord would result in prosperity at all levels. Poverty and physical suffering were taken as indications of discord with God. "To the Hebrew the body-situation was also a soul-situation; a leper-situation was a sin-situation" (Jones, 1961, p. 104). In the New Testament, this way of thinking is reflected in the response of Jesus' disciples to the blind man they encountered: "Who did sin, this man or his parents, that he should be born blind?" (John 9:2). Holiness, in this way of thought, is a condition of wholeness which involves health at a bodily, mental, and spiritual level.

Jay Adams (1970, 1973, 1975) is perhaps the best known proponent of the view that holiness and mental health are ultimately the same. To Adams, mental disorders are the result of disunity with God and are to be primarily treated on a spiritual level. Howard Clinebell, another psychologist in the vein of Adams, also takes the position that spiritual health and mental health are "inseparably related." He states:

Spiritual health is an indispensable aspect of mental health. The two can only be separated on a theoretical basis. In live human beings, spiritual and mental health are inextricably interwoven. Whatever hurts or heals one's relationship with oneself and others will tend to hurt or heal one's relationship with God, and vice versa. (Clinebell, 1965, p. 20)

In response to such a position, I would resonate the counterargument set fort by Vernon Grounds in his article entitled "Holiness and Healthy-mindedness" (1974). Grounds responds:

Some Christians, one is almost tempted to think, have never heard about Job. They hold the opinion of his three would-be comforters, an opinion which God Himself refutes and repudiates, that a pious man must assuredly enjoy peace and prosperity. Some Christians apparently share the conviction of those three well meaning friends that sickness is proof of personal sin. (p. 3)

The suffering which Job experienced, on both a physical and mental level, was expressly not a "result" of his disunity with God. If we learn nothing else from Job's story, we must certainly realize that his physical and emotional ailments were not caused by his sin or unholiness. In the same regard, we must remember that when the disciples of Jesus naively attributed the blind man's condition to sin, Jesus was quick to correct them (John 9:3). Job's suffering and the man's blindness were divinely purposed. At least in these situations, health and holiness were not "inextricably interwoven" (Clinebell, 1965, p. 20).

I have argued thus far against a total separation or a total equation of health and holiness, and so we are now left with the idea that they are different things which share some relationship. Our next question concerns the degree and nature of whatever correlation is involved. Two possibilties emerge: (1) there is a positive correlation, so that the presence of holiness coincides with a condition of health; or (2) there is a negative correlation, so that the presence of holiness coincides with an unhealthy condition.

There does seem to be evidence that holiness and health might be positively correlated (Hiltner, 1963; Grounds, 1974; Allport, 1950). Grounds writes:

Highly impressive is the case for Christianity's value as a reservoir of emotional health and healing . . . . A striking correlation exists between holiness and healthymindedness, sanctity and serenity, piety and self-actualizing personality. (1974, pp. 6-7)

Others, however, would claim that religion and personal holiness correlate negatively with physical and mental well-being. They would argue that true holiness most often coincides with persecution, physical and emotional abuse, intense sensitivity, and a religious passion which, by contemporary definitions of mental health, would resemble neurotic or even psychotic pathology. Jesus himself was "a man of sorrows," and if we examine the lives of dedicated disciples, we often find emotions, thought processes, and other "symptoms" which modern psychologists would eagerly diagnose as abnormalities. "The true Christian experience may be considered a queer, unhealthy type of morbidness, according to the generally approved conception of mental healthy-mindedness" (p. 10). It is difficult to resolve this correlation issue because of the various possibilities of interaction between holiness and health. My own impression is that there is most likely a positive correlation (holiness tends to coincide with health), but that the degree of correlation is probably small. By this I mean that holiness would usually co-exist with a condition of mental health, but that holiness could be present without health and health without holiness.

The final issue we need to look at is the question of causality. Correlation is rarely, of itself, a clear indication of causality, and so we need to ask whether holiness is caused by health or whether health is caused by holiness. It seems clear that the first alternative is not a viable one. It may be true that being in good mental and physical health might facilitate movement toward God but so might suffering. As I have said before, holiness has no existence apart from God, and so a person's holiness can only be actualized in relationship with God. Health, on the other hand, seems to be a variable which can be present in one who is godly or ungodly. To approach the task of promoting holiness by simply trying to produce psychological health is to work from the false presupposition that health will cause movement toward holiness. It may or may not.

The other possibility is that growth toward holiness will result in better psychological health. Again I must say, in light of modern definitions of mental health, that this may or may not be true. My opinion, however, is that there may be some causality operating in this direction. Union with God involves God's regenerative work in man at all levels. Our progression toward holiness is ultimately a progression toward wholeness and health, even though the full realization of this condition may not occur until a much later point in our eternal future. Man's movement toward holiness ultimately moves him toward a healthier position, yet we need to realize as Christians that God's methods of making us holy may involve rather drastic means. We may need to go through experiences of tremendous stress and anxiety before true dependence upon God and true holiness become possibilities for us. We may experience psychological disorder and pathology along the road to holiness and wholeness, yet our faith must assure us that God is indeed carrying out his redemptive purposes in us as he works to conform us to the image of his holy Son (Rom. 8:29).

I would conclude that holiness ultimately yields wholeness and soundness of mind, but that our experience of holiness as a progressive reality does not always involve a condition of mental stability and health. The fact that we are on the road toward holiness in no way insures the absence of either mental or physical problems, yet the ultimate reality is that our final state of holiness will have produced (caused) a final condition of psychological wholeness.

In summary, I would like to restate several conclusions of this discussion. First, I feel it essential to focus the question of integration on the relationship of holiness and health. This relationship is neither one of full identity nor of full independence, but it is rather correlational (positive) and does involve some degree of causality. The degree of correlation is small in light of interactional possibilities, but nevertheless we would generally expect that holiness would coincide and work to facilitate a condition of mental health. Exceptions to this are prevalent (thus the small correlation), but nevertheless they are exceptions.

Finally, it is imperative, from a Christian perspective, to recognize the total priority of holiness over health. The promotion of health at any level is in no way a substitute for the promotion of holiness, and when modern notions of mental health come into opposition with that which would promote holiness, such notions must be re-evaluated and strongly confronted. The ultimate value of holiness is infinitely and eternally greater than health and must be preserved above all.

References

Adams, J. E. *Competent to Counsel.* Nutley, N. J.: Presbyterian & Reformed Publishing Co., 1970.

――――. *The Christian Counselor's Manual.* Grand Rapids: Baker Book House, 1973.

――――. *Your Place in the Counseling Revolution.* Grand Rapids: Baker Book House, 1975.

Allport, G. W. *The Individual and His Religion.* New York: The Macmillan Co., 1950.

Clinebell, H. J. *Mental Health Through Christian Community.* Nashville: Abingdon, 1965.

Connery, J. R. "Sin, Sickness, and Psychiatry." *America,* 1960, *102* (16), 493-95.

Dicks, R. *Towards Health and Wholeness.* New York: The Macmillan Co., 1960.

Doniger, S. (ed.). *Religion and Health.* New York: Association Press, 1958.

Geiger, K. *Insights into Holiness.* Kansas City, Mo.: Beacon Hill, 1962.

Grounds, V. C. "Holiness and Healthy-Mindedness." *Journal of Psychology and Theology,* 1974, *2* (1), 3-11.

Hilgard, E. R., Atkinson, R. C., and Atkinson, R. L. *Introduction to Psychology* (5th ed.). New York: Harcourt Brace Jovanovich, 1953.

Hiltner, S. "Mental Health/Spiritual Wholeness." *Christian Advocate,* 1963, *7* (15), 7-8.

Jones, O. R. *The Concept of Holiness.* New York: The Macmillan Co., 1961.

Koberle, A. *The Quest for Holiness.* Minneapolis: Augsburg Publishers, 1938.

Lewis, C. S. *Mere Christianity.* New York: The Macmillan Co., 1943.

———. "Meditation in a Toolshed." In W. Hooper (ed.), *God in the Dock.* Grand Rapids: Eerdmans, 1970.

Miller, M. S., and Miller, J. L. *Harper's Bible Dictionary.* New York: Harper & Row, 1952.

Millon, T. (ed.). *Theories of Psychopathology and Personality* (2nd ed.). Philadelphia: Saunders, 1973.

Oden, T. C. "What Is Mental Health?" *Journal of Pastoral Care,* 1960, *14* (4), 193-202.

Parsons, M. *The Call to Holiness.* London: Darton, Longman, and Todd, 1974.

Ryle, J. C. *Holiness: Its Nature, Hindrances, Difficulties, and Roots.* Grand Rapids: Kregel, 1952.

U.S. Department of Health, Education, and Welfare. *Bibliography on Religion and Mental Health 1960-1964.* Washington: U.S. Government Printing Office, 1967.

PERSONALITY AND CHRISTIAN MATURITY: A PROCESS CONGRUITY MODEL

John D. Carter

Recently there have been a number of works attempting to integrate psychology and a biblical view of man from a variety of perspectives such as Daim (1963) and Wagner (1974) from a broad analytic perspective; Tweedie (1963) and van Kaam (1968) from an existential perspective; and Craine (1970) and Hodge (1967) from a broad client-centered perspective. These works should be examined for their penetrating insights by anyone seriously interested in the task of integration. However, in keeping with the current interest in psychology on model building in personality theory (Maddi, 1972; Rychlak, 1973; Wiggins, Renner, Clore and Rose, 1971), this paper will analyze several theorists, Gendlin, Rogers, and Jung, whose constructs form a model. The common principles or processes—self-actualizing process and congruence—underlying these three theorists will be examined and proposed as a model for integration since these processes are implicitly and explicitly referred to in the Scripture as basic to Christian maturity. Though there may be other psychological theorists who share the model common to Jung, Gendlin, and Rogers they cannot be considered here.

Personality and Self-Actualization

The theories of Jung, Gendlin, and Rogers are fundamentally similar in that they postulate an in-process internal frame of reference or internal data level as the basic level of personality. Gendlin (1964) describes this internal data level as a feeling process, i.e., inwardly sensed, bodily felt events. This felt process or flow of bodily sensing is the direct reference of experience and contains implicit, felt meanings. These felt meanings function implicitly in most thinking and behavior, i.e., most behavior and thinking occurs without verbalizations. When felt meanings interact with verbal symbols, the meanings become explicit. Felt meanings are "in awareness," but are incomplete until they are symbolized. These implicit meanings must interact with work, behavior or symbols to be carried forward to completion (made explicit). Thus implicit meanings are not hidden conceptual units, but are boldly patterned readiness for organized interaction. Just as physical life is an interaction between the body and the environment so psychic life or experiencing is an interaction between feelings and the symbols which complete or carry the feelings forward.

Experiencing is always in process and as such is implicitly functioning. The continuous interaction between feelings and events (verbal sounds, others' behavior, and external occurrences) carries forward the process. Consequently others' responses are very important to the process in that they provide the events which carry forward felt meanings. Only if there are events (interpersonal responses, which provide symbols for making meanings explicit, is an example of a very large class of events) can there be an ongoing interaction process. If there are not responses then at least some feelings are not carried forward and those aspects of experience cease to be in process. They become structure bound. However, since feelings are many faceted some aspects interact with some events to carry forward the process of experience in a somewhat restricted fashion. The importance of others for experiencing should not be minimized for several reasons according to Gendlin. One, the events available for interaction are different when one is alone and when one is with another. Two, others influence the manner in which the individual's experiencing occurs. Critical or annoyed listeners tend to produce constricted, general, and shallow experiencing. Three, rejection of an individual by another ignores the individual's felt meanings and they are not carried forward. Thus, others are important for the experiencing process because their responses influence the carrying forward of feelings.

The self, or more correctly the self process, is another important concept for Gendlin. The person exists in interaction with interpersonal events before there is a self. These interpersonal events or responses interact with the individual's felt meanings. In time the individual develops the ability to respond to his own feelings. This ability or self is not a learned set of behavior, but a response to one's own feelings. These responses then carry forward the implicit feelings. If the individual is unable to respond to his feelings or responds in such a way as to skip or stop the process, he then needs others' responses to carry forward or reconstitute his feelings. It is important to note that others are significant, not for their attitudes or appraisals, but because their responses (assuming they are appropriate) carry forward the individual's felt meanings.

Since Gendlin borrowed from Rogers' (1959) theory of personality, it seems appropriate now to consider internal process from his perspective. Rogers describes this process in terms of experiencing which constitutes the full range of sensations, perceptions, meanings, and memories and is referred to as the internal frame of reference. This frame of reference is the internal data level of an organism whose only motive is to actualize its potential. Coupled with the internal frame of reference is the organismic valuing process which applies the actualizing tendency as its criterion for values. The experiencing process involves symbolization which is representing in some accurate form at the conscious level the internal frame of reference. Symbolization may be more or less accurate and more or less complete. Experience and feelings are closely connected for Rogers. Feelings refer to the unity of emotion and cognition which is experienced inseparably in the moment. Experiencing a feeling fully involves congruence of the feelings in awareness and the symbolization and the expression of it.

Before a discussion of the importance of others in personality development or change can be undertaken, Rogers' concept of the self must be examined. The self is a process, a changing gestalt "composed of perceptions of the characteristics of the 'I' or 'me' and the perceptions of the relationships of the 'I' or 'me' to others and to various aspects of life, together with the values attached to these perceptions" (Rogers, 1959, p. 200). The self is available to awareness though not necessarily in awareness. As the awareness of self develops, there emerges in the individual a need for positive regard, the need for warmth, liking, respect, sympathy, acceptance. Since others provide these attitudes and behaviors, others are important to the individual. However, if others do not supply positive regard unconditionally, conditions of worth are set up. The individual realizes he is prized in some aspects but not in others. Gradually he assimilates this attitude into his self-regard complex. Once the conditions of worth have been assimilated they become part of the self and are subject to the self-consistency principle. Experiences tend to be denied to awareness to the degree that they are incongruent with the self. Thus, for Rogers, others are important to the individual in that they provide positive regard or conditions of worth which in turn control the access of experience into awareness.

In the limited space available for the topic it may appear pretentious to discuss Jung's theory of personality. Nevertheless, those aspects which are relevant for the purpose of the paper will be examined. Jung (1960) describes personality in terms of consciousness and unconsciousness. The former is composed of a stream of sense perceptions and direct adaptations to objects. The latter is composed of two parts: (1) the personal unconscious, all forgotten or repressed contents; and (2) the collective unconscious, those contents (archetypes) inherited from the race. The archetypes are inherited tendencies to feel and symbolize in a certain way, just as a dry riverbed predisposes water to flow in a particular path. The core of the actualization process for Jung is the assimilating or integrating of the unconscious contents which are inherited archetypes. Dreaming, painting, or any means of expressing these inner contents is helpful in making these contents available for assimilation. Since the conscious process has become so directed and rational, it cannot be the means of obtaining the inner irrational aspects. However, once the inner meanings (unconscious contents) have become available in symbolized form they need to be integrated with the conscious contents. Symbolization for Jung means archetypical representation which then needs to be interpreted, to be understood and assimilated. Symbols are something the individual produces which express his unconscious. Associations and interpretations of a dream, for example, can render its symbolic expression understandable in consciousness. Jung's explanation of the transformation of unconscious contents to conscious ones is not in conflict with Gendlin's concept of symbolization. However, Jung's transformations—symbolization and interpretation—occur in two steps, while Gendlin and Rogers propose a single step process—symbolization—which appears to be close to Jung's interpretation though it can be nonverbal (behavioral or circumstantial).

Archetypes are the *a priori*, inborn forms of "intuition." They are typical modes of apprehension and are essentially feeling-values inherited from the race. Though they cannot be known in themselves, archetypes are represented in consciousness as ideas or images (Jung, 1960). Thus, archetypical representations are symbolized feelings or apprehensions or inner (unconscious) psychic life. The similarity of archetypical representations to Gendlin's and Rogers' theory of symbolization of feelings is obvious, but the differences must not be overlooked. Feelings, for Gendlin and Rogers, are nonspecified or general, i.e., the nature, structure or character of felt meanings is never described. On the other hand, much of Jung's work has been the elaboration of the nature and forms of archetypes in dreams, schizophrenic thought, and mythology.

Developmentally as part of the actualization or individuation process consciousness emerges out of unconsciousness and becomes one-sided because of its directedness to objects and its rational functioning. This one-sidedness or imbalance in the conscious attitude and functioning is compensated for by the unconscious. If balance is not restored then psychic energy becomes redistributed and unconscious contents break into consciousness. Jung (1960) describes the integrating of conscious and unconscious contents as the transcendent function. By means of dreams, artistic production, or behavior, the unconscious contents can be made available to consciousness. By means of analysis and associations these contents become interpreted and understood in conciousness. However, the ego as the center of consciousness must maintain its position of equal value to the counterposition of the unconscious. Neither must overbalance the other if the integration of the individuation process is to continue.

Jung (1939) describes the self as both the center and periphera of personality, i.e., it is both the focus or axis and the integrated totality. The unification of the personality in a functioning whole in which neither consciousness nor unconsciousness dominates is the goal of personality. "In the last analysis every life is the realization of a whole, that is, of a self, for which reason this realization can also be called 'individuation' " (Jung, 1953, p. 222). The emergence of the self in middle life is thus the final "step" in the individuation process. With the emergence of the self as the center of personality the ego loses its central place to the self which dwarfs the ego in scope and intensity by the afflux of unconscious contents vitalizing the personality (Jung, 1960). Unfortunately not everyone develops a self, in fact many do not, particularly those who do not become separated from the collectivity of the masses in society and those who do not "work at" the development of their personality. The self for Jung is thus not the social side of personality nor is it a superego. It is the integrative totality of all psychic functions which develops as a culmination of the individuation process and as the ultimate transcending function.

A comparison of the three theories under consideration is now in order. The most obvious similarity is that all three are process theories and the nature of this process is actualizing one's potential or self-actualization. For Gendlin (1964) the process consists fundamentally of the ongoing felt meanings as they are carried forward by interaction with external events. This is a psychic process and it is parallel to the process of physical life which is an interaction of body and environment. The fundamental process for Rogers is the self-actualization which evaluates events in terms of their value to the process. In place of Gendlin's internal datum level, Rogers describes an internal frame of reference whose contents must be symbolized in consciousness for experiencing to take place. Thus, for both Rogers and Gendlin symbolizing of internal feelings is an important and necessary aspect of the ongoing process.

Rogers (1959) recognizes a defensiveness which distorts or denies incongruent experiences to awareness. Gendlin differs from this in that he argues there is no such thing as repression which pushes material out of consciousness into unconsciousness. Rather, material which is said to be repressed is in reality not symbolized, i.e., not completed, not carried forward or structure bound. There is also a difference in the role others play in these theories. For Rogers, others may set up conditions of worth which become incorporated within the person producing incongruence and anxiety. Gendlin, however, conceives of others as important only because they are events or symbol-producing agents, thus, completing or reconstituting the felt meanings. In spite of their differences they agree: (1) personality is a process, (2) symbolizing one's inner feelings carries the process forward, and (3) others' responses impair or enhance the functioning of the process.

For Jung (1960) personality is a process of actualization or individuation. It is the totality of the psychic functioning. It includes the conscious as well as the unconscious. Jung describes the process of individuation as the process of developing a particular or individualized integration from the collective aspects of the personality in the unconscious, and the specific or unique aspects of personality resulting from conscious experiences. Thus individuation is actualizing synthesis of all that it means to be human (collective aspects) with all that it means to be a particular individual.

Thus Jung is very similar to Gendlin and Rogers, but there are some differences. One difference lies in the concept of symbolization. Jung has emphasized both aspects of the continuum of inner feelings (archetypes or felt meanings) and the outer (conscious interpretive understanding or symbolization), while Gendlin and Rogers have emphasized the connection (in nonspecific terms) between feelings and symbols. That is, they have emphasized the upper half of the continuum. Shlien (1970) has also described Rogers' theory in this way and calls the continuum the Literal-Intuitive axis. Thus, Jung's theory is broader in scope and richer in content; that is, Jung's conscious-unconscious range of psychic functioning is broader than Gendlin's and Rogers' level of awareness, and Jung (1960) has described in specific terms the structure and dynamics of the psychic contents at all levels of functioning.

In spite of the difference between Gendlin's and Rogers', and Jung's description of how the process of symbolization works, there are very basic similarities. These similarities may be summarized as follows: precognitive felt meanings exist at some inner psychic level; these meanings become explicated in symbols; the explication is a completing, fulfilling and/or integrating of the inner feelings with the outer aspects of the person which leads to fuller psychic functioning; the blocking of the symbolizing process has a debilitating effect on the person; and the therapist (another person) can greatly assist a "patient" whose psychic functioning has become impaired or can assist a "normal" person in becoming a more fully functioning organism. These similarities in the symbolizing process rest on the essential agreement by these three theorists that personality is an ongoing, in-process, internal feeling level which becomes articulated or symbolized at a more external or conscious level of awareness. Consequently it is the similarities or the phenomena of the process which will be retained in the construction of a model of personality. However, the model building must wait until an additional process has been delineated.

Personality and Congruence

Congruence (consistency or balance) is another process which is common to all three theorists. For Rogers congruence is the consistency in the symbolization of feelings and the experience of those feelings. It also refers to the consistency between the perceptions of the self and the actual experiences. The state of incongruence between self and experience is a state of tension and internal confusion because the individual is trying to actualize his self (i.e., he consciously wants to do something) which is inconsistent with his inner experience. In simpler terms the individual's symbolization of himself is inconsistent with his experience. Gendlin does not have much to say about the congruence of feelings and symbols which is different from Rogers. However, he does argue that an individual senses (feels) the rightness of a symbolized felt meaning; part of the sensed rightness is an easing of anxiety (Gendlin. 1964).

Because Jung's theory of personality is broader and more complex, so is his concept of balance. In its directedness and rationality, consciousness tends to emphasize one attitude and certain functions rather than the others. The unconscious compensates for this imbalance up to a point. If the imbalance is continued there is an energy redistribution such that the imbalance appears to become greater, but then the unconscious contents break through and overcome the imbalance. Furthermore, Jung's idea of the transcendent function is basically a combination process-balance notion in which discrepant conscious and unconscious material is brought together and synthesized in such a way as to transcend the original level carrying forward the process of individuation (self-actualization). The self also creates a balanced totality by synthesis of the divergent parts into a new whole and is thus the ultimate transcendent function. It is of interest to note at this point that Rogers (1959) asserts that in a general way, integrated, whole, and genuine are synonymous with congruence.

In summary, it has been shown in this section that there are two fundamental processes in Gendlin's, Rogers', and Jung's theories of personality which can be conceptualized as a model. First, all three maintain that there is an inner psychic level of felt meanings which is an ongoing process and needs to be symbolized at some more conscious level for psychic health and development. This process as a totality is self-actualization. Second, all three also maintain that congruence or balance between the inner feelings and their symbolizations is also necessary for psychic health and well being. However, in each case Rogers' and Gendlin's theories show greater similarity to each other than Jung's more complex theory does to either.

Christian Maturity and Self-Actualization

The detailed analysis of Rogers', Gendlin's, and Jung's thought was undertaken to establish the basic underlying structural similarity of their theories of personality. This common structure or core tendency (as Maddi [1972] would call it) forms a model upon which the detail of personality and individual differences can be grounded. It is this model which provides the framework in which Christian maturity can be integrated because the same two principles of personality described above also are basic to the scriptural understanding of Christian maturity. In addition, the New Testament appeal and rationale for holy living is grounded in these two principles. While dominion over the created order (Gen. 1:28) can be thought of as the actualization of human nature, this paper will focus on salvation as an actualization process. There are three basic words in the New Testament used to describe salvation: to save (*sozō*), to sanctify (*hagiazō*), and to glorify (*doxazō*). These words are all used in a past, present, and future sense: the Christian was saved, sanctified, and glorified. The process of salvation had a point of beginning which is called regeneration (Titus 3:5). However, what was started at one point continues. Hence, the present tense of these verbs is used to stress this fact. While the process continues it will not be completed until Christ returns. Table 1 contains a list of at least one Scripture verse for each word used in each sense. The verses appearing in table 1 and their context will not be discussed. It is sufficient for the purpose of this paper that these three words, used in the past, present, and future tense, represent the core and bulk of the New Testament discussion of salvation. It should also be noted that the future tense is rare in New Testament Greek and the aorist tense, particularly the infinitive, is used to indicate the future. The context may also indicate a future or past event. This occurs in the case of the additional word which is shown in table 1: to make conformable to (*summorphaō*). This word is included in the discussion for two reasons: (1) it occurs only three times in the New Testament but once in each sense; and (2) Paul uses it as a motive in the model of Christian maturity which will be described later in this paper. Being made conformable to Christ was God's predestined purpose from eternity past (Rom. 8:29), it now characterizes the mature Christian (Phil. 3:10), and it will finally fully occur when Christ returns (Phil. 3:21).

Thus, the central focus of salvation in the New Testament is that it is a process which began in each believer and which is moving toward completion. However, the total integration of salvation as self-actualization is made clear in Ephesians 4:24 and Colossians 3:10 where salvation is described as the renewal of the image of God (Gen. 1:27), which was marred or warped by the Fall. Salvation is the process of the restoration of the image in each believer. Therefore, most clearly salvation is the process which allows the believer to begin to actualize his full potential: to be what he was created to be, to become what he is—a son of God, being in the image of him who created him.

TABLE 1
Illustrations of the Basic Words Related to Salvation
as They Appear in Different Tenses in the New Testament

	Sōzō (save)	*Hagiazō* (sanctify)	*Doxazō* (glorify)	*Summorphaō* (to make like)
Past	2 Timothy 1:9	2 Timothy 2:21	Romans 8:30	Romans 8:29
Present	1 Corinthians 15:2	Hebrews 10:14	1 Peter 4:11	Philippians 3:10
Future	Romans 5:9, 10	Revelation 22:1	Romans 8:17, 18	Philippians 3:21

A second aspect of the biblical concept of actualization is evident in the New Testament word for maturity (*teleios*) which is translated "perfect" in the King James Version but "mature" in most modern versions. The word is noncomparative in character; instead, it refers to the development of the potential of the object. "Be ye therefore perfect even as your father in heaven is perfect" (Matt. 5:48) does not mean we are to become divine or as holy as God but to be as complete or fully developed as he is. In secular Greek fruit was spoken of as mature *(teleios)* when it was ripe. Thus, the word refers to developing potentialities and not relative to achievement compared to others. Consequently Paul says his goal as an apostle was to present everyone *mature* in Christ (Eph. 4:13). Christ is described in the epistle to the Hebrews as the author and maturer *(telewten)* of the faith (Heb. 12:2). Hence Christian maturity clearly is a self-actualizing process.

The nature of this process becomes even more evident when the biblical model of maturity as outlined in Philippians 3:4-15 is analyzed. Paul uses his own experience to outline this model. The descriptive statement of this passage as a model appears in verse 15: "Let those of us who are mature be thus minded; and if in anything you are otherwise minded, God will reveal that also to you." Or to paraphrase it in a more contemporary vain, "This is the way the spiritually mature think and if you don't think this way God will show you that this is the way it is." There are three focuses or phases in this model. Phase one involves verses 4-9. All of Paul's accomplishments ethnically, culturally, socially, and religiously in Judaism are discarded for the surpassing worth of knowing Christ. This involves a reorganization of behavior, values, and self-perceptions. In the second phase Paul (as a model) describes his current desires and experience, "That I may know him and the power of his resurrection, and may share his sufferings, becoming like him in his death" (Phil. 3:10). The mature Christian is to be characterized by the desire to know Christ, his power and his sufferings (for others), and at the same time is in the process of becoming like Christ in his death (to sin). At this point it should be noted that table 1 shows that *summorphaō* (to make conformable) appears in verse 10. It occurs as a present participle which is the way to express continuing action or process in Greek when connected with the durative force of the main verb (to know). It is in the passive voice indicating a process which occurs without the control of the subject. Thus, the mature Christian consciously wills to know Christ while the divine dynamic is transforming him. The processes are parallel but occur at different levels within the person. Hence they have a different quality. Maddi (1972) divides self-actualization of personality theories into two categories which he calls actualization theories and perfection theories. The former may be described as becoming what one is while the latter involves becoming what one chooses. The second phase of the biblical model shows how the two aspects of biblical actualization merge into one. More will be said later about the integrating of these two aspects of self-actualization.

The third phase of the model of biblical maturity (vv. 12-14) flows directly out of the second. This phase involves the personal goals of the Christian or more specifically the process-goal. "I press toward the mark for the prize of the high calling of God in Christ" (v. 14). The image here is the Greek long-distance runner moving through the race to the finish line. The runner forgets what is behind and does not consider himself to have arrived but presses forward toward the goal. This is similar to the growth process of self-actualization. The past becomes irrelevant because the person is moving forward realizing that his goals are not yet achieved. Thus there is an awareness of one's progress without a sense of either failure or arrival. The focus of Christian maturity is the present, but with the knowledge that one is currently moving toward the goal. This goal is self-chosen. The mature believer wills or chooses to follow Christ and he becomes his choice. Thus the biblical concept of salvation in its various facets parallels the psychological process of self-actualization described by Rogers, Gendlin, and Jung.

Christian Maturity and Congruence

The principle of congruence (consistency or balance) described above is also a biblical principle and it is related to salvation and Christian maturity. While the Bible does not use the language of personality theory it does describe human congruent functioning in its own terms. (For purposes of this paper human functioning will be described in terms of three general aspects: thinking and cognitive process, emotion and affective process, and behavior with its antecedent motives.) The congruence emphasized in the Scripture usually involves a consistency between cognitive, affective, and/or motivated behavior. For example, "Faith without works is dead" (James 2:26); "Let us love not in word or tongue but in deed and in truth" (1 John 3:18); "If you love me keep my commandments" (John 14:15); and, "out of the abundance of the heart the mouth speaks" (Matt. 12:34). In each of these examples consistency between inner aspects of the person and outer behavioral aspects is either described or encouraged as the art of Christian living. Furthermore, congruence in the Christian life is described by such concepts as fruit of the spirit (Gal. 5:22-23) and the new man (Eph. 4:24; Col. 3:10). In each case a consistent pattern of behavior, attitudes, traits, and/or motives is described. Each is also contrasted with an antithetical pattern of the works of flesh or the old man. In addition there is strong biblical exhortation and encouragement not to try to live incongruently. Regular incongruent living is biblically described as carnal (1 Cor. 3:3), or double-minded (James 1:8; 4:8). Finally congruence in the Christian life is one of the major themes of the book of 1 John. Three criteria are given to determine who a believer is and these criteria are repeated in a cyclical fashion three times in the book. The criteria are: (1) loving the brothers; (2) practicing righteousness; and (3) believing the truth, namely that Jesus is the Christ. The criteria form a consistent pattern in which all must be present or the person in whom one or more is presently absent is simply not a believer. While more evidence could be cited, enough evidence has been given to indicate that the Scripture represents the mature Christian as living a congruent or consistent life in which his thoughts and beliefs, motives and feelings, and his attitudes and behavior are consistent with each other and with the Scripture.

To summarize, the Scripture grounds Christian maturity in two processes: actualization and congruence. Actualization has two aspects: (1) the process of salvation which is described in terms of being saved, being sanctified, glorified, and being made like Christ; and (2) the Scripture also uses the word *teleios* (perfect, mature, complete) to describe maturity. The process of salvation focuses on something which God causes to happen to the believer while *teleios* seems to focus on the believer's choice or will (Phil. 3:14-15). Hence, the mature Christian becomes what he is—a son being renewed after the image—and becomes what he chooses—pressing toward the mark of the high calling of God.

The second process of Christian maturity is congruence, integrity, or consistency. The mature believer is characterized by the fruit of the Spirit. His actions and words flow consistently out of an inner thought and emotional life which has been committed to Christ. Since the mature believer lets the mind of Christ dwell in him his actions follow congruently (Phil. 2:5-8); i.e., they are both Christ-like and self-congruent.

The Integrated Model

This paper has established that actualization and congruence are processes which form the model of both personality and Christian maturity. However, it is important to recognize that personality and Christian maturity are not the same things. The same process operates in both spheres but their contents are different. Only when the same principles or processes operate in both psychology and Christian thought is it possible to speak of integration. This point must be heavily stressed since some writers tend to reduce psychology to the Bible (Adams, 1970) while others reduce the Bible to psychology (Mowrer, 1961).

The contents of the actualization and congruence processes for personality (theory) are that each individual person is developing all his motives, capacities, and potentialities. The content of the actualization and congruence processes is that the image of God in the person is being renewed or developed. The salvation process is the restoration of the image of God in the Christian believer which was marred in the Fall (Eph. 4:24; Col. 3:10). It is coupled with congruent functioning modeled after Christ. Thus congruence is for the mature Christian not only internal congruence but congruence with the pattern Christ gave for the Christian. In willing to do God's will the mature believer does both God's will and his own will.

From a biblical perspective actualization and congruence in personality (psychological maturity) involve developing a person who was created in God's image but who is fallen and is marred. The individual can become as actualized and congruent as human nature and the situation with all the assets and liabilities, will allow. The Christian has from a biblical perspective greater potential than the non-Christian. While the image in which he was created has become marred it is now being renewed. The imperfection or marring is in the process of being transformed and congruence has a new focus around a creation (2 Cor. 5:17). The non-Christian is being actualized as a created and fallen person and the Christian is being actualized as a created, fallen, and redeemed person. Since congruence is always consistency among the capacities and functioning of the individual, congruence is different in content for the Christian and non-Christian. Figure 1 helps illustrate the difference and the similarity between maturity in terms of personality theory and Christian maturity though graphic illustrations of personality are limited and should not be pressed.

FIG. 1. An illustration of the similarity and difference in actualization and congruence in the Christian and non-Christian.

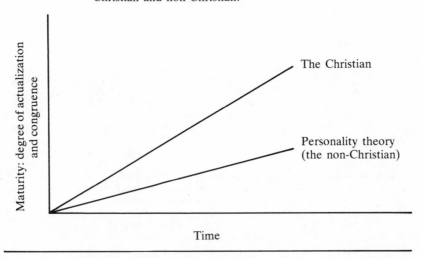

Both the Christian and the non-Christian (as conceived by personality theory) increase in maturity over time. The line of development for the Christian increases at a faster rate since his potential (renewed image) and resources (divine assistance) are greater. Nevertheless the absolute degree of maturity may be higher for the nonbeliever since he may have been in process longer. The use of freedom, choice, and responsibility, as well as developmental life factors, also influence maturity, but they have been presumed to be constant across Christian and non-Christian lines in this illustration. However, there is a sense in which it is inappropriate to compare Christian maturity and psychological maturity, because their contents and dynamics are different. The meaning of behavior cannot be evaluated apart from its motivation. Often comparisons are made in terms of social or interpersonal behavior, but Christian maturity involves a specific content in motivational, affective and cognitive function of a person which may not be immediately apparent in behavior, i.e., there may be different dynamics behind the same behavior. The cup of cold water given in Christ's name (whether verbalized or not) is different from the cup of cold water given for other reasons.

In conclusion, actualization and congruence are described as basic underlying structures of the personality theory. This paper utilizes these principles or processes to construct an integrated model of both personality theory and Christian maturity. It is also maintained that genuine integration of psychology and biblical thought involves a communality of principle (or process) but a difference in content as illustrated in this discussion of maturity.

References

Adams, J. *Competent to Counsel*. Grand Rapids: Baker Book House, 1970.
Craine, W. E. *Where God Comes In: The Divine "Plus" in Counseling*. Waco: Word Books, 1970.
Daim, W. *Depth Psychology and Salvation*. New York: Fredrick Unger, 1963.
Gendlin, E. T. "A Theory of Personality Change." In P. Worchel, and D. Byrne (eds.), *Personality Change*. New York: John Wiley, 1964.
Hodge, M. B. *Your Fear of Love*. Garden City, N.Y.: Doubleday, 1967.
Jung, C. G. *The Integration of the Personality*. New York: Farrer and Rinehart, 1939.
———. *Psychology and Alchemy*. The Collected Works. Vol. 12. New York: Pantheon, 1953.
———. *The Structure and Dynamics of the Psyche*, The Collected Works. Vol. 8. New York: Pantheon, 1960.
Maddi, S. R. *Personality Theories*. Homewood, Ill.: Dorsey, 1972.
Mowrer, O. H. *The Crisis in Psychiatry and Religion*. New York: Van Nostrand, 1961.
Rogers, C. "A Theory of Therapy, Personality and Interpersonal Relationship, as Developing the Client-Centered Framework." In S. Koch (ed.), *Psychology: The Study of a Science*. Vol. 3. New York: McGraw-Hill Book Co., 1959.
Rychlak, J. F. *Introduction to Personality and Psychotherapy*. Boston: Houghton Mifflin, 1973.
Shlien, J. M. "The Lateral-Intuitive Axis and Other Thoughts." In J. T. Hart, and T. M. Tomlinson (eds.), *New Directions in Client-Centered Therapy*. Boston: Houghton Mifflin, 1970.
Tweedie, D. F. *The Christian and the Couch*. Grand Rapids: Baker Book House, 1963.
van Kaam, A. *Religion and Personality*. Garden City, N.Y.: Doubleday, 1968.
Wagner, M. *Put It All Together*. Grand Rapids: Zondervan Publishing House, 1974.
Wiggins, J., Renner, K., Clore, G., and Rose, R. *The Psychology of Personality*. Reading, Mass.: Addison-Wesley, 1971.

SELF-ACTUALIZATION AND SANCTIFICATION

James A. Oakland

This article will commence with a summary of the theological concept of sanctification derived from three reformed theologians (i.e., Hodge, Strong and Berkouwer). Following will be a discussion of John Wesley's concepts on sanctification and perfection. There are obviously differences among these theologians, particularly between the reformed group and Wesley, but insofar as possible, these differences will be minimized. Ultimately, the *possibility* of negotiations between theology and psychology around the common topic of "growth" will be discussed. For the theologians, sanctification seems to be the appropriate category; for the psychologists, self-actualization (or self-realization, etc.) is the appropriate domain.

Strong (1907) defined sanctification as "that continuous operation of the Holy Spirit, by which the Holy Disposition imparted in regeneration is maintained and strengthened" (p. 869). While justification is a "forensic act"—God acting as judge, declaring justice satisfied so far as the believer is concerned—and regeneration is viewed as the instantaneous work of God whereby a change of heart (or of the governing disposition) occurs, sanctification is a process, a continuous process, which removes more and more of the principles of evil still infecting our nature and which simultaneously sees the growth of the principle of spiritual life until it controls the thoughts, feelings, and acts, and brings the soul into conformity to the image of Christ. Sanctification is to regeneration as growth is to birth. The growth, however, continues *throughout* the remaining life of the believer. Sanctification is seen as necessary because of the existence in the believer of two opposing natures, continually giving rise to conflict; it is in this conflict that the Holy Spirit enables the believer, through increasing faith, to more fully and consciously appropriate Christ, and thus progressively to make conquest of the remaining sinfulness of his nature. The importance of the indwelling Spirit of Christ is crucial, as is the

This paper was presented at the Institute on Depth Christianity, Enumclaw, Washington, August 13, 1972, and at the First Annual Convention, Western Association of Christians for Psychological Studies, Santa Barbara, California, May 25, 1974. © *Journal of Psychology and Theology,* 1974, *2,* 202-9. Used by permission of the author.

believer's faith. The object is Christ himself, being like Christ, being in close union with Christ, knowing him, etc.

Note the following Scripture selections:

Being confident of this very thing, that he who began a good work in you will perfect it until the day of Jesus Christ. (Phil. 1:6)

Speaking the truth in love, we may grow up in all things unto him who is the head, even Christ. (Eph. 4:15)

The Lord make you to increase and abound in love toward one another, and toward all men. (1 Thess. 3:12)

But grow in grace and in the knowledge of our Lord and Savior Jesus Christ. (2 Peter 3:18)

Walk by the Spirit, and ye shall not fulfill the lust of the flesh. (Gal. 5:16)

Till we all attain unto the unity of the faith, and of the knowledge of the son of God, unto a full grown man, unto the measure of the stature of the fullness of Christ. (Eph. 4:13)

From the aspect of the believer, it seems several things are important. First faith—this might imply freedom from tension. At the phenomenological level, it appears not to be greatly different from Rogers' "trusting one's organism," and not too far removed from a comfort with oneself, a freedom to be oneself. A second factor has to do with "union with Christ" or "the indwelling of the Spirit," and here it appears, phenomenologically, that one aspect of this would be peak experiences. A third part has to do with "means of grace" and the sacraments, and if these are explored as to the significance to the believer, we are again close to peak experiences (as well as "plateau-experiences" of which Maslow speaks, 1964; 1970).

Spelling out more specifically the results of sanctification, Paul speaks in Galatians 5 of the fruit of the Spirit: love, joy, peace, patience, kindness, goodness, faithfulness, gentleness, self-control, not terribly different from self-actualization characteristics such as spontaneity, humor, acceptance, democratic character structure, social interest, deep interpersonal relationships, resistance to enculturation, life mission, and ethical awareness. (This similarity will become clearer further on.) In Ephesians 4 and 5, Paul further talks about unity, knowledge, honesty, and forgiveness as other characteristics.

John Wesley* wished to emphasize perfection in a way different from the reformed theologians. He cited Scriptures such as:

Be ye therefore perfect, even as your father which is in Heaven is perfect. (Matt. 5:48)

*Grateful acknowledgement is given to LaMont Lee and Stephen Meyer for their assistance in the preparation of the section on John Wesley.

But let patience have her perfect work, that ye may be perfect and entire, wanting nothing. (James 1:4)

In understanding this conception of perfectionism it must be understood that to Wesley there are two kinds of sin: (1) that of breaking relationship with Jesus Christ, and (2) not doing the perfect will of God. The true believer can be perfect in the sense that he does not break fellowship with Christ, though he cannot conform fully or perfectly to the will of God. Wesley maintains that

the perfect Christian is holy, not because he has risen to a required moral standard, but because he lives in this state of unbroken fellowship with Christ. (Williams, 1960, p. 175)

The Christian who is perfect is free from sin, not according to the objective standards of justice, but according to the measure of personal relationship with Christ. (p. 178)

There is in Wesley's theology a freedom from all known sin, at least the conscious committing of sin. Both the inward disposition as well as the conscious act of sin seemed to be done away with. This is not a process, but a state of being, given to us daily from Christ. In his mind, this was possible because love expels sin and governs the heart; this love cannot be conjured up by man but comes as a gift. The perfect man receives a love from God which expels sin and allows unbroken fellowship between man and God.

The expectation of the fulfillment of the promises of Christ in our lives is the essence of Wesley's doctrine of holiness. The faith that leads to perfection is essentially a conviction "that what God hath promised he is now able to perform, and that he is able and willing to do it now." Perfection does not occur at the instant of death but can be experienced by the believer now.

There is therefore implied in Wesley's doctrine of perfection a concept of freedom—that is freedom to accept a perfect relationship to Jesus Christ and experience perfection daily. The sense that man can experience this potential on the spiritual level would give him more freedom to help his fellowman and serve society better than the nonperfect man. By daily acceptance, man could also properly direct his freedom to serve toward being in and working in and with the world which is quite imperfect. He would be better able, particularly spiritually, to aid the imperfect, to be a model for society, and to be an effectual child of God.

The picture of perfection is as follows: A person has led a self-centered and fruitless existence, then comes into a relationship with God's love at a level of significance in all likelihood known only to himself; at first grows in an unstable manner alternately believing on and ignoring God's love; comes to a point were living with God becomes the only reasonable way to live; and embraces God's love on a day-to-day basis—which is the state of perfection according to Wesley.

Before leaving the doctrine of sanctification, it is appropriate to examine the continuously recurring themes in the Bible of "know and grow." The analogy with physical growth, particularly from infancy, if frequent, including types of nourishment appropriate to different levels of growth (i.e., "milk," "meat"), (e.g., Heb. 5:11-14; 1 Peter 2:2; 1 Cor. 3:13). Similarly, the analogy of plant growth is often found, including the production of fruit (e.g., Eph. 3; 2 Cor. 9:10; John 15). Further, there are concrete exhortations to grow and develop (e.g., Heb. 6:1, "Let us go on"; 2 Peter 3:18, "Grow in grace and in knowledge"; Eph. 4:15, "We are to grow up in every way into Christ").

Similarly, "know" is an important part of the experience and exhortations of biblical characters. For example, in the Book of Acts, believers were called "disciples"—meaning learners—for many years until the term "Christian" came into usage. Jesus stated in Matthew 11:29, "Learn of me"; Paul stated in Philippians 3:10, "That I may know him"; Paul prayed (e.g., 2 Cor. 1:5) that believers would increase in their knowledge of God; Jesus prayed in John 17:3 that they may know God and Christ. Old Testament writers such as Jeremiah, Hosea, Micah, etc., emphasized knowing God. And to all of these biblical references, one might add libraries of writings of the followers of Christ throughout the history of Christianity.

Now, let us examine self-actualization. This concept has a long and varied history, with many of the ideas contained in the writings of Alfred Adler, but more specifically spelled out by Karen Horney, Kurt Goldstein, Carl Rogers, etc. The concept will be discussed, however, in terms of Maslow (1970) for two reasons: (1) Maslow is quite comprehensive and leaves out very little that other writers discuss, and (2) his discussion of the concept is based on extensive observations of particularly healthy people. The fifteen aspects of self-actualization that he discusses will be organized into three clusters.

The first cluster has to do with being a relatively open person, both in the sense that the world outside of oneself can be perceived without distortion, and the world inside of oneself is integrated, interrelated, permeable, not constricted, not boxed up or tightened by multiple anxieties. Thus the self-actualized person has a more efficient perception of reality and more comfortable relations with it. He has an unusual ability to detect the spurious, the fake, the dishonest, to see concealed or confused realities more swiftly and more correctly, to be unthreatened by the unknown, etc. Second they have a continued freshness of appreciation, to see the basic goods of life freshly and naively, with awe, pleasure, wonder, and even ecstasy. Third, they easily accept themselves, others, and nature, not in a self-satisfied manner but rather as a straight forward acceptance of what is; they seem to have a uniformly good appetite, sleep well, enjoy their sexual lives, give and receive love without questions, lack defensiveness or pose, have a distaste for artificialities in others, dislike playing games or trying to impress in conventional ways. It is basically an acceptance of reality with a healthy sense of goal orientation. Fourth, they are characterized by a philosophical, unhostile sense of humor, not making people laugh by hurting someone, or laughing at someone else's inferiority, or defying authority through humor, but the ability to laugh at themselves, at the human predicament, at the foolishness of so much of human life with the noise, movement, turmoil, hurry, and bustle, all of it going no place. Fifth, they have the mystic or peak experiences. Sixth, they can be described as relatively spontaneous in behavior and even more spontaneous in their inner life, thoughts, impulses, etc. Their behavior is marked by a simplicity in naturalness, by a lack of artificiality or straining for effect; conventionality is accepted easily but can be cast aside equally easily when desirable. A seventh characteristic is creativeness, not the special talent creativeness of the genius but more like the naive and universal creativeness of children; the products of their creativeness may or may not be visible to anyone besides themselves and may or may not be regarded as valuable by others but these factors are not particularly important.

In the second cluster there appears to be a strong belief system. Thus they customarily have some mission in life, some task to fulfill, some problem outside themselves which enlists much of their energies, a "calling"; they are strongly focused on problems outside themselves rather than concerned about themselves (in contrast to the ordinary introspectiveness that one finds in insecure people). Second, they have an exceptional ethical awareness, definite moral standards, though these may or may not be the conventional ones.

The third clustering is a balance between individuation and social relationships. First, on the individuated side, is the quality of detachment and a need for privacy—they can be solitary without harm to themselves and without discomfort; in fact, they positively like solitude and privacy to a definitely greater degree than the average person. Second, they have a sense of autonomy, of independence of culture and environment, of free will, of being strong rather than weak, of being an active agent rather than being helplessly "determined" by others. Third, there is a resistance to enculturation, a transcendence of any particular culture, a certain inner detachment from the culture; while they fall well within the limits of apparent conventionality and choice of clothes, language, food, ways of doing things, they are not *really* conventional, certainly not fashionable or smart or chic; they are hardly authority rebels in the adolescent or hot sense, but can fight when necessary—the impression is that they are not against fighting but only against ineffective fighting.

On the social side of the balance is a strongly democratic character structure, an ability to be friendly with anyone of suitable character regardless of class, education, political belief, race, or color; they find it possible to learn from *anybody* who has something to teach them, they possess a humility of a certain type; in addition, there is a certain tendency to give a certain quantum of respect to *any* human being just because he is a human individual. Second, they have for human beings in general a deep feeling of identification, sympathy, and affection in spite of occasional anger, impatience, or disgust; there is a genuine desire to help the human race, a genuine feeling that all are members of a single family. Third, they have deeper and more profound interpersonal relations than other adults with more fusion, greater love, more perfect identification, more obliteration of the ego boundaries than other people would consider possible; they have especially deep ties with rather few individuals, as relationships require a good deal of time; they have an especially tender love for children, in fact, for all mankind; this love does not imply lack of discrimination—they can and do speak realistically and harshly of those who deserve it and especially of the hypocritical, the pretentious, the pompous or the self-inflated; some seem to attract admirers or friends or even disciples or worshipers.

Maslow does not minimize the fact that self-actualizing people have many imperfections. They sometimes have silly habits, can be boring or stubborn, are by no means free from vanity and temper outbursts, may forget ordinary social politeness, are not free of guilts, anxieties, sadness, self-castigation, internal strife, and conflict. Further none of them possess all of the above mentioned characteristics of self-actualization (or all the just mentioned imperfections).

Maslow distinguishes between deficiency-motivation and growth-motivation. He sees every human being possessing a set of very basic needs including his physiological needs, needs for safety and security, needs for love and belongingness, and needs for self-esteem. Because these needs are inadequately met, we think, feel, and act in many ways, consciously or unconsciously seeking relief from the tension of the ungratified need. In contrast to that, he sees growth motivation not arising out of any deficiency in the person, but rather a flowering of the inner potentials of the person. It is this growth motivation that leads toward self-actualization.

The general "flavor" or "feel" of this picture of self-actualization is not much different from that of sanctification. This can be illustrated and emphasized by going back over the above description of self-actualization, and examining whether and to what degree Christ exemplifies self-actualization. Think of Christ as he is pictured in the Gospels; then substitute his name (or an appropriate pronoun) in the appropriate places in the preceding description of self-actualization (pp. 8-12), and reread it.

It is the opinion of this writer that with few qualifications Christ is a magnificent example of a self-actualizing person. Adding to this the awareness of the biblical passages on becoming like Christ (e.g., Eph. 4:13, "Till we all attain unto . . . a full grown man, unto the measure of the stature of the fullness of Christ"), and that Christlikeness is a significant, if not *the* significant, result of sanctification, one can conclude that self-actualization and sanctification are very close indeed.

Let us go one step further in our consideration of self-actualization. Maslow (1970) devoted a whole separate chapter to love in self-actualized people. (Incidentally, keep Jesus as well as the primacy of love in Christianity in mind here as well.) Maslow's definition of love is subjective: a feeling of tenderness and affection with great enjoyment, happiness, satisfaction, elation, and even ecstasy. There is a wanting to get closer, to be more intimate, to touch and embrace, to share with, to yearn for the loved person. This person is perceived in some desirable way—beautiful, good, attractive, etc. There is specific, conscious sexual desire. There is a special taste for privacy. There is the pleasure of giving and pleasing. There is a desire for fuller knowledge. Beyond these descriptions, there is in *self-actualizing* love relationships an absence of anxiety, ("I can let my hair down—just be completely myself"), less maintenance of distance, mystery, glamour, reserve, secrecy, an absence of hostility between the sexes, an improvement of the relationship with length of involvement. There is a power to love and the ability to *be* loved. There is a profoundity and even mysticism in sexual intimacy. There is a "pooling of needs," such that each person feels the other's needs as if they were his own, and an easy ministering to the need state, whether in oneself or the other. There is fun and gaiety, acceptance and respect for the other's individuality, a frequent sense of wonder and awe in the love relationship, an ability of each partner to have a detachment and an individuality (i.e., self-actualizing people are simultaneously the most individualistic and the most altruistic, social, and loving of all human beings).

Now, if we review the writings of the Christian mystics and the like, again we find striking similarity. Let us focus on one aspect: Their experience of God is marvelously like the love relationship above. God was not a way-off, reserved, and distant being. Consider the easy relationship between Abraham and God: They could talk over things, and when God told the aging Abraham he would have a son, they could laugh about the absurdity of it—an easy laugh of faith, not cynicism, and Abraham ends up calling his son "Laughter" which is what Isaac means.

Here again we can tie into the significance of peak experiences/God experiences. We can perhaps sense more clearly what Wesley meant in describing perfection as a perfect relationship to Jesus Christ, experiencing (note that word) that perfect relationship daily. We could say that Wesley wished to facilitate peak-experiences (as well as plateau-experiences).

Focusing more on the processes involved, how does all this come about? There are certain limitations in Maslow, viz., the fact that his approach has been descriptive of self-actualized people means that his focus has been more on result than process. However, if we go to therapists (who are more involved in the process) we find them describing the way toward self-actualization. These processes, not surprisingly, are those familiar in therapy: an acceptant, warm, nourishing relationship with at least one other person, a chance to explore one's inner feelings and conflicts, to have support and help in this, to gain insight and to implement that insight into living, to find straightforward and regular ways of getting one's needs met in reciprocal relationships, to become at ease with the flow of feelings and impulses, to develop a solid sense of identity, to let one's potential unfold. Therapy and encounter groups are important as well as quality relationships and a life setting relatively low in chronic stress. More recently, quasi-religious activities such as meditation and transpersonal experiences have been quite visible. Reading, while seldom overtly noticed as part of the process, is usually significant in practice.

The similarity of these processes to those leading to sanctification is self-evident. To even further emphasize this we can look at Oden's (1972) comparison of classical pietism (those particularly interested in sanctification) with contemporary encounter groups.

TABLE 1
Comparison of Classical Pietism with Contemporary Encounter Groups

18-19th Century Religious Group Leaders	*Current Encounter Group Leaders*
Rules of the Bands: Is it your desire and design to be, on this and all other occasions, entirely open, so as to speak everything that is in your heart without exception, without disguise and without reserve? Have you nothing you desire to keep secret? (Wesley, 1977)	The pursuit of honesty is begun by asking the couples to think of three secrets they have never told their mate and that would be most likely to jeopardize their relationship. During the course of the workshop they tell these secrets. (Schultz, 1971)
Beware of resting in past experience. (Newstead, 1943)	Nothing exists except the now. (Perls, 1969)
Many, many a time, in immediate answer to prayer, in the classroom, so intensely burns the heart with love to God and man, that the whole class is quickened by the subduing and stirring testimony given, and the very classroom seems to be a mansion of glory. (Rosser, 1855)	Participants feel a closeness and intimacy which they have not felt even with their spouses or members of their own family, because they have revealed themselves here more deeply. (Rogers, 1970)
I have been at meetings where the whole congregation would be bathed in tears; and sometimes their cries would be so loud that the preacher's voice could not be heard. Some would be seized with trembling, and in a few moments drop on the floor as if they were dead; while others were embracing each other with streaming eyes, and all were lost in wonder, love and praise. (Lee, 1810)	. . . participants almost unanimously speak of marathons, immediately afterward and a year afterward, as a worthwhile and moving experience. The words, "I felt reborn," are often uttered. (Mintz, 1967)

In summary, making a broad scope comparison between self-actualization and sanctification, we can see that both attempt to describe a long-term process in individuals whereby certain characteristics become increasingly prominent; both describe these end-characteristics in a general way but there appears to be almost complete overlap; both describe similar intro- and interpersonal states which are the means to the end. The major difference, of course, is that in sanctification God is the agent, working in a believer whose role is secondary, viz., cooperation; while in self-actualization no God is necessary and the individual person is primary, with the process unfolding from within.

This difference is not so great, it would seem. Clearly, "God sends the rain on the just and the unjust." Theologians discussing human depravity, have always made room for the obvious empirical fact that there is much that is noble in fallen man, attributed directly or ultimately to God's work. On the other side, consider this: Maslow and the host of other humanistic psychologists have shown how empty a reductionistic and mechanistic psychology is—that we need to allow for such previously discarded concepts such as choice and the significance of the experiential.

Now, even though Maslow takes the lead in wanting to keep at a naturalistic (vs. supernatural) level, his good friend Bertocci has chided him (1965) for being unduly reductionistic and just as arbitrary and limiting as the mechanistic behaviorists.

If Maslow is to be faithful to his own concern for non-reductionism, he may need to keep his humanistic-naturalism from tempting him to reduce the phenomena of religious experience into what might well be the lowest-common-denominator of a humanism that still is rather arbitrarily defined. (p. 450)

It has not been uncommon for encounter groups to have overt religious activities and experiences; even a new journal (*The Journal of Transpersonal Psychology*) has been started as an outlet for discussion of this by the same people who ten years earlier began the *Journal of Humanistic Psychology*. This does not include the tremendous amount of activity arising out the "importing" of encounter groups into the churches.

The nonreligious people in humanistic psychology have become strikingly more religious, and the theologians have always spoken of God's work throughout his creation, not just in the church.

Does Christianity offer something uniquely additional or significantly facilitative? My belief is that it does and that an intensive study of sanctification in the history of Christianity will unearth some very significant and helpful discoveries for growth-oriented people.

References

Bertocci, P. "On Deeper Dimensions." Review of A. H. Maslow, *Religions, Values, and Peak Experiences. Contemporary Psychology*, 1965, *10*, 449-51.

Maslow, A. H. *Religions, Values, and Peak Experiences.* Columbus: Ohio State University Press, 1964.
————. *Motivation and Personality.* 2nd ed. New York: Harper & Row, 1970.
Oden, T. C. "The New Pietism." *The Journal of Humanistic Psychology,* 1972, *12,* 24-41.
Strong, A. H. *Systematic Theology.* Philadelphia: The Judson Press, 1907.
Williams, C. W. *John Wesley's Theology Today.* New York: Abingdon Press, 1960.

INTIMACY AND SPIRITUAL GROWTH

Clark Barshinger

Our contemporary society is characterized by loneliness and isolation. Within the church, as well as at large, people struggle to maintain masks of success and well being, while deeper human needs, such as love and relatedness, go unmet and often unnoticed. In the society, superficial life styles are both the symptom and the cause of personal alienation. They are the symptom in that the injustices in society are hidden by the diversions of apparent success and by the legion of amusements. They are cause in that the superficial life styles allow the setting of patterns of noninvolvement personally. The counterpart in the culture of the church is the superficial, well-adjusted Christian. The "sins" and "distractions" of the "world" are rejected, but the worldliness of living for other people's notice is the same. Pasted over our own unhappiness is the assurance that we are getting along better than the others. The result of such an external view of the meaning of our lives has been a continuation of our separateness from one another.

In light of this, it has been of interest to me to observe an apparent correlation between success in psychotherapy and spurts in spiritual growth. I have observed, as have many others, that Christians who have reported seemingly no "life" in their faith, have, after making significant headway in therapy, reported a renewed sensitivity in their spiritual life. Numbers of times, I have found myself disliking the manner in which some Christian clients of mine used God like a "yellow pages" for coping with life. If their struggles, or those of someone else, become too difficult to face, they simply "turned it over to God" and went on their way, relieved to know there was a simple answer of faith to every difficulty. As these clients of mine began to genuinely wrestle with what they said, did, and felt, it was amazing to watch the increasing honesty and realism with which they reviewed their own values and their relationships with others. The easy answers of "beating out the Joneses" or of "victorious Christian living" melted away before a growing hunger for personal and interpersonal realness. These people frequently experience a similar process of reviewing where they are spiritually with the same candor they are facing their social presentations.

Perhaps because I am a psychologist rather than a minister (and perhaps not), I seem to meet more Christians who have moved from a new honesty and realism in looking at their life before others to a renewed candor regarding their spiritual life than Christians who have moved in the opposite direction. In other words, more Christians I meet "feel the presence of God." In times of revival, the two events seem to be simultaneous; that is, feeling the presence of God and getting right with one's neighbors seem to occur at the same time and to reinforce each other.

One common phenomenon in the personal growth that occurs, emotionally, socially, and spiritually, is the breaking down of facades, false images of self and others, and isolation and estrangement patterns that characterize most of society's social relationships give way to more intimacy. Rather than being primarily invested in creating and maintaining a "social self" oriented around the culture's values of importance (i.e., money, physical attraction, social status, and power), the individuals growing in personal and/or spiritual maturity become invested in genuine human contact (i.e., honesty, self-disclosure, realism, and integrity).

Intimacy and Spiritual Growth

The conclusion that I drew was that intimacy precedes personal growth, whether personal-emotional or spiritual. I am defining intimacy as the ability to let yourself be known by others, God, or yourself. Most of us desire to have a very close relationship with others in our lives, but tend to have instead rather guarded acquaintances. We want the security of a friend who sees all yet loves and accepts us. However, we are afraid of the vulnerability that comes with genuine transparency. It sometimes appears as if only the healthiest persons among us can muster the ego-strength to risk spontaneous sharing of themselves with others. Yet, I am coming to believe that any person can begin the process of greater openness by allowing him/herself to slowly see him/herself. In other words, for most people, the beginning of genuine intimacy with life is the courage to really look at his/her own person. Without such courage, only those who are fortunate enough to be raised in love and intimacy or those who have God and/or others consistently reach out . . . to them in sacrificial ways, are able to find an intimate life. In short, unless a person is willing to risk an honest look at herself, she will probably never reach an intimate relationship with others or God either.

This, I think, is why I so often observe spiritual growth following personal-emotional growth. Until one has some idea of what it is he or she is bringing to God and needs from God, his or her relationship with God will be limited in intimacy by the "ways" of other people before. It means that the more we must depend on other people's approach to God, the less genuine intimacy we can have with God. In short, easy spirituality (just like easy friendships) is shallow. I remember one client, when talking about positive feedback she had gotten on her warmth and depth, saying with deep emotion, "I don't want to believe it about me unless it's really true." It is as if she were saying, "I want this particular aspect of me to be true so badly, I cannot accept it until 'I know' it is true." There is a sacred dimension to an attitude such as this. It is as if all the pretense and facade is temporarily washed away and the person stands utterly willing to let the truth be known.

For me, it is a hard thing to express clearly what I sense to be the overwhelming issue here: the courage to say, if only for a moment, I want to know what I really am and I want to be what I really am. It reminds me of Luther's "Here I stand; I can do no other." One thing I am sure of, real personal *power* comes from moments such as these. There is a profound humility present when a person reaches moments of self-knowledge and a transcendent power and peace that follows when the person walks away being full of the liberation that such self-realization brings. I am not talking of self-actualization or the optimistic tyranny of the "fully-aware person." I am speaking of the strength and simplicity of persons honestly looking at who they are and how they are really responding to others.

Last year at the Christian Association for Psychological Studies Convention in Santa Barbara, I read a paper on "Natural Revelation Revisited." In that paper, I argued that perhaps God's most common means of speaking to us is through other people. Perhaps the biggest single relatively unexplored area of God's revelation to man and womankind is human interaction and its accompanying subjective experience. Here, I think, is the key toward intimacy for most of us. The way to come to know ourselves is to become known by others. When I allow you to see me in more transparent glimpses than I usually allow, I also come to see and better understand myself. But, perhaps even more important, as I have the courage to allow myself to be seen by you, in moments in which I do not know what will emerge or how it will appear to you, I become released from the prison of my own isolated fear of my fundamental vulnerability. First, I come to respect my own courage to let you see what is really there, for I know that the best of my facades cannot change that. It takes courage to allow myself to be exposed to your good will when I do not know if I am strong enough to defend myself against your misuse of my vulnerability. Second, I open myself to the profound healing that can take place when I open my wounds, pains, and fears to the loving touch of another.

But the question that emerges is why I am so filled with terror at the thought of your having even a glimpse of my moments of horrible uncertainty about myself. What do I fear you will do? What will happen to me? Of all people, why can I not trust you? I do not know the answer to these questions, but I do know they have something to do with the bigger question of intimacy in looking at and seeing myself. If I back away from letting you see me because I am afraid of seeing myself, I will indeed not see myself. But I will be haunted by the faces of my own frightened self, from which I ran when I ran from you.

So to grow toward a greater intimacy with my own self, I must be able to risk intimacy with you. And I have no doubt that this is fundamentally a spiritual journey. As a general rule, the arms God uses for holding me are yours.

Religious Spirituality and Intuitive Spirituality

Another question raised by this discussion is how all this talk of intimacy with myself and others relates to real, religious spirituality. Is not this simply a psychological gospel? I think not. I have come to believe that there are at least two kinds of spirituality (or perhaps they are stages). The first is what I will call religious spirituality and the second is intuitive spirituality. I think both forms of spirituality may exist in metaphysically false, as well as true, religious beliefs. In other words, I am referring to the manner in which a religious belief system is experienced. During the times I am in the religious spirituality mode, I look for "ways" and "methods". Religious spirituality specializes in "spiritual skills," such as devotional times, witnessing, Bible reading programs, and obedience to those whose authority is over me. As new Christians, we all live primarily in this mode, but as time passes and we grow, we live in this mode less frequently.

During times I am in the intuitive spirituality mode, I am more intent upon experiencing the presence of God and upon living out what I see as the implications of my faith for my own life values. My experience in this spiritual mode centers upon knowing God, either directly by intimate contact with God or indirectly by representing Christ to others or by receiving Christ's representatives to me. In intuitive spirituality, my focus is less on the specific socialization demands of my religious culture, and more on the universal nature and demands of my faith. My faith's demands now go beyond the clear issue of social morality to the inner struggles of my heart and to the universal issue of justice and mercy in the world.

Religious maturity can be matured by a wide range of experience, but most often it centers around growth through behavioral obedience, often in compliance to the wishes of a local Christian leader. For me, religious spirituality shows itself when I feel guilty for not going to church or when I feel as if I must act in a certain way to give the proper impression to a religious leader I am with. Now, this is not necessarily a bad thing. Often, especially early in our Christian life, we learn how to walk successfully as Christians by heeding the warnings and advice of other Christians. The problem lies in allowing the *forms* of religious spirituality to become so set or fixed that our inner spiritual life becomes static and predictable. We become religious rather than spiritual. In such circumstances, religion actually blocks spirituality. To grow spiritually, I would have to at times break out of my religious bubble.

At the times I make such breaks in my spiritual life I believe I am moving toward intuitive spirituality. My own spirit is responding to the leading of the Holy Spirit and leading me into personally unchartered waters. There is less certainty very often, although at times there is overwhelming sureness. In either case, when I am experiencing intuitive spirituality, I am operating at my "growth edge" spiritually.

Intuitive spirituality is closely related to intimacy. The experience of intuitive spirituality is similar to the vulnerability experienced in genuine intimacy. At the same time there is a closeness and oneness with the "other" and a vulnerability in its/his/her presence. There is frequently an experience of fusion or unity with the other person or force. When approaching God, who is beyond all our categories, the intimacy of intuitive spirituality evolves both a profound boldness and a profound sense of awe and humility. Intimacy and a sense of unity are essential characteristics of intuitive spirituality. Just as I need to be radically open to you if I am to experience personal growth, so I must be open to God and the immense domain of his/her natural revelation to me. In fact, I believe that my ability to be really intimate with other persons leads naturally to more intimacy with God. It is not an easy thing to really feel the presence of God, and if it should occur for us, it is not an easy thing to experience. Often, the presence of God is very frightening, not because it is dangerous but because it is so intimate. Perhaps this is why Rudolph Otto, in speaking of such intimate contact with God, refers to the experiencing of God as "the tremendum."

Sadly, in our religious spirituality, this sense of awe and intimacy in the presence of God is often missing. It is replaced by "programs," committees, sentimental ("heart-warming") special music, talks, and by authority figures who meet God for us and filter the impact of God's presence down to levels we can tolerate. To replace or purify all this, we need courage. Courage is a vital ingredient of spiritual maturity. It takes courage not only to discipline oneself in the pursuit of your spiritual goals, but it also takes courage to seek out and endure the spiritual moments of truth with other persons and with God. Religious life without intimacy is spirituality without soul.

Blocks to Intimacy and Spiritual Growth

Granting that intimacy may well be a vital aspect of spiritual growth, what would explain the infrequency of genuine intimacy in our culture. I suggest there are at least three aspects of ourselves that block intimacy and spiritual growth. The first is personal guilt and the culturally trained tendency to cover up our guilt. There appears to be a human predisposition to hide and protect the secret areas of guilt in which we feel we are our worst. Hobart Mowrer suggests that our personality is like a bank account, with both asset and liability accounts. If our manner of living accentuates "spending" our good traits for social advancement and hiding our weaknesses or liabilities to assure social approval, we end up living lives that are spiritually bankrupt. Matthew 6 tells that those who pray on the street corner for the recognition of others should not expect spiritual reward for their efforts since "they already have their reward." Self-help movements have means to inner healing. It is significant that all grass roots healing movements, whether social-psychological in nature or spiritual revival, have stressed "getting right" by "coming clean." All genuine revivals have been characterized by floods of confessions that have promoted interpersonal intimacy and resulted in spiritual closeness to God. When God is moving in persons' lives, personal confession and getting right with others is frequently involved. Therefore, I suggest that one block to spiritual growth is the fear of intimacy that would result if I allow you to see the parts of me about which I feel ashamed. There is a powerful will within us to resist the release of aspects of ourselves that arouse the emotion of shame. Dealing with our shame in a therapeutic, loving community also releases a powerful sense of forgiveness and healing. I shrink back from you when I feel you are near areas of which I am ashamed, but I am overwhelmed with love when I sense you have seen even that part of me, yet continue to approach me. Spiritual growth in this sense is somewhat like going to the dentist. You want to avoid the pain, but the pain is the only route to healing.

I think it was Carl Jung who said that we are fast to confess the lesser sin when we sense the presence of a much greater sin. When dealing with a religious faith that may confront the limits of our own shame and spiritual nakedness, it is often helpful to become preoccupied with our "lesser" behavioral sins. In fact, it is even safer to become preoccupied with someone else's behavioral sins. By focusing on getting right with God in various behavioral codes, I can sometimes avoid the deeper issues and questions of my life as a child of God. Fear of my personal guilt and shame may lie at the core of this block to spiritual intimacy with God and others. It also blocks my spiritual unity with God and others.

Secondly, the fear of the holiness of God can block my approach to spiritual intimacy. For many of us, God has been presented to us as either cold and rejecting or a nice person who does us good deeds if we ask for them properly. Yet, as we search Scripture more deeply, we find God's mercy and righteousness is accompanied by his being wholly other. I feel that evangelical Christianity has largely underplayed this aspect of God in favor of the personal interest, salvation-granting aspects. Yet, it is an awesome thing to reflect on the power and holiness of God. We justifiably avoid the working of demons in deference to their power, yet God is far greater in other-worldly power. We are told to approach God with the innocence of little children, but when we remember our own condition and our own sins, God looms before our lives in an awesome holiness. There is a mystery here of how we can both respect the significance of our relationship with God and approach God with the trust of a child.

Finally, our openness to spiritual intimacy is often blocked by our fear of our own deeper aspects of ourselves. Abraham Maslow speaks of our "Jonah Complex" in which we fear our own greatness. There is in us a tendency to be afraid of our own unknown strengths or abilities. This may result as much by our not wanting to believe unwarrantedly in certain strengths of ours, as in actually being afraid of those strengths. If I believe there is hope I can accomplish much and I am being very unrealistic, I am also heading for deep disappointment. Whether or not this is true, fear of what I may find within myself tends to block my openness to intimacy.

In each of these problem areas, courage is needed to take the first step of intimacy with others. We are all afraid of intimacy, but we can help each other by offering encouragement and loving support. And we can help each other by being willing to take the risk of sharing our real selves with each other. But, we must develop intimacy within our spiritual union together or we never find God's power and healing for our present lives.

References

Ellens, J. Harold. *Models of Religious Broadcasting*. Grand Rapids: Eerdmans, 1974.

Ellison, Craig W. (ed.). *Self-Esteem*. Oklahoma City: Christian Association for Psychological Studies, 1976.

Florio, Anthony, *Two To Get Ready*. Grand Rapids: Baker Book House, 1978.

Hockema, Anthony A., *A Christian Looks at Himself*. Grand Rapids: Eerdmans, 1975.

Smedes, Lewis B., *Sex for Christians*. Grand Rapids: Eerdmans, 1976.

SECTION FOUR

RELIGIOUS UNDERSTANDING AND THOUGHT

The five articles in this section are a sample of the current theoretical, research, and applied work in the area of religious understanding and thought. Much of the writing is theoretically based in the work of such cognitive-developmental theorists as Jean Piaget and Lawrence Kohlberg. Their developmental stage perspectives provide the framework for the first four articles in this section. The final article is not based on a specific developmental theory, but is a straight empirical research study dealing with several significant variables in the area of psychology of religion.

In two companion articles, Fleck, Ballard, and Reilly have proposed three Piagetian stages of cognitive development (i.e., preoperational thought; concrete operational thought; and formal operational thought) as a model for: (1) explaining research findings on the development of religious concepts in children and adolescents, and (2) teaching religious concepts to children and adolescents. Research findings on conceptions of God, prayer, religious denomination, and religious thinking in general are presented as fitting such a model. In addition, results of studies dealing with concepts of heaven, hell, and death published since the present articles appeared follow a similar developmental pattern.

In the article on teaching religious concepts Ballard and Fleck stressed the importance of presenting biblical material appropriate to the cognitive level of the child or adolescent. Examples of biblical content and teaching methods appropriate for each of the three stages are presented. Emphasis is placed on teaching content closely related to the child's present needs and world of experiences.

These two articles may stimulate a number of questions in the mind of the reader. Are there other major religious concepts that should be investigated from a similar developmental perspective? With intensive religious education in the church, home, and school, can religious conceptualization proceed more rapidly than general cognitive development? Are the religious education curriculum materials used by the average church consistent with the research findings on the development of religious understanding in children and adolescents? What effect has your own religious education had upon fixing your present level of cognitive functioning concerning critical spiritual concepts?

In contrast to the broad Piagetian stage approach to religious conceptualization presented in the first two articles of this section, the next two articles deal with a single concept, moral judgment, from the perspective of two different cognitive-developmental theorists: Jean Piaget and Lawrence Kohlberg.

In the first article Clouse has used the teachings of Jesus in the Gospels as the ultimate in mature moral judgment in an attempt to determine if Piaget's cognitive-developmental view of moral maturity is consistent with these Scriptures. Six age-related Piagetian categories of moral judgment were examined: (1) intentionality, (2) relativism, (3) independence of sanctions, (4) use of reciprocity, (5) use of punishment as restitution and reform, and (6) naturalistic views of misfortune. Clouse concluded that the teachings of Jesus and Piaget's concept of mature moral judgment are very similar and involve the same type of reasoning.

In the second article Motet has attempted to integrate Kohlberg's six-level theory of moral development with Old Testament and New Testament accounts of God's work to raise human moral judgment. A variety of biblical examples have been cited that illustrate the six-level progression of moral judgment. Motet concluded the article by applying Kohlberg's theory to Christian conversion and growth, pointing out that Jesus set the example by adjusting his message to the moral judgment level of his audience.

Are Clouse and Motet correct in claiming that Kohlberg's stages of moral judgment integrate well with Christianity? Can a Christian function at a universal-ethical-principle level (Stage 6) or is that level of functioning incompatible with biblical teaching? Is there a relationship between moral judgment level and the sophistication of our understanding of the religious concepts discussed in the first two articles of this section? Can the church present its message in a manner that will foster higher levels of moral judgment?

The final article in this section by Paloutzian, Jackson, and Crandall represents a solid example of empirical research in psychology of religion. They have raised significant questions such as: (1) Does Christian conversion make a difference? and (2) Does type of conversion experience and type of belief system relate to personal, social, and religious attitudes? In an attempt to answer these questions they have assessed the relationship between type of religious belief system (ethical versus born again), type of conversion experience (sudden versus gradual versus unconscious), and four attitudinal dependent variables (purpose in life, social interest, religious orientation, and dogmatism) in both a college and a general adult sample.

Does a religious commitment that is intense, mature, and personal foster good mental health? Or, is mature religious commitment a result of healthy personality development?

THE DEVELOPMENT OF RELIGIOUS CONCEPTS AND MATURITY: A THREE-STAGE MODEL

J. Roland Fleck
Stanley N. Ballard
J. Wesley Reilly

The research findings concerning the development of various religious concepts clearly fit into a three-stage Piagetian developmental progression from the prelogical, global, egocentric, perception-bound thinking of Piaget's preoperational child, to the concrete, logical, reversible thinking of the concrete operational child, to the abstract, theoretical, propositional thinking of the formal operational child.

Religious Concepts

Ernest Harms

Ernest Harms (1944) was the first researcher to present empirical evidence of age differences in the conceptualization of God. Harms asked his subjects (ages 3-18) to draw how God would look to them, if they were to picture him in their mind, or to imagine the appearance of the highest being they thought to exist. Older children (i.e., adolescents), who apparently objected to imagining God as such, were given the option of drawing what to them represented religion or the highest ideal expressed in religion. Harms arrived at three broad classes of drawings which were related to age and reflected what he assumed to be universal stages of religious development (see table 1).

1. *Fairy-tale stage* (3-6 years). Children expressed their version of the deity as a fairy-tale conception. God was pictured as a king, the "daddy of all children," or living in a golden house above the clouds. God is a fairy-tale imagination glorifying the highest fantasies which the child at this age can catch with his mind.

2. *Realistic stage* (7-12 years). Children expressed God in terms of the concrete teachings and concepts of institutional religion. Conventional

This article is an adaptation of papers presented at the 1975 California State Psychological Association Convention, Anaheim, California, March 6-9; the 22nd Annual Convention of the Christian Association for Psychological Studies, Oklahoma City, April 12-14, 1975; and the 2nd Annual Convention of the Western Association of Christians for Psychological Studies, Santa Barbara, California, May 30-31, 1975. Used by permission of the authors.

symbols such as the crucifix and the Jewish Star were the most frequently chosen representations of God. Somewhat less often these children drew priests or priestlike persons serving as mediators of God. God, angels, or saints were depicted as human figures who were helping, assisting, influencing, and supervising people on earth. "Realism" seems to refer to a concrete personalization of deistic conceptions.

3. *Individualistic stage* (13-18 years). Adolescent religious expression had such great diversity that Harms divided the adolescent subjects into three groups: (a) Group A expressed its religious imagination in a conventional and conservative way in line with the prevailing religious dogma. Typical portrayals included the crucifix, the madonna, gates of heaven, synagogue scenes, Moses and the burning bush, etc. (b) Group B's religious expression was highly original and unique. Abstract or semiabstract drawings with unconventional symbolism was typical. Drawings included a sunrise, light breaking through a dark sky, and rainbows or doors leading to heaven. (c) Group C expressed its religious imagination through religious and cult motifs which were never directly experienced by the individuals who drew them and which were quite foreign to the milieu of their upbringing. Drawings included those representing essential contents of early Egyptian cults, Persian mythology, Chinese Buddhist concepts, Celtic sun cult, German beliefs of the Middle Ages. The three stages identified by Harms seem to correspond closely to the prelogical, egocentric thinking of Piaget's preoperational child, the concrete, logical thinking of the concrete operational child, and the abstract thinking of the formal operational child.

Jean-Pierre Deconchy

Jean-Pierre Deconchy (1965) employed a word-association procedure to study the development of ideas about God in 4,733 children ranging from 7 to 16 years of age. The task was to write five word associations to six inductor words, one of which was "God." The associations to the inductor word "God" were grouped into 29 categories and along three dimensions: attributivity, personalization, and interiorization. These three dimensions characterize the three stages of religious development identified by Deconchy (see table 1).

1. *Attributivity* (7-10 years). The child thinks of God chiefly in terms of his attributes: (1) objective attributes such as greatness, omniscience, omnipresence, and creator; (2) subjective attributes (qualities of God) such as goodness and justice; and (3) affective attributes such as strength and beauty. The theme of this stage seems to be God's transcendence.

2. *Personalization* (11-14 years). The child thinks of God as a person. The themes of fatherhood, redeemer, master, and sovereignty predominate.

3. *Interiorization* (14-16 years). The child thinks of God in terms of subjective abstract themes such as love, trust, doubt, and fear.

The three stages mark the transition for the child from the God of his thoughts (attributivity) to the God of his life (interiorization).

Deconchy does not appear to have tested children young enough to be able to identify a stage of religious development parallel to Piaget's preoperational thought stage. The stage of attributivity and its emphasis on the attributes of God would seem to parallel Piaget's concrete operational stage, and the stage of interiorization and its emphasis on subjective, abstract themes concerning God appears to parallel formal operational thinking. The middle stage of personalization serves as a transition between the concrete stage of attributivity and the abstract stage of interiorization. The God-themes of this middle stage are similar both to the affective attributes of attributivity and the internal qualities of interiorization.

David Elkind

David Elkind (1961, 1962, 1963) defined "religious identity" in terms of the spontaneous meanings children attach to their religious denomination. In three separate studies Elkind investigated the growth of religious identity among Jewish (1961), Catholic (1962), and Congregational Protestant (1963) children. Piaget's semiclinical interview technique was used as each of the more than 700 children was individually interviewed and asked six questions. The questions were, with the appropriate denominational term inserted: (a) Is your family . . . ? Are you . . . ? Are all boys and girls in the world . . . ? (b) Can a dog or cat be . . . ? (c) How do you become a . . . ? (d) What is a . . . ? (e) How can you tell a person is . . . ? (f) Can you be . . . and American at the same time?

It was possible to distinguish three fairly distinct stages in the attainment of religious identity which held true of Jewish, Catholic, and Protestant children. These three stages appear to closely parallel Piaget's preoperational, concrete operational, and formal operational stages (see table 1).

1. *Global stage* (5-7 years). The child has only a global, undifferentiated conception of his denomination as a kind of proper name. "Although he acknowledges being a Jew, Protestant, or Catholic, he confuses these names with the terms for race and nationality." (1971, p. 677).

(a) What is a Jew? "A person." How is a Jewish person different from a Catholic? "Cause some people have black hair and some people have blonde." (1971, p. 677)

(b) How is a Jewish person different from a Catholic? "He comes from a different country." Which one? "Israel." (1961, p. 211)

(c) Are you Jewish? "Yes." And is your family Jewish? "Yes, uh, all except my dog, he's a French poodle." (1961, p. 215)

(d) Are all boys and girls Catholic? "No." Why not? "Some are Irish, some are Russian." (1962, p. 188)

At this stage the child regards having a denominational name as incompatible with possessing a racial or national designation. For example, it was common for the child to reply, in answer to the question about being an American and a Jew (Protestant, Catholic) at the same time, "You can't have two." That is to say, because you can't have two names (1971, p. 677). Like the preoperational child, children in this stage are unable to develop classifications.

2. *Concrete stage* (7-9 years). The child has a concretely differentiated conception of his denomination. His conception is concrete in the sense that he uses observable features or actions to define his denomination and his conception is differentiated because he uses these same observable features to distinguish among persons belonging to different denominations (1971, p. 678).

(a) What is a Jew? "A person who goes to Temple or Hebrew school." (1961, p. 212)

(b) What is a Catholic? "He goes to Mass every Sunday and goes to Catholic school." (1962, p. 187)

(c) What is a Protestant? "They go to different churches" or "He gets bap-a-tized" or "He belongs to a Protestant family." (1963, p. 294)

(d) Can you be a Catholic and a Protestant at the same time? "No." Why not? "Cause you couldn't go to two churches." (1962, p. 188)

Children at this second stage said they could be an American and their denomination at the same time. The reasons given were concrete and personal to the effect that "You can live in America and go to church" or "I'm an American and I'm a Protestant" or "Because you can live in America and be an American Jew" (1971, p. 678).

3. *Abstract stage* (10-12 years). The child demonstrates an abstract, differential conception of his denomination. "It is abstract in the sense that these children no longer define their denomination by mentioning names or observable activities but rather by mentioning nonobservable mental attributes such as belief and understanding" (1971, p. 678).

(a) What is a Catholic? "A person who believes in the truths of the Roman Catholic Church." Can a dog or cat be Catholic? "No, because they don't have a brain or intellect." (1962, p. 188)

(b) What is a Jew? "A person who believes in one God and doesn't believe in the New Testament." (1961, p. 212)

(c) What is a Protestant? "A person who believes in God and Christ and is loving to other men." Can a dog or cat be a Protestant? "No, because they can't join a church or understand what God is." (1963, p. 295)

When third-stage children were asked the question as to whether they could be American and their denomination at the same time, they replied that one was a nationality and the other was a religion and that they were two different things.

Long, Elkind, Spilka

Long, Elkind, and Spilka (1967) used an interview procedure in studying children's understanding of prayer. One hundred and sixty boys and girls between the ages of 5 and 12 were interviewed. In order to explore developmental changes in the form of the prayer concept, the following semistructured questions were employed: (1) Do you pray? Does your family pray? Do all boys and girls pray? (2) Do dogs and cats pray? (3) What is a prayer? (4) Can you pray for more than one thing? (5) What must you do if your prayer is answered? (6) If it is not? To explore developmental changes in the content of children's prayer activity and the fantasies and affect associated wih such activities, the following set of six incomplete sentences and questions was employed: (1) I usually pray when . . . , (2) Sometimes I pray for . . . , (3) When I pray I feel . . . , (4) When I see someone praying I . . . , (5) Where do prayers come from? (6) Where do prayers go?

The results suggested three major developmental stages in the child's understanding of the prayer concept. Again, these three stages appear to closely parallel Piaget's preoperational, concrete operational, and formal operational stages (see table 1).

1. *Global, undifferentiated stage* (5-7 years). The child has only a vague and indistinct understanding of the meaning of prayer: (1) "A prayer is about God, rabbits, dogs and fairies and deer, and Santa Claus and turkeys and pheasants, and Jesus and Mary and Mary's little baby"; and (2) "A prayer is God bless people who want to say God bless. Now I lay me down to sleep" (p. 104).

2. *Concrete, differentiated stages* (7-9 years). Prayer is conceived in terms of particular and appropriate activities (e.g., verbal requests). Prayer is very concrete and children in this stage never think beyond the mechanics of prayer to its cognitive and affective significances, which, to the older child and to the adult, are the essence of prayer. Prayer is seen as an external activity: What is a prayer? "That we should have water, food, rain and snow. It's something you ask God for, water, food, rain and snow" (p. 105). The child mistakes the form of prayer (its verbal component) for its substance (the thoughts and feelings associated with it).

3. *Abstract, differentiated stage* (10-12 years). Prayer is abstract in the sense that it is regarded as an internal activity deriving from personal conviction and belief. Prayer is understood as a kind of private conversation with God involving things not talked about with other people. Prayer has become first and foremost a sharing of intimacies in which petitionary requests are of only secondary importance: "Prayer is a way to communicate with God. Sometimes you just wait to talk to somebody, you just can always go to God and talk to him" (p. 106).

With increasing age the content of prayer changed from egocentric wish fulfillment (e.g., candy and toys) to altruistic ethical desires (e.g., peace on earth).

At the same time the affects associated with prayer activity become less impulsive and more modulated among the older children while prayer comes to be a deeper and a more satisfying experience. The fantasy activity associated with prayer changed from a belief that prayers were self propelled missiles to the view that they were a form of direct communication with God. (p. 101)

Ronald Goldman

Ronald Goldman (1964) studied religious thinking in 200 white Protestant children in England (10 boys and 10 girls at every age level from age 6 through 16). Goldman constructed a Picture and Story Religious Test which consisted of three pictures (a family entering church, a boy or a girl at prayer, and a boy or a girl looking at a mutilated Bible) and three Bible stories (Moses and the burning bush, the crossing of the Red Sea, and the temptation of Jesus). Each child was individually interviewed and following the presentation of each picture or story, the child was asked a standardized set of questions about the material. Goldman has identified three stages in the development of religious thinking that closely parallel the three Piagetian stages of interest in this article (see table 1).

1. *Preoperational intuitive thought* (-7/8 years mental age): Unsystematic, fragmentary thinking, leading to illogical and inconsistent conclusions because all the evidence has not been considered (i.e., centering). For example, why was Moses afraid to look at God? "God had a funny face" (p. 52).

2. *Concrete operational thought* (7/8-13/14 years mental age). The child focuses on specific and concrete features of the pictures and stories. For example, why was Moses afraid to look at God? "Because it was a ball of fire. He thought it might burn him." "It was the bright light and to look at it might blind him" (p. 56).

3. *Formal (abstract) operational thought* (13/14 years mental age). The child has the capacity to think hypothetically and deductively without the impediment of concrete elements. Thinking is now possible in symbolic or abstract terms. For example, Why was Moses afraid to look at God? "God is holy and the world is sinful." "The awesomeness and almightiness of God would make Moses feel like a worm in comparison" (p. 60).

Religious Maturity

Russel Allen (1965) and Allen and Bernard Spilka (1967) in attempting to determine the particular styles of religious belief and behavior which might differentiate between religious persons high in social prejudice identified dichotomous religious orientations or styles or religiosity. Allen and Spilka labeled these dichotomous styles "committed" and "consensual" religious orientation. A thirty to forty minute interview with ratings of subjects' responses was employed to identify religious orientation.

The "committed" style involves a personal and authentic commitment to religious values wherein the full creed with the attendant consequences are internalized and expressed in daily activities and behavior.

The "consensual" style involves a conformity or acquiescence to religious values wherein the full creed is not meaningfully internalized with respect to consequences for daily activities and behavior. (Allen, 1965, p. 13)

Allen and Spilka differentiated between committed and consensual religious orientation in terms of five structural components: content, clarity, complexity, flexibility, and importance (see table 2).

In terms of these five structural components,

the "committed" orientation, on the one hand, reflects an emphasis on the abstract, relationship qualities of religious belief which tend to be nonambiguous, well differentiated or multiplex, and diversity-tolerant. It would also involve a personal devotional commitment to religious values which suffuse daily activities. (Allen, 1965, p. 14)

The position of this article is that committed religious orientation is mature and that consensual religious orientation is immature.

Allen and Spilka's results support this maturity-immaturity thesis: (1) Consensual subjects scored significantly higher on the Prejudice scale; (2) Committed subjects scored significantly higher on the World-mindedness scale (a world view of the problems of humanity, with mankind, rather than the nationals of a particular country, as the primary reference group); (3) Consensual subjects had a greater tendency to express ideas reflecting a lack of personal worth or meaningfulness, and a loss of self-determination or adequacy; (4) Consensual subjects manifest greater mistrust of other people, doubt, and confusion; (5) Consensual subjects tend to lack assurance regarding the importance and authentic nature of an interiorized, integrative religious outlook which has ultimate importance in their life and daily activities. All of the above findings concerning consensual subjects would seem to support a basic immaturity of religious orientation.

The characteristics of the committed religious orientation in terms of the five cognitive structural components would seem to parallel the cognitive thought processes characteristic of Piaget's formal operational stage (i.e., abstract, well differentiated, diversity-tolerant, theoretical, hypothetical, deductive, integrated, and internalized). (See table 2.)

The characteristics of the consensual religious orientation in terms of the five cognitive structural components would seem to quite closely parallel the cognitive thought processes characteristic of Piaget's preoperational and concrete operational stages (i.e., concrete, literal, global, nondifferentiated, monopolistic, centered, restrictive, diversity-intolerant, magical, and egocentric). (See table 2.)

Further research is needed to see if three distinct religious orientations or levels of religious maturity can be identified which closely parallel the cognitive thought processes characteristic of Piaget's preoperational, concrete operational, and formal operational stages.

TABLE 1
The Development of Religious Concepts

JEAN PIAGET	Ernest Harms (1944) God	Jean-Pierre Deconchy (1965) God	David Elkind (1961; 1962; 1963) Religious Denomination	Long, Elkind & Spilka (1967) Prayer	Ronald Goldman (1964) Religious Thinking
Preoperational Period (2-7 years)	Fairy-Tale Stage (3-6 years)		Global, Undifferentiated Stage (5-7 years)	Global, Undifferentiated Stage (5-7 years)	Preoperational Intuitive Thought Stage (-7/8 Mental Age)
Concrete Operational Period (7-11 years)	Realistic Stage (7-12 years)	Attributivity (7-10 years) — Personalization (11-14 years)	Concrete, Differentiated Stage (7-9 years)	Concrete, Differentiated Stage (7-9 years)	Concrete Operational Thought Stage (7/8-13/14 Mental Age)
Formal Operational Period (11-adulthood)	Individualistic Stage (13-18 years)	Interiorization (14-16 years)	Abstract, Differentiated Stage (10-12 years)	Abstract, Differentiated Stage (10-12 years)	Formal (Abstract) Operational Thought Stage (13/14- Mental Age)

TABLE 2

Characteristics of the Committed Versus the Consensual Religious Orientation in Terms of Structural Components (Adapted from Allen, 1965, pp. 30-32; Allen and Spilka, 1967, pp. 199-200).

Committed	*Consensual*

Content

Refers to the way the individual conceptualizes the topic area.

Abstracts-Relational: Religiosity seems to be largely anchored in abstract principles and relational expressions. There is use of general categories, philosophical notions, or formulated theology.	*Concrete-Literal:* Religiosity seems to be rooted in concrete, specific, or literal statements and judgments.

Clarity

Refers to the precision and coherent structure of the beliefs of the individual. The relative ability to perceive meaning and implications clearly.

Discerning: Tends to order religious concepts and to express ideas in a discerning manner. Answers to questions or discussion of topics is clear and exact in meaning and reference.	*Vague:* Tends to give nonreferential or routine answers. Discussion of topics is vague, obscure, or unclear in meaning and reference.

Complexity

Refers to the number of categories, elements, or aspects of religiosity which the individual uses. The degree to which there is a differentiation among and between various aspects of religion.

Differentiated: Religiosity tends to be composed of a relatively large number of categories or elements. Ideas tend to be multiple rather than simple, global, or overgeneralized.	*Monopolistic-Dichotomous:* Religiosity is composed of a relatively small number of categories or elements. Ideas tend to be typologized and global. May make repeated reference to a single concept or think in terms of diametrical opposites.

Flexibility

Refers to the adaptable or accommodating quality of ideas, beliefs, or attitudes when the individual compares his beliefs with others' or his own belief-disbelief components.

Candid-Open: A relatively greater tolerance for diversity. A tendency to examine or thoughtfully consider in a frank straightforward manner different opinions, beliefs, or feelings.	*Restrictive:* Relatively inaccessible or closed to differing ideas. Apparently tries to narrow or encapsulate religiosity by rejection, distortion, or a "screening out" of different ideas and practices.

Importance

Refers to the strength, importance, or value of religious beliefs in the everyday functioning of the individual.

Relevant: Religiosity is a matter of personal concern and central attention. Ideals and values incorporated in the religious beliefs seem to account for or be relevant to daily activities.

Detached-Neutralized: Religion is considered thoroughly important, but is mainly severed from substantial individual experience or emotional commitment. Religion is primarily an emotional "clinging," a magical or encapsulated feeling tone which is not meaningfully related to daily activities.

References

Allen, R. *Religion and Prejudice: An Attempt to Clarify the Patterns of Relationship.* Doctoral dissertation, University of Denver, 1965.

Allen R., and Spilka, B. "Committed and Consensual Religion: A Specification of Religion-Prejudice Relationships." *Journal for the Scientific Study of Religion,* 1967, *6,* 191-206.

Deconchy, J. P. "The Idea of God: Its Emergence Between 7 and 16 Years." In A. Godin (ed.), *From Religious Experience to a Religious Attitude.* Brussels: Lumen Vitae Press, 1965.

Elkind, D. "The Child's Conception of His Religious Denomination I: The Jewish Child." *Journal of Genetic Psychology,* 1961, *99,* 209-25.

————. "The Child's Conception of His Religious Denomination II: The Catholic Child." *Journal of Genetic Psychology,* 1962, *101,* 185-93.

————. "The Child's Conception of His Religious Denomination III: The Protestant Child." *Journal of Genetic Psychology,* 1963, *103,* 291-304.

————. "The Development of Religious Understanding in Children and Adolescents." In M. Strommen (ed.), *Research on Religious Development: A Comprehensive Handbook.* New York: Hawthorne Books, 1971.

Goldman, R. *Religious Thinking from Childhood to Adolescence.* New York: Seabury Press, 1964.

————. *Readiness for Religion.* New York: Seabury Press, 1970.

Harms, E. "The Development of Religious Experience in Children." *American Journal of Sociology,* 1944, *50,* 112-22.

Long, D., Elkind, D., and Spilka, B. "The Child's Conception of Prayer." *Journal for the Scientific Study of Religion,* 1967, *6,* 101-9.

C H A P T E R   1 4

THE TEACHING OF RELIGIOUS CONCEPTS:
A THREE-STAGE MODEL

Stanley N. Ballard
J. Roland Fleck

In the realm of child psychology, the age-stage hypothesis suggests that children's development proceeds through behavioral stages which are progressively more mature and better defined. These stages are usually associated with particular ages (Rogers, 1969). The age-stage concept has been applied to various aspects of personality development. Havighurst (1953) posited a series of life stages which emphasized the developmental tasks to be accomplished at each stage. If an individual was to function effectively at any given stage, he must have accomplished the tasks appropriate to preceding stages. Erikson (1950) proposed a series of psychosocial stages of ego development in which the individual had to establish new basic orientations to himself and his social world. Kohlberg (1964) has constructed a developmental system in an effort to explain moral development. His research has indicated that the development of morality also has stages. It is Piaget (1932), however, who has done more than anyone else to emphasize the age-stage concept. He perceived children as progressing through sequential stages of conceptual development. The majority of studies in the aforementioned areas support the age-stage hypothesis; that is, children seem to go through generally invariant stages in certain areas of development.

Since this article is based upon Piaget's model of cognitive development, it would be wise to examine his theoretical system in more detail. As a general model, the system of Piaget outlines how the child makes cognitive progress at any stage in his development. In any cognitive encounter with the environment, the child assimilates the relevant environmental events to his existing cognitive structures—roughly to those organized systems of capacities and propensities for responding to or construing his milieu which have been built up in the course of past encounters and which are operative at this particular moment in his developmental history. At the same time, the structures modify and adjust themselves slightly to encompass whatever novel realities are present in the events. That is, they also accommodate to the events and, in so doing, get transformed into

This article is based on a paper presented at the 22nd Annual Convention of the Christian Association for Psychological Studies in Oklahoma City, April 12-14, 1975. © *Journal of Psychology and Theology*, 1974, *3*, 164-71. Used by permission of the authors.

somewhat different structures. This is the way the child makes intellectual progress. It is through a childhood of such assimilative and accommodative bouts with the milieu that cognitive structures are born, develop, and change into new structures. The crowning structure of each major Piagetian era of development (sensorimotor, preoperational, concrete operational, and formal operational) is said to achieve a certain state of equilibrium, roughly translated as a state of balance or homeostasis between assimilatory and accommodatory actions in the structure—environment transaction. If the gap between the child's assimilatory structural wherewithal and what he is supposed to assimilate and accommodate is not too large, cognitive progress can take place. If the gap is too large, even the most carefully planned training is unlikely to be effective.

The most pressing question for Christians is whether or not Piaget's stages apply to the development of spiritual concepts. There is research to indicate that there appears to be a goodness of fit between the Piagetian stages of cognitive development and the development of religious concepts and religious maturity. The findings of Harms (1944), Deconchy (1965), Long, Elkind, and Spilka (1967), and Goldman (1964, 1965) are indicative of support for a Piagetian model of religious concept development. Christian educators such as Joy (1975) and Wakefield (1975) are two contemporary writers who have seen the relevance of Piaget's work for the development of mature biblical concepts in the home and church context.

Cognitive Characteristics of Piaget's Developmental Stages

Having determined in general fashion the relevance of Piaget's cognitive developmental model of religious conceptual development, it is now imperative to ascertain some of the specific cognitive characteristics of each stage. The stages of intellectual development are as follows:

1. Sensorimotor Stage (birth to about 2 years)
2. Preoperational Stage (2 to 7 years)
3. Concrete Operational Stage (7 to 11 years)
4. Formal Operational Stage (11 years and after)

Since most research in the development of religious concepts has focused on the latter three stages, the thrust of this article deals with the same three stages (i.e., the preoperational, concrete, and formal). This emphasis is not to imply that religious conceptual development is totally nil during the first two years of life.

The most salient intellectual characteristics of the preoperational, concrete, and formal stages can be seen by referring to table 1. Even a cursory perusal of these statements highlights the child's limited mental capacities. Is it conceivable to postpone his Christian education until his thought processes are more fully matured? Should parents and teachers make the attempt to introduce children to biblical material which appears to confound their mental abilities? Goldman (1964, 1965), while not advocating a total lack of biblical content for the teaching of children up to the age of 12, nevertheless holds to the position that the content of religious education for this age group is to be child-centered in terms of meeting the child's cognitive, emotional, and social needs. He sees the Bible as a major source book for Christianity for adults. In an effort to clarify his position, Goldman (1964) states:

When we say that religious education needs to be more child-centered this is not to minimize the importance of the Bible. It is an observation based upon the demonstrable fact that the Bible itself, although not the ideas and persons of which it speaks, must be introduced in a systematic manner later in the child's development than has been previously practiced. . . . (pp. 227-88)

TABLE 1

An Outline of Piaget's Stages of Intellectual Development

Stage	*Approximate Ages*	*Some Characteristic Cognitive Developments*
Preoperational	2-7 years	*Object constancy.* Once language and internal representation of the world begin to develop, mental as well as physical objects acquire permanence. The child realizes an object continues to exist even when he does not perceive it.
		Little capacity to grasp time, distance, and numbers.
		Thinking has *little flexibility* and usually proceeds step by step in only one direction. Thinking is transductive. He cannot group ideas together and draw a central principle. The child's thought is characterized by *syncretism.* Syncretistic thinking links items and events together that do not belong together. Thought is dominated by *centering.* This is a tendency to focus attention on one characteristic or feature of an idea or experience and fail to see other important aspects.
		Thinking is *"irreversible."* The child can follow a sequence of operations but cannot trace a sequence back to the original starting point.

The child is *egocentric* in his thinking.

The child *cannot assimilate* another person's point of view.

Perceptions dominate the child's thinking. He is greatly influenced by what he sees, hears, or otherwise experiences at a given moment.

Concrete Operations	7-11 years	The child becomes less egocentric in his thinking.

The child understands and uses certain principles or relationships between things and ideas. This type of thinking is still rooted to events and objects that are concrete (visual experience and data apprehended through sensory activity).

Thinking is reversible. Thus, in certain learning situations the child can check on his conclusions.

The child begins to master conservation abilities. Substance, weight, length, area, volume, and number remain the same (are conserved) even when changes are made in arrangements and positions.

Formal Operations	11 years and after	The individual can think in terms of abstract symbols instead of having to base his thoughts on concrete things and events.

The individual can entertain concepts with which he has had no real experience such as the notion of infinity.

The individual is free to move in his thoughts and is flexible. He is not stuck with his perceptions or his conclusions.

The person can think about his own thinking.

While recognizing the difficult task of teaching children certain biblical concepts, there are Christian educators who disagree with Goldman on this point. Some of these are LeBar (1952), Haystead (1974), Richards (1970), and Wakefield (1975). Their point is that even in teaching young children with limited cognitive abilities the curriculum should remain Bible-centered but at the same time being cognizant of the child's total developmental needs and limitations at any stage of life. The authors of this article concur with this position.

Scriptural Cognitive Content Appropriate to Each Developmental Stage

Some of the major sections of the Bible, such as prophecy, most poetical books, and a great deal of the logical teaching of the New Testament, are beyond a child's intellectual ability to comprehend. Why then is there the insistence in this article for the curriculum in the church and the teaching in the home to remain Bible-centered? As Richards (1970) suggests:

Even though much of the Bible is beyond children, God does have something to say in His Word to our six-year-olds, our sevens and eights, our nines and tens and elevens. And it's our task to communicate what He is actually saying to them. (p. 179)

Continuing in this vein, he further states:

It's not only adults who have needs that must be met by the Lord, children do too. Trust in God and personal experience with Him do not suddenly come into style when a person reaches his teens. . . . Since God's point of communication with us all is the Word, it's clear that the Bible must be for children too. It's through the Bible that children come to know the person of God, to understand His love and steadfastness, to discern His character and care, and to know His will that they might be guided in their responses to Him in daily life. Through the Bible children, too, can become aware of the God Who reveals Himself there. (p. 181)

In reviewing the Bible in this connection, it does say some highly potent things to parents and educators concerning their teaching responsibilities. The Bible commends and even commands the teaching of the faith to children. The following passages are instructive.

Exodus 12:24-27. In this passage Moses instructed the elders in the proper procedures for the Passover observance, not just for that single occasion, but as a permanent celebration. "And you shall observe this event as an ordinance for you and your children forever" (v.24). The objective of the annual repetition of the ritual was to portray physically that historic event in such a way as to arouse questions among the children. Their questions were to then provide opportunity to explain the significance of the symbols.

Deuteronomy 6:4-9. Here Moses presents Israel with the essence of God's commandments, indicating a methodology for teaching them to children. The instruction was to be in the form of speaking both indoors and outdoors, visual reminders bound to foreheads and wrists, and written text on the doorposts of the houses and on the gates. Parents were to obey the commandments themselves and to make them the subject of conversation "when you sit in your house and when you walk by the way and when you lie down and when you rise up" (v.7).

Other passages of Scripture which continue this theme are Psalm 78:5-6; Proverbs 4:1-4; Matthew 18:1-10; and 2 Timothy 1:5; 3:15. In the last passage Paul speaks of Timothy's childhood—the time when Timothy had become acquainted with the Bible. Paul commends Timothy's mother—and grandmother—for having provided the impetus for Timothy's youthful faith.

Parents and educators, then, must present the Word of God even to the very young. Joy (1975, pp. 17-23) records a series of observations about the importance of ministering the Word to children. Some of these are as follows:

1. Children are our gift from God.
2. Children are open to God.
3. Jesus placed a high value on children.
4. The early years set the tone for life-long values.
5. Children deserve to be helped to moral and spiritual maturity.
6. Early, consistent saturation in a warm Christian environment helps children respond personally to Christ's call to salvation.
7. The child's emerging life needs are best met in the Christian fellowship.
8. The child's development is best understood, appreciated, and ministered to in the loving environment of the family of God.

In bringing together what research has shown concerning the emerging cognitive abilities of children and the view of this article that Bible-centered material is to be presented to children, the statement of Wakefield (1975) is most appropriate:

The Christian educator must always respect the inner supernatural working of the Spirit of God in the life of the child. Christian educators should be careful not to limit what they think a child can do, because of research by behavioral scientists. At the same time, the discerning Christian educator may be aware of human behavior and child development. (p. 122)

Preoperational Stage (2-7 years)

Based upon the cognitive characteristics of this stage, several implications emerge. Parents and educators must not expect too much of children at this age. The child does have difficulty in developing and relating biblical concepts. He utilizes precepts and images, but his thinking is fragmentary and discrete. He tries to understand biblical material, but his intellectual powers are not sufficiently developed to piece all the information together.

The biblical information that is given must be accurate and broken down to the preoperational child's level of comprehension. In spite of limitations the Word and words of God cannot be neglected. Even during this stage the child—in terms of his interaction with the environment—is building a world view. It is an excellent time to create an awareness of God. Young children gain a preconceptual awareness of the nature of God through observing others who express the love of God through their behavior. The modeling behavior of both parents and Christian educators is crucial at this time. As Joy (1975) concludes:

. . . During this time, children have difficulty distinguishing between reality and fantasy. They are creative and imaginative and indulge in magical explanations, inventing a wide range of supranatural persons and events. This capacity makes them highly susceptible to belief both in Santa Claus and in God. We cannot unravel the mystery of this particular stage of development, nor can we separate the child's orthodox religious belief from his unbridled fantasy. It will be important that his religious environment be stable during these years and that he have wide exposure to authentic adult faith. Where these conditions exist, he will separate fantasy from faith naturally and easily as his mind grows. (p. 17)

Content is crucial but for the preoperational child the methodology of content presentation is also important. Teaching must not rely solely on verbal explanations. The Bible must be related to the firsthand experiences of the child. Deuteronomy 6:1-9 is instructive at this point. The teaching is that childhood education was comprehensive in scope and made virtually all of life a school. It indicates that children were to be immersed in a total curriculum of experience and that God was to be related to the totality of experience.

In recognizing the above principles, Goldman (1965) suggests spiritual content which is related to the experience and spontaneous questions of children in this age group. In connection with the everyday experiences of the child and his spontaneous questions, the concept of God is to be simply and frequently expressed to the child. These expressions involve the concepts of a God who loves us and cares for us, and a God who has provided for us in this earthly home and who is always with us. In the home environment—where there is a great deal of interaction between parent and child—the aware parent can capitalize quite easily on this approach. In the church context, teachers may accomplish the same ends by establishing various learning centers in the classrooms which deal in simple fashion with the questions and needs of the child.

Beers (1975) is convinced that the preoperational child can learn certain theological concepts. These concepts deal with God, Jesus, the Bible, home and parents, church and Sunday school, and others. As an example of Beers' approach, he feels that the preoperational child can learn that God loves him, God provides sun and rain, God made the world, God made him, and that he should please and obey God. This approach is feasible if one remembers the cognitive characteristics of the preoperational child.

Memorization of specific scriptural content is also a viable possibility with this age group. Such themes as the child's behavior ("Love one another," 1 John 4:1), creation ("God created the heaven and the earth," Gen. 1:1), the Lord's attitude to us ("He careth for you," 1 Peter 5:1), and our attitude to the Lord ("I will love thee, O Lord," Ps. 18:1) would be specific examples. Again, these efforts in memorization are to be related to the everday experiences of the child.

Since children in this age group enjoy fantasy, play, and motoric involvement, the utilization of story playing offers a great opportunity to teach specific Bible content. When children can dramatize a story in simple form, they can more readily cognitively understand the story. The event becomes more real in story play. The drama involved is not necessarily practiced but can be spontaneous. Possibilities for story playing are illustrated by the following: (1) how Joshua conquered the land of Canaan (Josh. 9–11), (2) the great ship that saved eight people (Gen. 6:1–9:17), and (3) Palm Sunday (Matt. 21:1-11).

Additional content, similar to that of Beers', is suggested by McDaniel and Richards (1975, pp. 46-48) for this age group. The key to utilizing these concepts is to relate them to all aspects of the world about which the child is naturally curious at this age. To be real, they must be presented at a personal, immediate level of experience.

Concrete Operational Stage (7-11 years)

In this stage the child is becoming more and more able to relate facts together, to generalize and classify his experiences, and to reverse his thinking processes. Limitations, however, still accompany the advancement of this period. When a child is asked to use verbal propositions rather than objects, he must consider one statement at a time in reasoning the proposition through. His generalizing cannot go beyond particular situations or examples. His intellectual abilities are restricted to physical actions which he can internalize. His skill at grouping common relationships is a significant factor during this period. Wakefield (1975) writes:

Now that the child is gaining skill at grouping information, notable features become evident. At about nine years of age, children are becoming more competent at developing hierarchy of classes and relationships. For example, a child now begins to grasp divisions in the Bible such as the Minor Prophets, the Gospels, and the Epistles. As he matures, he gains facility at working with multiplication of classes, such as the second of the Pauline epistles. (p. 127)

When teaching content to the concrete operational child, it must be remembered that the child is concerned with concrete people, actions, and situations. Because this is true, factual information can be presented. Facts pertaining to the sources and people of the Christian faith would be appropriate at this time. Possible content might be drawn from the following: (1) life of Jesus, (2) what is the Bible (Bible background facts), (3) the story of a beautiful garden: creation (Gen. 1–3), (4) the beautiful baby who was found in a river: Moses (Exod. 1–2), (5) Gideon and his brave three hundred (Judg. 6:1–8:28), (6) the shepherd boy's fight with the giant (1 Sam. 17:1-54), (7) Daniel in the den of lions (Dan. 6), (8) the manger of Bethlehem (Matt. 1:18-25), (9) the earliest missionaries (Acts 11:19-30; 13–14), and (10) Stephen with the shining face (Acts 6–8:3).

In teaching the aforementioned concepts, the emphasis is upon the children doing things, finding out, experimenting, and thinking creatively.

The Formal Operational Stage (11 years and above)

At this stage the individual develops the mental ability for mature conceptual thinking. There is present the capacity to think in abstract terms, utilizing the world or propositions. Problems can be approached in a systematic manner and solved by using logical procedures which are expressed in abstract form. In this stage the person is concerned with the theoretical, the remote, and the future.

As to content, it is important to link it in some way with the real life experiences and needs of individuals going through this stage. What about the opposite sex? What about the problems of science? What about ambitions for life? What about happiness? Where does God fit into what I am doing? Biblical content must be correlated to these issues of life.

Many biblical themes can be explored at this time. Some of these would be as follows: (1) the inspiration in the Bible, (2) parables, (3) the attributes of God, (4) Satan: his personality and power, (5) man: his creation and fall, (6) sin: its character and universality, (7) the second coming of Christ, (8) the study of any individual book of the Bible, (9) Who am I according to the Bible?, and (10) the biblical concept of marriage.

Conclusion

In concluding this article, several principles clearly need to be emphasized. The whole subject of facilitating mature spiritual concepts is extremely complicated but several factors appear to stand out. Bible-centered content must be present, but at the same time methodology of presentation is crucial. The way in which biblical material is conveyed to children is of utmost importance. Parents and educators must model the content they are attempting to teach. The scriptural material that is presented must be appropriate to the cognitive level of the child. That which is taught should be part and parcel of the child's real world in that the content is related to his present needs and experiences. Words are to be matched with experience and experience with words. The child is to be helped to gain an enriched meaning of basic scriptural truths rather than the aim being cyclopedic understanding.

References

Beers, V. G. "Teaching Theological Concepts to Children." In R. B. Zuck and R. E. Clark (eds.), *Childhood Education in the Church.* Chicago: Moody Press, 1975.

Deconchy, J. P. "The Idea of God: Its Emergence Between 7 and 16 Years." In A. Godin (ed.), *From Religious Experience to a Religious Attitude.* Brussels: Lumen Vitae Press, 1965.

Erikson, E. H. *Childhood and Society.* New York: W. W. Norton, 1950.

Goldman, R. *Religious Thinking from Childhood to Adolescence.* New York: Seabury Press, 1964.

————. *Readiness for Religion.* New York: Seabury Press, 1965.

Harms, E. "The Development of Religious Experience in Children." *American Journal of Sociology,* 1944, *50,* 112-22.

Havighurst, R. J. *Human Development and Education.* New York: Longmans, Green, 1953.

Haystead, W. *You Can't Begin Too Soon.* Glendale, Calif.: Regal Books, 1974.

Joy, D. M. "Why Teach Children?" In R. B. Zuck and R. E. Clark (eds.), *Childhood Education in the Church.* Chicago: Moody Press, 1975.

Kohlberg, L. "Development of Moral Character and Moral Ideology." In M. L. Hoffman and L. W. Hoffman (eds.), *Review of Child Development,* Vol. 1. New York: Russell Sage Foundation, 1964.

LeBar, L. E. *Children in the Bible School.* Westwood, N.J.: Fleming H. Revell, 1952.

Long, D., Elkind, D., and Spilka, B. "The Child's Conception of Prayer." *Journal for the Scientific Study of Religion,* 1967, *6,* 101-9.

McDaniel, E., and Richards, L. O. *You and Preschoolers.* Chicago, Moody Press, 1975.

Piaget, J. *The Moral Judgment of the Child.* New York: Harcourt, Brace, 1932.

Richards, L. O. *Creative Bible Teaching.* Chicago: Moody Press, 1970.

Rogers, D., (ed.). *Issues in Child Psychology.* Belmont, Calif.: Brooks/Cole, 1969.

Wakefield, N. "Children and Their Theological Concepts." In R. B. Zuck and R. E. Clark (eds.), *Childhood Education in the Church.* Chicago: Moody Press, 1975.

THE TEACHINGS OF JESUS AND PIAGET'S CONCEPT OF MATURE MORAL JUDGMENT

Bonnidell Clouse

Those of us who call ourselves evangelical Christians hold to the basic tenets that Jesus Christ is Lord and that the Holy Scriptures are the inspired Word of God, the only unerring guide of faith and morals. Psychology, as a science, is not prepared to deal with "faith" but has shown an increasing interest in the area of morality and in methods for assessing moral development. It would follow, then, that psychologists and those of other disciplines who hold to the historic Christian position would look to the life of Jesus as the ultimate example of moral conduct and to his words as recorded in Scripture as a guide to the most advanced thinking possible in the realm of moral discernment.

The scope of theoretical statements and research investigations in the area of morality has become so great that one must limit any particular study to only a portion of the total picture. Kohlberg, Professor of Psychology at Harvard University and considered by many to be the leading authority on moral development theory, suggests that the research emphasizes either the behavior, the emotions, or the judgments of individuals (1964). As would be expected, what a person does and the emotions he experiences or the judgmental processes he exhibits are interrelated, and studies lend support to this fact (Kohlberg, 1964; Krebs, 1968; Sears, Rau, and Alpert, 1965; Ziv, 1975). But, each way of assessing morality is a legitimate study in its own right and adds to the overall picture of what constitutes a mature and responsible life.

With the current interest in the topic of morality increasing at a rapid pace, there has come a more careful analysis of ideas generated in years past. Among references often cited is *The Moral Judgment of the Child,* written in 1932 by the eminent Swiss philosopher, Jean Piaget. Piaget's interest was in portraying ontogenic changes in the moral concepts of children, and the method he used was to observe children at play (e.g., boys engaged in a game of marbles) or to present a story involving a dilemma (e.g., which boy is naughtier, John who accidently broke eleven cups while helping his mother or Henry who broke one cup while stealing jam?) and to listen to the reasoning of the child as he interacted with his

© *Journal of Psychology and Theology,* 1978, 6 (3), 175-82. Used by permission of the author.

peers or gave his opinion concerning appropriate punishment for clumsy behavior.

Although Piaget did not adhere to separate and discrete stages of moral development, by observing children between the ages of four and thirteen, he noted that older children gave more mature responses to questions than did younger children. "Though we could not point to any stages properly so called, which followed one another in a necessary order, we were able to define processes whose final terms were quite distinct from one another. These processes might mingle and overlap more or less in the life of each child, but they marked nevertheless the broad divisions of moral development" (p. 171). Young children regard rules as sacred and untouchable. Rules emanate from adults and must last forever. The child may throw a tantrum or refuse to play if rules are changed. At this early age, the child is a moral realist. To be good is to be obedient, and actions are judged according to their material consequences.

Older children, after the age of 8 or so, respect rules in order to be fair and loyal to others and say that rules may be changed on the condition of enlisting general opinion on one's side. Rules are due to mutual consent and for the well being of those who abide by them. The child becomes a moral relativist and judges others according to the circumstances in which the action occurred.

Piaget thus sees moral development as proceeding from *heteronomy,* or the constraint of an external authority, to *autonomy,* or self rule. Although heteronomy is legal, it is never moral. Genuine morality, by definition, is never imposed. Autonomy, being guided by internal controls, represents a more mature level of judgment. Responsibility is subjective, and actions are judged by motives rather than by objective consequences.

Beginning at ages eleven or twelve, the child progresses to an even higher concept of justice called *equity* in which there is mutual respect as well as mutual consent. At this level, reciprocity may include benevolence and understanding of universal love and forgiveness. Rules that do not help people should be changed. The law was made for man, not man for the law.

Piaget makes it clear that his concern is with "moral judgment . . . not moral behaviour or sentiments" (p. vii). Moral judgment has to do with how the child reasons, with the thinking processes involved, and with what the child says is right or wrong. As was mentioned, this does not mean that what a person thinks or verbalizes is not related to what he does or to the emotions that he experiences, but it does mean that special attention is given to the mental processes involved in moral development.

The Teachings of Jesus

Jesus is the only one who ever walked this earth who was without sin. As the Son of God as well as "the son of man," no fault was found in him. As our only example of perfection, any serious student in the area of moral judgment would do well to go to the teachings of Jesus as recorded in the Gospels to determine the ultimate in mature moral judgment. To do this, one must study what Jesus *said*. Although not unrelated to his work of kindness or to his emotions of sorrow or anger, the teachings of Jesus are the focus of our attention.[1]

The Gospel writers make it plain that those who heard Jesus were profoundly affected by his words. Matthew[2] records that the people were "astonished" (7:28; 13:54; 22:33) and "amazed" (12:23) and that the multitudes "marvelled" (9:33; 22:22). "What manner of man is this?" they asked (8:27). "It was never so seen in Israel" (9:33). He taught them as one having authority (7:29), as one who had great wisdom (13:54), and as one who could make even the winds and the sea obey him (8:27). Some were "offended" (13:57), and those who tried to trick him by presenting their own set of moral dilemmas turned and went their own way. But whether the response of the people was positive or negative, it was never neutral. The words of Jesus reflected a level of moral maturity far in advance of any views before expressed. The gracious words that proceeded from his mouth showed a reasoning and concern never before presented to mankind.

By knowing the teachings of Jesus, one is in a position to determine the validity of the writings of those in the area of moral judgment. His words are the criterion reference, so to speak. Would we find, for example, that Piaget's cognitive-developmental view of moral maturity is in keeping with the Scriptures, or is there a discrepancy between the two?

In the *Moral Judgment of the Child,* Piaget mentions a number of ways in which younger children and older children differ in their responses to stories involving a moral dilemma. Lawrence Kohlberg has put these differences into eleven categories but sees only six of the eleven to be specifically age related across all cultural and class groups, that is, older

---

[1]Jesus closely related actions and feelings with words spoken. He told the Pharisees that, "Out of the abundance of the heart the mouth speaketh" (Matt. 12:34). And to his disciples he said, "A good man brings good out of the treasure of good things in his heart; a bad man brings bad out of his treasure of bad things. For a man's mouth speaks what his heart is full of" (Luke 6:45).

Writers in the area of moral development are also aware that verbalizations and thought processes relate to behavior. Piaget recognized that "theoretical moral reflection does constitute a progressive conscious realization of moral activity properly so-called" (1932, p. 173), and John Dewey (1929, p. 265) has stated that "judgments about values . . . will determine the main course of our conduct, personal and social." Kohlberg writes that the same variables which favor advance in moral judgment also favor resistance to temptation and moral autonomy (1964, p. 409). "In our studies, we have found that . . . the man who understands justice is more likely to practice it" (Kohlberg, 1968, p. 30). Kohlberg (1976) further mentions the need to deal with justice issues directly and gives as examples racial integration, school bussing, and compensation for theft.

[2]All scriptural references will be from the Gospel According to Matthew unless otherwise specified.

children giving more mature responses than younger children (Kohlberg, 1964). For purposes of brevity, we will look at these six rather than all eleven: first, in terms of Piaget's findings and then in terms of Jesus' teachings on each issue.

Intentionality

Piaget noted that young children judge an act as bad in terms of the actual physical consequences of the act. When told about the misfortunes of John and Henry, the child will say that John is naughtier because he broke more cups. It is easy to see that eleven broken cups is worse than one. By attending to the material results of any given piece of behavior, the child is unable to differentiate the consequences of an action from the action itself or from the motives underlying the action. The intellectual level of the younger child prohibits his taking into consideration more than one point of view. The older child, by contrast, having a higher cognitive organization takes into account the circumstances that surrounded the accident. He will say that Henry is naughtier even though fewer cups were broken. John's intention was to help, whereas Henry's intention was to steal. One's intention counts far more than the material consequences of the deed.

Although the level of judgment is related to age, some older children and even some adults remain at a low level of moral maturity. Piaget noted that the average housewife "in the very poor districts where we conducted our work" (1932, p. 37) showed more anger over several cups being broken than over one. By fixing on the consequences of an act, the parent may ignore the circumstances in which the inappropriate action occurred. In this way, the adult "leads the child to the notion of objective responsibility, and consolidates in consequence a tendency that is already natural to the spontaneous mentality of little children" (p. 189). Unless a child has more mature models to emulate in other adults or older peers, he may grow up to be "as stupid with his own children as his parents were with him" (p. 191).

Do we find that intentionality is important in the teachings of Jesus? A study of the Gospels will show that it definitely is. On numerous occasions Jesus emphasized the inward desires and motives of the individual as opposed to outward visible signs and objective consequences. He told the Pharisees that the amount of money put into the coffers did not matter as much as the sacrifice involved. In God's sight the widow gave "more" for she gave "all . . . that she had" (Luke 21:3, 4). He told the woman at the well that the place of worship was not important but that worshiping God "in spirit and in truth" was. He condemned the Pharisees in that they made a pretense of piety and "All their works they do for to be seen of men" (23:5). These religious leaders of the day thought that long robes and good seats and pleasant greetings and the carrying of Scripture on their foreheads would declare their righteousness to the lesser elements of the society. But, Jesus was quick to let them know that even the children were closer to the kingdom of God than they were. He who would be great must first be a servant (20:27; 23:11), and he who would receive a reward from the Father must not display his works publicly (6:1). They were instructed to clean themselves on the inside (23:26) before taking concern for external appearance. The thoughts and intents of the heart are in God's sight more important than outward forms and ceremonies.

Relativism

The young child sees an act as totally right or totally wrong and thinks everyone sees it the same way. If there is a discrepancy in views, he will say that the adult view is the right one. This is exemplified in his response to the following Piagetian type story: A lazy pupil is forbidden by his teacher to receive help from his friends. A classmate, not knowing the teacher has said this, helps the lazy pupil with his homework. The child is asked if the teacher thought it was right or wrong for the pupil to receive help? Did the lazy pupil think it was right or wrong? Did the friendly classmate think it was right or wrong? In answering the questions, the young child will say that it was wrong and that the teacher, the lazy pupil, and the friendly classmate all knew that it was wrong. As a moral realist, he is unable to put himself in the place of others and can fixate on only one viewpoint at a time. An older child, by contrast, is aware that people have different views depending on their respective positions. Able to analyze a variety of situations and anticipate outcomes, the older child is a moral relativist and is fully aware that there may be more than one perspective in a given situation.

Although adults have the capacity to be moral relativists, this does not assure that they will function as such. They may be so certain that their way of looking at things is right that they are unwilling or unable to put themselves in the place of others and see things from a different perspective. Then, too, it makes one feel very good to be sure of what is right and what is wrong and to convince others that they are obligated to assume the same position if they, too, wish to be "moral" or "loyal" or "good" or "know the will of the Lord." Those who are in charge of any institution, be it the home, the church, the school, or a business seem to be especially tempted to assume that they know the truth on any matter thus assuring their continuance in a position of authority.

The religious leaders in Jesus' time were no exception to this proclivity. They had the power; they interpreted the Scripture; they set up the list of "do's" and "don'ts." No occasion, however small, escaped their attention or their judgment. "Is it lawful?" they often asked. Is it lawful for a man to put away his wife (19:3)? Is it lawful to pick corn on the sabbath (12:2)? Is it lawful to pay taxes to the Roman emperor (22:17)? Is it lawful to heal on the sabbath (12:10)? They quoted Scripture making sure that the interpretation worked to their advantage. But, Jesus confronted them face to face. He told them they were not to judge lest they be judged (7:1), that their perceptions were so blurred by the beam in their own eye that they were hardly in a position to take out the splinter in someone else's eye (7:3). The Samaritan woman, the publican praying in the temple, the blind beggar, and the little child, all had their way of looking at things, and these perceptions also must be taken into consideration. Because Jesus is omniscient, he knew everyone's thoughts (12:25) and, thus, was aware of all possible views. As God, he knew how the Father perceived any occasion. He knew by what authority he did what he did (21:23) and by his example reprimanded the disciples for their jaundiced beliefs as to who was not fit for them to talk to (John 4:27) or the best way for money to be spent (26:8-9).

This does not mean that one view is as good as another. Relativism in judgment is not a relativity of truth depending on one's perspective. Jesus made it plain that God's view is the right one. But, he also showed that just because a person is a leader or in charge of others, the adult, so to speak, in no way assures that his perceptions are to be preferred to those who follow or that he is exempt from considering the views of those who are in a more dependent position. Quoting the Bible and interpreting it to one's advantage does not assure that one knows the truth and is thinking God's thoughts after him. Jesus said that one must not set himself up as the judge. Only God has that right.

Independence of Sanctions

A small child says that an act is bad because it will elicit punishment. When asked by Piaget, "Why must we not tell lies?" a six-year-old responds, "Because God punishes them." When asked, "And if God didn't punish them?" the answer is, "Then we could tell them" (p. 164). An older child says that an act is bad because it may hurt another person. One should not tell lies, "Because if everyone lied no one would know where they were" or "Because you can't trust people anymore" (p. 168). The older child can make moral judgments independently of sanctions. An act is not judged as right or wrong on the basis of the rule itself or on the consequent rewards and punishments meted out by a higher authority but rather in terms of the effects on other people. Mutual trust and concern assume greater importance than the edict of the law.

Jesus told the crowds that he came not to destroy the law but to fulfill the law (5:17). He did not criticize the obeying of a law but rather encouraged it

(5:19). However, he chided the teachers of the law for attending to the lesser elements of the law and not considering the weightier matters of justice, mercy, and honesty (23:23). When asked if it was lawful to heal on the sabbath (12:10), he told his inquisitors it was lawful to do well on the sabbath (12:12). When told that the disciples transgressed by not going through the ritual of washing (15:2), he rejoined that eating without the ceremony of hand washing would not defile a man (15:17-20). It was not the sanction that determined its importance in the teachings of Jesus so much as the resulting consequences in one's relationship to others and to God.

Use of Reciprocity

The young child advocates concrete forms of reciprocity and takes the view that one should "do unto others as they do unto you." One repays evil with evil and good with good. Action is based on retaliation or an expectation of return for favors. If asked, "What should Mike do if Kevin hits him?" the usual response is that Mike should "hit him back." The older child, being able to put himself in the place of others, sees such action as marring personal relationships and may say that Mike should tell Kevin he will no longer be his friend if he continues to hit. In its most mature form, reciprocity becomes the golden rule. You "do unto others as you would have them do unto you." By taking motives and circumstances into account, concern may center as readily on the culprit as on the victim.

Mature forms of reciprocity seem too idealistic to most people to be practical. They are unable to comprehend or cope with the seeming ramifications of such action. Advocates of the Golden Rule are considered to be hopeless visionaries who do not understand the real world. The multitudes who listened to Jesus were no exception to this way of thinking. Besides, they had the Old Testament which advocated an eye for an eye and a tooth for a tooth (Exod. 21:24). So when Jesus told them to turn the other cheek (5:39), go the extra mile (5:41), and love their enemies (5:44), their reaction was one of amazement. Jesus showed concern for the blind, the lame, the women, and the children—those members of the society who could not reciprocate with money or power. He told the people to invite to their homes those who could not return the favor (Luke 14:13, 14) and to give a coat to someone who took you to court (5:40). When the devil offered him concrete forms of reciprocity in exchange for worship, Jesus told him that the words of God and the worship of God were more important than food for the body or "all the kingdoms of the world" (4:8). Jesus, the only holy and perfect one on the face of this earth, both taught and practiced mature forms of reciprocity and asked that those who would follow him do the same.

Use of Punishment as Restitution and Reform

Younger children advocate severe and painful punishment when told a story of some misdeed. They feel that punishment is just and necessary and the sterner it is, the more just it is. Older children, however, advocate milder punishment and are more in favor of measures which will lead to the reform of the culprit.

Piaget tells the story of a boy who was asked by his mother to fetch a fresh loaf of bread for supper. But, the child continues to play and does not obey. The father is not pleased and thinks of three possible punishments. The first is not to take the boy to the fair the next day; a second is not to let the boy have any of the little bit of bread left from the day before and thus he will not have much supper; and third is to refuse to help the boy the next time the child asks for it. Younger children, knowing how much children love the fair, will advocate the first of the three punishments because they perceive that that will hurt the boy the most. The boy must suffer for his wrongdoing. It does not concern them that there is no relation between the content of the guilty act and the nature of the punishment. Older children may choose either the second punishment which makes the guilty one endure the natural consequences of his behavior or the third punishment which involves reciprocal treatment and thus conveys the message that mutual cooperation is important in human relationships.

As with the other areas of moral judgment, those of all ages including adults may favor the attitudes of the immature child. It is not unusual to hear people recommend harsh penalities for infractions of the law. It is as though the only way to bring one back to his duty is by a sufficiently powerful method of coercion imposed upon him from without. If punishment is great enough, if one has suffered enough, then he has paid for his wrongs. Such individuals advocate a back-to-the-woodshed approach to keep the child in line and vote into office those judges who promise to give stiff sentences to delinquents. The emphasis is on hurting the accused rather than on methods that would encourage him to change his ways or make restitution to the victim.

The teachers of the law and the Pharisees brought to Jesus a woman caught in the act of adultery and asked Jesus what should be done with her (John 8:3-5). They were quick to remind him that the law said she was to be stoned to death. They knew from previous encounters that Jesus quoted Scripture as the Word of God and yet had very liberal views concerning relationships between groups of people and the way each person should be treated. They thought that in this way they could trick him because in their minds the two positions were mutually exclusive. How could one be conservative in doctrine and at the same time liberal in social matters? But after writing on the ground Jesus said, "He that is without sin among you, let him first cast a stone at her" (John 8:7). Jesus communicated to them that by their very law each of them would also have to be stoned. And so they left, one by one, until all were gone. Jesus did not imply that the nature of the misdeed was not a serious one, but he was aware that the method of punishment they desired would annihilate the wrongdoer rather than lead to a changed life. Jesus showed that he cared about her as a person when he said to her, "I do not condemn you . . . but do not sin again" (John 8:11). It was this element of kindness and understanding that deeply affected the lives of many with whom he came in contact. Punishment simply for the sake of punishment was not prominent in Jesus' dealings with others.[3]

Naturalistic Views of Misfortune

Younger children view physical accidents and misfortunes occurring after misdeeds as punishments willed by God. It seems natural to the child that a fault should automatically bring about its own punishment. This idea of "immanent justice," as Piaget calls it, seems to occur in all children without any direct influence on the part of the adult but may continue longer in those children whose parents encourage this type of immature judgment. Linking an accident (e.g., falling down) with disobedience ("I told you to tie your shoestrings") strengthens the bond between the physical hurt and an offense. Unless the parent has actually seen the child trip on the shoestrings, such "serves you right" comments only encourages faulty reasoning. Older children, however, do not confuse misfortunes with punishment. They realize that sometimes wickedness goes unpunished and virtue remains unrewarded. Children fall and get hurt whether or not shoestrings are tied, and natural calamities come to both the righteous and the unrighteous.

Piaget tells the story of a boy who was stealing apples. When a policeman came, the child ran away; but, while crossing a rotten bridge, it collapsed and he fell into the water. In response to the question, "Why did he fall in?" the young child says, "God made him . . . because he had eaten the apples." When asked, "If he had not eaten the apples, would he have fallen into the water?" the answer is, "No . . . because the bridge would not have cracked" (p. 252). The older child when asked the same questions will say that he fell in because the plank was worn out and that "He'd have fallen in just the same" (p. 253).

The teachings of Jesus support both the concept of immanent justice and

[3]On numerous occasions Jesus showed himself to be gracious and kind when others would have scorned or ignored. The woman at the well, the "publicans and sinners," the demoniac, and the lepers are but a few examples. An exception to this, however, came when he witnessed the money changers using the house of the Lord for personal gain. Appalled by what he saw, he overturned the money tables and drove them out, calling them thieves (Mark 11:15-17). His wrath came not upon the less fortunate members of the society but on those who took advantage of their religious connections to profit financially, and in so doing, they desecrated the place of worship.

the concept of naturalistic views of misfortune. There is both disagreement and agreement with Piaget's view of mature moral judgment as it pertains to a cause-effect relationship between behavior and subsequent fortune or misfortune. Jesus told the Pharisees that they would be punished for their part in the murders of the prophets (23:34), and he told his followers that faith was related to the healing process (8:13; 9:22). But he also said that persecution would come to those identified with him (5:10; 24:9) thus relating misfortune with desirable conduct. When it came to individual problems, Jesus showed that these are sometimes linked to the person's behavior and sometimes not. He told the crippled man at the pool of Bethesda, "Sin no more, lest a worse thing come unto thee" (John 5:14). But when asked about the man born blind, "Teacher, whose sin caused him to be born blind? Was it his own or his parents' sin?" Jesus answered, "His blindness has nothing to do with his sins or his parents' sins" (John 9:2, 3).

Jesus was also careful to show that natural events may bear no relationship to those individuals affected by them. One knows that whether one builds his house upon the sand or upon a rock determines how long the house will stand, but the storms will come to both (7:25, 27). "He makes his sun to shine on bad and good people alike, and gives rain to those who do good and to those who do evil (5:45). Jesus told the people that the Galileans whom Pilate killed were not worse sinners than other Galileans and that the eighteen who died when the tower of Siloam fell were not more wicked than others living in Jerusalem (Luke 13:2-5). Because adversity comes does not necessarily mean that God is judging a person for his sins. One need not assume a cause-effect relationship between the circumstances he finds himself to be in and his relationship with God unless he has good reason to believe otherwise.

Conclusions

The teachings of Jesus and Piaget's concept of mature moral judgment are remarkably similar. In his omniscience, Jesus knew all things and represented the most advanced thinking possible in the area of morality. Piaget's cognitive-developmental approach, although not religious in nature, approximates the same type of reasoning.

Even though mature forms of moral judgment are positively related to age, it is not unusual to find adults functioning at the lower levels. They appear to be locked into less developed forms of thinking, and, unaware of their state, they encourage the same immaturity in others. An act is judged according to objective consequences rather than according to intent. The viewpoint of the one in authority, be it parent or teacher or minister, is said to be the right one with little regard given to the perspectives of those within their charge. An act is said to be good or bad in terms of whether or not it violates a rule or a law, while relationships between people as a consequence of that act is given little attention. Concrete forms of reciprocity take on great importance; there is a call for more severe forms of punishment for the recalcitrant; and misfortunes are immediately linked with personal inadequacies.

One might expect that those who call themselves Christians would strive for the mature moral judgments so beautifully given in Jesus' teachings and exemplified by his life. Unfortunately, this does not appear to be the case. The world and our own selfish desires are too much with us. And, like the Pharisees, we can readily quote Scripture, interpreting it to our advantage and thus feel complacent and even smug in our "righteous" but immature world. A perusal of recently published articles and books by Christian authors reveals a high number that advocate ideas and behaviors typical of low levels of moral judgment. The impact of this literature on the Christian world is tremendous and serves to secure the reader at immature stages of cognition. Jesus has given us an example that we should follow in his steps. What better place to go than to Jesus himself? No parent or minister or Christian writer can usurp that position. Only by looking unto him can we expect to attain desirable levels of moral judgment.

References

Dewey, J. *The Quest for Certainty: A Study of the Relationship of Knowledge and Action.* New York: Minton, Balch & Co., 1929.

The Gospels According to St. Matthew, St. Luke, and St. John, King James Version and Today's English Version.

Kohlberg, L. "Development of Moral Character and Moral Ideology." In M. L. Hoffman (ed.), *Review of Child Development Research,* Vol. 1. New York: Russell Sage Foundation, 1964.

————. "The Child as a Moral Philosopher." *Psychology Today.* Sept., 1968, *2,* 24-30.

————. "The Quest for Justice in 200 Years of American History and in Contemporary American Education." *Contemporary Education,* 1976, *48,* 5-16.

Krebs, R. L. "Some Relationships Between Moral Judgment, Attention, and Resistance to Temptation." Doctoral dissertation, University of Chicago, 1968.

Piaget, J. *The Moral Judgment of the Child.* London: K. Paul, Trench, Trubner & Co., 1932.

Sears, R., Rau, L., and Alpert R. *Identification and Child Rearing.* Stanford: Stanford University Press, 1965.

Ziv, A. "Measuring Aspects of Morality." *Journal of Moral Education,* 1975, *5,* 189-201.

KOHLBERG'S THEORY OF MORAL DEVELOPMENT AND THE CHRISTIAN FAITH

Dan Motet

Kohlberg's theory is one of the most interesting approaches to the subject of moral development. His views, although criticized by some, are generally received by psychologists and have found large application in education. Considering the fact that moral education is one of the important objectives of the church, this article attempts an integration of Kohlberg's ideas with the Christian faith. The first part of this article describes some analogies between the theory and scriptural material. The second part includes some hypotheses concerning the generalization of Kohlberg's theory from moral reasoning to motivation in general with possible application to evangelism.

Kohlberg sees the moral development occurring in six stages. The following will consider his earlier definition (Kohlberg, 1975) of the stages as being clearer than the latest modification (1976).

Stage 1: The punishment-obedience orientation—In this stage the individual acts in order to avoid punishment and out of deference to power.

Stage 2: The instrumental-relativist orientation—Right action is that which satisfies one's own needs and occasionally the needs of others, especially when something in return is expected. Elements of reciprocity are present but interpreted in a physical, pragmatic way. Human relationships are seen in marketplace-like terms.

Stage 3: The interpersonal concordance or "good boy-nice girl" orientation—In this stage a seeking for approval by others is characteristic. Good behavior is that which pleases and helps others.

Stage 4: The "law and order" orientation—This stage involves respect for authority and obedience towards fixed rules for their own sake. The maintenance of the social order and doing one's duty are important.

Stage 5: The social-contract orientation with utilitarian overtones—The general individual rights and standards which have been critically examined and agreed upon by the whole society are important. It is still an emphasis upon the "legal point of view," but the laws are seen as being more flexible and can be changed if they are not adequate.

© *Journal of Psychology and Theology*, 1978, 6 (1), 18-21. Used by permission of the author.

Stage 6: The universal-ethical-principle orientation—The individual is guided by his conscience in accordance with the self-chosen ethical principles. These principles are abstract and ethical, as the Golden Rule, rather than concrete moral rules like the Ten Commandments. Universal principles of justice, reciprocity and equality of human rights, and respect for the dignity of human beings as individual persons are stressed.

The person progresses through these stages in succession from one to six without skipping any of them. Therefore, the immediate purpose of moral education should be to raise the student to the stage next superior to the one in which he functions at that moment.

It should be mentioned that Kohlberg's hierarchy relates to moral judgment not necessarily to moral behavior, but the two are positively correlated, and behavior can be an indicator of moral judgment.

Kohlberg's approach is analogous to what we find in Scripture, where we can follow God's work to raise human moral judgment through the six stages. The events that started with the Exodus are a good example. After the destruction of the Pharaoh's army, the people accepted Moses' leadership because "they feared the Lord" (Exod. 14:31). They had seen the Egyptian gods and magicians humiliated during the plagues, and the mighty army of the "Son of the Gods," the Pharaoh, annihilated in a spectacular and miraculous way by Moses' God. Yahweh was stronger, and nobody could oppose him without consequences. So they obeyed Moses out of deference to power; and in order to avoid sharing the fate of Pharaoh's army, they "feared the Lord," not in the sense of awe as usually this fear is understood in Scriptures, but they actually were afraid of the physical consequences of disobedience. Their moral judgment was in Stage 1. This lowest level of moral development was probably due to the stifling effect of slavery and oppressing conditions in which survival was the highest on the hierarchy of values.

Later, during their wandering in the wilderness, the Hebrews murmured against Moses and Aaron complaining about the lack of food (Exod. 16:2-3). We see that the obedience out of deference to power changed into a motivation based on the satisfaction of one's own needs characteristic to the second stage of instrumental-relativistic orientation. The elements of marketplace-like exchange in human relationships are seen in their longing for Egypt, with the willingness to give up freedom for the desired food.

The third stage of moral development, in which the main motivation is seeking for approval by others, is illustrated by Aaron himself when he gives up to the request of the people and makes them a golden calf (Exod. 32). When Moses returns from the mountain, he finds among the Hebrews a group that declares itself on the Lord's side. They were strong enough to slay the stubborn idol worshipers, but where were they during the golden calf worship episode? Probably, they joined in or remained neutrally motivated by the need for approval. Maybe it was the same motivation that brought them on Moses' side once he showed up.

God's work to bring the Jews to the fourth stage, the "law and order" orientation, is illustrated by the giving of the Ten Commandments (Exod. 20:1-17) and the Law in general. It is at this fourth stage that later the Pharisees remained fixated, and many of the conflicts between them and Jesus arose because he tried to bring them to the superior levels of moral judgment. One example was his interpretation of the laws concerning the Sabbath as being flexible (Matt. 12:1-14). By this Jesus was trying to bring the fourth level people to the next superior one, the fifth level.

Stage 6, the universal-ethical-principle orientation is illustrated best by the great personalities of the Scriptures. Moses follows his conscience and his decisions are based on self-chosen principles. Contrary to his upbringing, but according to his conscience, he defended the Hebrew against the Egyptian. He accepted Yahweh as his God only after he was convinced that he is the true God, the God of his ancestors. Even in his interaction with God, Moses first tries to understand and internalize a principle, then follows it faithfully. He also pleads with God for his people; selflessly and loyally he risks his own future for them (Exod. 32:11-13, 31, 32).

There are other numerous examples in the Scriptures that illustrate Kohlberg's stages and how people occasionally act at levels inferior to the one in which they are or even regress for a longer period of time. In reference to this, David is an interesting example. Although he puts his trust in God (Stage 4), he also inquires repeatedly about the reward promised to the one that would kill Goliath, a Stage 2 motivation (1 Sam. 17:22-30). Later, when David finds his enemy Saul defenseless in a cave, he spares his life because Saul was his king chosen by God (Stage 4); but, we also find in his thinking elements of Stage 3 as he cuts a piece of the king's robe which will be used to prove his noble deed and obtain the favors of Saul (1 Sam. 24). Stage 5 is displayed by David when he restores to Mephibosheth, the grandson of his enemy Saul, all his wealth, rights, and honors (2 Sam. 9), or earlier, when starving with his men, he eats the sacred bread from the Temple (1 Sam. 21), bending the ritual laws. However, this great man displayed regression to Stage 2 when he sent Uriah to be killed in order to marry his wife, Bathsheba (2 Sam. 11). Still, after his repentance, David reaches the sixth stage reflected in the beautiful lines from Psalm 51:10: "Create in me a clean heart, O God, and put a new and right spirit within me."

One of the problems that a Christian faces in accepting Kohlberg's theory is that Stage 6, following your own conscience, is often claimed by adherents to the "do your own thing" philosophy frequently synonymous with a hedonistic playboy philosophy. The answer is relatively simple because of two reasons: First, the "do your own thing" people are not following universal-ethical-principles but rather their own principles made so that their own needs and desires would be satisfied, which is analogous with Stage 2. Second, according to Kohlberg, in order to reach Stage 6, one has to pass through all the previous stages including Stage 4 that involve the acceptance of an authority. Still the "doing your own thing" person is nearly always scoffing at any authority if not outrightly rebellious which indicates that he never reached Stage 4.

One interesting aspect we might consider is related to a phenomenon that puzzles some observers, namely the great variety of evangelical approaches to which different individuals respond and become converted. A first group responds to a hell, fire, and damnation preacher, while others are turned off by such an approach; a second group is those who respond to Jesus, the Savior and God, as a satisfier of all human needs; the third group is brought into the Christian flock by the believer's love and acceptance and by the idea of a loving God that accepts the lost sheep as well as the righteous; a fourth group accepts Jesus at once as both Savior and as Lord and submit unquestioningly to God's authority; we see, on the other hand, a fifth group who first need to understand the marvelous complexity and liberating power of the gospel and the approach to human wholeness; finally, a sixth group needs to understand and first internalize the Christian theology to accept its teachings as true and then the conversion occurs. Looking at these different groups, it is tempting to hypothesize that they belong to the six stages of moral thinking.

If this hypothesis, still untested, is true, it brings us to a very interesting insight into the psychological concomitants of Christian conversion and growth. An individual would respond best to a message girded to his level of moral judgment or at the level immediately above it. This explains also why some people easily accept Christ as Savior but have a hard time to accept him as Lord: They are only at the second stage and must grow more before a total commitment. On the other hand, we should not ignore God's power to help some "babes" grow fast through the stages; and in this case, we have one of those spectacular changes in the personality of the individual. This power should not be stifled, but the new convert should be helped to grow through the fourth stage of acceptance of authority. Interesting is the fact that Kohlberg observes that very few people are above Stage 4. Indeed, this stage seems to be a stumbling block for many. Some reject it and remain in Stage 3 or even regress to 2.[1] Others grow into Stage 4 but remain fixated in a legalistic form of Christianity.

It appears that Jesus himself gauged his audience and spoke appropriately to all stages. He spoke of hell more than any personality in the Bible, addressing himself probably to the Stage 1 audience. He told the people to ask and it will be given to them as for Stage 2 listeners. Then he spoke about belonging to the body of believers, an idea attractive to the 3 stage people. For the fourth stage he proved his authority and deity. In the fifth stage he presented the Law as being made for man and not man for the Law. He tried to help them to follow the spirit instead of the letter of

[1]It is true that lately Kohlberg seems to reject the possibility of regression. Still, if we accept the existence of regression at least from stages 3 or 2, many of the cases I observed in counseling would be explained.

the Law. Finally, for the sixth stage, he gave the high ethical principle of self-sacrificial love of which he himself was the highest example.

Another element that requires an explanation is the meaning of the conscience that leads the Christian who functions in the sixth stage. We have to accept that for a Christian the universal-ethical-principles that lead him are the scriptural ones. We find both in the Old Testament and in the New Testament some enlightening verses that pertain to this aspect. We have already seen David's prayer from Psalm 51:10. Also,

I hold fast my righteousness, and will not let it go; my heart does not reproach me for any of my days. (Job 27:6)

When Gentiles who have not the law do by nature what the law requires, they are a law to themselves, even though they do not have the law. They show that what the law requires is written on their hearts. . . . (Rom. 2:14, 15)

My conscience bears me witness in the Holy Spirit. (Rom. 9:1)

While I leave it to the theologian to decide, it is a tempting hypothesis that the Christian's conscience is either the indwelling Holy Spirit that guides him and "convicts him of sin and righteousness and of judgment" (John 16:8-10) or represents the internalized God-given universal-ethical-principles. That may be one of the rich meanings of Jesus' words given to us in John 14:20: "I am in my Father, and you in me, and I in you."

References

Kohlberg, L. "The Cognitive-Developmental Approach to the Moral Education." *Phi Delta Kappan,* 1975, *56,* 670-77.
———. "Moral Stages and Moralization: The Cognitive-Developmental Approach." In T. Lickona (ed.), *Moral Development and Behavior.* New York: Holt, Rinehart, and Winston, 1976.

CONVERSION EXPERIENCE, BELIEF SYSTEM, AND PERSONAL AND ETHICAL ATTITUDES

Raymond F. Paloutzian
Steven L. Jackson
James E. Crandall

Does conversion make a difference? From the earliest research on conversion (James, 1958; Starbuck, 1899), there has been speculation regarding the ways that the individual's personal and social life change as a function of conversion. The most fundamental comparisons reported in this article are between people who claim to be Christian converts and those who make no such claim.

Conversions are not necessarily all the same, however, and do not all have the same effects. The following two factors differentiate types of conversion: (a) the type of belief to which converts may be committed, and (b) the type of conversion experience. Underlying the present research is the general hypothesis that belief systems and types of conversion experiences are related to personal, social, and religious attitudes. Specifically, the present research explores the relations between different types of Christian commitments ("ethical" vs. "born again" belief systems), different conversion experiences (sudden, gradual, or unconscious), and attitudinal measures of purpose in life, concern for others, intrinsic and extrinsic religious orientation, and dogmatism.

Belief Systems

Professing Christian converts sometimes define their faith in different terms and sound as though they are committed to different belief systems. Some individuals view themselves as Christians because they follow the Christian moral code. Other persons claim to be Christians because they have accepted Jesus Christ as personal savior. In the present study, the former is termed "ethical" Christianity, and the latter is termed "born again" Christianity.

Of the many ways in which ethical and born again converts may differ, the following are relevant to the present article. First, the Christian who

© *Journal of Psychology and Theology*, Fall 1978, 6 (4), 266-75. Used by permission of the authors.

adopts the born again belief is by implication also committed to Christian ethics even though the ethics might be regarded as secondary. The reverse is not true, however. Adopting Christian ethics as primary does not necessarily imply born again belief; the personal relationship with Christ may be either secondary or absent.

Second, there is a difference in the degree to which the primary object of commitment is personal. Ethical conversion implies commitment to a more-or-less impersonal code, whereas born again conversion involves commitment to a person believed to reside inside the convert. This difference could affect the internalization of the belief system. For example, converts who try to follow impersonal ethical codes may be less likely to internalize the belief system than those who commit themselves to a person believed to have taken up residence within themselves.

Different predictions may be made regarding which type of convert would score higher on measures reflecting Christian ethics and intensity of commitment. On the one hand, we would expect ethicals to score higher because for them the ethical principles take on primary importance. On the other hand, born agains might score higher because they have a greater probability of internalizing their faith. The present studies were designed to test these possibilities.

Types of Conversion

Three types of conversion experiences have been outlined by Scobie (1973, 1975): sudden, gradual, and unconscious. Sudden conversion takes place in a very short period of time, sometimes within only a few hours, and is thought of as being emotionally based. Gradual conversion takes place over an intermediate length of time, wherein the person moves from a point of rejection to a point of acceptance of the faith and is thought to involve a more cognitive and rational process. Unconscious conversion, in which the individual cannot remember ever not believing the faith, is thought to be a result of social learning.

Different types of conversions may affect the intrinsicness, meaningfulness, and maturity of the religious commitment. For example, if unconscious converts acquired their faith through social learning, they might have a more extrinsic, utilitarian, or reinforcement-directed orientation to their faith than other converts. Also, sudden and gradual conversion may result in a greater experience of meaning for the individual than unconscious conversion. This effect could be due to (1) a greater perception of decision and personal choice in adopting the religion in the case of sudden and gradual conversions, and (2) the satisfaction of previously unmet emotional needs or cognitive needs for meaning. The present research explores these issues.

Dependent Measures and Hypotheses

Frankl (1955, 1963) proposed that a sense of purpose or meaning in life may be a consequence of a mature religious sentiment. Indeed, one of the theories of conversion is based upon the idea that religious conversion satisfies a cognitive need for meaning (Argyle and Beit-Hallahmi, 1975; Scobie, 1975). The Purpose in Life Test (PIL) (Crumbaugh and Maholick, 1964, 1969) was designed to measure this construct. Prior research has consistently shown a positive relation between commitment to Christianity and high PIL scores (Crumbaugh, 1968; Crandall and Rasmussen, 1975; Soderstrom and Wright, 1977; Paloutzian, 1976). Therefore, in the present study, it was hypothesized that Christians would score higher on PIL than non-Christians. Differences in PIL between born agains and ethicals and among the three conversion types were also assessed.

It has been proposed (Scobie, 1975) that different types of conversion experiences are associated with different degrees of religious maturity. Scobie (1975) argued that sudden and gradual converts are more likely to have an intrinsic religious orientation (Allport and Ross, 1967) because of "inner feelings" associated with their more dramatic religious experiences. Scobie further suggests that unconscious converts are more extrinsic or conventional since their religion has been acquired through a social learning process which may not have fostered a very strong personal commitment to the beliefs. Therefore, in the present research, it was hypothesized that sudden and gradual converts would score more intrinsic and less extrinsic than unconscious converts on the Religious Orientation Scale (Allport and Ross, 1967). Also, since three studies report data associating intrinsicness with high PIL (Bolt, 1975; Crandall and Rasmussen, 1975; Soderstrom and Wright, 1977), it was expected that intrinsicness and PIL would be positively correlated.

Conversion to the Christian belief system implies a commitment to Christian ethics. The concept of social interest was developed by Adler (1964) as one type of ethical attitude. By "social interest," he meant concern for the welfare of others, an idea clearly part of Christian ethics. The Social Interest Scale (SIS) was developed by Crandall (1975) to measure this concept. SIS scores are positively related to peer ratings, cooperative and altruistic behavior, empathy, and interpersonal attraction (Crandall, 1975, 1977; Crandall and Harris, 1976). Of more immediate relevance, the SIS correlated positively with the PIL ($r = +.32$) (Crandall, 1975). As related to conversion, Morris and Morris (1976) found that "saved" Christians scored significantly higher on SIS than persons who answered negatively to being a "saved" Christian. Among the "saved" group, those reporting a conversion experience scored higher on SIS than those not reporting a conversion experience. These findings suggest that a conversion experience may have some beneficial effect in increasing one's concern for others. In light of this, in the present research it was hypothesized that Christians would score higher on SIS than non-Christians, and that sudden and gradual converts (who are more likely to report having had a conversion experience) would score higher on SIS than unconscious converts.

There is some evidence to indicate that type of conversion experience is related to cognitive style. Stanley (1964) found a small correlation ($r = +.19$) between Rokeach's (1956) dogmatism scale and sudden conversion. Wilson (1976) found that sudden converts were more dogmatic than gradual converts. Morris and Morris (1976) found that college students reporting a conversion experience were higher in dogmatism than those not reporting such an experience. In the present research, it was hypothesized that sudden converts would score higher on a measure of dogmatic cognitive style than unconscious converts.

Study 1: College Students

Method

Subjects. A total of 84 students in an Introductory Psychology course at the University of Idaho received course credit for participating as subjects. There were 49 females, 32 males, and three people who did not identify their sex. Ages ranged from 18 to 33, with a mean of 19.5 years. Participation was voluntary and anonymous.

Instruments and procedure. Subjects were tested in a small classroom in groups of five to ten. The assessment device was a self-administered questionnaire. It consisted of a face sheet with instructions and questions on sex, age, and educational level and a back sheet asking for information on religious experiences and beliefs. Counterbalanced between these were the four dependent variable scales:

1. The Purpose in Life Test (Crumbaugh and Maholick, 1969), consisting of 20 items, each rated from 1 (low purpose) to 7 (high purpose). Average group means typically fall between 100-108 on this test.

2. The Intrinsic-Extrinsic Religious Orientation Scale appearing in Robinson and Shaver (1973).

3. The Social Interest Scale (Crandall, 1975), consisting of 24 pairs of traits, including 15 scored items and 9 buffer items. Subjects must choose the one trait of each pair that they value more. The SIS score is the total number of social interest traits chosen.

4. The Short Dogmatism Scale (Troldahl and Powell, 1965), consisting of 20 items scored from -3 to $+3$.

On the last page of the questionnaire, Christian status was assessed by asking, "Do you profess to be a Christian?" Subjects could circle "yes" or "no." If they answered "yes," belief system and conversion type were then measured. Assessment of born again versus ethical belief system was done by placing subjects in a forced choice situation, wherein they had to choose one and only one of the following statements:

1. "I respect and attempt to follow the moral and ethical teachings of Christ" (ethical statement).
2. "I have received Jesus Christ into my life as my personal Savior and Lord" (born again statement).

Assessment of type of conversion experience was accomplished with the procedure used by Scobie (1973). Subjects first read brief descriptions of the three conversion types and then chose the description that most clearly represented their own experience.

Results and Discussion

Data analysis. The data were categorized in three ways.[1] First, they were placed into Christian and non-Christian groups. Second, the Christian group was divided into born again and ethical subgroups. Third, the Christian group was divided into sudden, gradual, and unconscious conversion subgroups. (No 2×3 [belief system × conversion type] analysis of variance was done due to an insufficient number of subjects in the ethical-gradual and ethical-sudden cells.)

TABLE 1
Mean Attitude Scores of Christians and Non-Christians

Study 1: College Students

Attitude Measure	Christian (N = 66)	Non-Christian (N = 18)	t
Purpose in Life	112.11	104.67	2.44*
Social Interest	9.94	7.33	3.08**
Dogmatism	-10.59	-14.67	1.14

Study 2: Adults

Attitude Measure	Christian (N = 147)	Non-Christian (N = 30)	t
Purpose in Life	115.33	102.57	5.29***
Social Interest	11.21	6.70	7.36***
Dogmatism	-8.75	-19.23	3.45***

Note: All of the scales are scored so that a higher number represents more of that construct.

*$p<.05$
**$p<.01$
***$p<.001$

[1]In addition to the analyses presented, the data were analyzed with sex of subject treated as an independent variable. Overall, sex differences were minor and nonsignificant.

Belief and conversion type. The mean scores for professing Christians and non-Christians on purpose in life, social interest, and dogmatism are summarized in table 1. Professing Christians had significantly[2] higher mean scores on both the purpose in life and social interest measures. The two groups did not differ significantly on mean dogmatism scores. The data are consistent with our hypothesis, and suggest that subjects who claimed to be Christians were higher in sense of purpose and social interest than those not claiming to be Christians.

The mean scores on purpose in life, intrinsic and extrinsic religious orientation, social interest, and dogmatism for the born again and ethical Christian groups are presented in table 2. Significant differences between born agains and ethicals appeared on three of the dependent measures. The born again group scored significantly higher than the ethicals on purpose in life, social interest, and intrinsic religious orientation. The

TABLE 2
Mean Attitude Scores of Professed Christians with Different Belief Systems and Different Types of Conversions

Study 1: College Students

	Belief System			Type of Conversion			
		Born		Uncon-	Grad-	Sud-	
	Ethical	Again	*t*	scious	ual	den	*F*
Measure	(N = 32)	(N = 34)		(N = 36)	(N = 25)	(N = 5)	
Purpose in Life	109.41	114.65	2.04*	112.14	110.68	119.00	1.27
Intrinsicness	28.84	35.56	3.72**	31.69	31.32	41.60	3.99*
Extrinsicness	33.03	30.21	1.67	32.11	31.68	27.20	1.10
Social Interest	8.94	10.88	2.59*	9.58	10.00	12.20	1.52
Dogmatism	-13.53	-7.82	1.81	-12.69	-9.20	-2.40	1.62

Study 2: Adults

	Belief System			Type of Conversion[a]			
Attitude		Born		Uncon-	Grad-	Sud-	
Measure	Ethical	Again	*t*	scious	ual	den	*F*
	(N = 42)	(N = 105)		(N = 67)	(N = 44)	(N = 33)	
Purpose in Life	113.40	116.10	1.29	114.69	114.20	117.12	0.70
Intrinsicness	30.43	41.11	12.30**	35.66	39.14	41.45	10.14**
Extrinsicness	34.19	24.87	7.51**	29.88	26.95	23.79	7.31**
Social Interest	9.71	11.81	4.06**	10.49	11.61	12.15	4.10*
Dogmatism	-13.57	-6.82	2.43*	-11.75	-7.75	-4.73	2.48

Note: All of the scales are scored so that a higher number represents more of that construct.
[a] Data for three subjects were not included due to incomplete information regarding conversion type.

*p < .05
**p < .001

[2] Unless otherwise stated, 2-tailed *t* tests were used to test the significance of differences between two groups.

differences for extrinsicness and dogmatism were nonsignificant. These results suggest that, as compared to the ethicals, the born again group may experience a greater sense of meaning in life and may be more intrinsically motivated toward their faith. Also, these findings are consistent with the notion that subjects who espouse a born again statement of belief are more likely to internalize the ethical system implied by their commitment.

Table 2 presents the mean scores on the dependent variable scales for sudden, gradual, and unconscious converts. For each of the scales, significance of differences among the three groups was tested with an analysis of variance. Significant differences were obtained on the measure of intrinsic religious orientation, with the sudden converts having higher intrinsicness scores than either the gradual or the unconscious converts. No other analysis in this series yielded significant differences. These data are consistent with our prediction that sudden converts would score higher on intrinsicness than unconscious converts, but they do not support our hypotheses that extrinsicness and social interest would be related to conversion type.

TABLE 3
Intercorrelations of Attitude Measures

Attitude Measure	Intrinsic-ness	Extrinsic-ness	Social Interest	Dogmatism
Study 1: College Students				
Purpose in Life	.34**	-.15	.25*	-.07
Intrinsicness		-.13	.53***	.14
Extrinsicness			.04	.18
Social Interest				.04
Study 2: Adults				
Purpose in Life	.37***	-.05	.44***	.05
Intrinsicness		-.40***	.50***	.22***
Extrinsicness			-.2**	.08
Social Interest				.27***

Note: All statistical tests are 2-tailed.
*$p<.05$
**$p<.01$
***$p<.001$

The intercorrelations among the five attitude measures are presented in table 3. The pattern of correlations indicates that purpose in life, intrinsicness, and social interest tend to cluster together to a moderate degree, and that these three are relatively independent of extrinsicness and dogmatism.

Study 2: Adults

Since the subject sample for study 1 included only college students, the generalizability of the findings to the full range of the adult population is limited. Study 2 was conducted in order to test whether the pattern of results obtained for college students would also be obtained for a more representative sample of the adult population.

Method

A total of 177 adults ranging in age from 21 to 82 participated voluntarily and anonymously. This sample included 86 people drawn from Sunday classes of local churches and 91 people randomly selected from the University of Idaho nonacademic staff. Several denominations were represented in the church sample. The total sample contained 110 females, 38 males, and 9 persons who did not identify their sex. The mean age was 35 years.

The instruments used in study 2 were the same as those used in study 1. Subjects from local churches were given the questionnaire at their Sunday classes and returned them in stamped, self-addressed envelopes. Subjects in the university staff sample were mailed the questionnaire via campus mail and returned it via campus mail.

Results and Discussion

Belief and conversion type. The overall pattern of results for study 2 largely replicates the results of study 1, with a few modifications. Table 1 summarizes the data for the Christian-non-Christian comparisons and indicates that professing Christians scored significantly higher on purpose in life, social interest, and dogmatism. These findings parallel those of study 1, with the addition of a significant difference in dogmatism for the adult sample.

Table 2 summarizes the data for comparisons between the born again and ethical groups. The born again group scored significantly higher on the scales of intrinsicness, social interest, and dogmatism and lower on the scale of extrinsicness. Unlike the results for college students in study 1, the born agains were not significantly higher on the purpose in life test than the ethicals. As in study 1, these data are consistent with the notion that a born again commitment fosters greater internalization of the belief system and, in addition, that these are associated with a slightly more dogmatic cognitive style than the ethical type of commitment.

The mean scores on the attitudinal measure for the three conversion types appear in table 2. Significant differences among means were obtained on three scales: intrinsicness, extrinsicness, and social interest. Sudden converts were the highest in intrinsicness and social interest and lowest in extrinsicness. The reverse pattern emerged for the unconscious convert group: they scored highest on extrinsicness, and lowest on intrinsicness and social interest. The gradual convert group scored between the other two groups on these scales. Post hoc Scheffe tests revealed that, for all three scales, the statistical significance was due to the difference between the sudden and unconscious groups and not between either of those and the gradual group.

Belief System-Conversion Type Relationship

Inspection of the means for adults in table 2 reveals that the three measures that yielded significant contrasts for conversion type also yielded significant contrasts for belief system. This raises the possibility that the significant differences on these measures for conversion type may not actually be due to conversion type but rather to covariation of conversion type with belief system. In order to explore this issue, additional analyses were run which were not run in study 1 due to a different pattern of significances and an insufficient number of sudden converts. A separate analysis of variance was performed on each of the dependent variable scales across the three conversion types within the born again group. No significant differences among means on any of the five scales was found among conversion types within the born again group. These findings suggest that the three significant overall analyses that appeared for conversion types could have been a function of an association between conversion type and belief system, particularly between the ethical belief system and the unconscious conversion type. The relationship between belief system and conversion type, presented in table 4, clarifies this issue. It can be seen in table 4 that conversion type and belief system are significantly associated. Only one out of 33 sudden converts consider themselves ethical believers. Almost 80 percent of those who espouse an ethical belief system fall into the unconscious convert category. The findings that no significant differences among means were found across conversion type within the born again group, and that the vast majority of ethical believers fall into the unconscious convert cell, imply that the overall significant differences obtained for conversion type are actually due to belief, that is, almost half of the unconscious converts also espoused an ethical belief system.

TABLE 4
Frequencies of Conversion Type by Belief System: Study 2

Belief System	Conversion Type			
	Unconscious	Gradual	Sudden	Total
Ethical	32	8	1	41
Born Again	35	36	32	103
Total	67	44	33	144

Note: Data for three subjects were not included due to incomplete information regarding conversion type.

$x^2(2) = 25.97$, $p < .001$

The relationships among the scales for the adult sample are presented in table 3. Purpose in life, intrinsicness, and social interest cluster together as they did for the college student sample. In adults, however, intrinsicness and social interest also seem to be mildly, but significantly, associated with dogmatism. Also, in the adults, intrinsicness and social interest are negatively associated with extrinsicness rather than nearly independent as in the college student sample.

General Discussion

The overall pattern of findings speaks clearly to the questions guiding the present research and supports some of the hypotheses. The finding that Christians scored higher than non-Christians on purpose in life is consistent with our predictions and with prior research (Crandall and Rasmussen, 1975; Paloutzian, 1976). The finding that Christians scored higher than non-Christians on social interest is understandable in light of the high degree of correspondence between the qualities that make up social interest as Adler conceived it (e.g., helpful, sympathetic, forgiving, patient) and the characteristics that are central in Christianity. It may be noted that the Christians increased in social interest from the college to the adult samples, whereas the non-Christians decreased slightly. This could imply that Christians adhere to Christian ethics increasingly with age. Table 1 reveals that the contrast between Christians and non-Christians increases with age on all three measures. The finding that, for adults, Christians were more dogmatic than non-Christians, even though both groups scored on the negative (nondogmatic) side of the scale, suggests that acceptance of Christian beliefs is associated with a more close-minded approach to information inconsistent with the Christian position. The non-Christian may be less certain about what he/she believes to be true and, consequently, may be more open to differing viewpoints. The nonsignificant difference in dogmatism for the college students suggests that there is no important difference between Christian and non-Christian students in the degree to which they are openminded. However, older Christians are apparently slightly more dogmatic, while older non-Christians are apparently somewhat less dogmatic.

Perhaps the most intriguing findings of the present research are those regarding born again versus ethical belief systems. The born again group scored higher in social interest in both age groups studied, even though they are primarily committed to the person of Christ, and are secondarily committed to the ethics. Via "common sense," one might predict that the ethicals would score higher on social interest since they are more directly committed to the ethics themselves. These results support the notion that the born again commitment fosters greater internalization of Christian ethics.

The finding that born-agains scored higher on intrinsicness also supports this view. A related finding is that the contrast between born-agains and ethicals on intrinsicness and extrinsicness increases from the college to the adult sample. Table 2 reveals that this effect is due primarily to an increase in intrinsicness and a decrease in extrinsicness for the adult born again as compared to those in the college sample. This could imply that the born again type of commitment is more likely to mature with age than the ethical type.

Regarding conversion type, the findings indicate that, in general, sudden converts have a more complete commitment to their beliefs than unconscious converts. Scobie (1973) may be correct in postulating that the "inner feelings" associated with sudden conversion result in deeper commitment to one's faith than the social learning process of unconscious conversion. As discussed previously, however, the differences obtained between sudden and unconscious adult converts were probably a function of the high proportion of ethical believers who were also unconscious converts. These relationships raise the possibility that unconscious conversion facilitates commitment to an ethical belief system and that sudden conversion does not.

Some of the relationships among the dependent measures are worthy of note. The positive association between intrinsicness and purpose in life is consistent with previous findings (Bolt, 1975; Crandall and Rasmussen, 1975; Soderstrom and Wright, 1977), as is the association between social interest and purpose in life (Crandall, 1975). Also of note is the association between intrinsicness and social interest, a finding parallel to the association between intrinsicness and racial tolerance (Allport and Ross, 1967). One unusual finding is a positive correlation between intrinsicness and dogmatism but not between extrinsicness and dogmatism. This result is contradictory to prior findings (Raschke, 1973) and common opinion that the extrinsic religious orientation is more associated with dogmatism. Also, probably inconsistent with common opinion is the positive relationship between dogmatism and social interest. Dogmatism is usually treated as though it is an essentially negative attribute, but the present relationships call this notion into question. What the individual is dogmatic about may be more important than the trait of dogmatism *per se,* at least for the range of people studied in the present research.

The idea of a religious commitment that is intense, mature, and personal may help to tie together the various results of the present studies. In the case of Christianity, such a commitment would foster dedication to one's beliefs, a sense of purpose in life, and concern for others. Finally, it would foster strong adherence to the beliefs in the face of opposing views or incongruent information. Future research should explore the effects of this type of commitment on mental health and on additional social action or ethical indicators. Assessing the behavioral effects of such commitment may be particularly revealing. Whether similar effects result from commitments to non-Christian religions also needs to be explored.

References

Adler, A. *Problems of Neurosis*. New York: Harper & Row, 1964.

Allport, G. W., and Ross, J. M. "Personal Religious Orientation and Prejudice." *Journal of Personality and Social Psychology*, 1967, *5*, 432-43.

Argyle, M., and Beit-Hallahmi, B. *The Social Psychology of Religion*. London: Routledge & Kegan Paul, 1975.

Bolt, M. "Purpose in Life and Religious Orientation." *Journal of Psychology and Theology*, 1975, *3*, 116-18.

Crandall, J. E. "A Scale for Social Interest." *Journal of Individual Psychology*, 1975, *31*, 187-95.

————. "Further Validation of the Social Interest Scale: Peer Ratings and Interpersonal Attraction." *Journal of Clinical Psychology*, 1977, *33*, 140-42.

Crandell, J. E., and Harris, M. D. "Social Interest, Cooperation, and Altruism." *Journal of Individual Psychology*, 1976, *32*, 50-54.

Crandell, J. E., and Rasmussen, R. D. "Purpose in Life as Related to Specific Values." *Journal of Clinical Psychology*. 1975, *31*, 483-85.

Crumbaugh, J. C. "Cross-Validation of a Purpose-in-Life-Test Based on Frankl's Concepts." *Journal of Individual Psychology*, 1968, *24*, 74-81.

Crumbaugh, J. C., and Maholick, L. T. "An Experimental Study in Existentialism: The Psychometric Approach to Frankl's Concept of 'Noogenic Neurosis.'" *Journal of Clinical Psychology*, 1964, *20*, 200-7.

————. *The Purpose in Life Test*. Munster, Ind.: Psychometric Affiliates, 1969.

Frankl, V. *The Doctor and the Soul*. New York: Alfred A. Knopf, 1955.

————. *Man's Search for Meaning: An Introduction to Logotherapy*. New York: Washington Square Press, 1963.

James, W. *The Varieties of Religious Experience*. New York: Mentor, 1958. (First published, 1902.)

Morris, H., and Morris, L. "Conversion: Conditions and Correlates." Unpublished study. Psychology Department, University of Idaho, 1976.

Paloutzian, R. F. "Purpose-in-Life and Value Changes Following Conversion." Paper presented at the American Psychological Association Convention, Washington, D.C., Sept. 4, 1976.

Raschke, V. "Dogmatism of Religiosity, Committed and Consensual." *Journal for the Scientific Study of Religion*, 1973, *72*, 339-44.

Robinson, J. P., and Shaver, P. (eds.). *Measures of Social Psychological Attitudes* (2nd ed.). Ann Arbor, Mich.: Institute for Social Research, 1973.

Rokeach, M. "Political and Religious Dogmatism: An Alternative to the Authoritarian Personality." *Psychological Monographs*, 1956, *43*, 70.

Scobie, G. E. W. "Types of Christian Conversion." *Journal of Behavioral Science*, 1973, *1*, 265-71.

————. *Psychology of Religion*. New York: John Wiley, 1975.

Soderstrom, D., and Wright, E. W. "Religious Orientation and Meaning in Life." *Journal of Clinical Psychology*, 1977, *33*, 65-68.

Stanley, G. "Personality and Attitude Correlates of Religious Conversion." *Journal for the Scientific Study of Religion*, 1964, *4*, 60-63.

Starbuck, E. D. *The Psychology of Religion*. London: Walter Scott, 1899.

Troldahl, V., and Powell, F. "A Short-Form Dogmatism Scale for Use in Field Studies." *Social Forces*, 1965, *44*, 211-14.

Wilson, R. "A Social-Psychological Study of Christian Experience and Conversion." Paper presented at the American Psychological Association Convention, Washington, D. C., Sept. 4, 1976.

Thanks to Patty Ward and Tim Jones for their assistance in this research.

SECTION
FIVE

COUNSELING AND THERAPY

The four articles in this section represent widely divergent attempts at integrating various approaches to psychotherapy with Christianity. In the first article Carlson has proposed Jesus' style of relating in the Gospels as a counseling or therapy model broad enough to include most current psychotherapy approaches. In the remaining three articles psycho-dynamic, cognitive, and Rogerian approaches to therapy are integrated with various aspects of Christianity. Narramore proposes psychodynamic therapy as the best approach to guilt reduction. Pecheur argues that cognitive therapy and spiritual sanctification are identical in process, and cognitive therapy should therefore be the most effective means of obtaining change in clients. In the final article the anonymous author presents a personal account from the client's perspective of the process of Rogerian Therapy.

Carlson has proposed Jesus' style of relating as a model that provides a wide range of interventive-redemptive approaches to healing people. The author's aim is to bridge the gap between various helping professions and to communicate with those in the church who are threatened by these mental health professionals. Carlson has called for going beyond theology and psychology to the development of a Christian mental health perspective. At present, he sees Christian professionals as caught between those who would transform psychology into theology and those who would transform theology into psychology.

It is Carlson's contention that it is a mistake to claim one style of relating or counseling as distinctively Christian or biblical, whether it be a directive, confrontive, preaching style or a nondirective, listening, reflective style. Carlson has referred to the former as "prophetic counseling" and the latter as "priestly counseling." He has represented counselors, Christian or non-Christian, as arguing either for this dichotomous approach emphasizing differences or for an eclectic one emphasizing similarities of counseling approaches.

In contrast, Carlson has presented what he perceives as a biblical view of counseling, one based upon Jesus' style of relating. This biblical view of counseling is seen by Carlson to be continuous rather than dichotomous and integrative rather than eclectic. This continuum moves from the "prophetic" on one end through the "pastoral" to the "priestly" on the other end. It is rooted in the belief that Jesus was never in a dichotomous bind but related to people at their point of need using a multivaried rather than monistic approach. Carlson has called for Christian professionals to expand their repertoire of interventive roles and therapeutic responses in order to provide more correctly a biblical style of counseling.

Is Carlson's biblical model of therapy broad enough to include the three secular approaches to therapy discussed in the three following articles in this section of the book (i.e., psychodynamic, cognitive, and Rogerian)? Did Jesus relate in one or all of these three therapy modalities? If so, cite biblical examples of each.

In a four-part series of articles Narramore has presented a psycho-dynamic model of guilt and interpreted it within a theological framework. The last of the four Narramore articles, contained in this book of readings discusses three therapeutic approaches for reducing guilt: (1) alteration of the ideal self, (2) alteration of performance, and (3) alteration of punitive guilt attitudes.

Narramore has argued that altering one's ideals or levels of performance will give only temporary or superficial symptomatic relief of guilt feelings. He has also discussed both psychological and theological weaknesses of these two therapeutic approaches for guilt reduction.

The third therapy approach, alteration of punitive guilt attitudes, is viewed by Narramore as providing the only avenue for long-term guilt reduction. It is a psychodynamic therapy model that gives primary attention to the origin and history of a patient's punitive guilt attitudes. It allows the therapist to focus upon the internalization of attitudes that allow patients to experience more completely the psychological significance of Christ's atonement.

Is Narramore correct in assuming that long-term psychodynamic-oriented therapy is the only approach useful in providing long-term guilt reduction? How would the cognitive therapist bring about guilt reduction? How would the Rogerian or other humanistic-existential therapists bring about guilt reduction? How would the strict behaviorist view guilt and its reduction?

Pecheur has presented a biblical rationale for cognitive therapy by proposing that the process posited by cognitive theorists to underlie change and growth in therapy is identical to the scriptural process of sanctification. Cognitive therapy and sanctification have been conceptualized by Peucheur as following the same four-stage process with differences only in content.

Cognitive therapy is viewed as a self-control technique whereby the individual develops the ability to regulate his own internal and external behavior in four stages: (1) The client is presented with the rationale for cognitive therapy; (2) the client becomes an observer of his thoughts, feelings, and behaviors by means of heightened awareness; (3) the process of self-observation lays the foundation for the client to emit a set of incompatible self-statements and images, and incompatible behaviors; and (4) the nature and content of what the client says to himself about the behavior change and its accompanying consequences determines the persistence and generalization of the treatment effects.

Sanctification is viewed as the process of restoration of God's image in each Christian, and this process of spiritual growth also occurs in four stages: (1) The Christian recognizes that his covert thoughts reflect the intents of his heart; (2) the Christian becomes an observer of his thoughts by means of heightened awareness and the Word of God; (3) the Christian puts off the old man and puts on the new man through the renewing of the mind; and (4) the Christian's growth is reinforced by the resources of Christianity.

Pecheur has argued that cognitive therapy makes explicit the process of growth indicated in Scripture and should therefore be the most effective means of obtaining change in clients.

Is Pecheur correct in assuming that cognitive therapy and sanctification are identical in process? Are other therapy approaches (e.g., psychodynamic or Rogerian) also compatible with Scripture in general and the process of sanctification in specific? Is Pecheur correct in arguing that, because of its biblical integration, cognitive therapy should be the most effective means of obtaining change in clients?

In the final article, anonymously written, the author has given the reader an inside look at her experiences as a Christian in therapy with a Rogerian therapist. She has equated her therapy experience to being reborn, to being led from darkness to light in a similar fashion as her original birth and later spiritual rebirth.

In relating the stages of therapy of the client the author has stressed the importance of client self-disclosure and the problems, especially for the Christian client, in handling the emerging relationship with the therapist. The therapist is perceived as almost Godlike, creating guilt and tension for the Christian client who may feel considerable distance from God at this point in life. However, the author has related how her horizontal relationship with an accepting therapist contributed to an exciting renewal in her vertical relationship with God.

Would experiences with therapists using other therapy modalities be similar to those experienced by this author with a Rogerian therapist? Is Jay Adams correct in seeing Rogerian therapy as unbiblical and inappropriate for the Christian client?

JESUS' STYLE OF RELATING: THE SEARCH FOR A BIBLICAL VIEW OF COUNSELING

David E. Carlson

As professionals in the mental health field, we have been separated from each other because of our differing academic preparations and theoretical orientations. But that is only part of a sad story. More importantly, we have been separated from a large part of the body of Christ who fear psychology.

This paper is directed toward the task of bridging the gap between various helping professions and dedicated to communicating with those in the church who are threatened by us. The major task facing us is integration between mental health professions and between Christian therapists and the Christian church. It is within this context—the need of integration—that I offer these thoughts regarding Jesus' style of relating.

Harry Blamires (1963) argues that there is no Christian mind. That is, there is no collective viewpoint from which Christians can begin talking with each other about the Christian view of the major issues of our day. I believe conferences and articles are a start in establishing a collective Christian mind. But we have several hurdles to overcome if we are to bridge the gap between the two cultures—one theological, the other scientific.

Culture Conflict

The first hurdle we must face is the problem of cultural conflict. Christianity has historically been confronted by challenges to faith. Often these challenges have come from within Christianity. Christians who are uncomfortable with the ambivalent position of being "in" the world but not "of" the world have historically presented much of the challenge. As evangelical Christians we are still struggling with an uneasy relationship to culture. Richard Niebuhr (1951) describes this as the Christ against culture position. If we are to accomplish integration, we must find ways to bridge this anticulture position. Some of us have ignored this issue by separating our counseling profession from our Christian faith. I don't believe this is an

Presented at a conference on "Research in Mental Health and Religious Behavior," Atlanta, Georgia, January 24-26, 1976. © *Journal of Psychology and Theology*, 1976, *4*, 181-92. Used by permission of the author.

adequate response to the challenge. But ignoring the Christ and culture controversy is no more satisfactory than the segregationist posture. We need to affirm and demonstrate that Christ is not necessarily against mental health perspectives, psychology, social work, sociology. We need to find ways for the church to cope with perspectives that appear threatening and challenging to its view of the world. I am convinced that if integration is to be accomplished, we need to rethink the question of the relationship of Christ to culture. It will mean that we do not confuse Christ with Christianity or cultural evangelicalism with Christian culture (Dolby, 1972).

At the heart of the problem of integrating Christianity with mental health, then, is the need for a reintegration of our two cultures—one theological and the other scientific. Some have abandoned the quest altogether as impossible, nonsensical, or anti-Christian. But the problem still faces us, how are we going to relate relation with research? It seems to me we need to try something that Constantine, Calvin, and a host of others attempted and succeeded to do with questionable results—to go beyond theology and psychology. We need to develop a Christian mental health perspective.

If we are to develop an integrated model, we can only do so by assuming a posture quite different from the Christ against culture perspective. While we need to maintain a commitment to the authority and inspiration of Scripture and belief in the corrupting, distorting, and destructive influence of sin in human thinking, we cannot long maintain a vital culture or community by renouncing everything which has its source in extra-biblical thinking or research. I assume that most of us submitted to the old evangelical culture of denial only to find out that as we acted out most of those ritualistic denials of knowledge and pleasure, they no longer contributed to our spiritual or mental health (Reiff, 1968, p. 254). It seems to me our efforts may be understood as an individual and communal attempt to stabilize our own ambivalent relation to our faith. We must be aware of a break in the continuity of evangelical culture and Christian community in order to take steps toward restoration and healing.

Cultural Lag

A second problem facing those of us who are interested in integration is cultural lag. Our techniques and tools for assisting hurting people are advanced beyond our theology. It seems to me we have a nineteenth century theology and a twentieth century methodology of helping people. I hasten to point out that I view theology as a changing interpretation of scriptural truth. That is theology is not a static view of Scripture. I am committed to propositional unchanging truth, but I believe our conceptions of truth change. What we need is a contemporary interpretation of Scripture which can relate to the developments and insights of contemporary mental health viewpoints.

To add to this difficulty, no systematic theologian as far as I know has addressed the problem of integrating the helping professions and biblical truth. There are literally hundreds of psychologists, psychiatrists, social workers, and others who have attempted to relate their discipline with Christianity. But where are the theologians' attempts at integration? I suppose one would recognize Tillich and the Niebuhrs as approaching integration from the theological left. And within the evangelical camp Carnell, Busell, and Henry could be recognized for some attempt at integration. But, most theologians seem to have little interest or preparation to discuss integration with those of us in the mental health professions. This has left most of us with having to develop our own scriptural and theological foundation to our counseling practice through informal or formal seminary education. We are in a curious position as Christian professionals; seemingly we are either professionals in the helping professions and amateurs in theology or professionals in theology and amateurs in helping theory. In this age of specialization, we need to engage in dialogue, to study and learn from each other. The job of integration is certainly too big for one person to develop competency in both fields.

Those of us who are attempting to integrate Christian theology and therapeutic theory must face our theological and psychological limitations squarely. We must be willing to reexamine our integration model. We must reject the temptation to defend our position through the use of overworked biblical texts proclaiming these as the only important words God has spoken. I'll let you supply your own illustrations of this problem to avoid the criticism of taking potshots at anyone. Yet, my point is that we must be willing to welcome controversy and debate because it is through these processes that our theory and practice are enriched, modified, and corrected.

Authority

A key problem confronting those interested in integration is the issue of scriptural authority and relevance. This question can be described in several ways. At one level the controversy is between a conception of Scripture as the only source of truth and ultimate source of truth. At a second level the controversy is over the relationship of special revelation to natural revelation. Often persons who hold this view tend to confuse scriptural data with theological interpretation. That is, they ignore the need to discover, study, and research the meaning of special and natural revelation. More specifically, the controversy can be expressed by asking three questions:

(1) What are the permissive limitations of man's creativity in counseling theory and technique beyond the biblical record? That is, is it permissible for man to create theory and technique beyond that which Scripture describes?

(2) Is Scripture our only legitimate source of information about counseling?

(3) What is the interrelationship between revelation and research? How should (can) these inform and enrich each other?

Within the evangelical community many are defensive about learning from extrabiblical sources and non-Christian persons. This posture often leads to a distorted and exaggerated set of claims for what the Bible says.

These persons attempt to discover a biblical basis or approach for counseling to the exclusion of clinical and experimental data. Others have bought a view of counseling to the exclusion of any biblical or theological input. I am concerned about both groups of people: those who have enthusiastically bought counseling as a legitimate methodology of ministry but continue to renunciate the sources of counseling theory as necessarily anti-Christian; and those who buy counseling theory and practice yet remain uncritical of its theological presuppositions or implications.

Hermeneutics

There are at least two other major integration problems both of which I will address more specifically later in the paper. One hindrance to integration is the issue of selective hermeneutics—that is, choosing only those portions of Scripture which support your particular view of counseling. The other hindrance to integration is the personality needs of the counselor which encourage the counselor to proclaim Jesus as the answer to all problems in an immediate sense. At the heart of the issue is this question: In what sense is Jesus the answer to problems immediately and/or ultimately?

Integration: The Basic Issue

I sense we are in a curious position—caught between those Christians who attempt to escape culture and the helpers who attempt to escape Christ. I see us Christian professionals caught between those who would transform psychology into theology and those who would transform theology into psychology. To me the process and problem of integration are quite different. I conceive of integration to be the conscious bringing together of the component aspects of psychology and theology without violating their individual autonomy or identity and without ignoring conflict, paradox, and mystery. In this view, integration is more than baptizing psychology with scriptural texts or lining up psychology and theology to see their points of correlation and convergence.

As I suggested earlier, integration is only a concern for the Christian who is willing to consider the relationship between special and natural revelation as informative, corrective, expanding, and interrelated holistically. I expressed this as going beyond theology and psychology.

The basic question, as I see it, for developing a model of integration is, what is the relationship between biblical and nonbiblical data? We must ask more than how Scripture and academic disciplines are related, compatible, or contradictory. We need to go beyond correlation and convergence to confluence and congruence. Integration is more than a harmonizing of Scripture and human research. Integration is built on the foundational belief that all truth is God's truth wherever it is discovered. If one assumes the relationship between Christianity and culture to be necessarily antithetical, then integration is defined as impossible. Taking this Christ against culture position prevents one from asking an essential question, Is there a larger reality or whole of which these disciplines, theology, psychology, psychiatry, and social work are merely the parts?

I would like to suggest a model which has the possibility of integrating doctrinal and theoretical counterpoints without rejecting them as dogmatic contradictions. If I have any unstated assumptions, I suppose they are: (1) that Christ is the living, functioning resolution of the differences between the disciplines, that Christ embodies this greater reality (Col. 2:4), that Christ, rather than one's theology, is the organizing principle because theology has led us all too often to our anticulture posture; and (2) that theology and science are compatible as long as they both direct their search toward what is, and as long as they both continue to assume that some consistent theory and system of description, explanation, and prediction is possible.

The Search for Jesus' Style of Counseling

The search for Jesus' style of counseling is, I suppose, an inevitability for evangelicals. With our high view of Scripture, we are rightly cautious about accepting a view or approach toward helping which is not first checked out with our absolute rule and guide for faith and practice. There is something authoritative, even romantic, in claiming that your style of counseling is biblical and follows our Lord's approach to people. Yet the search for a biblical style of counseling has its pitfalls. For example, to claim an approach is biblical may lead to a wholesale uncritical acceptance of the position. Also, it may be overly optimistic to think one can define Jesus' style of counseling with any more preciseness than defining the New Testament church. And third, one must remember that Jesus was more than a man. Whatever his techniques of counseling, he possessed something quite unique, God-power and God-perspective and God-understanding.

Did Jesus Have a Style of Counseling?

Did Jesus have a style of counseling? Originally, I titled my paper, "Jesus' Style of Counseling." I've reconsidered that idea from both the biblical and current uses of the word "counseling." I now believe it is more correct to talk about Jesus' style of relating. Biblically, the word counseling is never used. When the word "counsel" is used, it is limited to giving or taking advice. The word "counselor" is used in both the Old and New Testaments. Of the three times used in the New Testament (*boulutees,* Mark 15:43, Luke 23:50; *sumboulos,* Rom. 11:34), it is descriptive of a person's employment as advisor. The same meaning is in the Old Testament (see Prov. 11:14; 15:22; 2 Chron. 25:16; Isa. 1:26; 9:6).

Strictly speaking, the twentieth century concept of counseling was foreign to the writers of the New Testament. Counseling as defined currently in the mental health field goes beyond advice giving and broadly describes a variety of interventive strategies. In this paper I choose not to get into the debate over the differences between counseling and psychotherapy. Rather, I prefer to use the concept "counseling" in its generic sense. That is, counseling is descriptive of a wide range of interventive, interpersonal relationships intended to bring about change in another person. Therefore, I conclude that given the current broad use of the word counseling and the narrow biblical use of the word counselor, it would be more precise to describe Jesus' style of relating than limit him to only advice giving or taking.

However, in the current debate among evangelicals, frequently it is claimed that Jesus had a style of counseling. Adams (1973, 1974) is among those who specifically claim Jesus' style of counseling was directive, confrontive, and one of preaching. One of these authors describes his style of counseling supposedly patterned after Jesus' model as, "I simply attempt to speak the truth and face the facts" (Jabay, 1967, p. 44). I have come to describe this position as "prophetic counseling."

On the other side are those authors (Hulme, 1956; May, Lake, and Clinebell, 1966; Hiltner, 1949) who claim their counseling is Christian and implicitly suggest they are modeling Jesus. I describe this counseling approach as "priestly counseling." For the sake of clarity I have outlined what I see to be the major differences between these two approaches:

Christian Counseling Approaches

Prophetic	*Priestly*
convicting	comforting
confronting	confessional
preaching	interviewing
lecturing	listening
thinking for	thinking with
talking to	talking with
proclaiming truth	affirming truth
disturbing the comfortable	comforting the disturbed

Broadly speaking, these two basic approaches could be described as directive and nondirective counseling regardless of their claims to be distinctively Christian. While I independently arrived at this conceptualization of Christian counseling approaches in the two categories "prophetic" and "priestly," they appear to be similar to Frank's (1963, pp. 147-48) two classes of therapeutic methods, directive, and evocative. Also, they largely parallel Wolberg's (1967) reeducative and reconstructive categories. This distinction in counseling positions, of course, has its historical roots in the 40s long before evangelical Christians accepted counseling as a legitimate ministry.

Christian therapists have generally recognized this distinction in their writing. However—and this is the *crux* of the issue—few counselors, Christian or non-Christian, view these divergent counseling approaches as an integrated continuum. For example, Christian counselors generally argue either for an eclectic or dichotomistic approach. On the one hand, the *similarities* of counseling approaches are emphasized, and, on the other hand, the *differences* between counseling approaches are also emphasized. The eclectic view often is an attempt to marry Christian and secular thought with the result that Christian thought often takes second place. The dichotomous view often is an attempt to preserve the authority of Scripture over secular thought with the result that the secular thought is described in almost demonic terms.

A Biblical View of Counseling

The prophetic and priestly approaches appear contradictory and are often claimed to be antithetical to one another. However, I would like to suggest that Jesus' style of counseling incorporated both of these divergent approaches. To assist in presenting my argument, I have utilized the sociological concept of role. For those of you unfamiliar with the concept, "role" can be defined as expected behavior of a person holding a specific social status (position).

I began my exploration of the question, What is Jesus' style of counseling by searching the Gospels to observe what approaches Jesus made to people. What I found is this: Jesus' style of relating to people was varied, not monistic. While it is true that Jesus used confrontation, it is equally accurate to describe Jesus' technique of relating as comforting. Jesus' approach was multivaried; that is, he taught from Scripture, listened, drew pictures, asked questions, told stories from which he asked his listeners to draw their own conclusions. As we take the whole counsel of God into consideration we begin to see that Jesus was not limited to one style of relating.

Reviewing Jesus' dealings with people, there appears an interesting relationship between the role Jesus chose to play and his style of relating. For example, when Jesus took the role of "prophet," he preached, taught, confronted, and called for repentance. When he took the role of "priest," he listened, forgave, mediated, and called for confession. When he assumed the role of "king," he paraded, ruled, and called for the establishment of the kingdom. When he chose the role of "lamb," he sacrificed, accepted ridicule and rejection, and called sinners to be healed by his stripes and bruises. When he submitted to the role of "servant," he washed feet, served food, gave of himself, and called for humility. When he played the role of "shepherd," he fed his flock, nurtured, protected, and called the lost to be found.

TABLE 1
Jesus' Role Repertoire

Status	*Role*
Prophet	Preaching, teaching, confronting, calling for repentance
Priest	Listening, forgiving, mediating, calling for confession
King	Parades, rules, calling for establishment of kingdom
Lamb	Sacrificing, accepting, ridicule, rejection, calling sinners to be healed
Servant	Serving food, nurturing, washing feet, caring for, giving self, calling for humility
Shepherd (Pastoral)	Nurturing, protecting, calling lost to be found

If we attempt to model our counseling or relating after Jesus' example, then, like Jesus, we should play a variety of interventive roles as we relate redemptively to hurting people. I submit that the biblical view of counseling is a multivaried one. It seems to me that if my analysis of Scripture is correct, then it is a mistake to claim one style of relating as distinctively Christian and biblical. It is a mistake in at least two ways: first, because it is based on selective reading and interpretation of Scripture, and second, because it limits the mobility of responses essential for helping.

"One of the measures of competence for the change agent is his ability to shift to another model when this is called for" (Seifert and Clinebell, 1969, p. 54).

A dichotomous view of Christian counseling then is unacceptable. But so is an eclectic view which tends to ignore paradox and conflict. I would like to suggest a biblical view of counseling which is continuous rather than dichotomous, integrative rather than eclectic. The model of counseling which I believe is more accurately descriptive of Jesus' style of relating than either the dichotomous or eclectic views can be conceptualized on a status-role continuum. Notice that the roles and technique are intimately related but technique is not exclusively limited to one role. Also notice that I have added a third descriptive term which I believe is a necessary conclusion from the biblical data.

TABLE 2
Jesus' Style of Relating

Statuses	Counseling: A Continuous View*		
	Prophetic	Pastoral	Priestly
R	Critic, preacher, teacher, interpreter, mediator, confronter,		
O	convictor, corrector, confessor, admonisher, advocate,		
L	sustainer, supporter, lecturer, advisor, burden bearer,		
E	listener, reprover, warner, helper, consoler, pardoner.		
S			

*Illustrative not exhaustive

By this model I am suggesting that our interventive roles can be the result of professional training and commitment or they can be personal characterstics and capabilities. Ideally, the range of therapeutic responses represents an integration of a person's professional role and personality so that the counselor does not merely act out a particular helping role but actually possesses the attitudes and feelings of that role. As you can see from this continuum of statuses and roles, therapists have many interventive role possibilities. Whatever our primary counseling role, whether it be prophetic, pastoral, or priestly, I see the need for us to expand our repertoire of interventive roles and therapeutic responses to include all three role models if it is to be correctly a biblical style of counseling.

I am arguing that the prophetic, pastoral, and priestly roles in counseling are different but they are not antagonistic. In Scripture each role is related to another role and is an integral part of the larger role network identified as the body of Christ (see Rom. 12; 1 Cor. 12). There is no organismic and functional relationship between these roles (see Eph. 4:11-16). The New Testament documents described these roles as gifts necessary for the development of each person in the Christian community. I conclude that Jesus' style of relating utilized the repertoire of roles now found in the church.

Whoever named the journal of the National Association of Christians in Social Work, *"Paraclete,"* understands my arguments. The cognate verb of this Greek word is often translated "to exhort," but as John Carter (1975) observes, "the concept is broad enough to support a variety of therapeutic techniques from crisis intervention to depth therapy, and it is a gift given to the church which is clearly different than the gift of the prophet or teacher." Another student (Ulrich, 1976) has observed, "this gift of the Spirit describes many forms of relating, ranging from the paregoric (consolatory) and encouraging, to the hortatory and paraenetic (admonitory)."

What Can We Learn from Jesus' Multi-role Ministry?

What can we learn from Jesus' multi-role ministry? First, therapeutic role integration is possible when one takes into consideration the whole counsel of God. Specific roles can be differentiated and distinguished from each other, but they cannot be logically or biblically segregated from each other. There are many interventive roles from which the Christian counselor can choose. Jesus' roles were not mutually exclusive, but they did have relative importance based on both who and why he was relating to a person. Jesus demonstrated role flexibility and variability. The implications of this for our Christian counseling is rooted in the observation that Jesus related to people where they were. Jesus was never in a dichotomous bind, having to choose between prophetic, pastoral, or priestly roles. The Christian counselor, for example, can be both directive and nondirective. He does not need to choose a directive approach which is dogmatic, that is, to the point of not being able to listen to where and why people hurt. He can be a listener without excluding teaching. The Christian counselor may be prophetic but not at the expense of the needs of the hurting person for a priest. He may reprove, correct, and instruct, but like prophets in Scripture, he must at times be the bringer of a message of consolation and pardon.

Granted that the Scriptures describe role variability in redemptive relationships, some counselors will have difficulty in achieving role flexibility largely for two reasons. First, the counselor may be inadequately socialized into other therapeutic intervention models. Second, the counselor may be unable to achieve role flexibility due to the rigidity of his personality. The first problem can be overcome through additional education and training, but the second problem poses more difficulties in bringing about change. If one's identity, self-concept, and ego-ideal are exclusively invested in one of the role models, then there will be a tendency to maintain the one particular role at all cost. I am suggesting that role integration is possible only if the personality of the counselor is integrated. In other words, integration between Christ and culture in the therapeutic encounter can be achieved only if the counselor can become an integrated personality.

Second, we can learn from Jesus' style of relating that one can "know" what the problems and solutions are and yet be willing to listen and understand. Because one has knowledge does not preclude a willingness to listen and understand. Nor does it suggest that a counselor must ignore his preconceived ideas of what the client needs. However, it does mean that one can be explorative without excessive explaining, and he can be confrontive without unnecessarily challenging or raising the person's defenses. Prophets bring a message as God's representative to man. The message relates to where the people are and what they are doing. Unlike the biblical prophets, the "prophetic counselor" gathers his data from the person he is serving rather than receiving privileged information about his client from God. Priests also bring a message from God to man, but his message of forgiveness follows man's confession to God, i.e., the priests' message to God. Like the biblical priests, "priestly counselors" must remember that listening only is never enough. Forgiveness and pardon must follow confession. And many times directives for restitution will also be part of the priestly counselor's role.

Third, Jesus' style of relating suggests that a counselor can be authoritative without being authoritarian. A danger of prophetic counseling is not the style of counseling as much as the personality needs of the counselor. The prophetic approach lends itself to be used by persons who need their counseling to be evidence of their authority. On the other hand, counselors may be attracted to a priestly style out of needs to avoid using their authority therapeutically. The implication is that authority is an intrinsic quality in each of the counselor roles and need not be avoided for effective counseling to take place.

Fourth, Jesus' style of relating indicates that one can be right without having to demand that the counselee accept and recognize the counselor's rightness. For example, most of the prophets were not heard, but that is not evidence that their message was incorrect. Often the issue for the counselor is not rightness as much as affirmation of one's worth and dignity. I might add this is often the issue for our clients also. Truth is truth regardless of another's acceptance of it. Most people can be led to the truth more easily than given the truth. While as counselors we may know the truth, our truth for another person cannot change his behavior until it becomes "his truth." That is, the client must hear the truth and understand it for himself before it will effectively change his behavior.

Fifth, Jesus' style of counseling raises the issue of the counselor timing his confrontations and interpretations. Jesus shared ideas, advice, and solutions without demanding his audience hear these before they were ready. The prophetic style counselor is often a person who expects he can change people by saying the right words regardless of their preparation and readiness. As one minister confessed, "When I entered the minstry, I held the rather firm conviction that the Bible possessed all the answers to every human need and problem. I was under the impression that all a counselor had to do was come up with the right Bible verse for the problem, and presto, the problem would be solved. I soon learned in the crucible of everyday ministry that problems are not solved that easily, nor feelings changed that simply." He goes on to claim, "This does not imply that I lost confidence in the authority of the Scriptures to deal with human needs. It does imply that I lost a great deal of confidence in the approach and method I was using. I saw that it was ineffective and too simplistic" (McDill, 1975).

Jesus teaches us also that sin and guilt are concerns equally important to all counseling roles. One can believe in sin and the importance of the consciousness of sin without necessarily playing the role of prophet. Many times clients are painfully aware of their sinfulness and wrongdoing. They are looking for one who can help them deal with their guilt and the negative consequences of their behavior. They come to the counselor craving for the intervention of someone whom they can trust to help them out of seemingly impossible feelings and circumstances. These clients come not because they need to be confronted with their sin but because they need to confront their sin through confession and repentance. This is the very fundamental difference between the prophetic counselor proclaiming truth previously unheard or rejected and the priestly counselor affirming truth the hurting person finds difficult to face. Yet, whenever confrontation is necessary, it is more than speaking the truth. To the Christian counselor confronting is speaking the truth in love (Eph. 4:15). "Always with grace, seasoned with salt" (Col. 4:6).

In addition, prophetic counseling will be convicting rather than condemning. The "paraclete," whether Jesus, the Holy Spirit, or a fellow Christian, plays the role of convictor. Therefore, the client will experience acceptance yet reproof and correction. Particularly for our Christian counselees we can proclaim, "There is therefore now no condemnation for those who are in Christ Jesus" (Rom. 8:1). It is imperative to remember, however, that while the truth is freeing (John 8:32) at first it often creates considerable discomfort. Also, I have found that when the client experiences condemnation, its sources are often self-inflicted or are the work of Satan or the result of family and friends trying to help the Holy Spirit with his role. The Spirit convicts; people and Satan condemn (see John 16:8). When a person is hurting, whether feeling convicted or condemned, it is at these times the counselor must be able to be a priest more than a prophet.

And last, we learn from Jesus' style of relating that the role of counselor-priest is to mediate between the divine and the human. He is man's representative to God. In counseling this priestly mediatorial function takes on the added dimension of assisting the Christian client to be his own priest, to develop his own priesthood abilities. We do want the client to be decreasingly dependent on the therapist and increasingly dependent on God to work out his own salvation. Hulme argues that the counselor "never violates the priestly prerogatives" of his clients to be their own priest (1956, pp. 120-21). While the counselor may mediate for his client, this is not to be the end of the therapeutic exchange. The counseling relationship should be a means to an end, the means to help clients do their own mediating, to develop their own confessional-prayerful relationship with God. "As the priestly function of the counselee becomes blocked, the (counselor's) task is not to jump in and mediate for him, but to (help him) remove the block so that he may resume his own mediatorship" (p. 130).

Conclusion: Advantages and Affirmations

I have argued for the integration of therapeutic roles. I believe there are several advantages to expanding our repertoire of interventive roles. We will avoid two important pitfalls. The pitfall for the nondirective priest-counselor is the temptation never to speak the words of comfort, forgiveness, and healing. The pitfall for the directive prophet-counselor is the temptation never to listen, to jump to conclusions, to speak the words of God before the person is ready to hear them. Bonhoeffer makes an important suggestion to both the prophetic and priestly counselor: "We should listen with the ears of God that we may speak the words of God" (1954, p. 99).

Another advantage to adopting this model of counseling is the dialogue it can facilitate between those of us who are at polar extremes on the status-role continuum. We do need to talk *with* each other. We need to end the debate regarding the biblical view of counseling by recognizing there are many approaches illustrated in Scripture. But we must go beyond an exclusivistic hermeneutic which limits man's creativity in developing counseling approaches. We need to affirm that Christ's creative work is to be legitimately continued by his creation, man. Let us affirm that human creativity and culture are good when they are produced to the honor and glory of God (Col. 3:16-17).

The third advantage of this integrated model is its potential to direct research. A key issue for research is: When are the various interventive roles most effectively utilized in the therapeutic process? We need to learn when to confront, comfort, speak, listen. Paul writes: "In all its complexity, the question toward which all outcome research should ultimately be directed is the following: *What* treatment, by *whom,* is most effective for *this* individual with *that* specific problem, and *under* which set of circumstances" (Patterson, 1973, p. 539). I am strongly suggesting that we end the argument whether there is a biblical view of counseling. We need to move on to research what specific interventions produce what specific changes in what specific clients by what kind of therapists.

A second research issue is the development of an integrated counseling model which is tested clinically and empirically. I have attempted to show that an integrated model is possible. Like Rogers, I believe, the divergences in counseling only "seem irreconcilable because we have not yet developed the larger frame of reference that would contain the polar extremes." Allport said it well, "The trouble with our current theories is not so much that they are wrong, but that they are partial" (Patterson, 1973, p. 532).

Jesus' style of relating suggests a wide range of redemptive approaches to helping people. What I have tried to suggest in this model of counseling is a repertoire and range of counseling roles which can legitimately be labeled biblical. The focus of this paper has been more on the various roles which can be played by Christian counselors and on their presuppositional view of Christ, culture, and Scripture than on counseling technique per se. I have argued for the recognition of a repertoire of counselor roles which can be described on a status-role continuum as prophetic to priestly. Counseling from a Christian perspective assumes an overall gestalt, a holistic view which recognizes, accepts, and uses various role relationships in the helping process. It assumes that Christ and culture are distinguishable (separate) but not necessarily divorced (contradictory). It recognizes that love, wisdom, kindness, listening are virtues of Christian relating and are common denominators between the prophetic and priestly counseling approaches. That is, Jesus' style of relating suggests that the principles of counseling are more importantly executed in spirit than method. This model of counseling assumes that one of the measures of competence for the counselor is his ability to shift to another counseling role when the client's readiness and needs indicate.

As we sort from the treatment maze which is called "Christian Counseling," let us recognize that the differences between the many counseling approaches are often more complementary than conflicting. Let us recognize that there are "differences" among counseling methods: different theoretical tenets, different words to express concepts and terms, and different mechanics to implement the various strategies. However, when considered in a broad perspective, these differences are almost inconsequential. Perhaps the real difference lies in the counselor—he understands some methods better than others, and because of his personal style and emotional comfort level, he can apply some methods better than others" (Peoples, 1975, p. 372). Perls reached the same conclusion, "by and large the various theories are not logically incompatible . . . (they) often nearly supplement and indirectly prove one another" (Patterson, 1973, p. 523).

In addition, as we take into consideration the divergences and convergences of counseling theory and technique, it is important from a Christian perspective to keep in mind that his spiritual gifts also dictate what style of relating the counselor may choose to utilize. I assume that all counselors will not possess the full range of "paraclete" gifts. When a counselor's spiritual gifts are limited, it is imperative that he utilize others in the body of Christ as co-therapists.

Let us affirm today that methodology is not supreme or sufficient in Christian counseling. What is important? You and I as the helpers. What are we like? How well do we relate? Truax and Carkhuff (1967) taught us eight years ago that approach is not the most important ingredient in counseling. What is? The personal characteristics of the counselor, such as accurate empathy, nonpossessive warmth, genuineness, congruence.

While the importance of relationship may not be equally recognized in directive (prophetic) and nondirective (priestly) techniques, it seems relationship is a common denominator in these divergent counseling approaches. Patterson, summarizing divergent counseling theories, concludes the counseling relationship is "characterized not so much by what techniques the therapist uses as by what he is, not so much by what he does as by the way he does it" (1973, p. 536).

Therefore, Jesus' style of relating is based more on who Jesus is than on *what* Jesus says or does. Whatever role Jesus plays—prophet, priest, pastor, king, savior—he is Christ. Whatever Jesus' approach to hurting, sinful people, he is Christ. Whatever role or approach we use in counseling, let us above all imitate Jesus' Christlikeness more than his techniques. Moreover, let us depend on "Christ in us" (Col. 1:27) as we counsel.

Jesus' style of relating provides a model for us today, but it does not necessarily provide a norm. There are no commands in Scripture to imitate Jesus' style of counseling. But there are commands to be like Jesus. "So if there is any encouragement in Christ, any incentive of love, any participation in the spirit, any affection and sympathy, ... Have this mind among yourselves, which you have in Christ Jesus" (Phil. 2:1-5).

References

Adams, J. *Competent to Counsel*. Nutley, N.J.: Presbyterian & Reformed Publishing Co., 1974.
————. *Christian Counselors Manual*. Grand Rapids: Baker Book House, 1973.
Blamires, H. *The Christian Mind*. New York: Seabury Press, 1963.
Bonhoeffer. *Life Together*. New York: Harper, 1954.
Carter, J. "Adams Theory of Nouthetic Counseling." *Journal of Psychology and Theology*, 1975, *3* (3), 143-55.
Clinebell, J. H. *Basic Types of Pastoral Counseling*. Nashville: Abingdon, 1966.
Dolby, J. R. "Cultural Evangelicalism: The Background for Personal Despair. *Journal of the American Scientific Affiliation*, 1972, *24* (2), 91-101.
Frank, J. D. *Persuasion and Healing*. New York: Schoken, 1963.
Hiltner, S. *Clinical Pastoral Training*. New York: Abingdon Press, 1949.

Hulme, W. E. *Counseling and Theology.* Philadelphia: Muhlenberg Press, 1956.

Jabay, E. *Search for Identity.* Grand Rapids: Zondervan Publishing House, 1967.

Lake, F. *Clinical Theology.* London: Darton, Longman & Todd, 1966.

May, R. *The Art of Counseling.* New York: Abingdon Press, 1939.

McDill, T. "Peer Counseling in the Local Church." Doctoral dissertation, Bethel Seminary, 1975.

Niebuhr, H. R. *Christ and Culture.* New York: Harper & Row, 1951.

Patterson, C. H. *Theories of Counseling and Psychotherapy.* New York: Harper & Row, 1973.

Peoples, E. *Readings in Correctional Casework and Counseling.* Pacific Palisades, Calif.: Goodyear, 1975.

Reiff, D. *Triumph of the Therapeutic.* New York: Harper & Row, 1968.

Rogers, C. *Counseling and Psychotherapy.* New York: Houghton Mifflin, 1942.

Seifert, H., and Clinebell, H.J. *Personal Growth and Change.* Philadelphia: The Westminster Press, 1969.

Truax, C. B., and Carkhuff, R. P. *Toward Effective Counseling and Psychotherapy: Training and Practice.* Chicago: Aldine, 1967.

Ulrich, J. "The Practice of the Gift of Exhortation According to the New Testament." Masters thesis, Wheaton College, 1976.

Wolberg, L. *The Technique of Psychotherapy.* New York: Grune & Stratton, 1967.

GUILT: THREE MODELS OF THERAPY

S. Bruce Narramore

In earlier articles (Narramore, 1974a, 1974b, 1974c) I have suggested a model of guilt encompassing both theological and psychological concep-tions of personality functioning. A diagrammatic summary (see figure 1) suggests that experience of guilt can be understood as the response of the punitive self when the individual's performance falls short of his internalized standards or ideals.

Two clarifications should be made at this point. The first is the need to distinguish between guilt feelings and what I call constructive sorrow. I consider all guilt feelings (comprised as they are of fears of punishment, rejection, and loss of self-esteem) to be negative, neurotic, or inhibitory. On the other hand constructive sorrow is a love-motivated ego function. Tournier (1962) and Pattison (1969) use the terms "true guilt" and "existential ego guilt" respectively to indicate the emotion I call constructive sorrow.

I prefer the designation constructive sorrow to the terms true guilt or existential ego guilt on two grounds. The first is a theological one. The Bible does speak of an emotion of constructive sorrow (2 Cor. 7:8-10) while it does not use guilt in an effective sense. My second reason for avoiding terms like true guilt and existential guilt is that in the neurotic sufferer they are too easily confused with neurotic guilt. I believe a totally separate verbal designation facilitates clearer communication of the essential differences between the negative emotion of guilt and the positive one of constructive sorrow.

The second clarification I wish to make is that when we speak of one's performance falling below his ideals we are speaking not only of external behavioral acts but of internal attitudes as well. In fact, a much greater portion of guilt is likely to arise from internal fantasies and wishes than it does from overt behavior.

In the above model of moral functioning we have three potential sources of maladjustment. The first is the set of ideals, goals, and aspirations (the

Presented at a conference on "Research in Mental Health and Religious Behavior," Atlanta, Georgia, January 24-26, 1976.

ideal self). The second is the individual's performance. And the third is the set of corrective attitudes we utilize to motivate acceptable behavior.

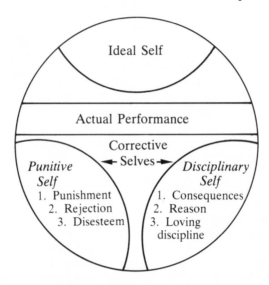

Having isolated these three possible sources of guilt emotions we are now in a position to note that therapeutic endeavors can be directed at any one (or all three) of these aspects of the personality. In fact, varying approaches to guilt reduction can be rather effectively classified according to which source of guilt is made the object of the therapeutic strategy. We can either lower the ideal, raise the performance, or change the punitive guilt emotion.

Alteration of the Ideal Self

The first seemingly logical approach to reducing guilt is to lower one's standards or aspirations. If the goal is lowered, so this reasoning goes, our performance will come nearer the standard, lessen the gap between the ideal and the real, and therefore reduce the guilt.

Unfortunately, this method seldom works and it is based on some serious misconceptions regarding the nature of guilt. To begin with, it postulates a positive correlation between the width of the gap between one's performance and his ideals and the amount of guilt experienced. In other words, it is based on the assumption that greater deviations from ideals result in greater degrees of guilt and that lesser deviations cause lesser amounts of guilt. All sensitive therapists know this simple formula is rarely true. Many people with exemplary behavior that in many ways closely approximates their ideals are riddled with neurotic guilt. At the same time others with huge gaps between their ideals and their performance experience (at least at a conscious level) very little guilt. The intensity of guilt is not so much a function of the gap between the ideal and the real as it is the nature of the corrective attitudes embedded in the personality. Slight deviations associated with punitive corrective attitudes produce great guilt. Large deviations in a personality without punitive attitude produce very little guilt.

A second problem facing therapists attempting to reduce guilt by the lowering of standards is the unconscious nature and origin of many of these ideals. The mere conscious adoption of a new set of standards usually does little to effect a dynamic change in a patient's guilt emotion. Take the rebellious young adult as an example. After living for years in what he considers a restrictive, guilt-inducing family (or subculture) he decides he has had all the guilt he can handle. He has tried to be good and it hasn't worked so he will throw off his parental standards and adopt a "new morality." For a moment he feels free. His new-found peer support gives him some help in combating his old ideals. But before long that old sense of guilt returns. While it may be focused on very different conscious issues, the painful accusations are just the same. The reason for this is the long-term nature and loving significance of the parental introjection. Fifteen years of internalizing parental values and standards do not easily give way to a drastically different set of values. Even though the parent-child relationship was not the best, it was still the closest and most significant human experience he has ever known. The habits, values, and attitudes learned there are exceedingly change resistant.

A third reason for the failure of therapeutic approaches directed toward lowering the ideals is that it ignores the fact that all men have some sort of built-in moral awareness. The observations of psychologists and sociologists about this truth are supported by the biblical statement that there is a "law written on the heart" of every man (Rom. 2:15). While we might endlessly debate the exact origin and content of this law, the Scripture is quite evidently teaching the universal existence of some universal moral standard or awareness that is not susceptible to ready removal by external means.

Alteration of Performance

A second apparent solution to the guilt dilemma is to improve one's performance. If people feel guilty because they fall short of their standards, it seems clear enough that one appropriate solution is to improve the behavior and thereby conform to the standard. Consider, for example, the following quotation from William Glasser (1965):

To be worthwhile we must maintain a satisfactory standard of behavior. To do so we must learn to correct ourselves when we do wrong and to credit ourselves when we do right. If we do not evaluate our own behavior or, having evaluated it, if we do not act to improve our conduct where it is below our standards, we will not fulfill our needs to be worthwhile and will suffer as acutely as when we fail to love or be loved. (p. xiii)

This sounds very good—and even Christian. In fact, it is a view that has been heartily endorsed by many Christian authors and large segments of the church. Therapeutic approachs that attribute man's emotional problems to unacceptable behavior (sin) and promise relief for improved behavior have great appeal to many Christians. Unfortunately this view also has serious theological and psychological weaknesses.

To begin with let's take Glasser's assumption that "To be worthwhile we must maintain a satisfactory standard of behavior." No matter how Christian this may sound it isn't biblical. The Bible does not say that if we want to feel good about ourselves we should improve our performance. Instead, it says we should possess a high sense of worth because we are created in God's image as creatures of worth and value. Because of this sense of worth and self-esteem— because of our being—we will desire to live up to our calling! This is exactly opposite the reality therapy viewpoint. The Bible says you are accepted—now perform. Reality therapy says perform if you want to be accepted. The theological fallacy of this approach is clearly laid out in Scripture. James writes, "For whosoever shall keep the whole law, and yet offend in one point, he is guilty of all" (James 2:10). And Paul wrote, "For as many as are of the works of the law are under a curse; for it is written, Cursed is every one who does not abide by all things written in the book of the law, to perform them" (Gal. 3:10). In other words the Bible plainly teaches that it is not the *degree* of deviation from the ideal that causes guilt but rather the very *fact* of any deviation. Therapeutic experience consistently bears out this same fact. Guilt feelings arise not from the extent of our failures but from their very presence.

The second weakness of this view of guilt reduction lies in its neglect of the punitive guilt feeling. Just as do efforts to reduce guilt by lowering the standard, attempts to reduce guilt by improving behavior miss the crucial issue. They attempt to resolve the punitive, neurotic guilt emotions indirectly. And in so doing they offer at best very short term or superficial solutions.

Alteration of Punitive Guilt Attitudes

We have now come to the key issue in effect—long-term guilt reduction. If a person is to be freed from neurotic guilt emotions, he must undergo some major changes in his punitive self-attitudes. The only way guilt can effectively and lastingly be resolved is for a person to replace his internalized threats of punishment, rejection, and disesteem with corrective attitudes based on loving self-acceptance, awareness of the consequences of misbehavior, and constructive reason. This, of course, is not an easy task. But our knowledge of the contents and childhood development of guilt give us some immediate guides.

To the degree that guilt feelings have their origin directly in the child's relationships with his parents we can easily see some of the needed therapeutic ingredients. Parental punitiveness, shame, and conditional acceptance help instill in the growing child the fear of punishment, rejection, and loss of self-esteem. It follows naturally that these patterns of thought and feeling are best dissolved by a new interpersonal relationship characterized by nonpunitiveness, unconditional acceptance, and mutual regard. These therapist variables are, of course, of well-recognized therapeutic value.

To the degree we repeat or even approach our client's parental condemnations, threats, and criticisms we will actually reinforce our patient's guilt responses. Even when these therapeutic tactics yield external behavior changes (as they often do), they do so on the basis of neurotic guilt motivation. Theologically, this therapist repeating of parental guilt motivations boils down to a reversion to the methods of law motivation. Law says change or else. Grace says you are totally accepted so you may now change for the good of yourself and others.

Having looked at these basic attitudinal ingredients we are now in a position to look at some other guidelines for therapeutic endeavors. Perhaps the single most important thing to keep in mind in reducing peoples' burden of guilt is to never minimize the feeling. Minimizing guilt tells a hurting person we really don't understand the depth of his psychic pain. In attempting to offer hope we actually do the opposite. Hope is best offered by acknowledging the depths of one's self-condemnation and guiltiness. Minimizing guilt is like a small band-aid on a deep psychic wound. It is no more than a slight temporary help. Only when the severity of a wound is seen are we in a position to begin to heal the problem.

Minimizing a patient's guilt also serves to reinforce defensiveness and prevents a confrontation with the depth of his guilt feelings. Painful as it may be the exploration of the depths of one's feelings of worthlessness, isolation, and desert of punishment are central to the final resolution of these very feelings. In fact, not until the depth of our conflicts and guilt are fully understood are we in a position to experience a genuine regret or constructive sorrow.

My therapeutic experience has consistently shown a predictable pattern in overcoming guilt. From a conscious awareness of some feelings of guilt a client begins to explore his problems and life style. This exploration turns up new areas of conflict, anxiety, and irresponsibility. As new conflict areas are explored guilt feelings may temporarily increase. But as an accepting therapeutic attitude prevails clients gradually begin to feel less guilt. As they are gradually freed of these neurotic guilt emotions new feelings of constructive sorrow take their place. An analysis of the original feelings of guilt, the devious ways of defending against them, and the true depth of our sinfulness, are, however, prerequisites for developing this constructive sorrow. Therapeutic methods that prevent exploration of painful guilt feelings and their origins only serve to reinforce old patterns.

This brings us to another crucial therapeutic task—that of unmasking the variety of defenses utilized to hide the inner presence and full extent of guilt's impact. In an earlier article (Narramore, 1974*b*) I suggested that guilt was in some way at the root of all psychological defense mechanisms. Not until tendencies toward rationalization, repression, reaction formation, intellectualization, isolation, and a host of other defenses are revealed in their true light—as ways of avoiding the frightening experience of guilt—can we begin to make significant progress in therapeutic guilt reduction.

This analysis of a client's defenses against guilt open him up to a deeper experience of the reality of God's forgiveness.

As a person sees his self-inflicted punishment and its origin in his early relationship with his parents, he is better able to accept the fact that Christ's atonement took care of the law's demands for his punishment. As he breaks, gradually gives up his neurotic defenses and experiences his therapist's acceptance he is better able to receive God's full acceptance. And as he finds himself valued, he is better able to accept God's high evaluation of himself.

One final word needs to be said about the therapy of guilt. We must continually keep in mind that our client's guilt feelings are not exact replicas of their parent's corrective attitudes. As discussed in the first article in this series (Narramore, 1974*a*) a person's guilt feelings are nearly always more severe than his parents' guilt-inducing methods of correction. The explanation of this fact lies in an understanding of the dynamics of projection and internalization. A child does not merely internalize his parents' attitudes. What he internalizes is his parents' attitudes *as he perceives them*. When a child is angry he naturally assumes (on the basis of projection) that his parents are angry. Then, as he internalizes his parents' attitudes he takes in both their actual punitive attitudes plus the anger he originally projected into them! Keeping these dynamics in mind aids us in avoiding the common therapeutic error of placing all the blame for our client's guilt problems onto their environment.

Summary

While altering one's ideals or level of performance may give temporary or symptomatic relief of guilt feelings, a therapeutic model that gives primary attention to the origin and history of a patient's punitive, corrective attitude is more likely to bring about lasting guilt reduction. This model is not only consistent with a dynamic view of guilt but also allows the therapist to focus upon the internalization of attitudes that allow clients to more completely experience the psychological significance of the atonement.

References

Glasser, W. *Reality Therapy*. New York: Harper & Row, 1965.

Narramore, B. "Guilt: Where Theology and Psychology Meet." *Journal of Psychology and Theology*, 1974 *a, 2,* 18-25.

———. "Guilt: Its Universal Hidden Pressure." *Journal of Psychology and Theology*, 1974*b, 2,* 104-15.

———. "Guilt: Christian Motivation or Neurotic Masochism?" *Journal of Psychology and Theology*, 1974*c, 2,* 182-89.

Pattison, E. M. "Morality, Guilt, and Forgiveness in Psychotherapy." In E. M. Pattison (ed.), *Clinical Psychiatry and Religion*. Boston: Little, Brown, 1969.

Tournier, P. *Guilt and Grace*. New York: Harper & Row, 1962.

COGNITIVE THEORY/THERAPY AND SANCTIFICATION: A STUDY IN INTEGRATION

David Pecheur

Psychology was alleged to have "lost its mind" with the advent of Watsonian behaviorism in the second decade of this century (Dember, 1974). However, there are numerous indications that psychology is presently undergoing a "cognitive revolution" (Dember, 1974; Mahoney, 1977; cf. Edwards, 1976; Lazarus, 1977). In the epigrammatic assessment of Dember, "psychology has gone cognitive."

It is important to note at the outset that the meaning of cognition as used in this article is not restricted to verbal statements but includes both verbal and nonverbal symbols (cf. Edwards, 1976).

Cognitive Theory

Humans, as uniquely language-creating beings, start to learn from early childhood to formulate thoughts, perceptions, and feelings in words, phrases, and sentences. "Practically all of us, by the time we reach adulthood, seem to do the majority of our important thinking, and consequently our emoting, in terms of self-talk or internalized sentences" (Ellis and Harper, 1975, p. 25).

It should not be concluded from the preceding quote that humans gradually move from an S-R model to an S-O-R model as they mature and approach adulthood. Brewer's scholarly review argues persuasively that there is not and never has been any convincing evidence for operant or classical conditioning in adult human beings (1974; Lazarus, 1977). The essence of his compelling argument is that conditioning in human subjects is produced through the operation of higher mental processes—through cognitive mediation—rather than vice versa (Brewer, 1974; Lazarus, 1977). He believes that a cognitive theory of conditioning will also be required for children. In fact, Brewer points out that the early work of Zener (1937) suggests the necessity of a cognitive theory to account for the Pavlovian conditioning of dogs (Brewer, 1974; Lazarus, 1977).

The crux of cognitive theory is capsulized in the simple but profound statement that our self-verbalizations essentially determine our emotional and behavioral responses. The salient point, in other words, is that what an individual says to himself governs the way he feels and acts (Rimm and Masters, 1974).

This fundamental precept has been conceptualized by Albert Ellis in his ABC theory of emotion. "A" refers to some external event to which the individual is exposed. "B" refers to the particular chain of thoughts (self-verbalizations) that he goes through in response to "A"; and "C" symbolizes the emotions and related behaviors that are a result of "B" (Rimm and Masters, 1974). Accordingly, what a person says to himself about a specific situation can differentially determine his emotional (and behavioral) reactions to that situation (Goldfried, Decenteceo, and Weinberg, 1974).

It is maintained that positive human emotions, such as feelings of love or elation, are often associated with, or result from, some variation of the phrase "This is good for me!" and that negative human emotions, such as feelings of jealousy or depression, are frequently associated with or result from sentences stated in some form or variation of the phrase "This is bad for me!" (Ellis in Goldfried et al., 1974). The maladaptive emotional reactions and concomitant ineffective behaviors we witness in our clients, then, are mediated by the specific nature of their self-statements about certain events (Goldfried and Sobocinski, 1975).

It should be pointed out that an individual is unlikely in many situations to literally "tell himself" various things consciously or deliberately when he is confronted with real-life situations. Because of the habitual nature of one's expectations or beliefs, it is likely that such thinking processes become as automatic and seemingly involuntary as any over-learned "set" (Beck, 1976; Goldfried, Decenteceo, and Weinberg, 1974; Goldfried and Sobocinski, 1975; Meichenbaum, 1975). Our clients' debilitating cognitions—negative, self-defeating, and anxiety-engendering self-statements—become habitual and in many ways are similar to the automation of thought that accompanies the proficiency of a motor skill such as driving a car. However, the therapist can make the client aware of such thinking processes (Meichenbaum, 1975).

If an experimenter induces individuals to modify their internal dialogue (i.e., self-statements or thoughts), they will significantly change their emoting and behaving (Ellis and Harper, 1975).

In sum, cognitive theory assumes that people can control what they think, and what they think can control how they act and feel (Strong 1976).

Research Evidence

A profusion of empirical research data has been amassed to date which cogently evinces the tenability of cognitive theory. This section will review a representative sample of that data which can be broken down into several different areas.

Self-Talk and Physiological (Emotional) Arousal

According to Schacher and Singer's (1962) theory of emotion, "emotional states may be considered a function of a state of physiological arousal and of a cognition appropriate to this state of arousal" (p. 398). The succeeding studies clearly indicate that the state of physiological arousal, necessary to emotional states, is a function of covert self-statements.

Rimm and Litvak (1969) investigated certain assumptions derived from Ellis' theory relating implicit verbalization to emotional (physiological) arousal. Emotional responses of Ss instructed to silently read sequences of affectively loaded sentences were compared with those of Ss who read neutral sentences. Results were that Ss showed significantly greater emotional arousal, as measured by respiration rate and depth to sequences of affectively toned sentences (e.g., "My grades may not be good enough this semester . . . I might fail out of school . . . that would be awful") than to sequences of neutral sentences (e.g., "Inventors are imaginative . . . Edison was an inventor . . . therefore he was imaginative").

Russell and Brandsma (1974) also tested the assumptions of Albert Ellis' ABC theory of psychopathology. Emotional responses of Ss asked to read aloud negatively toned dyads of sentences were compared with those of Ss's who read neutral, impersonal sentences. An overall pattern of results favorable to Ellis' assumptions was obtained. In particular, the mean responsiveness of the experimental subjects, as measured by galvanic skin conductance, to affectively loaded statements was significantly greater than the mean responsiveness of the matched group of controls to statements consisting of neutral, impersonal content.

In a study conducted by May and Johnson (1973), the effects of internally elicited thoughts on autonomic nervous system activity was investigated. Ss were divided into two groups. Group 1 subjects generated thoughts to a series of numbers, arousal (stressful) words, and neutral (nonstressful) words. Group 2 subjects generated thoughts to a series of numbers, inhibitory (relaxing) words, and neutral (nonstressful) words. The results indicated that internally evoked thoughts produce physiological changes; heart rate and respiration were found to change as a function of the affective nature of the cognitive event.

These studies point out unmistakably the influence of covert statements on physiological (emotional) arousal.

Self-Talk and Emotion

A cardinal feature of cognitive theory is that the content of a person's thinking affects his mood (Beck, 1976). The following studies amply demonstrate that the emotions experienced by subjects are a function of differentiative self-statements.

Goldfried and Sobocinski (1975) studied the relationship between the tendency to hold certain irrational beliefs and the likelihood of becoming emotionally aroused in various types of situations. The first experiment was correlational and discovered a positive relationship between irrational beliefs and paper-and-pencil measures of interpersonal examination and public speaking anxiety. The second experiment centered on one specific irrational belief—the overriding importance of social approval—and investigated the likelihood of emotional arousal occurring among individuals who ascribed to this belief. When instructed to imagine themselves in social situations that might be interpreted as involving rejections by others, subjects holding this belief reported feeling significantly more anxious and angry than those who did not. This study revealed, essentially, differential susceptibility to emotional arousal by individuals varying in the irrationality of their expectations.

In an experiment performed by Schachter and Singer (1962), a state of physiological arousal was experimentally induced through an injection of epinephrine. It was hypothesized that given a state of physiological arousal for which an individual has no explanation, he will label this state in terms of the cognitions available to him. This implies that by manipulating the cognitions of an individual in such a state his feelings can be manipulated in diverse directions. Experimental results corroborated this proposition for, following the injection of epinephrine, those subjects who had no explanation for the bodily state thus produced gave behavioral and self-report indications that they had been readily manipulated into the disparate feeling states of euphoria and anger. It was concluded that cognitive factors are major determiners of the emotional labels we apply to a common state of sympathetic arousal.

The theoretical goal of an experiment conducted by Velten (1968) was to test a central tenet of "semantic" therapy, that the constructions of interpretations people place upon events determine their affective responses. His subjects read self-referent statements which varied in content. One group read and concentrated upon 60 self-referent statements intended to be elating (e.g., "This is great—I really do feel good—I am elated about things"); a second group read 60 statements intended to be depressing (e.g., "I have too many bad things in my life"). A third group read 60 statements which were neutral, that is, they were neither self-referent nor pertaining to mood (e.g., "Utah is the Beehive State"). Using verbal report as well as performance in a variety of different tasks, including writing speed, decision time, reaction time, a word association test, and spontaneous verbalizations, mood was found to change as a function of the type of emotionally toned statements (depressive, elated, or neutral) read by subjects.

In summary, these three studies point to the conclusion that the self-verbalizations we generate from an event mediate our emotional response.

Self-Talk and Behavior

The other cardinal feature of cognitive theory is that an individual's self-statements determine his behavioral responses. The research subsumed under this area will be organized according to the different ways in which the validity of this basic assumption has been confirmed.

(1) Self-talk and behavior modification techniques. Meichenbaum and his colleagues have conducted a series of studies designed to evaluate the role of cognitive factors in behavior modification. Their general research strategy has been to assess the efficacy of "standard" behavior therapy procedures relative to behavior therapy procedures which included a self-instructional component (Meichenbaum and Cameron, 1974).

In a laboratory operant training program (Meichenbaum, 1969), a group of hospitalized schizophrenic patients were trained to emit "healthy talk" in an interview setting. The effects of operant training were generalized over time to a follow-up interview administered by the experimenter, to a post-test interview administered by a patient confederate, and to additional verbal tasks (e.g., proverbs test, word association test) administered under neutral conditions. A rather serendipitous and provocative finding was that a number of the schizophrenic patients who had been trained to emit "healthy talk" repeated aloud and spontaneously the experimental instruction "give healthy talk, be coherent and relevant" while being tested on the generalization measures. This self-instruction appeared to mediate generalization by aiding the subject in attending to the demands of the task, thus preventing any internally generated distracting stimuli from interfering with his language behavior. It was concluded that the direct training of self-instructional statements provides a promising approach for the modification and generalization of behavior.

Vygotsky and Luria have proposed three stages through which the initiation and the inhibition of voluntary motor behaviors come under verbal control. During the first stage, the speech of others, generally adults, controls and directs a child's behavior. The second stage is characterized by the child's own overt or external speech becoming an effective regulator of his behavior. In the last stage, the child's covert or inner speech comes to assume a self-governing role (Meichenbaum and Cameron, 1974). From this hypothetical developmental sequence, Meichenbaum and his associates developed a self-instructional training program. It proceeds as follows: first, the experimenter performs a task talking aloud while the subject observes (cognitive modeling); then, the subject performs the same task while the experimenter instructs the subject aloud (overt, external guidance); next, the subject is asked to perform the task again while instructing himself aloud (overt self-guidance); then, the subject performs the task while whispering to himself (faded, overt self-guidance); and finally, the subject performs the task while guiding his performance via private speech (covert self-instruction). In short, functional interiorization of the subject's private speech is trained (Meichenbaum and Goodman, 1971; Meichenbaum and Cameron, 1973; Meichenbaum and Cameron, 1974; Meichenbaum, 1974; Meichenbaum, 1975).

The efficacy of this cognitive self-instructional training procedure in altering the behavior of "impulsive" school children was examined in two studies (Meichenbaum and Goodman, 1971). The results of study 1 indicated that the self-instructional group improved significantly relative to attentional and assessment control groups on a variety of psychometric tests which assessed cognitive impulsivity, performance IQ, and motor ability. The improved performance was evident in a one-month follow-up assessment.

Study 2 examined the efficacy of the components of the cognitive treatment procedure in altering the impulsive child's performance on a measure of cognitive impulsivity. The results indicated that the addition of explicit self-instructional training to modeling procedures significantly altered the attentional strategies of the impulsive children and facilitated behavioral change.

The findings of these two studies demonstrate that a cognitive self-guidance technique which explicitly trains an impulsive child to talk to himself is capable of bringing his nonverbal behavior under his own cognitive control.

In two other studies, Meichenbaum and Cameron (1973) used the same modeling and overt-to-covert cognitive rehearsal paradigm as the impulsive children received to train schizophrenics to talk to themselves. In study 1, the self-instructional group was trained to use such self-instructions as "pay attention, listen, and repeat instructions, disregard distraction." The results showed that this group improved relative to practice and assessment control groups on a digit symbol substitution task and on an auditory distraction digit recall task.

The second study evaluated the therapeutic efficacy of extended individualized self-instructional training (viz., six hours) in changing a range of behaviors. This training emphasized practice in monitoring intra- and interpersonal behaviors with a view to supplying the schizophrenic with cues for emitting task-relevant self-statements. The results showed that the self-instructional group relative to a yoked practice control group improved on a variety of measures including amount of "healthy talk" emitted in a structured interview, level of proverb abstraction, level of perceptual integration of responses to an inkblot test, and digit recall under distraction conditions. This consistent pattern of improvement for the schizophrenics who received self-instructional training was clear-cut in a three-week follow-up assessment.

The outcomes of these two studies denote that a cognitive self-guidance program which trains schizophrenic patients to talk to themselves is effective in modifying their behavior on a variety of attentional, thinking, and language tasks.

With the impulsive children and schizophrenic patients, appropriate self-instructional statements appeared to be missing from the Ss' repertoires before training. Self-instructional training was employed to develop the "interiorization of language" in these populations. However, a large population of clients, who usually fall under the rubric of "neurotic," seem to emit a diversity of maladaptive, anxiety-engendering self-statements. Consequently, the goal of intervention is not to remedy the absence of self-statements (as with the schizophrenics and impulsive children), but rather to make the "neurotic" patients aware of the self-statements which mediate maladaptive behaviors and to train them to produce incompatible self-statements and behaviors (Meichenbaum and Cameron, 1974).

The following series of studies shows that a variety of "neurotic" populations have been explicitly taught to talk to themselves in order to develop self-control. The Ss were trained to (a) become aware of their negative, self-defeating, anxiety-engendering self-statements and (b) emit incompatible self-statements which would engender self-control and facilitate behavior change (Meichenbaum, 1972).

Speech anxiety. An experiment in treating speech anxious clients (Meichenbaum, Gilmore, and Fedoravicius, 1971) was designed to evaluate the relative merits of a semantic "insight" therapy approach versus systematic desensitization. In each case, treatment was conducted on a group basis. Results indicated that the insight group was as effective as the desensitization group in significantly reducing speech anxiety over control group levels as assessed by behavioral, cognitive, and self-report measures administered immediately after post-treatment and later at a three-month follow-up.

Test anxiety. The relative efficacy of a group cognitive modification treatment procedure in treating text-anxious clients (Meichenbaum, 1972) was ascertained by comparing it with group desensitization and a waiting list control group. The cognitive modification group combined an insight-oriented therapy which was designed to make test-anxious Ss aware of their anxiety-engendering thoughts with a modified desensitization procedure which utilized (1) coping imagery on how to handle anxiety and (2) self-instructional training to attend to the task and not ruminate about oneself. Results indicated that the cognitive modification group was most effective in significantly reducing test anxiety as assessed by (1) test performance obtained in an analogue test situation, (2) self-reports administered immediately after post-treatment and later at a one-month follow-up, and (3) grade point average. Following treatment, the test-anxious Ss in the cognitive modification group did not significantly differ from a group of low test-anxious Ss on the performance and self-report measures. It was concluded that the desensitization procedure can be both successfully modified and supplemented by treatment procedures designed to change the self-labeling or cognitive process of the client.

In both of the preceding studies, a comparison was made between the group versus individual administration of the "insight" treatment procedure. In both instances group administration of the "insight" treatment procedure was found to be as effective as individually administered "insight" treatment. In fact, the group administration of the "insight" treatment method appears easier and somewhat more efficacious than individual administration. In the group administration, the Ss can readily contribute and benefit by a shared exploration of the personalized cognitive events which they emit and the incompatible cognitions and behaviors they must emit to decrease anxiety and improve performance. In addition, group pressure can be therapeutically exercised to encourage and reinforce behavior change (Meichenbaum, 1972; Meichenbaum and Cameron, 1974).

Low creativity. Meichenbaum (1972) appraised the adequacy of his cognitive self-instructional training procedure in modifying the behavior of low, creativity college students. The self-instructional training was effectuated by means of group discussion, modeling, and rehearsal. The results indicated that the self-instructional training group, relative to two control groups, manifested a significant increase in originality and flexibility on tests of divergent thinking, an increase in preference for complexity, a significant increase in human movement responses to an inkblot test, and concomitant changes in self-concept. In short, the Ss who received self-instructional training altered both their self-perceptions and performance in the direction of more creativity.

The following three studies did not employ Meichenbaum's two-stage self-instructional training procedure to assess the ability of self-statements to mediate behavioral change.

Phobics. Meichenbaum (1971) examined the use of modeling therapy to modify the self-statements of snake phobic clients. The modeling study was designed to examine the differential efficacy of having models self-verbalize (i.e., the express modeling of self-statements the client could use) versus the absence of any model verbalizations. A second factor included in the study was the modeling style: multiple models demonstrating coping behaviors (i.e., initially modeling fearful behaviors, then coping behavior, and lastly mastery behavior) versus mastery models demonstrating only fearless behavior throughout. Behavioral and effective self-report measures revealed that observation of coping models was significantly superior to mastery models in enhancing fear reduction. The addition of the models' self-verbalization to the coping condition significantly enhanced treatment effectiveness. The results pointed out that a coping self-verbalizing model was the most effective model to reduce avoidance behavior.

Dating skills. Glass, Gottman, and Shmurak (1976) compared the effectiveness of a response-acquisition treatment with a cognitive self-statement modification treatment, a combination of these two treatments, and a waiting-list control group. Training in cognitive self-statement modification comprised a model of effective self-statement coping and reinforcement. Assessment included in vivo measures made by women phoned by the subjects, questionnaire measures, and ratings of role-play performance in taped, laboratory, problem situations. A six-month follow-up assessment was also included. The results denoted that subjects trained in cognitive self-statement modification showed significantly better performance in role-play situations for which they were not trained, made significantly more phone calls, and made a significantly better impression on the women than subjects in the other groups. These effects were basically maintained at follow-up, and the cognitive self-statement groups' performance on the role-play measures improved from post-treatment to follow-up. It was concluded that a cognitive self-statement modification treatment can result in significant changes (in vivo dating behavior as well as in increased transfer of training).

Cigarette smokers. Steffy, Meichenbaum, and Best (1970) conducted a study in which the aversive conditioning paradigm was elaborated in order to modify what Ss (smokers) say to themselves. The results demonstrated substantial and significant improvement for the treatment group whose attention to covert verbalizations was accentuated as compared to a standard aversive conditioning group. The addition of having the Ss verbalize an image while smoking and then making the onset and offset of shock contingent upon the verbalized covert processes was highly effective in modifying what clients say to themselves and in reducing smoking behavior.

The results of the studies in this section clearly indicate that cognitions can be directly modified by Ss and that these modifications can result in significant changes in behavior (cf. Glass et al., 1976). Thus, Ss' overt behavior can be brought under their own discriminative control by developing the self-regulatory function of private speech (Meichenbaum et al., 1971).

These studies also show that the efficacy of behavior modification techniques is enhanced by means of focusing treatment on the Ss' self-verbalizations (Meichenbaum, 1975). Therapeutically attending to the S's self-statements leads to significant behavioral change, greater generalization, and persistence of treatment effects.

(2) *Self-talk and empathy training.* Emphasizing the impact of self-verbalizations on emotions and behavior, Cabush and Edwards (1976) employed training in facilitative self-responding as a means of helping clients alter what they say to themselves. The training was compared to empathy-based individual counseling for personal-social problems with college students. The two treatment groups were compared on post-tests of (1) empathy, regard, genuineness, and concreteness of their self-help

responses; (2) self-ratings and observer ratings of interpersonal functioning; and (3) self-ratings and observer ratings of improvement on specific counseling goal behaviors. Results showed that minimally facilitative levels of self-responding and positive change as rated by observers was attained only by the group trained in facilitative self-responding. This indicated the use of the technique for self-help training. It was concluded that a client who can create an environment of facilitative self-talk for himself is more likely to experience the new learning essential to breaking neurotic patterns of behavior.

(3) *Self-talk and assertive behavior.* Schwartz and Gottmann (1976) analyzed the components of assertive behavior. Content knowledge of an assertive response, delivery of the response under two conditions, heart rate, self-perceived tension, and the incidence of positive and negative self-statements were assessed. Differences on these variables between low-, moderate-, and high-assertive groups were analyzed to determine the nature of the response deficit in nonassertive subjects. The results suggested that the most likely source of nonassertiveness in low-assertive subjects could be related to the nature of their cognitive and negative self-statements. A greater number of negative and fewer positive self-statements were reported by low compared to moderate- and high-assertive subjects. It was concluded that some type of cognitive restructuring or manipulation of cognitive self-statements would be an appropriate form of treatment for nonassertiveness.

(4) *Self-talk and verbal operant conditioning.* Farber (1963) conducted an experiment in verbal operant conditioning which revealed, as Dulaney has aptly put it, "that a human subject does what he thinks he is supposed to do if he wants to . . ." (p. 192).

(5) *Self-talk and problem-solving.* The relationship of self-talk to problem-solving has been investigated by Gagné (1970) and Gagné and Briggs (1974). After evaluating the relevant research, he concluded that it was reasonable to suppose that cognitive (i.e., self-instructional) strategies are learned and used by individuals in solving any kind of problem. Gagné has defined a cognitive strategy as an internally organized skill which governs the learner's own behavior.

Conclusions from the Research

It has been evinced from the research findings cited that the fundamental tenets of cognitive theory are supported by a solid empirical foundation. This conclusion receives cogent corroboration from Edwards' (1976) incisive review of research relevant to the practice of psychotherapy which documents the central role of cognition in emotion and behavior. Self-talk, evidently, does mediate our feelings and behaviors. Were this not so, psychotherapy as a verbal exercise would be useless (Strong, 1976). The research, in effect, strongly supports the efficacy of the cognitive self-statement modifications approach to therapy.

It should be apparent by now that, on the one hand, as Farber has pointed out, "the one thing psychologists can count on is that their Ss will talk, if only to themselves; and not infrequently whether relevant or irrelevant, the things people say to themselves determine the rest of the things they do" (Meichenbaum and Cameron, 1974, p. 115). On the other hand, the evidence has convincingly demonstrated that the experimenter can significantly influence what the client says to himself; now it is time for the therapist to directly influence what the client says to himself (Meichenbaum, 1972).

Cognitive Therapy: Process

The neurological concept of *final common pathway* elucidates how behavior change follows from diverse therapy procedures. It is suggested that clients who see therapists of wholly different persuasions go through similar psychological processes in attaining behavioral change. The final common pathway to behavior change is the modification in the internal dialogues in which our clients engage. Behavioral change, in essence, is mediated by means of alterations in our clients' covert verbalizations (Meichenbaum, 1975). Therapy can thus be defined as a "learning process through which a person acquires an ability to speak to himself in appropriate ways so as to control his own conduct" (Shaffer quoted in Meichenbaum and Cameron, 1974).

Cognitive therapy can be conceptualized as a four-stage process.

Stage 1: Presentation of Rationale

It is always necessary to present to clients the idea that what we think determines how we respond to situations (Strong, 1976). Relevant examples can be offered to illustrate the point that our feelings and behaviors are the result of what we tell ourselves about situations rather than the situations themselves (Goldfried, Decenteceo, and Weinberg 1974).

In describing and illustrating the basic rationale, it is helpful for the therapist to point out that in many situations one may not literally "tell oneself" things which lead to emotional arousal. Because of the well learned nature of our associations with particular situations, our self-statements may have reached the point where the labeling process is more or less automatic (Goldfried, Decenteceo, and Weinberg 1974).

I have not yet found a client who was aware of thinking anything before becoming depressed, anxious, angry, and the like. I explain that they have never paid attention to how they evaluate the situation: they have simply done so and become aware of their reactions. While they have not been aware of evaluating, they were evaluating just the same, and our task is to root out what they are saying to themselves, examine its reasonableness, and change it if necessary.[3] (Strong, 1976, n. 1, p. 357)

Stage 2: Self-observation

The next step in the change process is the client's becoming an observer of his own behavior. It is recognized that the force and prominence of maladaptive thoughts appear to increase in measure with the severity of the client's disturbance. In severe disorders, the thoughts are typically salient and may, in fact, occupy the center of the ideational field as in acute or severe cases of depression, obsession, anxiety, or paranoid states (Beck, 1976). Thus, one of the things that already characterizes some clients prior to therapy is a heightened awareness, a self-preoccupation, and general egocentrism. But, what these clients attend to and say to themselves about their behavior prior to therapy are qualitatively and quantitatively different than what they will observe and how they will appraise their behavior following therapy (Meichenbaum, 1975).

A client experiencing a mild to moderate disturbance in his feelings or behavior, in contrast, may not be aware of his maladaptive thoughts—even though they occur within the realm of conciousness. In such cases, the maladaptive thoughts do not attract his attention—although they regulate how he feels and acts. By shifting his attention to these thoughts, however, the client becomes more aware of them and can specify their content (Beck, 1976).

A basic procedure for helping a client identify his "automatic" thoughts is to train him to observe the sequence of external events and his reactions to them. Generally, there is a gap between the stimulus and response. The emotional and/or behavioral response becomes understandable if he can recollect the thoughts that occurred during this gap (Beck, 1976).

Ellis describes the following techniques for explaining this procedure to the client. He labels the sequence "A, B, C." "A" is the "Activating stimulus" and "C" is the excessive, inappropriate "Conditioned response." "B" is the "Blank in the client's mind," which, when he fills it in, serves as a bridge between "A" and "C." Filling in the blank becomes the therapeutic task (Beck, 1976).

In sum, through heightened awareness and deliberate attention, the client monitors, with intensified sensitivity, his thoughts, feelings, and/or interpersonal behaviors. In the ensuing stage of the change process, this self-observation of the client's inappropriate actions will, upon the occurrence of a maladaptive behavioral event, serve as a signal, or cue, to produce thoughts and behaviors incompatible with the continuation of the inappropriate cognitions and behaviors. The process of self-observation is a necessary but not sufficient condition for change (insight is not enough.) (Meichenbaum, 1975).

One of the byproducts of the increased self-awareness, however, is that the client gains a sense of control of his emotional state and behavior; he feels that he is an active contributor to his own experience and not a defenseless victim of his thoughts and feelings and the reactions of others. A sense of hopefulness and "faith" are stimulated. A key component of effective psychotherapy is the client's experience of having increased his control over his own emotions and overt behavior (Meichenbaum, 1975).

Stage 3: Incompatible Thoughts and Behaviors

Once the client has become an effectual observer of his behavior, the third stage in the change process takes place. The process of self-observation becomes the cue or discriminative stimulus for the client to emit differing cognitions and behaviors. If the client's behavior is to change, then what he now says to himself and/or imagines, must initiate a new behavioral chain, one that is incompatible with his maladaptive behaviors (Meichenbaum, 1975).

After therapy, the client no longer responds impulsively, in an S-R-like manner, to externally or internally generated events. Rather, a salubrious mediational process is elicited by stimuli, and such internal processes now precede the emission of the overt response (Meichenbaum, 1975).

Stage 4: Cognitions Concerning Change

The fourth step in the change process, what the client says to himself about his newly acquired behaviors, determines whether the behavioral change will be maintained and will generalize. As the client endeavors to behave differently, he will frequently elicit different reactions from significant others. What the client says to himself and imagines about these reactions and his own behavior change will affect the stability and generalizability of the treatment (Meichenbaum, 1975).

It is hypothesized that consistency of behavior across situations or treatment generalization is a function of the extent to which the individual emits a set of similar self-statements and/or images across situations. What is being extended is a concept-formation view of personality. Insofar as the same mediators (i.e., appraisals, attributions, self-statements, and images) are elicited across events, one will observe behavioral similarities (Meichenbaum, 1975).

Summary

In summary, a four-stage process of behavioral change is offered: (a) the client is presented with the rationale for cognitive therapy; (b) the client becomes an observer of his thoughts, feelings, and behaviors by means of heightened awareness; (c) the process of self-observation lays the foundation for the client to emit a set of incompatible self-statements and images, and incompatible behaviors; (d) lastly, the nature and content of what the client says to himself (i.e., his self-statements and images) about the behavior change and its accompanying consequences determines the persistence and generalization of the treatment effects (Meichenbaum, 1975).

The therapeutic picture which is proffered is that through monitoring and modifing his thinking (i.e., self-statements and images), a client can effectively change his behavior (Meichenbaum, 1975). Cognitive modification may thus be viewed as a self-control technique whereby the individual develops the ability to regulate his own internal and external behavior (Goldfried et al., 1974).

Sanctification: Process

When God first created man, he said: "Let us make man in our image, after our likeness . . ." (Gen. 1:26). The image of God in man was marred or warped by the fall, but God has never changed in his purpose for man. His purpose is still to conform each human being into one image—the image of his Son: "In sanctification man is 'being renewed unto knowledge after the image of him that created him' (Col. 3:10). Of course, this renewal begins in regeneration; but it is continued in sanctification" (Thiessen, 1949). Sanctification is, thus, the process of the restoration of the image in each believer; it allows the believer to be what he was created to be, to become what he is—a son of God, being in the image of him who created him (Carter, 1974).

It is maintained that as the image in each believer is being renewed, his self-talk becomes more Christlike and less carnal. The biblical conceptualization of this change process patently appears to be the same as the conceptualization formulated by the cognitive theorists.

Stage 1: Presentation of Rationale

The Scripture verse which most manifestly supports the theoretical framework of cognitive therapy is found in Proverbs: "For as a man thinketh in his heart, so is he" (23:7). It follows, then, that "the thoughts of the righteous are right, but the counsels of the wicked are deceit" (Prov. 12:5), "for they that are after the flesh do mind the things of the flesh; but they that are after the Spirit, the things of the Spirit" (Rom. 8:5). ("Mind" is from the Greek word *phroneo* meaning "to think, or to be minded in a certain way" [Vine, vol. 3, 1940].) Since Scripture teaches that what we think reflects either our old nature or our new nature, it behooves us to become aware in what type of self-talk we are actually engaging.

Stage 2: Self-observation

The Psalmist seems to be actively involved in the process of becoming cognizant of his covert verbalizations: "Search me, O God, and know my heart, try me, and know my thoughts; and see if there be any wicked way in me, and lead me in the way everlasting" (Ps. 139:23-24). The implement which God has given us to apprehend our underlying thoughts is his Word, "for the word of God is living, and powerful, and sharper than any two-edged sword, piercing even to the dividing asunder of soul and spirit, and of the joints and marrow, and is a discerner of the thoughts and intents of the heart" (Heb. 4:12).

The heart is the center of the intellectual and volitional life of man (Rom. 10:9-10; Holloman, 1976). It is noteworthy, therefore, that the Bible distinctly teaches that the thoughts of our hearts fall within the purview of consciousness (see Matt. 9:4; 15:19; Mark 7:21, 22; Luke 2:19; 2:51; 5:22; 9:47; 24:38; Acts 8:21, 22). Although inner thoughts occur within the field of consciousness, a person may not observe or notice them. By shifting his attention to these thoughts, however, he becomes more aware of them and can delineate their content (Beck, 1976). Thus a believer who is relatively open and nondefensive is quite capable of being an accurate observer of the thoughts emitted from his heart.

Identifying the operative sinful cognitions that are sources of difficulties precedes replacing these thoughts and attitudes with more Christlike ideas and their behavioral consequences (Strong, 1976): "Let the wicked forsake his way, and the unrighteous man his thoughts, and let him return unto the Lord" (Isa. 55:7), "bringing into captivity every thought to the obedience of Christ" (2 Cor. 10:5).

Stage 3: Incompatible Thoughts and Behaviors

The key role that cognitions play in the process of sanctification is highlighted in Paul's instructions to the Ephesians: "That ye put off concerning the former manner of life the old man, which is corrupt according to the deceitful lusts, and be renewed in the spirit of your mind; and that ye put on the new man, which after God is created in righteousness and true holiness. Wherefore, putting away lying, speak every man truth with his neighbor; for we are members one of another" (Eph. 4:22-25). The renewal here mentioned *(ananeoo)* is not that of the mind itself in its natural powers of memory, judgment, and perception, but "the spirit of the mind," which, under the controlling power of the indwelling Holy Spirit, directs its thoughts and energies Godward in the enjoyment of "fellowship with the Father and with His Son, Jesus Christ," and of the fulfillment of the will of God (Vine, vol. 3, 1940).

Similarly, Paul directs the Romans: "And be not conformed to this world, but be ye transformed by the renewing *(anakainosis)* of your mind, that ye may prove what is that good, and acceptable, and perfect, will of God" (Rom. 12:2; cf. Phil. 3:15). "The renewing (of your mind)" designated here signifies the adjustment of the moral and spiritual vision and thinking to the mind of God, which is designed to have a transforming effect upon the life. Whereas the Ephesians passage stresses the operation of the indwelling Spirit of God, the Romans passage stresses the willing response on the part of the believer (Vine, Vol. 3, 1940). The believer, then, assumes an active role in the process of renewing his mind and, concomitantly, in restoring the image of God in him.

The believer's active role in focusing his mind upon Christlike thoughts is evident in Colossians 3:1-2: "If ye, then, be risen with Christ, seek those things which are above, where Christ sitteth on the right hand of God. Set your affection on things above, not on things on the earth." "Set your affection on," which is the translation of *phroneo,* means to think or set the mind on (Vine, Vol. 1, 1940).

It is explicit from the verses examined above that the thoughts of the flesh are antagonistic to the thoughts of the Spirit. The condition resulting from each pattern of thought is diametric, "for to be carnally minded is death, but to be spiritually minded is life and peace" (Rom. 8:6). (The Greek word for minded in this verse is *phronema,* which denotes what one has in the mind, the thought [the content of the process expressed in *phroneo,* to have in mind, to think], or an object of thought [Vine, Vol. 3, 1940].)

In terms of what it means to be spiritually minded, we are told, "finally brethren, whatever things are true, whatever things are honest, whatever things are just, whatever things are pure, whatever things are lovely, whatever things are of good report; if there be any virtue, and if there be any praise, think *(logizomai)* on these things" (Phil. 4:8). That is, make those things the subjects of your thoughtful consideration (Vine, Vol. 4, 1940).

A word of caution concerning the implementation of "Spiritual self-talk" comes from Meichenbaum and his colleagues' work with schizophrenics as well as other clinical populations.

It is important to insure that the subject does not say the self-statements in a relatively mechanical, rote, or automatic fashion without the accompanying meaning and inflection. This would approximate the everyday experience of reading aloud or silently when one's mind is elsewhere. One may read the paragraph aloud without recalling the content. What is needed instead is modeling and practice in synthesizing and internalizing the meaning of one's self-statements." (Meichenbaum and Cameron, 1974, p. 106).

This caution is obviated if we can proclaim with the Psalmist, "Thy word have I hidden in mine heart, that I might not sin against thee" (Ps. 119:11). Therefore, "let the word of Christ dwell in you richly . . ." (Col. 3:16) and you will "let this mind be in you, which was also in Christ Jesus (Phil. 2:5; cf. 1 Cor. 2:16).

The preceding verses lucidly attest the central role of biblical truth in preventing sin and in promoting growth in sanctification. However, in line with "Meichenbaum's caution," merely memorizing various passages of Scripture in a rote manner does not guarantee that positive change will take place. In fact, no change will be the most likely outcome. In order for the Word of God and "spiritual self-talk" to be genuinely implanted (internalized) within the believer's heart, there should be an accompanying awareness of one's identity as a child of God (John 1:12; Rom. 8:15-16; Phil. 2:15; 1 John 3:1-2). This fundamental realization enables the believer to view God's word and his "sanctified self-talk" as accordant with and as a true reflection of his innermost self. He, therefore, does not employ the "Word" and his "words" as implements of defense in order to ignore or cover up underlying sinful cognitions. Such a use would only serve to promote deception of and dishonesty with one's self (1 John 1:8, 10). Instead, in the process of self-exploration (which occurs during stage 2), the Christian's sinful cognitions are recognized and confessed, being seen as ego-dystonic (ego-alien) and as utterly incompatible with his new divine nature (2 Peter 1:4) and his new identity (1 John 3:9). And (in stage 3) the Word of God and "sanctified self-talk" are emitted and impressed (upon the Christian's psyche), being seen as ego-syntonic in that they both perfectly express the nature of his core self as well as faster growth in sanctification. This being the case, the believer will have, in effect, synthesized and internalized the meaning of Scripture and of his "spiritual self-statements."

Stage 4: Cognitions Concerning Change

A believer's self-statements about his spiritual growth are bound to be positive if he continues to appropriate the resources that are available to him in Christianity, that is, the Word of God (2 Tim. 3:16), corporate fellowship (Heb. 10:25), and fellowship with God the Father, and with his Son, Jesus Christ (1 John 1:3). The exercise of these resources by the believer will not only maintain his growth but will foster it as well.

Since "body life" is a sine qua non of Christianity, it follows that the process delineated in the preceding four stages will be greatly facilitated within the group context, that is, the body of Christ. It was noted previously that Meichenbaum discoverd that the efficacy of his self-statement modification procedure was enhanced in a group setting.

Summary

A four-stage process of spiritual growth is proposed: (1) the believer recognizes that his covert thoughts reflect the intents of his heart, (2) the believer becomes an observer of his thoughts by means of heightened awareness and the Word of God, (3) the believer puts off the old man and puts on the new man through the renewing of his mind, (4) the believer's growth is reinforced by the resources of Christianity.

It is felt that this process of change which takes place in sanctification is the same as the process of change which occurs in cognitive therapy. Parenthetically, striking verification of the compatibility between cognitive theory and therapy and biblical truth comes from the systems of counseling developed by Crabb (1975, 1977) and Strong (1976)—two Christian psychologists. Although in formulating a model for counseling theory and practice Crabb primarily relied on special revelation, that is, Scripture and Strong primarily relied on general revelation, that is, what he had learned in counseling and in teaching, research, and theorizing about counseling, both models are based on the same fundamental tenets. (This should not really be surprising in view of the fact that "all truth is God's truth.") In addition, both ideational structures can accurately be labeled—from a psychological frame of reference—cognitive models of the change process.

The Role of the Will in Change

The intrapsychic agency which initiates an act, which converts intention and decision into action, is "will." Will is the fundamental "responsible mover" within the individual. Although modern metapsychology has chosen to stress the "irresponsible movers" of our behavior (i.e., unconscious motivations and drives), it is difficult to do without the idea of "will" in our understanding to change (Yalom, 1975).

Knowingly or unknowingly, every therapist assumes that each client has within him the capacity to change through willful choice. The therapist, using a variety of strategies and tactics, attempts to escort the client to a crossroad where he can choose, choose willfully in the best interests of his own integrity. The therapist's task is not one of creating will or of infusing will into the client. This, of course, he cannot do. What he can do is to help remove encumbrances from the bound or stifled will of the client (Yalom, 1975). The act of will, of the client changing himself, is at the core of successful therapy (Strong, 1976).

In sum, the individual is the agent of change in his life (Strong, 1976). The role of the therapist (or group) is to help motivate and strengthen the client's will to change.

It should be pointed out that in sanctification, the Christian is not the sole agent of change. Rather, an interdependent and interactive relationship exists between himself and God, although he (the Christian) is the initiator of change, that is, of growth, in sanctification. Thus, the Christian first wills to do God's will, and, in response, God wills to work his will in the Christian's life (Phil. 2:12-13; Holloman, 1978). God, in effect, provides the necessary willing and the power to do the right according to his will (Phil. 2:12-13); for the human will, by itself, may will to do the right, but it may lack the capability of doing the right (Rom. 7:18; Holloman, 1976).

A Christian Rationale for Cognitive Therapy

Cognitive therapy appears to make explicit the process of growth indicated in Scripture. Consequently, it should be the most effective means of obtaining cognitive change and, concomitantly, emotional and behavioral change in clients. The research cited in this article strongly supports this assumption.

In addition, the philosophical presuppositions underlying cognitive therapy are very compatible with the biblical view that each person is ultimately reponsible for his behavior. Cognitive therapists assume that each client is personally responsible for the emotional and behavioral problems he is encountering, that these problems are traceable to and directly caused by his thoughts, beliefs, and perceptions, and that he can change them (Strong, 1976).

The client is thus seen as the source and responsible agent for his problems (Strong, 1976).

By removing personal responsibility from the individual, causal explanation focuses on events the person cannot control, and he is left without tools to deal with his problems (Strong, 1976, n. 1). A client could only lose hope and surrender if he believed historical events were *the* cause of today's problems. He cannot change his history. He can only change what he thinks and does now. Therefore, the effective cause must be something about what he thinks and does now (Strong, 1976, n. 1; cf. Johnson and Matross, 1975). Helping the client see how he can change gives him hope (Strong, 1976, n. 1).

. . . one thing I do—forgetting what is behind and reaching out for what lies ahead, I push on to the goal for the prize of God's heavenly call in Christ Jesus. Let those of us, then, who are mature have this in mind . . . . (Phil. 3:13-15)

References

Beck, A. T. *Cognitive Therapy and the Emotional Disorders.* New York: International Universities Press, 1976.

Brewer, W. F. "There Is No Convincing Evidence for Operant or Classical Conditioning in Adult Humans." In W. B. Weimer and D. S. Palermo (eds.), *Cognition and the Symbolic Processes.* New York: Halsted Press, 1974.

Cabush, D. W., and Edwards, K. J. "Training Clients to Help Themselves: Outcome Effects of Training College Student Clients in Facilitative Self-Responding." *Journal of Counseling Psychology,* 1976, *23,* 34-39.

Carter, J. "Personality and Christian Maturity." *Journal of Psychology and Theology,* 1974, *2,* 190-201.

Crabb, L. J., Jr. *Basic Principles of Biblical Counseling.* Grand Rapids: Zondervan Publishing House, 1975.

———. *Effective Biblical Counseling.* Grand Rapids: Zondervan Publishing House, 1977.

Dember, W. N. "Motivation and the Cognitive Revolution." *American Psychologist,* 1974, *29,* 161-68.

Edwards, K. J. "Effective Counseling and Psychotherapy: An Integrative Review of Research." *Journal of Psychology and Theology,* 1976, *4* (2), 94-107.

Ellis, A., and Harper, R. A. *A New Guide to Rational Living.* Englewood Cliffs, N.J.: Prentice-Hall, 1975.

Farber, I. "The Things People Say to Themselves. "*American Psychologist,* 1963, *6,* 185-97.

Gagné, R. M. *The Conditions of Learning* (2nd ed.). San Francisco: Holt, Rinehart and Winston, 1970.

Gagné, R. M., and Briggs, L. J. *Principles of Instructional Design.* San Francisco: Holt, Rinehart and Winston, 1974.

Glass, C. R., Gottman, J. M., and Shmurak, S. H. "Response-Acquisition and Cognitve Self-Statement Modification Approaches to Dating-Skills Training." *Journal of Counseling Psychology,* 1976, *23,* 520-26.

Goldfried, M. R., Decenteceo, E. T., and Weinberg, L. "Systematic Rational Restructuring as a Self-Control Technique." *Behavior Therapy,* 1974, *5,* 247-54.

Goldfried, M. R., and Sobocinski, D. "Effect of Irrational Beliefs on Emotional Arousal." *Journal of Consulting and Clinical Psychology,* 1975, *43,* 504-10.

Holloman, H. W. *Theology 2.* La Mirada, Calif.: Talbot Theological Seminary, 1976.

————. Personal communication, June 30, 1978.

Johnson, D. W., and Matross, R. P. "Attitude Modification Methods of Helping People Change." In F. H. Kanfer and A. P. Goldstein (eds.), *Helping People Change: Methods and Materials.* New York: Pergamon Press, 1975.

Lazarus, A. A. "Has Behavior Therapy Outlived Its Usefulness?" *American Psychologist,* 1977, *32,* 550-54.

Mahoney, M. J. "Reflections on the Cognitive-Learning Trend in Psychotherapy." *American Psychologist,* 1977, *32,* 5-13.

May, J. R., and Johnson, H. J. "Psychological Activity to Internally Elicited Arousal and Inhibitory Thoughts." *Journal of Abnormal Psychology,* 1973, *82,* 239-45.

Meichenbaum, D. H. "The Effects of Instructions and Reinforcement on Thinking and Language Behavior of Schizophrenics." *Behavior Research and Therapy,* 1969, *7,* 101-14.

————. *Enhancing Creativity by Modifying What Ss Say to Themselves.* Manuscript, University of Waterloo, 1972*a.*

————. "Examination of Model Characteristics in Reducing Avoidance Behavior." *Journal of Personality and Social Psychology,* 1971, *17,* 298-307.

————. "Cognitive Modification of Test-Anxious College Students." *Journal of Consulting and Clinical Psychology,* 1972*b, 39,* 370-80.

————. "Self-Instructional Strategy Training: A Cognitive Prothesis for the Aged." *Human Development,* 1974, *17,* 273-80.

————. "Toward a Cognitive Theory of Self-Control." I. G. Schwartz and D. Shapiro (eds.), *Consciousness and Self-Regulation: Advances in Research.* New York: Plenum Press, 1975.

Meichenbaum, D., and Cameron, R. "Training Schizophrenics to Talk to Themselves: A Means of Developing Attentional Controls." *Behavior Therapy,* 1973, *4,* 515-34.

————. "The Clinical Potential of Modifying What Clients Say to Themselves." *Psychotherapy: Theory, Research and Practice,* 1974, *II,* 103-17.

Meichenbaum, D. H., Gilmore, J. B., and Fedoravicius, A. "Group Insight Versus Group Desensitization in Treating Speech Anxiety." *Journal of Consulting and Clinical Psychology,* 1971, *36,* 410-521.

Meichenbaum, D., and Goodman, J. "Training Impulsive Children to Talk to Themselves: A Means of Developing Self-Control." *Journal of Abnormal Psychology,* 1971, *77,* 115-26.

Rimm, D. C., and Litvak, S. B. "Self-Verbalization and Emotional Arousal." *Journal of Abnormal Psychology,* 1969, *74,* 181-87.

Rimm, D. C., and Masters, J. C. *Behavior Therapy: Techniques and Empirical Findings.* San Francisco: Academic Press, 1974.

Russell, P. L., and Brandsma, J. M. "A Theoretical and Empirical Integration of the Rational-Emotive and Classical Conditioning Theories." *Journal of Consulting and Clinical Psychology,* 1974, *42,* 389-97.

Schachter, S., and Singer, J. E. "Cognitive, Social, and Physiological Determinants of Emotional States." *Psychological Review,* 1962, *69,* 379-399.

Schwartz, R. M., and Gottman, J. M. "Toward a Task Analysis of Assertive Behavior." *Journal of Consulting and Clinical Psychology,* 1976, *44,* 910-20.

Scofield, C. I. (ed.). *Holy Bible.* New York: Oxford University Press, 1969.

Steffy, R. A., Meichenbaum, D., and Best, J. A. "Aversive and Cognitive Factors in the

Modification of Smoking Behavior." *Behavior Research and Therapy*, 1970, *8*, 115-25.

Strong, S. R. "Christian Counseling." Manuscript, University of Minnesota, 1976.

Thiessen, H. C. *Introductory Lectures in Systematic Theology*. Grand Rapids: Eerdmans, 1949.

Velten, E. "A Laboratory Task for Induction of Mood States." *Behavior Research and Therapy*, 1968, *6*, 473-82.

Verkuyl, G. *The Modern Language Bible*. Grand Rapids: Zondervan Publishing House, 1969.

Vine, W. E. *An Expository Dictionary of New Testament Words*. Old Tappan, N.J.: Fleming H. Revell, 1940.

Yalom, I. D. *The Theory and Practice of Group Psychotherapy* (2nd ed.). New York: Basic Books, 1975.

Zener, K. "The Significance of Behavior Accompanying Conditioned Salivary Secretion for Theories of the Conditioned Reflex." *American Journal of Psychology*, 1937, *50*, 384-403.

The author would like to thank William Britt III and Glenn Goldberg for encouraging him to seek publication.

THE THERAPIST AND CHRISTIAN CLIENT
IN RELATIONSHIP

I have been born three times—once from the womb, once by the Spirit, and once out of therapy. I remember nothing, of course, about the first, a good deal about the second, and very much about the third because it was yesterday that I closed the door of the therapist's office for the last time. All three births led from darkness to light. Because I am a committed Christian, all three are inextricably bound together. As I view my life now, to make one birth more vital than another fleetingly reflects the odd necessity some find to decide whether Jesus' incarnation, death, or resurrection was most significant. It is difficult to put priorities on the pivotal experiences of any life.

As I experienced emotional healing in therapy, the phrase "born again" often thrust itself into my mind and while it may be theologically untenable, existentially, it is an appropriate designation of my new life. As I continue to grow and change and "find myself," I want to write about the therapeutic experience in relationship with the therapist. Before it fades, I want to clarify and settle it for myself and hope it may be of some significance to therapists or clients who come to some touchy and sensitive stages in their progress together.

Physical and spiritual births are always both unique and common. In my own experience and in my contacts with other clients who are in therapy, I have found it to be so with emotional "births" as well. I tell only my own story, but I am aware that it also reflects the stories of others.

Willing self-disclosure on the part of the client is, of course, an essential ingredient for success in therapy. Paul Tournier warns of crossroads at which the client may refuse to go forward.

It is easy to unburden oneself up to a point to someone who is neutral and kindly disposed. Sooner or later, however, . . . (there are) feelings the acknowledgment of which seems almost impossible. At that point, any loophole of escape or deception can decisively jeopardize the cure, while on the other hand, the courage to retain absolute frankness even to the bitter end will open the door to a great deliverance. (1962, p. 29).

The client is faced with the decision of what to tell, whether to withhold. At any point in self-disclosure, the client can balk—the truth is too painful, the risk too great. Tournier is speaking in the context of handling feelings of guilt which are dredged up from the past, but the principle he lays down applies in crises that develop in the client/therapist relationship.

In addition to disclosing whatever relates to the necessity for therapy, the client is faced with telling or not telling, dealing or not dealing, with the stages of involvement which arise in relationship with the therapist. This relationship adds a whole new dimension to self-disclosure, and with it an entirely different set of decisions. For the Christian this new dimension can be extremely threatening: the Christian often comes into therapy somewhat reluctantly because of the confusion between spiritual and emotional problems; the client may be scarcely convinced that it is acceptable to have something in life go sour. Then a depth and acceptance in relationship which has perhaps never been experienced before looms into existence and can become morally questionable: is it all right to form an emotional attachment with the therapist? A hornet's nest of resulting conflicting feelings must be sorted out, in itself a possibly intimidating process.

Identification with the Therapist

Definitions of "transference" seem personally inadequate to define my experience with the therapist, if indeed I was experiencing "transference" in its technical sense at all. "Transference" is a term I disliked because it seemed so impersonal, so clinical, so often identified with negative experiences of the past, and because my identification with the therapist was loaded with positive personal feelings. I will always be in revolt against Dr. Jay Adams' description of whatever smacks to him of the Rogerian approach: a caricature of an uncaring and detached counselor, "nodding and grunting" acceptingly (Adams, 1972, p. 90). Even given a modified Rogerian approach, Adams says Rogers "must be rejected in toto" (p. 104).

From the very beginning I was unlocked by the acceptance of the psychologist, and his intent and careful empathy produced a flood of confidence on my part. It is not hard to recall the persistent reflection of my self-disclosure which in turn allowed me to really hear myself. In no time I was a willing captive of the process as we began to dig together not into the past, but the dense layers of my present. In very little time I was a "captive" of the therapist as well, intensely involved in relationship. I spoke of this involvement freely almost from its onset. I wrote it in letters. The therapist took this devotion (such shallow and need-oriented devotion) kindly and without evaluation.

For a few months the therapist was in effect not only the most important person on earth but God as well. My struggle to maintain meaningful relationships to God and the important people in my world was not my reality. I had no sense of sin about my attitude toward the counselor, felt no conscious need to make an evaluation, because overriding even this relationship was intense relief that I was working at the problems which had plagued and driven me for so long. For me the therapeutic process answered desperate prayer; it was all in God's will.

Although there is a sense in which all effective therapy is a two-way street, I do not know the therapist's story—I can only tell my own. The entire healing structure would have come crashing down had the therapist expressed anything (negatively or positively) other than a steady caring-while-neutral interest. I would guess my feelings were not particularly appreciated or agreeable, and I look back with amazement at such balance on the therapist's part: to accept without feedback. Perhaps it helped that my expression was only verbal.

I know Christian clients who have terminated therapy at this point of emotional involvement—it becomes too sinful, too hard to handle. Guilt enters. It is one of the first places in self-disclosure that can become a stumbling block. It is easily possible that an experienced but unacknowledged warm response to the counselor can begin to cripple the process. This has happened to a friend, and the suspecting therapist asked her in what way their personal relationship might be affecting therapy. It was an opportunity for her to express this response and to discover that it was a common and understandable part of the therapeutic process, nothing more. If emotional involvement becomes overwhelming before it is out in the open, it is more difficult to handle.

Although it was a tenuous time spiritually, my relationship to God grew positively upon the firm ground of my acceptance by the therapist in the face of *all* the "unacceptables—the hitherto undisclosed weaknesses and difficulties in life, and the added identification with the counselor. I reasoned: if a human being can be that accepting, the loving Creator of us both must be more accepting still. It is incredible that a relationship with the living God can be unexciting, yet dullness (to say nothing of hate) with God is common. Rewarding human relationships are so pleasurable; it is not hard to realize that when they begin to happen they may take the place of a relationship to God that has never been exciting or has lost its joy. As emotional healing occurred in terms of daily life, I benefited spiritually in the long run because of willingness to work through my feelings about the therapist. An exciting human relationship had renewed an excitement with God.

The Credibility of the Therapist

I became conscious of a second phenomenon in relation to the counselor a few weeks into therapy. It was an amazing credulity concerning anything he said. I was stunned with the statement, "You are depressed," because committed Christians do not become depressed, yet I knew he was correct. Because I discovered the things he said were accurate in my situation and because of the identification, I began to accept everything he said as gospel truth. I began to equate any casual words from the therapist with considered statements. On two occasions casual remarks threw me into a panic because I took them at face value. This panic was severe enough to leave me with no "cope" and was relieved only by clarification on the phone between sessions.

I think this undiscerning ascribing of such authority to the therapist is somewhat typical: there is the psychologist's professional status (much as the status of the physician, which we seldom question); the lay person can have some vague idea that a psychologist is a mind reader; and evangelical Christians in particular tend to trust authority. Because of this the client can even jump to catch any phrase that will reinforce a prior bias—e.g., to launch into some activity or relationship a client was already determined to pursue, or to have a negative reaction if one was initially reluctant to undertake therapy or the truth becomes too unpleasant. Christians are especially susceptible to discomfort with the whole internalizing process. Clients who react to the therapist's "authority" negatively can use these reasons as rationale to terminate prematurely.

The "Friendship" Syndrome

Well into therapy, to the place where healing was obviously taking place, came a most demanding and tenacious "need"—the need to establish some reciprocal acknowledgement of "friendship" on the psychologist's part, a conscious desire to be the counselor's peer in a social relationship. I am conscious only in retrospect of two things that caused this to happen. First, when a measure of healing was in sight, I looked back to my pretherapy self with distaste: "The real me is not that muddled, mixed-up, and unacceptable person. It will be a proof of ok-ness if the therapist will have me for a friend." Second, although healing was on the way, it was not accomplished, and if I got well, I would have to leave this vitally important person: "If I can become a friend, I will not have to sever this relationship."

It is important to recognize that these two reasons were not at all clear at that time, but it is safe to assume that as long as a client is deeply concerned with the relationship to the counselor (for whatever reason), therapy is not finished. One proof of healing is freedom to let the therapist go.

This desperate need to be a friend was heavy for the therapist: only he could authenticate me and only by this "friendship." It was a position of power which he had no desire to occupy. For me this became the balking place. I tried to run by taking a leap of faith and declaring a premature state of good health by canceling my "last" appointment. If I could immediately demonstrate a wholeness, I could become acceptable as a friend. In a moment of truth with myself, I knew I could not stop therapy unless the relationship was put to rest. In some confrontive sessions we did that "putting to rest" together, getting to the truth of the "friendship" problem.

Terminating

The point where termination takes place is an important one. If therapy is to be concluded successfully it is in large part a satisfying conclusion to the client/therapist relationship. The problems of life will never end and every "normal" Christian would benefit from a continued relationship with a person skilled in how minds and emotions "work." As I read Scripture and look at our world and live in deep involvement in the church, I don't need the gift of prophecy to know the truth: Tensions and pressures will increase for the Christian and handling them well may call for more insight than most of us have. The door to the psychologist needs to remain as open as the door to the physician; there may be a need in the future I don't anticipate now. If I had stopped therapy, not "finished" with the therapist, there is little likelihood I would go back again.

It took a few weeks in a group situation to give me the objectivity I needed to move out "on my own." It was very helpful to see the counselor in meaningful relationships with other counselees. It took still longer to come, as Tournier expressed it, to the "bitter end." When I left the office for the last time I felt ambivalence—at once a little fearful and yet consciously determined that the leave-taking would somehow be as definite and as clean-cut as the snap of the closing door—finished, done, the sooner forgotten the better. This is another stumbling block for Christians—a true acceptance of one's current state. Was something deep within still at war? Could I as a Christian really accept all the emotional intimacy of that relationship? Is it good to forget healing or its source? Jesus thought not. I'm sure the one grateful leper, the one who held his healing in consciousness and thanked God for it, was the one who benefited most. My mechanics are not mechanical and "forgetting" didn't help; working it *clear* through with self-acceptance did.

I believe that there may be deeper meaning and healing through my relationship with the psychologist than in the application of principles to specific problems, though those applications were most helpful and practical and I use these principles in daily life. I want to affirm my therapeutic experience, and in particular to affirm the relationship to the counselor. I accept the humiliations, the struggles, and release, as a very valid part of Christian experience. My vulnerability and selfishness clearly represents my condition before God; the patient work of the therapist clearly represents the long-suffering of God. The integration of Christian experience with the therapeutic experience is worth exploration.

References

Adams, J. *Competent to Counsel.* Nutley, N.J.: Presbyterian & Reformed Publishing Co., 1972.
Tournier, P. *Grace and Guilt.* New York: Harper & Row, 1962.

SECTION SIX

HUMAN SEXUALITY

There has been relatively little scholarly material written from a Christian perspective in the area of human sexuality, and only a small portion of this material integrates psychological and theological concepts concerning human sexuality. The four articles in this section are representative of this rather limited number of integrative attempts in the area of human sexuality. The first article presents a broad three-dimensional model of psychosexuality by which various sexual attitudes, behaviors, and practices can be evaluated. The next two articles focus in on the subject of homosexuality, probably the human sexuality issue of most concern presently to the Christian community. The final article deals with Christian perspectives on the treatment of human sexual dysfunction.

Court and Johnston have presented a three-dimensional model of psychosexuality which they contend is superior to the one- or two-dimensional proposals of secular psychologists. The three dimensions proposed are: (1) homosexuality-heterosexuality, (2) orientation-activity, and (3) moral-immoral. They argued that the spiritual aspect of man (i.e., the moral-immoral dimension) must be included in order to understand fully the relevant issues in the area of human sexuality.

The authors have viewed the three dimensions as being independent of each other and continuous rather than categorical. On the one hand, they enumerated potential semantic and theological problems inherent in this continuous rather than categorical view of psychosexuality. On the other hand, they illustrated how a continuous dimension viewpoint provides grounds for therapeutic optimism in treating homosexuality. Court and Johnston presented the specific case of homosexual behavior to illustrate the utility of their three-dimensional model in understanding the relevant issues in relation to homosexuality.

This three-dimensional model of psychosexuality may stimulate a number of questions in the mind of the reader. Is this model equally applicable to other sexual practices such as adultery, bestiality, bisexuality, and incest? Does this model conflict with biblical teaching against certain sexual practices which are labeled sin? Are there any behaviors that two homosexuals may engage in without sin? Are there additional dimensions that should be included in a more complete model of psychosexuality?

281

The articles by Evans and Vayhinger focus specifically on the issue of homosexuality. Evans has attempted to articulate a Christian ethic on homosexuality based on biblical material and results of psychological research. Vayhinger has approached homosexuality from the perspective of the treatment issues involved for the Christian psychotherapist.

Evans has made a sharp distinction between the homosexual condition and homosexual behavior. He has cited results of psychological research which indicate that the condition of homosexuality is not hereditary but is rather the result of an early and complex learning pattern brought about most typically by a pathogenic family pattern. The affected individual is a passive recipient of this learning process rather than an active participant.

Evans has defined homosexual behavior as the willful engagement in homosexual activity and has cited scriptural references that indicate that the biblical condemnation of homosexuality refers to homosexual behavior and not to the homosexual condition. He has further noted that the Christian community has failed to make this distinction between homosexual condition and behavior, and has called for the church to change its attitude from condemnation to compassionate forgiveness.

Vayhinger has explicated three issues which the Christian psychotherapist must resolve when treating a person who manifests homosexual behavior: (1) an understanding by the therapist of the many causes and forms of gender and homosexual life-style, (2) an open sharing of the definition of what is sought in the therapy and a contract which is functional for both patient and therapist, and (3) an accurate understanding of the biblically and psychologically sound definition of human potential as to what is possible in psychotherapy.

Vayhinger has cited research evidence indicating a relatively optimistic perspective on the treatment of homosexual behavior as compared to the treatment of alcoholism, criminality, schizophrenia, and other serious conditions. The treatment emphasis appears to be on change rather than cure, with the chief prerequisite being the patient's desire for change. The inference can be drawn that change for the majority of patients is in homosexual behavior rather than condition.

Is the distinction made between homosexual behavior and condition a valid biblical distinction? Does the Bible condemn the homosexual condition as well as homosexual behavior? What role if any should the church and Christian community play in helping to bring about change in the homosexual? Should the church place any restrictions on the repentant homosexual who is homosexual in condition but not behavior?

David and Duda have articulated an approach to the treatment of human sexual dysfunction in which they employ four permission-giving Christian concepts: (1) separateness versus unity, (2) coupleness, (3) in God's image, and (4) letting go. They have successfully used these concepts to aid patients, regardless of their religious affiliation or lack of it, in overcoming therapeutic resistances such as the notion that sexual pleasure is basically narcissistic and selfish. The authors have proposed the couple's commitment to marriage as a covenant to be the underlying essential ingredient for integrating the four permission-giving Christian concepts and desired sexual functioning.

Are there other biblical concepts that would be useful in treating human sexual dysfunction? Should the Christian sex therapist treat sexual dysfunction in people who have no commitment to marriage? Are there certain sex therapy procedures (e.g., the use of sexual surrogates, sexual fantasies, sexual literature, pictures, and movies) that are inappropriate for the Christian therapist to employ?

PSYCHOSEXUALITY:
A THREE-DIMENSIONAL MODEL

John H. Court

O. Raymond Johnston

Model-building plays an important part in scientific exploration. A good model permits testable hypotheses to be explored and further predictions to be made. Evidence as it accumulates can bring modifications or require a total rejection of a model when the available data prove incompatible.

Models in psychology are both widespread and important since so much research relates to hypothetical constructs not open to direct test by the sense or by instrumentation. The effects of conjecture, presupposition, expectation, and value judgment distort perception so much that the need to create and test models is essential in coming to understand human behavior as it is rather than as we suppose it might be.

In recent years implicit models of psychosexuality have been changing though research reports rarely mention them. Debate about findings can easily descend to acrimony when initial presuppositions create a hidden agenda. Scientists ostensibly arguing about the evidence can actually be in disagreement over more fundamental issues such as the purpose of sex, the limits of sexual freedom, and whether we are autonomous or subject to the will of God.

Clarification Through Models

Popular ideas about the nature of psychological reality can be refined by appropriate experimentation. An inadequate model may mean that we jump to conclusions. It can also mean that certain kinds of hypotheses are just not tested. In clinical settings, the therapist who unwillingly acts according to the suppositions of an inadequate model may be led to inappropriate treatment. Simplistic models can generate half-truths which obscure important unrecognized features.

An example from the last 40 years has been the controversies surrounding depressive illnesses. Psychiatrists ask whether there is one

© *Journal of Psychology and Theology,* 1978, *6* (2), 90-97. Used by permission of the authors. Research support provided to the first author by the Nationwide Festival of Light, England, is gratefully acknowledged.

type or two—neurotic (or reactive), or psychotic (or endogenous). Can we identify two distinct clusters of symptoms, or is there some kind of gradation such that the obviously different manifestations merely represent extremes of a continuum? These and related issues are of more than theoretical interest. Whichever model is implicitly assumed generates its own predictions about diagnosis, therapy, and prognosis. Psychologists ·may approach depression using a quite different model. Seligman's (1975) learned helplessness model is one example which proposes quite different antecedents as well as alternative modes of intervention based on reinforcement.

Psychosexuality Models

Assumptions about sexuality derived from the Christian tradition are being widely challenged. Often the underlying premises are hidden, but the conclusions are clear enough.

The best of Christian teaching has assumed that sexuality is God-given and for our enjoyment as well as for procreation. It has emphasized a differentiation between male and female with each complementary to the other and each of equal dignity and worth. It has clearly identified some aspects of sexual behavior as right and others wrong. It has stressed marriage as a special relationship between a man and a woman but including in this the spiritual significance of marriage as a sacred relationship which should, therefore, be indissoluble.

Into these basic propositions there has come a new generation of sex research, social psychology, and anthropology. The study of sexual patterns in animals, in people of other cultures, the clinical research relating to sexual disorders, especially transsexualism, as well as changing patterns of social life, have all led to reappraisals. Behind most of this sex research the fundamental assumptions have not been those of the Christian. They have been secular, expressing a humanistic view of man which prefers to avoid such distinctions as "good" and "evil," favoring tolerance and acceptance of others. The "Humanist Manifesto II" (1973) says *inter alia*:

The many varieties of sexual exploration should not in themselves be considered "evil." Without countenancing mindless permissiveness or unbridled promiscuity, a civilised society should be a *tolerant* one. (p. 13)

In this context, it follows logically that there have been strong pressures in society to accept homosexuality as merely one of the many variations of sexual adjustment. The contemporary secular orthodoxy says that:

There is no issue of public morals involved, and the law has no business to interfere. To seek an emotional or sexual relationship with a person of the same sex is simply an indication of an alternative life-style and nothing more. (Royal Commission Report, 1977, p. 98)

This area of homosexuality is one which confronts the Christian psychologist more obviously than many other aspects of sexuality partly due to the clinical responsibilities of many in the profession and partly because of public statements being advanced by many in the profession about homosexuality. Differences in view expressed within the profession, and even by Christians, appear to arise not so much from disagreements about evidence as from a failure to identify an underlying model of psychosexuality.

Even among apparently Christian writers, there has been divergence of views in recent years regarding quite basic questions about homosexuality. Many of the more liberal theological positions are supported by a hidden agenda. That is, behind any factual debate, those proclaiming that Scripture contains no moral condemnation are commonly responding either with a personal compassion for others, enlightened by the teachings of situation ethics, or are providing for themselves a rationale into which they can accommodate their own homosexuality. For example, it was as recently as April 1977, that Norman Pittenger identified himself as homosexual during a BBC-TV discussion. His theological writings are among the most widely quoted by Christian homosexual activists.

Personal involvement is no way to create a rational model for understanding—any more, one should add, than is a hostile antihomo-sexual orientation. The psychologist must in all honesty stand in awe of the facts. The Christian psychologist must go further and interpret the data with such enlightenment as Scripture offers. His interpretation will not disregard the scientific evidence, but he may well reach different conclusions because the model he uses will be less simplistic in the sense that it is neither randomly chosen nor based on any dogmatic reductionist or materialistic view of human nature, but includes the spiritual, Godward axis which Christians have always included in their overall assessments and explanation of human behavior.

Dimensions of Homosexuality

To do justice to the psychological debate about homosexuality, it is proposed that an orthogonal three-dimensional model is necessary. A great deal of apparently scientific debate is conducted as if only one dimension were involved. More sophisticated, scientific debate recognizes two dimensions are necessary. The Christian psychologist will find these two together with a third are necessary in order to understand the relevant issues. Additional dimensions are necessary in other contexts and will be briefly noted below.

First Dimension

Homosexuality-- Heterosexuality

This representation itself immediately dismisses the older view that psychosexuality is categorical. It now appears from evidence, notably that of Kinsey et. al. (1948), that a continuous dimension more adequately fits the picture. His development of a method of rating people on a scale from 0 to 6 (exclusively heterosexual to exclusively homosexual) made it clear that a very large number of adults report data giving them intermediate ratings. It appears, therefore, that we need a model of psychosexuality which identifies everyone at some point along a continuum with a potential for homo- or heterosexual activity. The model must also allow for the possibility of migration along this dimension either way since self-reports of young people and adults indicate patterns of behavior which are affected by such parameters as age and environment.

It is not helpful to identify a person's position on a continuum by combining data from past experience with data relating to present adjustment. The impression resulting from this is of a normal curve of distribution; whereas, among mature adults a distribution heavily skewed towards heterosexuality is more appropriate.

It is one of the more confusing paradoxes of the subject that activists in homosexual movements typically favor the continuum view over the older categorical one, yet still debate behind the drawn battle lines of "us" and "them." Their insistence on usage of "homosexual" or "gay" constantly carries with it the implication of difference from others, which at the same time is, at another level, denied.

Christian apologists have traditionally adopted a categorical assumption and written of homosexuals as being different and separate from heterosexuals. This has appeared to be necessary in order to sustain the oral arguments of Scripture. However, this may be a false perception based on an over-simple model. The introduction of a second dimension overcomes some of the semantic and theological problems.

One should note in passing that the result of placing people on a single dimension on the basis of life experiences gives a spurious impression of large numbers of adults of bisexual tendency. While many adults can recall events and fantasies from their adolescence which indicate homosexual potential, these should not be unduly weighted when assessing the mature adult's position on the 0-6 dimension.

Even with this single dimension, a great deal of unnecessary controversy can be avoided if protagonists identify whether they are adopting categorical or dimensional assumptions. The acrimony of confrontation implicit in polar opposites (homosexual *versus* heterosexual) can give way to rational discussion with the assumption that we all have a psychosexual nature of some sort in common. O'Donovan (1977) emphasizes that:

It is a false philosophy which regards "heterosexual" and "homosexual" relationships as alternatives exclusive of each other. A proper discussion of homosexuality . . . must include the observation that, though genital love-making between members of the same sex represents a distortion of God's purposes for human sexuality, warm and emotional friendship does not, and is entirely compatible with the so-called "heterosexual" orientation. The tragedy of the homosexual lies not in what he has, but in what he has lost. (p. 104)

This distinction is especially important in discussions relating to the possibility of change. A categorical view would imply that the homosexual is irrevocably fixed with an orientation from which change is impossible and leads to nihilistic assumptions about treatment. A continuous dimension gives grounds for therapeutic optimism, with the possibility of shifting from one position to another. Such a conviction needs to be more fully documented in the professional literature with careful follow-up reports on those who have rejected their homosexual life-style. While secular therapists dispute the validity of such experiences, the reality is clear enough to such groups as Exodus in California, and Pilot, the Homosexual Counselling Service in Poole, England.

Second Dimension

Orientation--- Activity

This dimension is largely irrelevant in determinist thinking. It is acknowledged by gay movements but not seen to be of great importance. It is crucial to conservative theology.

It is an unfortunate feature of the Kinsey investigations that the 0-6 rating is derived from a combination of responses, some of which refer to disposition or inclination (orientation) while others relate to overt practices (activity). This conflation of orientation with activity was recognized but not resolved in the original study when it was stated that "it will be observed that the rating which an individual receives has a dual basis. It takes into account his overt sexual experiences and/or his psychosexual reactions . . . In each classification there are persons who have had no experience or a minimum of overt sexual experience, but in the same classification they may also be persons who have had hundreds of sexual contacts" (Kinsey et al., 1948, p. 647). It makes for greater clarity of thought to separate these two components by introducing this second dimension which is skewed in the adult population towards heterosexual activity.

By relating the two dimensions orthogonally, one can think in terms of everyone being located in one of four quadrants: heterosexually oriented and inactive, heterosexually oriented and active, homosexually oriented and inactive, homosexually oriented and active.

The third category makes provision for the "latent homosexual" as well as those with a strong disposition towards homosexual relationships who do not engage in homosexual practices. An intrinsic difficulty in using the categorical terminology of homosexual and heterosexual is that individuals can also exhibit both types of attraction and behavior. The term bisexual is appropriate for refering to those who are not clearly identified with a psychosexually differentiated role. It should not be assumed (as the Kinsey model might lead one to suspect) that there is here a normal curve of distribution in the adult population with the largest number of adults found in the intermediate, bisexual part of the continuum. It is rather that individuals may shift along the continuum during psychosexual development, and ultimately, most adults are to be found clustering at the heterosexual end of the psychosexuality dimension.

At a scientific level, it is clearly useful to distinguish between orientation and action if measurement criteria are to be established. It is also helpful theoretically to incorporate homosexuality along with heterosexuality in the same matrix of ideas; to separate them a priori is to make a value judgment ahead of the evidence. The distinction is disliked by those who are advocates for the homosexual life-style. Their assumption is that if one has a tendency to homosexual arousal, this will logically lead to its expression and, indeed, should not be inhibited. The same free expression is also widely advocated for the heterosexual.

Such a position can be logically argued from the assumption of these two dimensions alone, and one should not be surprised that a large number of secular psychologists follow the view that the homosexual should be free to follow his sexual inclinations. If further distinctions are to be made, some additional information is required.

Third Dimension

Moral---Immoral

The secular psychologist is hard-pressed to find a basis for saying, "This behavior is abnormal (or deviant, or perverted)." He has no basis at all for saying behavior is moral or immoral, but finds himself conceptually tied to descriptions which implicitly contain value judgments, even when conventional moral judgments are rejected. Hence, while many psychologists and psychiatrists retain the conviction that homosexuality represents a departure from the norm (Morris, 1977), the reasons for this vary widely from a disease concept to an "aberrant behavior pattern." There is a singular absence of adequate scientific criteria by which such differences may be resolved.

The Christian psychologist, on the other hand, does have clear biblical teaching on psychosexuality generally, and homosexuality in particular. Fornication, adultery, and homosexual practices are clearly condemned as sinful (Bockmühl, 1973; Court, 1973; N.F.O.L., 1975). In the Old Testament, homosexual episodes are recorded on two occasions (Gen. 15:5-9; Judg. 19:22-23) and in each case judgment follows. Efforts to reinterpret and deflect the force of such passages by liberal theologians are rejected by Smith (1968) who believes the Hebrew is quite clear in its meaning. More direct injunctions against homosexuality along with other sexual practices such as incest and bestiality are present in Leviticus (18:22-23; 20:13–16).

Against the argument that such statements are only of temporary or local significance are the complementary New Testament references to sexual sins (Rom. 1:26-32; 1 Cor. 6:9-10; 1 Tim. 1:8-11; 2 Peter 2:6-7). These passages include homosexual acts within a broader perspective of psychosexuality which identifies all manifestations of illicit sex as sin.

. . . against the proper use of our bodies (I Corinthians 6:18) which are intended to operate sexually in a divinely ordained bond which reflects a supernatural relationship and which have already been possessed by the Spirit in anticipation of this idea (I Corinthians 6:19f.). (Smith, 1969, p. 22)

The force of these passages is such that they present not specific applications but normative, ethical principles.

It has to be emphasized, of course, that this biblical condemnation applies to activity not orientation—the distinction contained within the second dimension above. There is nothing in Scripture to suggest that the person with a homosexual orientation is under condemnation of the moral law of God. It is activity which is condemned, though it is clear from Jesus' teaching in Matthew 5:28 that activity must be construed to include the cognitive component of lustful fantasy.

Integration

On the basis of a biblical moral code, it is possible to evaluate the other dimensions, represented together in figure 1.

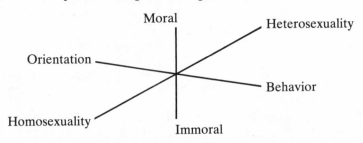

Figure 1. Three dimensions of psychosexuality

Monogamy, chastity, and a lifelong commitment to marriage are portrayed in Scripture as the norm (1 Cor. 7; Eph. 5:21-33; Heb. 13:4). There is also a significant place for the single person, male or female, living a creative and fulfilled life (1 Cor. 7:7-9; N.F.O.L., 1975; O'Donovan, 1977). This includes people of predominantly homosexual as well as heterosexual orientation, all of whom are equal in the sight of God.

Moral distinctions are the most important in relation to the orientation-activity dimension. The man who is strongly tempted to adultery but resolutely resists this is under no moral condemnation. In the same way, the homosexual strongly attracted to another of the same sex who resists the temptation to go further is equally free. The requirement of moral purity applies equally to homosexual and heterosexual alike.

Without this third dimension, a rational basis for social sanctions against homosexual behavior is difficult to find. It is not surprising that an understanding of sexuality based simply on observation of what *is* fails to provide a basis for determining what *ought* to be. The provisos of consent and harm to others are often introduced in ethical discussions in order to separate acceptable from unacceptable sexual behavior, but both lack clarity and are open to gross abuse. The concept of consent, which implies freedom of choice, is psychologically problematic and, indeed, strangely defended by those with a basically determinist view of behavior. The concept of harm to others is too limited if physical harm alone is intended. Psychological harm, and, for the Christian, moral harm, must be among the considerations.

The question of the harmfulness of homosexual behavior is a vexed one since one must take account both of the impact of the homosexual on others as well as the converse. Some, at least, of the postulated adverse consequences of homosexual behavior, such as discrimination and stigma, are heavily dependent on society's attitudes. Others, such as the increased incidence of venereal disease, often said to be associated with homosexual acts, may be more resistant to change. At the sociological level, arguments are advanced in relation to an adverse impact on family life-styles and to the effect that homosexual behavior profoundly confuses the function of sex in human relationships.

All such arguments are open to criticism if examined without reference to a moral dimension. Even if harm were conceded, this would give no clear indication what should be done. It would be as logical to argue for changes in society as for restraint of certain sexual behavior. Only inasfar as one acknowledges that a moral principle is involved can the sources of harm be identified.

The logic which defends homosexual behavior can equally be used in support of bestiality or, under some circumstances, necrophilia. The question of consent arises neither with animals nor corpses, nor could one demonstrate physical harm to either as a result of a sexual relationship. Again, only with a moral dimension to one's thinking can approval of such behavior be questioned.

Implications

This three-dimensional model includes some potential confusion and fails to deal with all aspects of psychosexuality.

(1) The use of a moral continuum could be found objectionable when we consider sin as categorical. Behavior is either sinful or it is not. One possible implication of the continuum is to identify some sins as more serious than others, and hence by implication follow the traditional view that homosexual acts are among the most heinous of sins. This is not the intention behind this continuum. In Leviticus 20, the compendium of sexual sins includes homosexual acts along with adultery, bestiality, and incest in an unequivocal way. Equally, however, it is listed in the New Testament with sins we commonly interpret as much less in importance. Smith (1968) says: "Homosexuality is not singled out for separate treatment or given special prominence. It is one sign—one symptom—among many" (p. 218).

A moral dimension rather than two categories may permit us to think more flexibly about those aspects of behavior where clear injunctions in Scripture are not to be found. That is, there are some areas of behavior where legitimate differences of opinion arise. In the past, Christian debate has focused on issues like smoking and drinking. Principles derived from 1 Corinthians 8 dealing with meat offered to idols and the principle of the weaker brother are invoked in support of both sides of such discussion. The same kind of debate over the morality of behavior arises today over such issues as abortion and divorce. Some see these issues as black and white; others believe a balance of moral arguments make them less clear cut.

The existence of such difficult moral issues should be sufficient to justify thinking about moral issues in continuous rather than categorical terms. The *danger* in doing so, however, is that something which is unequivocally sinful in Scripture is shifted away from the immoral end of the continuum to become a matter of relativity and debate. The end result is that what was clearly sinful first becomes sometimes sinful and then not simply morally neutral, but ultimately something to be positively rejoiced in. This is the sequence we have seen in the thinking of "gay" Christians, who not only reject the notion of biblical condemnation but proclaim their life-style as one to be encouraged and promoted.

A continuum view must not be used for such purposes. The morality of behavior must be established not by personal inclination, or intuitive appeal to reason, but on the basis of biblical revelation. This unchanging authority is the only protection against a dilution of truth which ultimately presents good as evil and evil as good.

(2) We may clearly specify homosexual acts as sinful, just as Scripture in the same context condemns bestiality and incest (Lev. 20).

It is important, however, always to balance the teaching of law with the teachings of love and grace. There has been little discussion of the kind of behavior which two homosexuals may engage in without sin. Just as Christian teaching has in recent years struggled with advice to teenagers and engaged couples on where to "draw the line" in sexual intimacies, the same kind of exploration is needed for homosexuals. Can two women live together in the same house without sin? Surely yes. Can two men share a flat together and enjoy each other's friendship? Surely yes. We find greater difficulty in responding to a homosexual couple who hold hands and show mutual affection in public. Is this morally wrong or simply breaking a social convention? Does such behavior, like alcohol, fall somewhere on the continuum such that issues of motivation and conscience determine its moral quality, value, and content?

(3) It is not suggested that a three-dimensional model will be sufficient for all purposes. It is proposed here as a basis for resolving the issues which arise in psychological debate.

There are other equally important contexts where other dimensions are relevant. In particular, in the psychiatric context the dimension of normal, pathological is debated, while among the legal profession the relevant issue is one of legality.

The pathological dimension is one which psychologists and psychiatrists have been debating for several years and finding enormous difference of opinion. Such controversy comes as no surprise if the moral dimension is disregarded, since one is then deprived of any final basis for significant decisions. Both the American Psychiatric Association and the American Psychological Association have in recent years backed off from calling homosexuality per se psychopathological. This does not preclude the possibility that some homosexuality (and some heterosexuality) can be psychopathological, both at the level of practice and of orientation. This dilemma of definition arises from the absence of a clear reference point. Hence, the Christian psychologist with a moral dimension derived from biblical revelation is in quite a different position from his secular colleagues.

(4) If it is true that professional discussion of psychosexuality is confused due to insufficient terms of reference, and if the moral dimension is crucial for the evaluation of other dimensions, then it follows that the Christian psychologist can make a significant contribution to clarity. Such a possibility also brings with it the responsibility to play an active role in professional discussion and decision-making since the absence of Christian moral voice in the debate will perpetuate the confusion and arbitrary decisions which currently prevail.

References

Bockmühl, K. "Homosexuality in Biblical Perspective." *Christianity Today,* Feb. 16, 1973, 12-18.

Court, J. H. "Homosexuality: A Scientific and Christian Perspective." *Interchange,* 1973, *13,* 24-40.

"Humanist Manifesto II." *Australian Humanist,* 1973, *28,* 10-15.

Kinsey, A. C., Pomeroy, W. B., and Martin, C. E. *Sexual Behavior in the Human Male.* Philadelphia: W. B. Saunders, 1948.

Morris, P. A. "Doctor's Attitudes to Homosexuality." *British Journal of Psychiatry,* 1977, *122,* 435-36.

N.F.O.L. *The Truth in Love.* London: Nationwide Festival of Light, 1975.

O'Donovan, O. "Marriage and the Family." In B. Kaye (ed.), *Obeying Christ in a Changing World.* Glasgow: Collins, 1977.

"Royal Commission on Human Relationships, Final Report" (Vol. 5). Canberra: Australian Government Publishing Service, 1977.

Seligman, N. E. P. *Helplessness: On Depression, Development, and Death.* San Francisco: W. H. Freeman and Co., 1975.

Smith, B. "Homosexuality in the Bible and the Law." *Interchange,* 1968, *1* (4), 218-22.

———. "The Normative Value of New Testament Ethics." *Interchange,* 1969, *2* (1), 19-23.

HOMOSEXUALITY: CHRISTIAN ETHICS AND PSYCHOLOGICAL RESEARCH

Ted D. Evans

At a time when there have been increasing pressures for the evangelical community to address itself to social issues, it is clear that a Christian ethic regarding homosexuality is required. There are perhaps few issues that elicit more emotion and misunderstanding than this sensitive area. As various homosexual groups have been seeking to gain political and legislative power, there have also been an influx of homosexual churches where homosexuals may exercise religious freedom and worship. Thus, to spend time thinking and researching in this area is certainly of value in terms of its relevance to society and particularly to the Christian, who desires to bring a sound ethical judgment to this issue.

Christian ethics is bound by scriptural ethics. All questions of morality and ethics must be examined in light of revelation and subsequent scriptural teachings. Being that Scripture is the basis of my ethical evaluation of homosexuality, I will cite biblical data that deals directly with homosexuality. Second, I will operationally define homosexuality, and with the aid of published psychological studies, I will describe and explain the typical processes by which one becomes a homosexual. An emphasis will be put on research which will supply us with valuable information so that our ethical conclusions will be based on inspired Scripture and scientific data.

If a man lies with a male as a woman, both have committed an abomination, they shall be put to death, their blood is upon them. (Lev. 20:13)

For this reason God gave them up for dishonorable passions. Their women exchanged natural pleasures for the unnatural and the men likewise gave up natural relations with women and were consumed with passion for one another, men committing shameful acts with men. (Rom. 1:26-27)

Do you not know that the unrighteous will not inherit the Kingdom of God? Do not be deceived, neither the immoral, nor idolaters, nor adulterers, nor homosexuals, nor thieves, nor the greedy, nor drunkards, shall inherit the Kingdom of God. (1 Cor. 6:9-10)

This article is a revision of a paper presented at the convention of the Western Association of Christians for Psychological Studies, Santa Barbara, California, May 24-25, 1974.

© *Journal of Psychology and Theology*, 1975, *3*, 94-98. Used by permission of the author.

These scriptural passages have a crucial bearing on our concern, and all condemn the committing of homosexual acts. Engaging in homosexual activity is outside of God's created ideal for man, and therefore, such a practice is in rebellion against God. There is no avoiding the fact that homosexual behavior is prohibited by Scripture and has no place in God's will. It is sin!

Here, however, we must make a distinction between the *condition* of homosexuality and homosexual *behavior*. Mamor (1965) defines the homosexual as "one who is motivated, in adult life, by a definite and preferential erotic attraction to members of the same sex and who usually, but not necessarily, engages in overt sexual relations." Homosexuality can be thought of as a condition of an individual who, in response to early and highly complex learning, finds himself (or herself) attracted to members of his (her) own sex. More recent research done in this area (Hooker, 1962; Pare, 1965; Pritchard, 1962; and Buss, 1966) has refuted earlier theories which attributed homosexuality to heredity or some hormonal imbalance. The hormonal imbalance theory of homosexuality has more or less been negated since it has been found that even though a small number of homosexuals have a hormonal imbalance (androgen-estrogen), these imbalances do not appear to be of etiological significance since nonhomosexuals show similar imbalances. Also, individuals may shift from a homosexual to a heterosexual pattern or vice versa without a change in hormone imbalance, and treatment with sex hormones to change endocrine balance does not alter the direction of sexual behavior. It is obvious that as one moves up the phylogenetic scale, the role of instinctual patterns and hormonal control diminishes to such an extent that even in cases of extreme deviation, social training takes precedence over physiological limitations. Lawrence Kolb (1973) states that the only commonality among homosexuals is not biological, but psychological. This commonality centers around difficulty in reconciling dependent and assertive drives, an ambivalent maternal relationship, and a high frequency of being reared in a broken home. In his review of research in homosexuality, Arnold Buss (1966) flatly concludes that none of the biological hypotheses have received support and have been discarded by most researchers.

It is explicit in the research that the *condition* of homosexuality is a socially learned process. While it is not my intent to present a comprehensive survey of the research on homosexuality, it is necessary to discuss the etiological factors of the homosexual condition since it is relevant to our ethical response.

A classical study done by Ivan Bieber (1962) yields valuable information regarding the etiology of the homosexual condition. He found that more than half of a group of male homosexuals had had homosexual experiences by the age of twelve as compared with only 20 percent of a control group of heterosexuals. I would not suggest that such early experiences determine the entire direction of later sexual development; however, it is important to note that etiologically, the factor of early sexual experience is a social, experiential factor, not a genetic one.

Bieber (1962) identifies the major etiological factor of the homosexual condition as being the pathogenic family pattern. He found a common pattern of family interaction in the background of homosexuals. Typically, the mother is frustrated by an unhappy marital relationship and establishes a close-binding, intimate relationship with her son to form an alliance against the father, who is often a distant, weak, and sometimes undesirable figure. Although Bieber says this type of pattern is common among homosexuals, he also found other patterns. For example, a mother who very much wanted a girl, will bring her son up as though he was a girl: keeping his hair lengthy, dressing him in girl's clothing, and generally inculcating in him typically feminine attitudes and interests. This author, who worked with male homosexuals in Hollywood, found this latter case to be true in many instances.

Finally, Bieber found that many of the homosexuals experienced peer group rejection and humiliation. Where the individual is ridiculed or meets with failure in his efforts to approach members of the opposite sex, he may turn to homosexuality as a safer source of acceptance and sexual outlet. While previous failure and embarrassment with the opposite sex does not bring about the homosexual condition in isolation from other facilitating variables, it is another factor which the research has uncovered to be a contributing factor in the developmental process of the homosexual condition.

Although the preceding discussion may not appear to be relevant to Christian ethics and its response to homosexuality, I have presented this data to emphasize that the *condition* of homosexuality is not hereditary, but is a *learned* process which involves many complex factors. The recipient of this learning process does not ask for the condition, rather, it happens to him. He is usually a passive recipient. Therefore, he is not responsible for its occurrence since it would be absurd to hold one responsible for the social interactions, role behaviors, and family patterns that characterize his early environment.

The reasons for the existence of this abnormal learning pattern can be evaluated on many levels: social, psychological, anthropological, etc. Nevertheless, it must be stated that the existence of pathogenic family patterns, on the theological level, is the result of a world separated from the holiness and perfection of God and therefore subject to the imperfection of sin, not the least of which is the homosexual condition. Here then, the homosexual condition is another manifestation of sin, sin being moral, personal, and social imperfection—all consequences of a broken relationship with the Creator-Redeemer. The imperfections in human relationships, which are then a manifestation of sin, create the homosexual condition. Thus, one who has the homosexual condition is responsible only insofar that he is a member of a natural order where such a condition can develop. He cannot be made directly responsible for being the recipient of a learning process he did not initiate or request. This conclusion should not result in the moral acceptance of homosexuality, but it should clarify the origin of the condition and thus make it more conducive to clinical focus and treatment. The church's attitude should also alter whereby the homosexual would come to be viewed as someone who has been victimized by familial-environmental components and not one who has amorally and voluntarily chosen a homosexual orientation.

Distinct from the homosexual *condition* is homosexual *behavior*. Like any other behavior where there is voluntary muscular control, there must be responsibility. While one is not accountable for possessing the condition, he is responsible for engaging in the behavior. One can accuse me of being unrealistic to assume that one could possess the condition without engaging in the behavior, especially when we are dealing with the sexual area, which is typically under the control of immediate gratification. However, ethically, this is a valid distinction. To engage in homosexual behavior is a volitional response. It is an act of the will and therefore held accountable. However, the Bible does not pronounce the condition of homosexuality as a sin. All scriptural references customarily cited to demonstrate the Bible's condemnation of homosexuality do so by condemning homosexual *behavior*. There is absolutely no question that the Bible condemns the practice of homosexual behavior as it prohibits any behavior which does not conform to the *imago Dei*.

It is the church's failure to make the distinction between condition and behavior that proliferates the attitude that the homosexual is inherently so and thus qualitatively different in his personhood. This tragic circumstance often robs the homosexual of any desire for repentance and drives him into a state of defensiveness and self-justification where autonomy is the only source of identity. This results in isolation from the healing community and God's redemptive Word.

Another consequence of this isolation is the rise of "homosexual churches" which allows for freedom of worship for the homosexual. However, in so doing, they have distorted certain scriptural teachings by sanctioning homosexual behavior and promiscuity which they hold to be entirely acceptable to God. This is blatant rebellion against God and requires a gross rationalization of his Word. The response of Christian ethics must be an emphatic no.

In order to avoid these consequences, the Christian community's response to the homosexual must radically change. The central factor that must change is attitude: the attitude of condemnation to the attitude of forgiveness. We cannot condemn a person for having a condition for which the research shows he is not responsible. The Bible is replete with texts on forgiveness:

Forgive, I say to you, the transgressions of your brothers and their sin. (Gen. 50:17)

For if you forgive men their sin, your Heavenly Father will also forgive you. (Matt. 6:14)

The element of forgiveness is crucial, for forgiveness carries potential healing and redemption. It is thus how the Christian confronts sin. Unfortunately, the church has not offered healing forgiveness to the homosexual. This may be due to the deviance that is associated with homosexuality and the fear induced by such a threat to one's own sexuality. But that takes us back to the research which shows that one does not choose to be a homosexual, but becomes homosexual through a complex learning pattern. Therefore, the church can be informed by the psychological research generated in this field and begin to compassionately offer forgiveness as Christ himself offered to the most miserable of sinners. It is this forgiveness which includes the homosexual in the fellowship of believers. This compassionate forgiveness may indeed diminish the defensiveness of the homosexual so as to develop a more open attitude concerning repentance.

An important exception to this is the homosexual who actively resists explicit biblical teaching (Lev. 20; Rom. 1; 1 Cor. 6) and natural revelation (Rom. 1) and firmly believes that homosexuality is not only desirable but entirely acceptable before God. Here, there is a willful refusal of repentance and an open desire to continue in sin. These people are "without excuse" (Rom. 1:20) and are truly immoral (Rom. 1:26). The responsibility of the church is to expel anyone who willfully continues in immoral behavior.

I wrote to you not to associate with immoral men, not at all meaning the immoral of this world . . . since then you would need to go out of the world. But rather I wrote to you not to associate with anyone who bears the name of brother, if he is guilty of immorality or greed . . . not even to eat with such a one. Drive out the wicked person from among you. (1 Cor. 5:9-13)

The unrepentant homosexual, as any unrepentant sinner, is immoral and "without excuse." Because of their entrenchment in immorality, they must be excluded from the fellowship of believers.

In summary, the following statements I believe are consistent with scriptural revelation and scientific data: (1) There is a difference between the condition of homosexuality and homosexual behavior; (2) the biblical injunction against homosexuality is on the level of behavior; (3) insofar as the individual is a passive recipient of such a learning process whereby he becomes a homosexual, he is not directly responsible for his homosexual orientation; (4) while the condition of homosexuality should not require guilt of the individual involved, overt homosexual behavior requires responsibility; (5) since homosexual behavior is prohibited by the Bible as a sin, the homosexual who desires to live his (her) life as God would have it must give up his homosexual behavior—any behavior that does not conform to God's will must be given up; (6) since the research indicates that homosexuality is not immorally chosen by the individual but rather is the result of a complex interactional learning pattern, the church must radically change its attitude from condemnation to compassionate forgiveness; (7) in exercising forgiveness and the potential healing it can bring, the isolation and defensiveness of the homosexual are no longer necessary and thus, the desire for repentance and a full embracement of Jesus Christ is more optimal; and (8) the unrepentant homosexual who actively believes that overt homosexual behavior is acceptable before God should be expelled from the fellowship due to his volitional involvement in what the Bible explicitly defines as immorality.

One last note, it is true that very few homosexuals successfully change and lead heterosexual lives. But it is also true that almost all attempted changes from homosexuality to heterosexuality are done outside of the redemptive power of the Holy Spirit. Henceforth, due to our theological affirmations, this is indeed a significant factor. At the same time, I do not want to minimize the overwhelming complexity of the homosexual orientation and the inherent difficulty in changing sexual preference. Nevertheless, God demands righteousness. The fact that psychological research indicates a poor prognosis for homosexuals desiring to change should not alter our attitudes regarding its moral undesirability; rather, it should motivate us to sharpen our therapeutic tools so as to inch closer to God's created ideal. While this is not an article devoted to therapeutic techniques regarding homosexuality, the reader is referred to Yates (1970) and Krasner (1969) for helpful suggestions.

References

Bieber, I. *Homosexuality: A Psychoanalytic Study*. New York: Basic Books, 1962.

Buss, A. H. *Psychopathology*. New York: John Wiley, 1966.

Hooker, E. "The Homosexual Community." *Proceedings of the 14th International Congress of Applied Psychology*, 1962, 2.

Kolb, L. *Modern Clinical Psychiatry*. Philadelphia: W. B. Saunders, 1973.

Krasner, L. *Psychological Approach to Abnormal Behavior*. Englewood Cliffs, N.J.: Prentice-Hall, 1969.

Mamor, J. (ed.). *Sexual Inversion: The Multiple Roots of Homosexuality*. New York: Basic Books, 1965.

Pare, C. M. B. "Etiology of Homosexuality: Genetic and Chromosomal Aspects." In J. Marmor (ed.), *Sexual Inversion: The Multiple Roots of Homosexuality*. New York: Basic Books, 1965.

Pritchard, M. "Homosexuality and Genetic Sex." *Journal of Mental Science*, 1962, *108*, 616-23.

Yates, A. *Behavior Therapy*. New York: John Wiley, 1970.

UNDERSTANDING HOMOSEXUAL BEHAVIOR AND LIFE-STYLES CLINICALLY AND RELIGIOUSLY

John M. Vayhinger

The continuum from strictly heterosexual to strictly homosexual attitudes, behavior, and life-styles is very apparent to clinicians in practice and becomes a concern to the Christian psychotherapist in acceptance, support, treatment, and therapeutic goals.

Therefore, the Christian interpersonal psychotherapist must resolve three factors when a person with a manifest, overt homosexual life-style contracts for treatment. There are many levels of heterosexual, homosocial, and homosexual life-style, as well as types of acting out which must be defined before treatment can begin. This definition cannot be just a logical definition but must be a clear understanding on the part of both persons in acceptance and goal setting for the psycho-therapeutic relationship to be effective.

The three factors are: (1) as clear an understanding as possible by the therapist of the many causes and forms of gender and homosexual life-style, (2) an open sharing of the definition of what is sought in the counseling and a "contract" which is functional for both patient and therapist, and (3) an accurate understanding of the biblically and psychologically sound definition of human potential as to what is possible in psychotherapy.

A Foundation

For the Christian and the scientist both take seriously the saying of Jesus as quoted by John (8:31, 32): "If you continue in my word, you are truly my disciples, you will know the truth and the truth will make you free." Both patient and therapist usually welcome a discussion of such crucial importance in the contemporary world as an open examination of life-style along with a description of symptoms and an exploration of the patient's background experiences. Psychological tests may further open the question of sexual identity to the patient.

© *The CAPS Bulletin*, 1978, *4* (3), 35-39. Used by permission of the author.

Sources of Sexual Identity

Human development begins with a tiny infant for whom pleasure (or release from pain) is the primary goal of life. With continuous maturing, the growing child develops his/her responses in behavior which is reinforced for creativity, responsibility, productivity, relationship, self-actualization, holiness, service, health, loving care, and such like, with pleasure increasingly becoming a second order reinforcement, as in the adult when loving relationship reinforces the "one flesh" actualized in marital relationships between a husband and wife. Pleasure, increasingly with maturing, becomes a supplement to these with happiness resulting, not from avoidance of pain, or sensuous and erotic stimulation by itself, but as the result of mature and productive living.

Thus, to make the pleasure of sexual stimulation—homo or hetero—the goal of life is to live continuously on an infantile level. The ultimate question facing us in this discussion is not, eventually, what stimulates the most pleasure for oneself, same or other sexual stimulation—but the meaning of life, which for decent persons and Christian individuals is loving God with heart and soul and mind, and one's neighbor as oneself (Deut. 6:5; Matt. 22:37-40).

While we cannot go into all of the questions raised as to the "normality" of sex styles in this short discussion, we must make two general observations: (1) most "masculine" and "feminine" activities are influenced by social customs and expectations; (2) and the scriptural and cultural sanctioning of heterosexual roles rest on values, not genes, glands, body build, or fetal influence.

To be more explicit, John J. McNeill's contention that the homosexual condition is divinely willed or genetically conditioned (p. 84) makes little sense to scientist or historian. In modern communist China, Ruth Tifany Barnhouse reports that homosexuality doesn't exist (pp. 155-56, 193-94), apparently due to Chairman Mao's decision to place all sexual behavior in a different perspective in socialist China and to change the role of women in the Chinese family. Nor does Troy Perry speak from bio-psychological fact when he refers to remembering that "while I rested in my father's loins" (p. 11), implying that he knew he was homosexual.

Two biological, developmental factors must be kept in mind before any discussion of homosexual life-style makes any sense. First, newborn infants are biologically divided into male and female by physiologically determined genital development, except for a very small number of those born with deformed or poorly differentiated genitalia. Then develops on a continuing progression what Mathis (1972, pp. 1-2) calls core gender, i.e., masculinity or femininity develops by the use an individual makes of his/her biological equipment and what is reinforced. Core gender is derived through complicated processes from (1) the anatomy and physiology of the external genitalia and (2) the attitudes of parents, peers, siblings, one's church, the mass media, education, significant persons, and chance experiences, and (3) what happens in the child's relationships in developing an awareness of himself/herself.

Second, heterosexual and/or homosexual functioning in the male depends on the anatomy of the boy and the signals, cues, or stimuli which become attached to the neural controllers of the venuous valve which facilitates retention of venuous blood in amounts of four or five times as much as ordinarily circulate, in the spongy erectile tissue (*corpora cavernosa penis*) of the phallus. This results in an "erection" which makes possible sexual intercourse of any kind. In the female a corresponding organ to the glans penis (center of sensitivity in the male) is the clitoris which, while not a necessary part of conception, makes possible the God-created pleasant experience of orgasm.

Crucial for our discussion is the process of identification and/or learning which provides the stimulus that triggers arousal. If during learning experiences of childhood, latency, and adolescence the cue, symbol, or stimulus is a member of the opposite sex, the individual learns to respond heterosexually; or if the cue, signal, or stimulus is same sex, the person then responds to the same sex. Unconscious motivation (close attachment to the mother for the boy), fear of penetration or pain (by the girl), sexual stimulation by the same sex, especially early seduction by older and/or skilled homosexual persons during critically vulnerable times may fix sexually arousing cues to the same sex or, if with heterosexuals, to the opposite sex.

In his autobiography Troy Perry, a preacher in the Metropolitan Community Church, tells of sexual experiences—with Daniel (1972, p. 24), with a merchant marine (p. 36), "more experimentation with homosexuality" (p. 48), with "the boys at the Pentecostal Church Camp" (p. 59), all before sixteen years of age—which were apparently effective for Perry.

Apart from biology, Karlen suggests, "So far, the most reasonable explanation of differences in sexual behavior is the incredible human capacity for learning. Human beings are born with a minimum of programed behavior; they must learn a great deal, coordinate what is programed and what is learned, and do it in interaction with other humans. They also show the greatest neoteny of all creatures—the extension of infant characteristics into adulthood, such as hairlessness, curiosity, and play . . . all (societies) have families of some kind, and they invariably involve an intimate, prolonged bond between the infant and the biological mother, and protection and support for them by the biological father and/or other *males*" (1971, p. 395). Learning, not instinct, plays the critical role in gender differentiation (sexual identity) and can override all biological programing for sexual choice (Birk, 1974, pp. 459-70). These facts not only describe how homo and hetero sexuality is attached to biological equipment but also provide a hope for relearning for the homosexual person who wishes to become heterosexual, or at least to change from his homosexual behavior.

At this point we need to define homosexuality or homosexual behavior and/or homosexual life-styles and homosociality. While definitions may vary somewhat, depending on whether the person making the definition is a psychologist, a "gay" person, a writer, a psychiatrist, a propagandist, a therapist, an ethicist, a theologian, we will here define "homosexual" to mean overt, acting-out sexual behavior between two or more persons of the same biological sex in which genitals and/or secondary sexual organs are involved for erotic purposes. "Homosocial," on the other hand, means a friendly companionship between two or more persons of the same sex in which no overt genital and/or secondary sexual contact of an erotic form is made.

"Homosocial" therefore covers the same-sex friendships and group-belonging of adolescent and adult ages in which persons of the same sex are involved. "Homosexual behavior" refers to erotic attraction carried through to behavior between two persons of the same sex. Mathis defines male homosexual practice as involving anal intercourse (pederasty, sodomy), oral genital contact (fellatio), intercrural intercourse, (between closed thighs), and mutual masturbation among males, plus various deviations such as sadomasochism (infliction of pain for sexual purposes), voyeurism, exhibitionism, fetishism, and incest. (1972, p. 17).

Among female homosexual persons (lesbians) contact usually takes the form of mutual masturbation, cunnilingus (oral-gental), rubbing of genitals together (tribadism), and the use of phallic substitutes (though this may represent transsexualism since it copies male-female intercourse).

The American Psychiatric Association's "Diagnostic and Statistical Manual II" has replaced "Homosexuality" with "Sexual Orientation Disturbance," and limited the diagnosis to individuals who "are either disturbed by, in conflict with, or wish to change their sexual orientation" (1975, p. 44). However, this change was predominantly arrived at on socio-political grounds rather than scientific, after a series of disruptive demonstrations by homosexual activists in the 1970s, and by ignoring the reports of some of the task forces who studied the matter. There was a mail ballot in which "dirty tricks" of a political sort were involved, the National Gay Task Force mailing a letter to the membership supposedly from the Board of Trustees, but actually written, paid for, and mailed by the Gay Task Force (see Barnhouse, 1977, pp. 43-76).

Evelyn Hooker, after reviewing the literature, defines male homosexuality of a committed kind as meaning: "They are erotically and emotionally attracted to, and engaged in, overt sexual behavior predominantly or exclusively with other males." And that they "rejected the possibility of a change in sexual pattern to that of heterosexuality and, in most instances, did not see such a change as being desirable" (1965, p. 27).

Daniel Cappon defines "homosexuality" to mean "the overt, acted-out homosexual behavior, in which the individual, male or female, habitually seeks and attains orgasm by means of sexual contact with a member of the same sex over a period of years, because of choice or preference for a sexual partner of the same sex, though this is not necessarily an exclusive choice. A single sexual act with the same sex does not necessarily constitute homosexuality" (1965, p. 7).

And finally, Bieber defines "homosexuality" as a "pathologic, bio-social, psycho-sexual adaptation consequent to pervasive fears surrounding the expression of heterosexual impulses" (1962).

So, we can recognize "homosexuality" as "a multi-motivated, many-caused, consistent, erotic response set in persons toward same-sexed individuals."

Types of Homosexually Oriented Persons

One enemy of understanding in discussing homosexual orientation is the simplistic approach. Just as there are thirty or forty heterosexual orientations, twelve or thirteen bisexual personality types, so there are many homosexual types.

1. *The multi-sexual person* is one who is involved in bi-, tri-, multi-homosexual and erotic behavior, where the libidinal urges are unfocused, or are polyfocused, and respond to anything that feels good. "The ego-centric sexuality of an infantile, pleasure-oriented, hedonistic individual."

2. *The classical homosexual personality* comes from a home with a domineering, seductive, manipulating mother and a weak, ineffectual, often absent father, where the boy has no adequate father figure with whom to identify, and a mother figure who cripples his normal outgoing responses.

3. *The early seduced person,* either boy or girl is one who, during latency or early puberty when mature sexual identity is vulnerable and just forming, is seduced by an experienced, skillful, older adult, sometimes a pedophiliac, which experience attaches the sexual pleasure arousing cues to the same sexed person.

4. *The "burned-out" or negatively conditioned person* is one who has had such a painful heterosexual experience that he or she cannot return to cross-sex relationships, i.e., the wife of a cruelly exploiting, sexually psychopathic husband or lover; a daughter sexually abused by a father or stepfather.

5. *The transsexual personality* is a person who "feels" like a male or female in the "wrong body," i.e., has female "feeling" in a male body, and who in homosexual relationship—or after transsexual surgery—"acts like" his/her opposite sex in intimate relations.

6. *The pseudo-homosexual* is one who, through misinformation, a

guilt-ridden infantile experience, or persuaded by argument or sexually oriented political pressure, or over-interpretation of a single or a few indistinct symptoms or minor "impulsive childish" homosexual incidents, "believes" him/herself to be homosexual, often with overwhelming guilt and/or shame.

7. *The isolated-deprived person* is one who in early life has had no cross-sex contacts with persons and is fearful, frightened, or ignorant of the opposite sex, i.e., a son born into a family of boys, isolated on a farm, whose mother dies while he is very young and who has had only male companionship.

8. *The situational homosexual person* is a person in prison or other one-sexed environment, who temporarily turns to homosexual "relief" while isolated, returning to heterosexual behavior when back "on the street."

9. The *"gay" or politically rebellious persons* is one who makes a crusade out of being "gay" and holds negative attitudes toward many societal or moral codes.

10. The *neurotic or psychotic acting-out persons* is one whose homosexual behavior can be incidental to his or her total illness, or intertwined with it, as in schizophrenia, obsessive-compulsive neurosis, anxiety hysteria, alcoholism, and the like.

The "types" overlap, are not mutually exclusive, and are not a complete list, but do point out that to speak of "the homosexual person" is to oversimplify any discussion.

What are the causes of homosexual personality pattern? Several, to be sure. One main source is discussed by Dr. Irving Bieber of the Medical Psychoanalysts in New York City from his research. He discovered that family patterns of homosexuals in treatment were "disturbed in characteristic ways which seldom appeared in the families of non-homosexuals; if the disturbance was seen at all in these matched cases, it appeared seldom in heterosexual families. The family patterns were made up of mothers who, from their son's earliest days, were destructively intimate by means of overprotectiveness and emotional and sometimes physical seductiveness. Also the fathers were emotionally detached and sometimes overtly hostile." Dr. Bieber goes on to say, "a constructive, supportive, warmly related father *precludes* the possibility of a homosexual son; he acts as a neutralizing protective agent should the mother make seductive or close-binding attempts" (1962, p. 50).

Dr. Lawrence Hatterer, a specialist in the field of homosexual study, grouped his findings as to the causes of homosexual behavior as: (1) relationship to mother and family and self as a search for male identity, (2) interfamilial relationships, (3) interpersonal relations with other-than-family, and (4) cultural and environmental pressures (1970, p. 2). Certainly homosexuality in persons is not a single clinical entity.

Hatterer points out that there is a "large undisclosed population (which) has melted into heterosexual society, persons who behaved homosexually in late adolescence and early adulthood, and who, on their own, resolved their conflicts and abandoned such behavior to go on to successful marriages and/or heterosexual patterns of adaptation" (1970, pp. 14-15). He goes on to say, "Homosexuality, like the divorce rate and other phenomena, is no more than a symptom of an underlying state of psycho-social distress. The 'cure' of this state on a broad scale can be effected only by altering the relevant social conditions," quoting Gordon Rattray Taylor. The importance of this may be seen in the current reports that there is *no* observable homosexual behavior either in communist China or in the Israel kibbutzim at this time.

Hatterer goes on to say, "More than a quarter century of research, including complete audio-taped documentation has shown that some homosexuals can become heterosexual . . . there are probably thousands of practicing homosexuals who, on their own, have changed their sexual orientation. I have listened to hundreds of accounts of committed homosexuals who have described members of their own families, lovers, friends, and casual acquaintances who have decided to abandon the 'gay' life to go straight" (1974, p. 151). This is this clinician's experience also, the acceptance of changeability, a belief in a power greater than oneself, i.e., God, and some real hard work can change most, if not all, persons with a homosexual orientation either into a heterosexual life-style, or enable them to sublimate their libidinal energies into healthier and nonadulterous behavior.

The evidence, when separated from wishful thinking, belief systems, and political considerations, Ruth Tiffany Barnhouse believes, indicates that "homosexuality, far from being an innate disposition which will inevitably assert itself in some proportion of any population is definitely the result of patterns of child-rearing and acculturation . . . since the eradication of homosexuality was not the primary aim of the Chinese leaders, and its disappearance was essentially a side effect of the effort to implement other, larger goals, such as eradication of venereal disease and the social problem of illegitimacy, homosexuality cannot be considered as an independent variable. Its incidence and the shapes of its manifestation are inevitably connected to the general cultural values and attitudes toward sexuality, including the role expectations for both men and women" (1977, p. 159).

An important consideration here is what Daniel J. Levinson calls the "novice phase" for males (17–33). During this second critical time for mature sexual identification, the teaching of homosexuality as a legitimate alternative to heterosexual marriage catches some persons looking for "role models."

As psychologists Freeman and Meyer write, "The perception and the payoffs provided in our society are crucial in determining whether or not individuals accept a homosexual adjustment." At least, this is true for many individuals without an adequate primary sexual identification during these ages.

The Historical Approach to Homosexual Life-Styles

Reading either the original manuscripts, journals, case reports, or books of Arno Karlen, one finds homosexuality far less acceptable, common, or desirable among civilized persons than some writers seem to think. Barnhouse points out that homosexuality in ancient Greece paralleled the badly deteriorated position of women who were not educated or encouraged to improve themselves in any way, only to bear children and keep house. Only in the city of Elis was it officially legal; the plays of Aristophanes treated it with withering contempt, which seems to have reflected the attitudes of the majority of citizens. In fact, homosexuality was considered deviant by most Greeks during most of their history. Plato himself condemned it as unnatural and degrading. And those who practiced it most would have been sent to jail in today's world, for adult males had sexual affairs (usually sodomy) with young boys (catamites), hardly ever with other adult males.

Karlen concludes that "in ancient Greece homosexuality was considered a deviation; it was given positive value only by a minority of homosexuals, bisexuals and apologists. Neither did its presence in Greece have any relationship to social, artistic or political health. The fact that homosexuality was a factor in the lives of many great men only speaks for its prevalence among the leisured, literate elite from which artists and statesmen came. A permissive or positive view of homosexuality must find other grounds than the myth that made everything Greek praiseworthy" (1971, p. 38).

In short, boys and women were the submissive receivers of pederasty and impregnation respectively.

If artistic and creative persons are cited as an apology for the homosexual life-style, one would also have to include the bestial and cruel persons who were also homosexual, like many of the Roman caesars (i.e., Julius, Octavius, Caligula, Tiberius), just as persons with heterosexual life-styles have a wide range of behavior, including the deviant (Karlen, 1971, pp. 12-43).

For the oft-repeated claim that famous persons have been homosexuals, probably some have, but there is no real evidence for even Michelangelo or Leonardo da Vinci, much less for Shakespeare (Barnhouse, 1977, pp. 24-27). The only "evidence" to support the notion of da Vinci's alleged homosexual life-style was drawn by what is now repudiated Freudian guesses as to "latent" tendencies.

References to supposed animal behavior to support the claim that homosexuality is a natural action can hardly be believed since such researchers as Konrad Lorenz, Nikolaas Tinbergen, Frank Beach, and Clelland Ford point out that no such thing exists in the animal kingdom as homosexual behavior which includes intermission and/or climax between male animals. Where such behavior appears to be, it is more likely to be "captivity or zoo induced" or to be part of elaborate dominant/submissive ritual behavior, in spite of C. A. Tripp's *(The Homosexual Matrix)* allegations that homosexuality is rampant throughout the animal world. However, as Barnhouse points out, "There are misrepresentations on nearly every page," and the book reflects Tripp's "inexcusable lack of scholarly accuracy" (Barnhouse, 1977, p. 38). Harry Harlow of the Primate Research Laboratory, Madison, Wisconsin, writes, "In the monkey there is no such thing as deviant behavior as we speak of it among humans . . . I'd guess that male homosexual behavior—if you want to call it that—is transient play or a token sexual gesture as a sign of friendship. . . . Anthropologists call what monkeys do Brittle Monogamy. I call it the Hollywood Mating" (Karlen, 1971, p. 400).

One new approach in this decade on the part of persons with a homosexual life-style is their involvement in the political arena as activists "to demand their rights." The current rejection of an ordinance in Dade County (Miami), Florida, which would have made mandatory the hiring of homosexual persons in public and private schools. The ordinance was repealed by 202,319 votes to 89,562. This event, projected Anita Bryant into the limelight. Scurrilous attacks on her by comedians, political gay groups, and others followed. The National Gay Task Force launched a $1-million fund-raising drive and education officials in San Francisco announced plans to "sensitize" students to accept—or at least tolerate—homosexual life-styles as just another way of living.

All this led Stanton Evans to write, "Miss Bryant's frequent arguments from Scripture confirm the view that she is deeply religious but refute the libel that she is any sort of a bigot. Her concern in the Miami squabble was not to persecute the 'gays' for deviant conduct, but to forestall their effort to legitimize their deviance as an 'alternative lifestyle.' She has paid a heavy price in terms of ridicule and professional ostracism but, as her autobiography makes plain, has no regrets. Would that we had a hundred others like her" *(National Review* Feb. 3, 1978, p. 169).

Miss Bryant herself, in two of her books, *Amazing Grace* and *Mine Eyes Have Seen the Glory,* reveals a sincerely Christian person, who invests herself in politics reluctantly but responsibly. Her Christian experience, "I was saved as a child of eight," and the descriptions of her family's prayer altar seem authentically Christian.

However, it would seem that the voting in Dade County was not so much about civil rights of individuals as it was about the social acceptability of homosexual behavior. The citizens of Dade County, editorializes the magazine *America,* reaffirmed the longstanding public consensus that homosexuality is a psychic aberration and a social evil, and holds that "the refusal by the voters to accept an ordinance both unnecessary and in conflict with community values was justified" (June 25, 1977, p. 558).

Also, to be kept in mind are national surveys of "conservative Christians" in many denominations including Roman Catholics, which found that most church persons support Anita Bryant's standing up against so-called "gay" rights legislation. A study taken by the United Methodist Task Force of the North Indiana Conference found that better than 90 percent of the sample would leave any church assigned a gay pastor. Other surveys found that better than 90 percent would object to gay teachers and ministers and that most felt that homosexuality, lesbianism, and bisexuality are "abnormal." While truth is not determined by survey or vote, it does indicate what would likely happen to any denomination, with few exceptions, who in moments of enthusiastic social concern would recognize homosexuality as simply an alternative life-style and knowingly assign such a minister to a congregation. To follow such an action see the *Daily Christian Advocate,* "Daily Proceedings of the 1976 General Conference of The United Methodist Church" held in Portland, Oregon.

Psychotherapy with Persons
Who Are Homosexual in Preference

To produce a change or "cure" in the homosexual person, John R. Cavanagh suggests he/she will have to (1) face the fact of the homosexual component in his/her personality honestly and frankly, (2) relinquish the false myth that the homosexual response is fixed and determined and that his/her homosexual energies are any stronger than any heterosexual exaggeration in behavior, (3) deliberately break contact with homosexual companions who may tempt him/her to acting-out or practicing overt homosexual behavior, (4) cease any homosexual behavior deliberately and consciously—which implies a strong decision to change, (5) search psychologically for the learning experiences and reinforcing factors which have involved him/her in past situations as well as in the present, (6) stress the independent, self-directed thinking which is not vulnerable to seduction or responsive to "group think" or suggestion, (7) avoid drugs, including alcohol, which leave one vulnerable to pressure and suggestion, (8) be personally involved in a "power greater than oneself," as Alcoholics Anonymous calls it, a belief in a loving God, and/or personal experience of salvation through Jesus Christ—and the moral devotion which goes with such a personal commitment, and (9) consciously develop a redirected style of life which develops either heterosexual relationships, as in marriage, *or* finds an acceptable sublimation which may "canalize" sexual impulses in more loving and ethically responsible channels.

Is it possible for every homosexually oriented person to change to heterosexual behavior? Theoretically it is, but the independent choosing of each person, just as in other behavior with moral or psychological implications, takes first of all conscious choice and a considerable amount of difficult working through, and some skillful relationships with a pastor and/or psychiatrically trained persons, and depends in part on age and the length of time of involvement in homosexual life-style.

Let us keep in mind that only a relatively small percentage of those persons who have had any homosexual experience are deeply conditioned to respond *only* to same-sex stimulation. Most persons, even in the "gay climate" are capable of redirecting and reconditioning their sexual preferences as much as they are their preferences for jobs, friends, denominational memberships, education, food tastes. There is only an untrue myth that homosexuality, like heterosexual behavior, is a determined, fixed, cemented characteristic of personality.

In fact, many heterosexually focused persons have remained continent during periods of separation from mates as in wartime, schooling, illness. Though a reconditioning and redirection through deliberate choice to heterosexual living may be the goal, there are a number of other alternatives, for sexual energy, unlike hunger or thirst, is one of the human needs redirectable into art, music, religion, social concerns, care for persons, and hard work.

Dr. Barnhouse points out that "approximately thirty percent of male homosexuals who come to psychotherapy for *any* reason can be converted to the heterosexual adaptation . . . strong motivations do sometimes cause such people to request psychotherapy in order to change their sexual orientation. Their reasons may be religious or social and may even include having formed a sufficiently deep friendship with someone of the opposite sex so that marriage could be contemplated if they were only able to engage in sexual relations. In such instances the prognosis for a successful therapeutic outcome is extremely good" (1977, pp. 97, 109).

Karlen reports on seventeen studies on homosexual patients in treatment, and all agree that a complete change occurs in a third of the patients and partial change in another third (1971, p. 583). There is, to be sure, a direct relationship between change and how exclusive a person's homosexuality was, and how early in life it was set. Therapists who specialize in the treatment of homosexual disorders: Irving Bieber, Lawrence Hatterer, Daniel Cappon, Harold Lief, Edmund Bergler, and others, agree that homosexuals can be helped and that the chief prerequisite for cure is the patient's desire for change. Note that these percentages are considerably better than those for alcoholism, criminality, schizophrenia, and other "conditions" treated by therapists.

Lee Birk reports that of a group therapy research with sixty-six patients, almost half made heterosexuality an explicit treatment goal, and if remaining in therapy for one-and-a-half years or more, 85 percent experience at least partial heterosexual shift and 52 percent nearly complete heterosexual shift.

As to the causes of homosexuality among men, Birk describes patients who come for therapy as men who "typically grow up in completely disordered family settings where as children they feel closer to their mothers than to their fathers; where the fathers are subtly, sometimes badly devalued by the mothers; where the sons find themselves caught between their mothers and their fathers so that they could not have both the man (father) and the woman (mother) at the same time . . . homosexual sons of these achieving fathers typically are not close to their fathers, and perceive them as dominated by their mothers" (1974, p. 46).

Probably most therapists think in terms of change, rather than cure for they, like Hadden, "regard homosexuality as only a symptom and its suppression without definite personality reorganization is of little value. . . . We should aim at personality reorganization rather than symptom control" (Cavanaugh, p. 250).

What Does the Bible Say About This Life-Style?

Biblically, the heterosexual life-style is assumed, and homosexual and other life-styles forbidden. Sociological explanations for this sound hollow in explaining away this clear direction. Outside of some tortured exegesis, nowhere is a homosexual life-style or experience either recommended or permitted. Sidewise looks at famous friendships between men fail psychologically, and certainly historically. Out of all the Scriptures that speak to homosexuality, three are particularly useful and typical.

1. Romans 1:26-27. "For this reason God gave them over to degrading passions: for their women exchanged the natural function for that which is unnatural (i.e., Lesbian), and in the same way also the men abandoned the natural function of the women and burned in their desires towards one another, men with men committing indecent acts (male homosexual behavior) and receiving in their own person the due penalty of error."

2. 1 Corinthians 6:9-10. "Or do you not know that the unrighteous shall not inherit the kingdom of God? Do not be deceived, neither fornicators (heterosexual or homosexual), nor idolators, nor adulterers (heterosexual or homosexual), nor effeminate, nor homosexuals (male or female), nor thieves, nor covetous, nor drunkards, nor revilers, nor swindlers, shall inherit the kingdom of God."

3. 1 Timothy 1:8-11. "But we know that the law is good, if one uses it lawfully, realizing the fact that law is not made for a righteous man, but for those who are lawless and rebellious, for the ungodly and sinners, for the unholy and profane, for those that kill their fathers and mothers, for murderers and immoral men and homosexuals and kidnapprs and liars and perjurers, and whatever else is contrary to sound teaching, according to the glorious gospel of the blessed God, with which I have been entrusted."

The Bible does indeed condemn homosexual practice, but it says little about homosexual thoughts, for the act, not just the thought, is the "sin". Not the temptation, but the response is the sin. Many persons may be afflicted by the psychological dynamics of homosexual learning who may not be responsible for the family conditions and early learning experiences that helped form the memories, but are responsible for choosing to act out those desires. There is a difference between the rules concerning mixing wool and cotton, as forbidden in the Old Testament, and the mixing of the love of man for woman with man for man, and the consequent life relationships as in Leviticus 18:22; 20:13. "Thou shalt not commit adultery," as in the Old Testament, or "He that looketh at a woman to lust after her, hath already committed adultery," as interpreted in the New Testament.

In Conclusion, Then

One of the cruelest things one human being can do is to carelessly and callously toss off another individual with such generalizations as, "Homosexuality is unchangeable, homosexuality is just another life-style, therapy is ineffective with homosexuality, or any woman raped wanted a forbidden sexual intercourse." All misinterpret the data and leave the individual in despair. Especially when there is very little fact or truth in any of these statements.

Jerry Kirk summarizes the church's point of view, "Although no orthodox Christian church could support the ethics of a homosexual lifestyle, we *must* respond to gays in a caring and helpful way—showing concern, compassion, and hope for a change. . . . Many of us struggle with self-love, but the gay struggle is of a greater intensity. In much of the literature that has been written, gays seem to put the blame for their lack of self-acceptance on the attitudes of the church and the society. . . . However, I also want to make a plea for the gays to look more honestly at themselves and more responsibly to the Scriptures. Because the underlying reasons for their lack of self-acceptance is sin, the true moral guilt that comes with it, gays need to know that all of us find it difficult to accept ourselves and love ourselves. We find it most difficult when we are rebelling against God and living in sin" (1978, pp. 100-103).

Adultery and fornication are selfishness and sin, whatever the sex of the partner. Dr. Val Clear, sociologist at Anderson College, in his writings, makes the clear statement that ethical and Christian behavior has a single standard for every person, man and woman, whether the underlying "feelings" are toward the same or the opposite sex.

For most clinicians and researchers, and most people increasingly are in agreement, the causes of homosexual behavior are not genetic or constitutional or glandular. Key roles in causation are played by the mind, the environment, and culture. For as newborns, we are delivered with the equipment of sexual experience but not specific attitudes or traits or personality factors formed, that is, without psychosexual identification, or at least very little. Societies form learning patterns that they have found function best, and the universal lesson is that cultures—that survive—are totally or predominantly heterosexual, and where human energy is invested in creativeness and productivity, and only small amounts are used in pleasure seeking.

Any discussion of homosexual life-style must include some information about promiscuity. Bell and Weinberg (1978, p. 308) of the Kinsey Institute describe the incidence of sexual relations in their sample of 1,500 homosexual persons studied as follows:

No. of Hsx Partners Ever Had	WHM	BHM	No. of Hsx Partners Ever Had	WHM	BHM
0: 1 partner	0%	0%	6: 25 - 49 partners	8%	6%
1: 2 partners	0%	0%	7: 50 - 99 partners	9%	18%
2: 3 - 4 partners	2%	4%	8: 100 - 249 partners	15%	15%
3: 5 - 9 partners	2%	4%	9: 250 - 499 partners	17%	11%
4: 10 - 14 partners	3%	5%	10: 500 - 999 partners	15%	14%
5: 15 - 24 partners	3%	6%	11: 1000 or more partners	28%	19%

This means that among white male homosexual persons, 28 percent had sexual contact with 1,000 or more partners, 43 percent had contact with 500 or more, and 60 prcent had sexual congress with 250 different partners or more. This promiscuity is also apparent among black male homosexual persons with 44 percent having sexual relations with more than 250 partners.

Many feel that the "gay life" is anything but gay. The great majority of homosexuals seem to vouch for the accuracy of its depiction in *The Boys in the Band,* a play replete with jealousy, competitiveness, insecurity, malice, tantrums, and hysterical mood shifts.

However, the problem won't just go away, the problem of the humanity of the homosexual and his/her worth as a person remains. Most of the scientific and biblical evidence for healthy and satisfying and matural sexual life-styles lies on the social support side for heterosexual life-styles. Certainly, society may show a humane tolerance of the different minority, but there is no value-free way to talk about homosexual, or for that matter, heterosexual patterns of conduct. And here is the really critical point, it is a clash between two differing values. The questions as to what forms of behavior are acceptable and encouraged in a democracy are based mainly on religions definitions of the worth of persons and cannot be made strictly on scientific grounds. Decisions must be made on the *results* of that behavior and on religious values. The two points of view, one historical and the other religious, must present accurate information upon which the members of our society can make these decisions.

So finally, it is as Benjamin R. Barber (1975) says: "Marriage cannot tolerate adultery—call it freedom or open marriage or mutual independence or what you will—but marriage will not stand for it by any name. That is the cost of our dependence, the price of our commitments, the sacrifice offered to trust. The cynics will scoff and the cosmopolitans will wink, but you will not find a woman who can love or trust completely a man who shares their common bed with others; or a man whose commitment will not be shaken by his wife's affair. Marriage is troubled enough in its present condition and sacred enough in its ideal state to warrant a rule that weakness may often infringe but that principle will not breach: marital fidelity and sexual infidelity are incompabitle" (p. 145).

Adultery, then, is the basic test for faithfulness or love: homosexual or heterosexual—and adultery negates the truly good, therefore, "If any one is in Christ, he/she is a new creation; the old has passed away, behold, the new has come" (2 Cor. 5:17).

What then, can be said about homosexual preference? It is a result of learning, a fixation at an early age of development, which can be re-learned at a later time. The Bible stands clearly against homosexual acting out though certainly as Enroth and Jamison write, "It is possible to demonstrate compassionate understanding of the homosexual's plight without having to discard sincere convictions about biblical norms . . ." for from the "experience of humanity and from the biblical record point to the conclusion that God ordained a hetereosexual life-style for humankind culminating and being perpetuated in the man-woman relationship" (pp. 138-40).

In short, we can conclude that *no one* has to "act out" any sexual behavior, whether it is heterosexual, homosexual, bestial, bisexual, or any other form. Just as an obese person may diet until a reasonable weight, a thief may "steal no more," an ignorant or naive person may gain an education, a racist or sexist may become an accepting, fair person, *so a homosexually oriented person may be re-educated, "healed," "converted," "adapted,"* in short, changed in life-style and behavior.

As Mark quotes Jesus, "From the beginning of the creation, God made them male and female, for this cause shall a man leave his father and mother, and shall cleave to his wife; and the twain shall become one flesh. So that in body they are no longer two people, but one. That is why man must never separate what God has joined together" (10:6-9 Phillips).

This means to accept the biblical model of monogamous, lifelong heterosexual marriage as the ideal (from which all other behavior is at best a sad, if humanly inevitable, departure, and at worst is exploitative lust), to be seen with compassion and forgiveness, but with discipline and responsibility. God teach us all.

References

Barber, Benjamin R.: *Liberating Feminism,* Seabury, 1975, $6.95, p. 145.
Barnhouse, R. T. *Homosexuality, a Symbolic Confusion.* New York: Seabury Press, 1977.

Bieber, Irvin et al. *Homosexuality: A Psychoanalytic Study.* New York: Random House, 1962.

Birk, Lee. "Group Psychotherapy for Men Who Are Homosexual." *Sex and Marital Therapy* Vol. 1. Fall, 1974, p. 46.

Cappon, Daniel. *Toward an Understanding of Homosexuality.* Englewood Cliffs, N.J.: Prentice-Hall, 1965.

Hatterer, Lawrence J. *Changing Homosexuality in the Male.* New York: McGraw-Hill Book Co., 1970.

———. In *Journal of Medical Aspects of Human Sexuality,* Nov. 1974, p. 151.

Hooker, Evelyn. "An Empirical Study of Some Relations Between Sexual Patterns and Gender Identity in Male Homosexuals." In Money, John (ed.). *Sex Research, New Developments.* New York: Holt, Rinehart and Winston, 1965.

Karlen, Arno. *Sexuality and Homosexuality.* New York: W. W. Norton, 1971.

Kirk, Jerry. *The Homosexual Crisis in the Mainline Church.* Nashville: Thomas Nelson, 1978.

McNeill, John J., S. J. *The Church and the Homosexual.* Mission, Kans.: Sheed Andrews and McMeel, 1976.

Mathis, James L. *Clear Thinking About Sexual Deviation: A New Look at an Old Problem.* Chicago: Nelson-Hall, 1972.

Perry, Troy. *The Lord Is My Shepherd and He Knows I'm Gay.* Los Angeles: Nash Publishing Co., 1972.

CHRISTIAN PERSPECTIVES ON THE TREATMENT OF SEXUAL DYSFUNCTION

James R. David
Francis C. Duda

Background

Western civilization has steadfastly clung to the idea that there is a duality within human beings, that we are comprised of a body and a soul. The Greek philosophers spent considerable time in deciding at what point the mind or soul was connected to the body. This dualistic thinking has permeated the Judeo-Christian tradition up until the present time. It has resulted in a second-class status for material things and a first-class status for spiritual or intangible matters. The theological result of this thinking is to put a pejorative emphasis upon the human body. There are many historical examples of Christian leaders warning of the dangers to be found in overindulgence in sexual matters. Even until the present time, there is a reluctance to accept human sexuality as a proper, God-given function.

The theological writings of Pierre Teilhard de Chardin constitute an abrupt departure from the traditional dualism. Teilhard was a Jesuit priest and a paleontologist who combined his scientific knowledge with theological training to present a view wherein all matter is good. It followed that if God is good, then everything he wills to be in existence will also be good. Teilhard's classic work, *The Phenomenon of Man,* optimistically celebrates the essential goodness of all created matter.

Within this historical perspective, it is somewhat easier to understand the type of reception that human sexuality has received from Christian writers. The Puritan tradition, which has so greatly impacted upon our American society, is certainly just a recent example of Christian disdain for material or bodily existence. Since Christianity has contributed to the current widespread repression of human sexuality which exists in our society, it only seems reasonable that a fuller understanding of the Christian message may be helpful in recognizing the essential goodness of human sexual functioning.

For the past eighteen months, we have treated individuals for sexual dysfunction at the Dwight David Eisenhower Army Medical Center, Fort Gordon, Georgia. We have found that 40 percent of our patients,

© *Journal of Psychology and Theology,* 1977, 5 (4), 332-36. Used by permission of the author.

regardless of their religious affiliation or lack of it, are aided in overcoming therapeutic resistances by some variation of the Christian concepts contained herein. This strategy was first employed with a twenty-five-year-old, white college graduate who was experiencing primary impotency. He was a very sincere Christian, and he very much wished to marry, but he had never in his life been able to experience penile erection or ejaculation. During the course of the treatment, the concepts enumerated upon in this article proved to be of pivotal importance in overcoming his sexual dysfunction.

Buyer Beware

The issues of applying Christian precepts as an integral part of a sexual treatment plan is particularly relevant during these times of shifting values regarding sexual behavior. Therapist knowledge and skill may be less relevant than integrity and ethical behavior. The absence of state or federal legislation regulating the practice of psychotherapy results in abuses as outlined in a recent issue of *Psychology Today*.

In our experience, many couples are skeptical about a treatment plan based solely upon individual fulfillment. They seem to want and/or need more rationale for investing their time and effort in an endeavor contrary to so many of the values contained in the Puritan ethic—hard work, rigid discipline, etc. These values oftentimes carry more weight than personal enjoyment and spontaneity. Many couples harbor the notion that sexual pleasure is basically narcissistic and selfish. When treated by a therapist who endorses individualism and what appear on the surface to be impersonal and mechanistic homework assignments, client motivation may be impaired.

Methodology

The patients treated for sexual dysfunction were referred to the Social Work Service by physicians of the family practice, obstetrics-gynecology, and urology clinics. The distribution of patients was approximately half women and half men and the same was true regarding whether the people came in as a couple or individually. The clients were seen once a week for an hour at a time. Detailed homework assignments were worked out with the patient. These consisted of graduated caressing exercises of increasingly more erotic portions of the body so as to gradually eliminate anxiety and to allow greater awareness of pleasurable feelings. Oftentimes, it was necessary to engage in marital therapy or assertiveness training prior to beginning the actual treatment of the sexual dysfunction. The approaches articulated by Virginia Satir (1967) and R. V. Fitzgerald (1973) were oftentimes used to develop the couple relationship so that they would be more receptive to completing the sexual treatment plan. The full range of sexual dysfunctions was treated to include: female general sexual dysfunction, anorgasmy and vaginismus; and the male sexual dysfunctions of primary and secondary impotency, premature ejaculation, and ejaculatory incompetence. Individuals seen ranged in age from 20 to 61 and were either active duty soldiers and their dependents or retired military members. Psychosexual treatment methodology included selected approaches articulated by Masters and Johnson (1966), Hartman and Fithian (1972), Helen Singer Kaplan (1974), and Lobitz and LoPicolo (1972).

Major Concepts

Self-Disclosure

The following ideas have enhanced therapeutic outcome when personalized in the self-disclosure tradition popularized by Jourard (1964). These concepts are not shared if they do not "spring up" spontaneously as a part of the interview; they must be genuinely felt as they are shared. The caring and authenticity of the therapist serve to elicit levels of patient involvement not otherwise reached. When suitable, these concepts are adjusted to make them relatable for nonreligious or non-Christian couples. Essentially, the tactic is a "permission-giving" experience. Acceptance is dramatically advanced when, for example, the sincere Christain sex therapist shares his or her enjoyment of a particular sexual activity.

Self-disclosure of the therapist not only enhances the outcome of his or her particular intervention but it models for the couple the kind of self-disclosure that is essential if they are to learn how to better bring pleasure to one another.

If openness of this sort is to take place, it must be encouraged by confidentiality in the therapy and mutual respect and positive regard within the sexual dyad.

Separateness Versus Unity

Erich Fromm's (1963) thinking regarding "separateness" and the Christian theological position that heaven consists of being merged or united with God is explained. This is relevant when addressing client resistances manifested as seemingly legitimate excuses for not completing intimate sexual touching assignments. Client assent is sought that all of us as humans suffer from separateness; that, as hard as we may try, we are unable to overcome our being separate from one another; and, that often our behavior manifests our yearning to overcome our separateness or aloneness and to experience the pleasant relief that occasions closeness with another human being.

Fromm's belief that man has inbred in him an insatiable desire to overcome this separateness, that he senses his incompleteness as an individual person, and the Christian belief that man will only be appeased by ultimately being united with God in heaven are woven together. We go on to say that it appears that the finest, most sublime foretaste of heaven (overcoming separateness and attaining oneness) lies in sexual intercourse and that God wants us to experience this joyful foretaste of heavenly unity.

Coupleness

Another effective way of establishing the sacredness of the human sexual relationship is to share the mystery of the fifth chapter of Ephesians:

Husbands, love your wives, as Christ loved the church. He gave himself up for her to make her holy, purifying her in a bath of water by the power of the world . . . Husbands should love their wives as they do their own bodies. He who loves his wife loves himself. Observe that no one ever hates his own flesh; no, he nourishes it and takes care of it as Christ cares for the church—for we are members of his body. (vv. 25, 28-30)

These thoughts must be shared spontaneously at the precise appropriate moment. We cannot offer a formula prescription for usage for what must be a creative endeavor. We point out that St. Paul used the oneness of the couple to get across the fact that Christ is the head of his body, the church, and that he is as intimately united with us, his church, as husbands and wives are united. He continues to depend upon couples to reveal the reality of his love relationship with his church. Couples do this best simply by being united; it is not what they do, rather it is who they are *with* and *for* one another. Just as God reveals himself to us through the Scriptures so he would have us reveal ourselves to one another in frank understandable human terms.

We combine this insight with Genesis verses which communicate the notion that God's plan for his people entails coupleness. "For this reason a man shall leave his father and mother, and shall cling to his wife, and the two shall be made into one" (2:24).

Another aspect regarding the desirability of attaining oneness as a couple is communicated by sharing John Powell's views regarding the etiology of the word "sex"; that the word "sex" comes from the Latin verb "secare," which means "to cut"; and, that men and women are figuratively "cut in half" and in again being joined together, they regain the wholeness they desire.

If couples are to put things back together again, it is necessary that each one know how things fit; one cannot expect to know how things fit unless the other clearly tells the partner in detail the delicate nuances of personal responses and preferences. We share the beauty we see in this and the serenity that it brings; it is comforting to see oneself as definitely living out God's desire.

In God's Image

A powerful concept, based upon the Genesis verse 1:27 that God made man in his image, is combined with an explanation of "God is love." This is often very effective in handling disavowals of the couple's call to be close. We share that we never understood what was meant by the often heard words, "God is love," until it was explained in the light of the Trinity; that God is love in the sense that he is three persons in an intimate love relationship; and, that we are called to be like God by also immersing ourselves in an intimate love relationship. We are most human and most Godlike when we are able to love fully as the Father, Son, and Holy Spirit. Even now, writing this, it is somewhat of a mystery but also reminiscent of Eugene Kennedy's (1974) observation that God reveals himself in ordinary, possible ways. The leap of faith comes in seeing God in the routine. The extraordinary and impossible events (miracles) rarely occur and then defy empirical verification.

Letting Go

Tyrell (1974), in his *Christotherapy,* talks at great length about the need to "let go," to surrender control, and to "trust in the Lord." We know how difficult this is for some clients. This is a central theme in facilitating the client's ability for sexual abandonment. It is particularly crucial in beginning phases of treatment when a shift is being made in patient goals from sexual performance to feeling fulfilled and simply staying with or "feeling the feeling." We are alert for borderline psychotic patients who may be unable to tolerate Gestalt techniques used to supplement behavioral homework assignments. The theological and psychological parallel between letting go sexually, as in orgasmic release, and in accepting one's dependence upon God is quite apparent. We sometimes teach Christian meditation techniques to introduce the steadfastly self-sufficient client to the possibility that it may be okay to relinquish control and "let go."

Conclusion

In our discussion to this point, you may have noticed the absence of the term: marriage. For many in our day and age, marriage and/or public enduring commitment to one's spouse is out of fashion. To some "status quo" Christians, marriage is seen as a lifeless contract drawn up and notarized in an attorney's office, a cold legalistic arrangement. With such a concept, it is little wonder why the institution of marriage is out of fashion. In addition to such an unattractive interpretation, which is occasionally seen in some Sunday schools and catechetical classes, another problem exists. The throwaway culture so popular today seems to favor the disposable and the idea of planned obsolescence regarding material things. This notion is now finding application as regards persons. What presumably works well for the economy (buy something new—throw away something old) should also work well for people (throw away an old spouse—try a new one).

To overcome this mentality of planned obsolescence, we suggest planned commitment. A significant element in reaching sexual fulfillment is the trust and security inherent in the full living set forth in Ephesians 5 as a model for marriage. Marriage needs to be seen, not as an antiquated prison that confines expression in legal restrictions, but as a protected workshop where two people can be secure—secure to grow, to experiment, to reveal, to expose, to make one's self vulnerable, to let go. No one in his right mind is going to "let go" unless he has some assurance, some faith that he will not be harmed; that there is a cushion for him to fall on; that an accepting protective embrace awaits him. The bilateral commitment of marriage can be that assurance, that covenant which allows a couple the necessary freedom to use these concepts outlined here in alleviating sexual dysfunction. Too often, in rigid attempts to ensure impartiality and client self-determination, therapists partition off their own personalities and beliefs in effecting therapeutic goals. Closeting one's religious or philosophic values may certainly be wise at times but sterile at other times. Integrating rather than compartmentalizing one's uniqueness serves to enrich the therapeutic use of self.

Summary

We have attempted to establish the destructive fallaciousness of viewing matter as separate from and inferior to so-called spiritual concerns. Dualistic thinking, which denigrates the physical, contributes to guilt and "dis-ease" regarding sexuality. The reasonableness of using Christian concepts to combat sexual dysfunction constitutes the main thrust of this paper: selected conceptualizations include *Self-Disclosure, Separateness Versus Unity, Coupleness, In God's Image,* and *Letting Go.*

We have concluded by mentioning that the underlying essential ingredient for weaving an interplay between the permission-giving Christian concepts enumerated herein and desired sexual functioning is the enduring commitment of marriage as a covenant.

References

Belliveau, F., and Fichter, L. (eds.). *Understanding Human Sexual Inadequacy.* Boston: Little, Brown, 1956.

Croft, H. A. "Sex Counseling by Physicians: Brief Office Treatment of Common Sexual Problems." Monograph. Fort Sam Houston, Tex.: Community Mental Health Activity, 1975.

Fitzgerald, R. V. *Conjoint Marital Therapy.* New York: Jason Aronson, 1973.

Fromm, E. *The Art of Loving.* New York: Harper & Row, 1963.

Hartman, W. E., and Fithian, M. A. *Treatment of Sexual Dysfunction.* Long Beach, Calif.: Center for Marital and Sexual Studies, 1972.

Jouard, S. M. *The Transparent Self.* Princeton, N.J.: Van Nostrand, 1964.

Kaplan, H. S. *The New Sex Therapy.* New York: Brunner Mozel, 1974.

Kennedy, E. *The Joy of Being Human.* Chicago: Thomas More Associates, 1974.

Koch, J., and Koch, L. "A Consumer's Guide to Therapy for Couples." *Psychology Today,* March, 1976.

Lobitz, W. C., and LoPicolo, J. "New Methods in the Behavioral Treatment of Sexual Dysfunction." *Journal of Behavior Therapy and Experimental Psychiatry,* 1972, *3,* 265.

Lukas, M., and Lukas, E. *Teilhard, the Man, the Priest, the Scientist.* Garden City, N.Y.: Doubleday, 1977.

Masters, W. H., and Johnson, V. E. *Human Sexual Inadequacy.* Boston: Little, Brown, 1966.

Powell, J. *The Secret of Staying in Love.* Niles, Ill.: Argus Communications, 1974.

Satir, V. *Conjoint Family Therapy.* Palo Alto, Calif.: Science & Behavior, 1967.

Shor, J., and Sanville, J. "Erotic Provocations and Dalliances in Psychotherapeutic Practice." *Clinical Social Work Journal,* 1974, *2* (2).

Towers, B. *Teilhard de Chardin.* Richmond, Va.: John Knox Press, 1966.

Tyrell, B. J. *Christotherapy.* New York: Seabury Press, 1974.

SECTION
SEVEN

CHRISTIANITY AND PSYCHOLOGICAL THEORIES

Much has been said already in this volume about the integration of Christianity and psychology, but little or no mention has been made of well-known or specific psychological theories. In this section four particular theories are reviewed and their compatibility with Christianity described. The authors of two of these theories, Freud and Frankl, had a great deal to say about religion; however, neither Rogers nor the behavioral theorist have much to say about religion.

Many Christians have read that Freud was critical of religion and was also an atheist. In addition, he wrote the book *The Future of an Illusion* in which he characterized religion as being a product of neurotic immature need. How then can Westendorf in the first article refer to "the" value of Freud's illusion or even "a" value in Freud's illusion? Westendorf is very much aware of Freud's criticism of religion as well as of religious psychoanalysts who in turn have been critical of Freud. Westendorf showed that Freud's criticism of religion was directed at religious practice rather than the truth of God's existence. While the criticism of religious practice may make the reader uncomfortable, perhaps it will also help the reader to recognize the difference between religious or social value in behavior and underlying truths about God. Finally, Westendorf discussed some of the implications of Freud's illusion for the church and the practice of psychotherapy.

Are there some actual religious practices which are neurotically immature? If so how can they be eliminated without threatening a person's Christian faith? Should that type of faith really be considered faith in God or faith in religious practice? Fleck's (chapter 4) distinction between consensual and committed might be helpful in clarifying these issues.

In contrast to a psychoanalytic view of man, Frankl has developed an existential or spiritual approach to the future of man. This spiritual dimension of man is described in terms of freedom, responsibility, and will-to-meaning. Shea not only described the spiritual aspects of Frankl's psychology but went on to discuss how Frankl maintains that the reductionistic psychology of Freud, Jung, and Adler has failed to come to grips with the transcendent dimension of human nature: the objective character of value and meaning which is what, in fact, has been repressed in the majority of men. These concepts seem so immediately sympathetic to religion and to Christianity and such a contrast to Freud's illusion described in the previous article that the reader may be tempted to embrace Frankl's view uncritically.

Perhaps the difference between Frankl and Freud is that the former views human nature from its transcendent and spiritual side and the latter views human nature from its weak, evil, and undesirable side. In the final analysis, can both perspectives be correct or should one be consistently embraced? For either case how can Bufford's emphasis on behavior (described later in this section) be integrated with either Freud or Frankl? Finally, is there a spiritual dimension to human nature which is separate from the psychological? If so, how can it be known?

Unlike other authors in this section, Jacobs has written from the perspective of having been a client rather than a practitioner of the theory she is discussing. Therefore, her article has a much more personal tone than the others in this section. Jacobs recognized that Rogers differs from her beliefs as a Christian at several points: Man is totally depraved; he needs someone larger than himself to rescue him; a relational God is more than organismic process; and the body of Christ is more than human islands touching. On the other hand, Jacobs has described her compatibility with Rogers. It is hard for Christians to overstress the importance of Rogers' emphasis on healthy human behavior which is expressed in such concepts as human worth, unconditional positive regard, empathy, personal congruence, and the need for acceptance of their humanity. Finally, Jacobs found Rogers' emphasis on "increasingly existential living" and St. Paul's ". . . I have learned in whatever state I am to be content" very congruent.

Does Jacobs' and Barshinger's (see chapter 12) emphasis on the subjective and personal really touch the central core of psychology and Christianity or does the subjective emphasis obscure the importance of evaluating the objective truth of the nature of the relationship between these conceptions?

While Bufford began his article with the less than serious reflection that God through the use of the Ten Commandments was the first behaviorist, he does seriously contend that Israel's history can be viewed as a series of periods of obedience followed by God's blessing alternating with disobedience followed by punishment. Blessing and punishment are interpreted as God's use of applied behavior modification.

Though Bufford concedes that behavior modification has an implicit ontology and metaphysics, he prefers to contend that it is primarily a technology which is consistent with biblical principles and can even be used to teach them. Bufford has illustrated the Bible's use of such behavioral principles as social influence, positive reinforcement, and self-control to establish positive desirable behavior; its use of substituting positive behavior for undesirable behavior, and punishment to eliminate negative behavior. After finishing this article, the reader may be surprised at the number of behavioral principles which can be illuminated from the Scripture.

Is Bufford in agreement with Clement (chapter 7)? They are both embracing a behavioral approach. More specifically, are they both operating from the same model (Carter, chapter 5) of integrating psychology and Christianity?

THE VALUE OF FREUD'S ILLUSION

Floyd Westendorp

Sigmund Freud wrote very extensively regarding religion and religious practices. He did this in spite of the fact that he had a completely negative attitude toward religion. In 1904, in his paper entitled, "The Psychopathology of Everyday Life," Freud laid the foundation on which he built in subsequent papers. That is, that religion is nothing other than psychological processes projected into the outer world. On this foundation he attempted to transform metaphysical constructs into metapsychological constructs in an effort to explain paradise, the fall of man, a concept of good and evil, and immortality.

Freud observed much similarity between obsessive acts associated with obsessive-compulsive neurosis and religious practices. The two primary areas that he compared are the rituals or ceremonials and the beliefs in certain dogmas. In 1907, in his paper, "Obsessive Acts and Religious Practices," he wrote that he was "struck by the resemblance between what are called obsessive acts in neurotics and religious observances by means of which the people give expression to their piety."

In this paper he pointed out three areas of comparison. The first area of comparison is relative to their origin. Freud felt that both the obsessive act and the religious ceremonial or ritual had their origins in guilt. "It is in the fear of pangs of conscience after their omission and the complete isolation of them from all other activities (the feeling that one must not be disturbed) and in the conscientiousness with which the details are carried out." He expressed this more clearly when he indicated that the individual performing the obsessive act is dominated by a sense of guilt and compared it to the sense of guilt seen in religious individuals as a consequence of continual temptation and anxious expectation in the guise of the fear of divine punishment. Freud thought that the knowledge of guilt feelings being associated with obsessive acts was a relatively new discovery. However, the guilt associated with religious rituals had been known for some time.

The second comparison of the obsessive act with religious rituals is that religious rituals appear to be public whereas obsessive acts generally appear to be private. Freud did not elaborate on this observation but rather used this comparison in his summary at the end of the paper.

The third comparison is that both the obsessive act and the religious ritual are symbolic. Even though religious ceremonials are full of meaning and are understood symbolically while obsessive acts appear to be silly and meaningless, he felt that they actually are the same. His argument was that most individuals participating in religious rituals carry them out without being concerned with their significance, even though priests and other investigators may be familiar with their meaning which is usually symbolic. This makes it very similar to the obsessive act because the individual performing the obsessive act is unaware of the meaning. Once psychoanalysis has been applied, the obsessive act no longer remains foolish and meaningless and one is able to see that obsessive acts arise from a well-thought-out process and all their details are full of symbolic meaning. Therefore, the obsessive acts are similar to the religious rituals in that they both are symbolic, have meaning and interpretation.

Because of the similarity that Freud saw between the obsessive act and the religious ritual, he interpreted the obsessional neurosis to be a pathological counterpart to the formation of a religion. Adding to this the observation that obsessive acts were generally private and religious rituals were generally public, he called obsessional neurosis a private religious system, and religion, in general, a universal neurosis.

Between 1907 and 1927 Freud wrote some significant papers in which he attempted to relate the need for a belief in a religion to the father complex. Among these papers is one in 1910 which is a study on Leonardo DiVinci in which Freud pointed out that he felt that psychoanalysis clearly shows that the personal god concept is psychologically nothing other than the magnified father. He drew this conclusion from the observation that young people often lose their religious faith as soon as a father's authority collapses. In 1919 Freud wrote the paper, "Psychoanalysis and Religious Origins," where he was even more specific relative to the father complex indicating that the oedipus complex and the attempted mastery of it, is the key dynamic. He drew his conclusion from the study of primitive religions, contemporary religions, and myths. In 1923, in his paper, "The Ego and the Id," Freud approached the father complex from a little different angle. Here he pointed out that the ego ideal is a substitute for the early longing for a loved father and as such contains a kernel out of which all religions are constituted.

In 1927 Freud's book, *The Future of an Illusion,* was published. This was, and still is, a much disputed work of Freud. In general, the book deals more with the nature and future of religion rather than its origin. He summarized quite succinctly the development of the need for the father complex in religion. He presented three reasons why man feels it necessary to develop religious beliefs. First, to defend himself against a crushing supremacy of nature. Second, the eager desire to correct the so painfully felt imperfection of culture. And third, everything is a son-father relationship. The last reason is explained by Freud's statement, "God is the exalted father and the longing for the father is the root of the need for religion."

In this book, Freud spent a great deal of time explaining the third reason for the necessity of man to develop religious beliefs. He went through the development of how initially the mother is the first love object for an infant and becomes the first protection against anxiety; however, as a child grows, this function is replaced by the stronger father toward whom the child has great ambivalence. Consequently, the father not only is feared but is also longed for and admired. As the child grows up and

finds that he is destined to remain a child forever because he can never do without protection against the unknown mighty powers, he invests these powers with the traits of the father figure. He creates for himself the god of whom he is afraid, whom he seeks to propitiate, and to whom he nevertheless entrusts the task of protecting him. Thus, the longing for the father explanation as a protection against the consequences of human weakness leads to the formation of religion.

Freud openly admitted that he was confronted with a problem if one accepts the fact that religion is a universal neurosis which has its origin in the father complex. The problem is, why is it that religious ideas have had such a strong influence on mankind? Freud said the answer rests in the dogmas professed by religion. He gave the religious explanation of a dogma as being the condensed result of a long process of thought which is founded on observation and on reasoning, a process that any individual can go through if one so desired and come up with the same result. However, he felt that most individuals accept dogmas, first, because our primal ancestors already believed them and, second, because we possess proofs which have been handed down to us from this very period of antiquity and, third, because it is forbidden to raise the question of their authenticity at all.

Freud viewed dogmas in a completely different perspective. He thought that, upon looking at the psychological origin of religious ideas, one finds dogmas not to be the product of experience and reflection, but rather that they are delusions or fulfillment of wishes and that the strength of the dogmas lies in the strength or intensity of these wishes. Once again he traced the wish to the father complex, the wish being protection, as illustrated in his statement.

We know already that the terrifying effect of infantile helplessness arouses the need for protection, protection through love, which the father relieved, and the discovery that this helplessness would continue through the whole of life made it necessary to cling to the existence of a father but this time a more powerful one.

Freud is careful to indicate that an illusion is not necessarily a falsehood; however, it is something that cannot be proved, neither can it be refuted.

Freud felt very strongly that illusions cannot be proven or refuted because of the lack of development of scientific knowledge, and that as scientific knowledge developed, the need for religious dogma would dissipate. He stated that the more the fruits of knowledge become accessible to man, the more widespread is the decline of religious belief. At first only of the obsolete and objectionable expressions of the same, then of its fundamental assumptions also.

A very brief summary of Freud's view on religion can be stated in four hypotheses. First, in general, most people need religion to cope with their fears of the power of nature. Second, all religion takes the form of a universal neurosis, it has its origin in the father complex, and the belief in God is nothing more than a belief in a magnified father. Third, all religious dogmas are illusions. Fourth, as scientific knowledge progresses, the need for religion will subside and ultimately science will replace religion.

From the very beginning Freud was subject to criticism by both his own colleagues and theologians alike with respect to his views on religion. These criticisms did not necessarily come from individuals who were opposed to Freud's basic psychology, but also from individuals who had high respect for Freud, close friends of Freud, who generally accepted his basic psychological principles.

One of these critics was Dr. Oskar Pfister, a Swiss Protestant theologian. Dr. Pfister carried on continuous dialogue with Freud primarily by means of letters from 1909 up until the death of Freud in 1939. Many of these letters were published in the book *Psychoanalysis and Faith* (1963), edited by Meng and Ernst Freud. Pfister was a student of Freud yet did not hesitate to be critical of Freud especially in the area of theology.

Pfister felt that Freud was mistaken in comparing religious rituals to the rituals observed in the obsessive-compulsive neurosis. He criticized Freud for drawing his conclusions on the basis of observations of primitive religions and emotionally unhealthy individuals. He agreed that in primitive religions one did observe rituals resembling compulsions but did not want to call this part of the religion, indicating that the magic preceding religion is not yet religion. The most interesting argument that he presented is that if obsessional fears were as widely present as Freud assumed, religious ceremonies would be much better attended than in fact they are.

Pfister thought that wishful thinking had no place in mature religion. Even though Pfister, as did Freud, observed that there is a lot of wishful thinking with respect to the life hereafter, he emphasized that Jesus eliminated the concept of waiting for a sensual life after death. He pointed out that Jesus preached that the highest ideal was the kingdom of God and that this ideal had the earth as a showplace and for its content ideal ethical and religious qualities which had nothing to do with instinctual wishes. This appears to be in full agreement with the statement regarding life everlasting in the Heidelberg Catechism, "even as I already now experience in my heart the beginning of eternal joy, so after this life I will have perfect blessedness such as no eye has seen, no ear has heard, no man has ever imagined, a blessedness in which to praise God eternally."

Pfister emphasized that religious dogmas are based upon reason and criticizes Freud for not recognizing the extent to which beliefs are due to man's continual search for meaning. Dogmas cannot be wishes in that they are continually tested against reality and although not all reality in either science or religion can be tested directly, Protestant theologians command free and critical thinking from their scholars. Therefore, he would strongly oppose Freud's statement as to why dogmas are so widely accepted.

Pfister also attacked Freud's metaphysics. He felt that Freud was unconscious of his metaphysical assumptions, that they are in any case invalid as they do not offer an adequate description of the whole man, including his religious potentials. Freud frequently made the statement that he had no beliefs. Pfister's reply is stated in a letter dated February 9, 1929. "Disbelief is, after all, nothing but a negative belief." Or, as Oliver S. Walters (1958) puts it in his paper, "Metaphysics, Religion, and Psychotherapy," "even to repudiate metaphysics is to affirm a significant metaphysical position" (p. 245).

Pfister accused Freud of erecting a messiahship of science without being aware that this illusion is also expanded into a faith, a faith which Pfister thought was much more lacking in security in that it was dependent upon the whole deceptive world of the senses which could not be compared to the world of spiritual order. Pfister pointed out that science lacks the ability to make an adequate description of the whole man including man's religious potential. Science lacks the ability to assess esthetic and ethical values and the power to produce them. Men are not merely thinking apparatus; they are loving, feeling, willing people. In science the purpose of character of human life is not taken into account. Pfister could only conclude that science is unable to replace religion with its enormous metaphysical background and future prospective with its divine sanctioning of the moral commandments and its gospel of forgiveness.

Dr. Gregory Zilboorg was a brilliant psychoanalyst, a very astute student of Freud, and a convert to Catholicism. He summarized his criticisms of Freud's religious thoughts in his book *Psychoanalysis and Religion* (1962).

Zilboorg first of all pointed out Freud's expression of ambivalence regarding his religious beliefs. This ambivalence is demonstrated in several manners. The first one that Zilboorg pointed out is that Freud, in his book *The Future of an Illusion* stated on several occasions that he was not questioning the truth of the claims made by religion and that even though he called religion an illusion this did not necessarily imply that it was a falsehood. Further evidence of Freud's ambivalence are the volumes that he wrote regarding religion. The best evidence of his ambivalence, I feel, is expressed in his letter to Dr. Pfister dated February 9, 1909, where he writes, "but you are in the fortunate position of being able to lead them to God and bring about what in this one respect was the happy state of earlier times when religious faith stifled the neurosis." In other words, Freud actually never refuted the existence of God or the natural laws involved in the development of morality and other tenets of religion. He merely considered all these tenets not acceptable because they seem to express themselves on the human plane in the manner human beings express themselves as a rule. Freud had described the process, the psychological ones, so well and with such insight, Zilboorg pointed out that perhaps Freud himself, and undoubtedly most of his disciples, failed to notice that the psychological mechanisms themselves cannot serve as a measure of religious truth nor of any truth for that matter.

One of the biggest criticisms that Zilboorg had of Freud was his equating the superego to the conscience. This criticism has far reaching implications for it is this very point that led Zilboorg to go beyond Freud. He did not feel satisfied; Freud had not gone deep enough. Therefore, Zilboorg turned to religion which he embraced humbly and seriously. Zilboorg described the development of the superego by means of a healthy resolution of the oedipus complex, but he emphasized that this does not mean that all conscience is a product of this mechanism. He could not understand how Freud could accept that reason integrated into personality and pervaded with object libidinous genital maturity would lead away from evil and toward that which is good. He wondered, did Freud assume the existence of values which would find their way into man's psychic apparatus by means of other psychological, biological, or cultural paths?

Zilboorg, however, emphasized that anyone who discards Freud on the score of moral philosophy is out of place since Freud never formulated and never attempted to formulate a moral philosophy.

Zilboorg was in total agreement with Pfister in his criticism of Freud's overemphasizing science. Zilboorg saw Freud as a great scientist but felt that Freud had a need to assert his scientific credo with an emphasis greater than was warranted, as if he had to assure his audience and his followers and, who knows, perhaps himself, that all there is is science and scientific knowledge. The rest, whatever it is, is fantasy and illusion.

In this paper I have presented only some of the negative criticisms that Pfister and Zilboorg expressed regarding Freud's religious views. In spite of the intensity of their criticisms, they did not find it necessary to throw Freud's observations away, or to sever their friendship with him. Rather, for each of them, it intensified their friendship, which tells us a lot about the beauty of the men involved. For both Pfister and Zilboorg, Freud's writings on religion led them on to new horizons. For Pfister, this led to his developing an entire new approach to pastoral counseling. To him it opened up another way to minister to the needs of his parishioners. Some called this the social gospel, and indeed it does have the potential to become just that. Whether it was for Pfister I do not know. For Zilboorg it initially led to dissatisfaction, feeling that depth psychology had not gone deep enough. It stimulated Zilboorg to turn to religion, and he became a Catholic convert.

The criticism that both Pfister and Zilboorg presented regarding Freud's overemphasis on science, and their strong belief that science will never replace religion, is strongly supported by the studies of various religious groups in the United States today, in a country that prides itself in its scientific development. Following are some illustrations of groups in the United States who are either reactivating old religious rituals or clinging very much to old religious rituals. Herman Wouk (1960), in his book *This Is My God,* describes the history of the rituals in Judaism and how, today, in the United States, after a prolonged period of rationalization as to why certain rituals need not be performed, they are being reactivated. A second illustration is what we observe among the Navajos in the southwest United States. There we see the younger educated Navajo attempting to re-establish the old Navajo rituals. This is especially true among the Navajos who are active in the group called AIM (American Indian Movement). The third illustration is taken from the black people in the South. There one observes that the rituals in the church appear to be no different than the rituals that we read about in the textbooks of history dealing with the Civil War. It would appear that the advancement of science does something to man that makes him all the more aware of the fact that he has a need of a God and seeks to have a relationship with that God that transcends science.

Even though it is easy to criticize Freud's conclusions, it is difficult to criticize his method of investigation and the observations he made with respect to religion. There are practical applications of his observations both in the area of religion as well as in the area of psychotherapy.

For one of the practical applications in religion I will quote a paragraph from Zilboorg (1962):

There are a number of earnest religious thinkers who are preoccupied with problems vital to religious life and the life of religion. Aggression, ambivalence, the constant clash between love and hate, esthetic dedication, the contemplative life, moral issues and personal, social and public life, and the relation of emotions to the problem of will and reason. A number of devout scholars are busy restudying all these problems with the utmost care, intellectual honesty, and profound faith. The aid of the added insight with which psychoanalysis provides them proves invaluable both to the further development of religious scholarship and the deeper understanding of the faith. (p. 97)

To those churches that continue to exercise church discipline, the insights gained through psychoanalysis can only help in understanding the delinquent parishioner and the church's role in contributing to the cause of the delinquency. It can also aid in the establishment of an approach that instead of pushing the delinquent further from the church will draw him back into the church.

A third practical application is in the entire area of proselytization. I have seen very little written regarding the application of psychoanalytic insights into mission outreach, but it seems to me that it is only a natural conclusion that if we have some insight as to why people have a need for a higher being, it is imperative that these be thoroughly researched and practical applications be made of them. This in no way degrades the power of the Spirit. Throughout Scripture our God has demonstrated himself to be a God of order and a God who utilized means. I strongly believe that God does use psychological methods to draw people to him. This leaves the responsibility to us to study the insights given to us through men such as Freud, Zilboorg, and Pfister and apply them to our mission methodology. Through this, what Freud calls an illusion, we can have the beautiful experience of being drawn closer to God and be instrumental in leading others to God.

Of what value is the illusion from a psychotherapeutic perspective? Freud did not utilize religious faith in the treatment of his patients as one would suspect; yet he was not averse to it, and in his letter of February 9, 1909, to Dr. Pfister, seemed somewhat jealous that he was not in a position to utilize religion. As he writes:

But you are in the fortunate position of being able to lead them to God and bring about what in this one respect was the happy state of earlier times when religious faith stifled the neurosis. For us, this way of disposing of the matter does not exist. Our public, no matter of what racial origin, is irreligious. We are generally thoroughly irreligious ourselves and as the other ways of sublimation which we substitute for religion are too difficult for most patients, our treatment generally results in seeking out of satisfaction.

John E. G. Irwin (1973), in his article, "Pfister and Freud: The Rediscovery of a Dialogue," points out a danger of misusing religion in therapy. Irwin states:

But if the goals in counseling, the ends of pastoral care, the moral ideas aimed at, the conception and means of salvation are dictated more by depth psychology than by the Christian gospel, then, of course, Christianity is being used as a *deus ex machina,* a resource and a scope of religious healing is reduced ethically and pastorally, until the question arises as it did for Pfister, as to whether this healing is but a higher form of mental hygiene. (p. 324)

This points out that the danger exists that religion could be used as a gimmick to aid in the therapy rather than the therapy being a means to make one's religion more meaningful.

Walters (1958) points out rather nicely that in order to do a complete task in psychotherapy one must address himself to both existential anxiety as well as the pathologic anxiety. His definition of existential anxiety arises out of Tillich's (1957) views of existential anxiety, that is, "an anxiety that grows out of the three-fold ontological threat of death, meaninglessness, and guilt." Walters (1958) states:

Existential anxiety is properly the object of priestly concern, while pathologic anxiety is the concern of the psychotherapist. The goal of both professions is to help the patient achieve full self-affirmation. They may collaborate fruitfully but neither should try to replace the other. (p. 247)

I would like to carry this one step further, based upon the work of Ferenczi (1951), who was a contemporary of Freud, a student of Freud, and one of the first psychoanalysts who attempted to integrate his psychoanalytic technique with his Christianity. He attempted to treat the neurotic by means of dramatization of the psychoanalytic technique, treating the patient as if he were a three-year-old and even talking baby talk with him, petting, him and so on. However, Ferenczi soon found that he could not give enough love to the patients, whose demand for love is insatiable. The psychotherapeutic results of the new method were disappointing and with his death in 1933 this method was given up. But the problem of neurotic need for affection remains unsolved.

Love plays a very important role in the development of a healthy personality. Ferenczi once made the statement "The unloved child dies and if it does not maybe it were better that he had." Theodore Reich (1963), after studying the research of Renee Spitz, Anna Freud, and Dorothy Burlingham, makes the statement, "Be loved or perish." The love relationships that exist between a child and his parents play an important role as to the development of a neurosis. This has led many therapists to approach the problem of treating neurosis in much the same manner as Ferenczi, that is, to teach the neurotic that he is lovable by showing him love, only to find that the demand for love is so insatiable that he gives up. This raises the question, can the Christian therapist be successful in these situations where other therapists have failed? If we accept Freud's observation that religion has its roots in the parental complex, and we accept the hypothesis that this observation of Freud could be a psychological means used by God to draw people to him, then why is it not possible for a Christian therapist to utilize the transference situation, to point the patient to the source of all love, namely God. Or, to put it in the words of Freud, to have the patient substitute his "personal neurosis" for the "universal neurosis." Almost all of us, at some time, have had some patients who have suddenly dropped out of therapy because they no longer felt a need for therapy; because they had experienced what they called a religious conversion. We, as therapists, are often inclined to look at this in terms of resistance or denial. It is not fair to generalize, for, on follow-up, we see some of these individuals making a very healthy adaptation and never requiring further therapy. We should examine how religious conversion does enable these patients' insatiable needs to be fulfilled and helps them live healthy adaptive lives.

References

Ferenczi, S. *Final Contributions to the Problems and Methods of Psychoanalysis* (Michael Balint, ed.). New York: Basic Books, 1951.

Freud, S. *The Future of an Illusion.* Garden City, N.Y.: Doubleday, 1957.

———. *Collected Papers.* New York: Basic Books, 1959.

Irwin, J. E. G. "Pfister and Freud: The Rediscovery of a Dialogue." *Journal of Religion and Health,* 1973, *12,* 315-327.

Meng, H., and Freud, E. *Psychoanalysis and Faith.* New York: Basic Books, 1963.

Reich, T. *The Need to Be Loved.* New York: The Noonday Press, 1963.

Tillich, P. *Dynamics of Faith.* New York: Harper & Row, 1957.

Walters, O. S. "Metaphysics, Religion, and Psychotherapy." *Journal of Counseling Psychology,* 1958, *5,* 243-52.

Wouk, H. *This Is My God.* Garden City, N.Y.: Doubleday, 1960.

Zilboorg, G. *Psychoanalysis and Religion.* New York: Farrar, Straus & Cudahy, 1962.

ON THE PLACE OF RELIGION
IN THE THOUGHT OF VIKTOR FRANKL

John J. Shea

In the introduction to *The Doctor and the Soul* **Viktor Frankl (1966) remarks that "every school of psychotherapy has a concept of the person** which should be made conscious" (p. xviii). He believes that the image of the person is an essential question in psychology and psychiatry, for whatever view of humanity is implicitly or explicitly adopted will determine the goals and techniques of therapy.

Throughout his writings Frankl insists that human existence is broader than its traditional psychoanalytic interpretation. His works, which are consciously philosophical, set forth a basically existential view of humanity within which he feels both therapy and psychoanalytic theory can be incorporated. Drawing mainly from Husserl and Scheler as well as from Heidegger and Jaspers, Frankl's approach is loosely phenomenological. Within this approach he sees the person as a situated freedom responsible for realizing objective values.

The Existential Analysis

Viktor Frankl situates his existential analysis within what he calls a "dimensional ontology." For him the person lives in at least three dimensions: the somatic, the psychic, and the spiritual or noological. At times he suggests a fourth, the religious dimension, but he seems reluctant to include this dimension in his existential analysis.

The somatic dimension is self-explanatory for it is simply the biological aspect of the person, and the psychic dimension is understood basically as including the phenomena described and interpreted by Freud. The spiritual dimension—which should not be understood as primarily religious—is what has been missing in psychoanalysis. It is that part of the person whereby he or she is human, and specifically, it is what Frankl is trying to uncover in his existential analysis. His purpose in this analysis is "to make the unifying image of man into a whole, a total image of true man, an image in all its dimensions, thus doing justice to that reality which

© *Journal of Psychology and Theology*, 1975, *3*, 179-88. Used by permission of the author.

belongs only to man and is called existence" (Frankl, 1967, p. 130).

Rooted in its own unconscious and given in prereflective or immediate awareness, the spiritual dimension is "the core or nucleus of the personality (Frankl, 1966, pp. x-viii)," an irreducible thing-in-itself which is unable to be explained in nonspiritual terms. Frankl sees this spiritual dimension as manifesting itself in terms of a human freedom and a concomitant responsibility which must be acknowledged as existential realities: "In actuality, man is free and responsible, and these constituents of his spirituality, i.e., freedom and responsibility, must never be clouded by what is called the reification or depersonalization of man" (Frankl, 1961, p. 8).

Human freedom, which is understood intuitively and prereflectively, stands in a unique relation to one's somatic and psychic dimensions:

Man is free to rise above the plane of somatic and psychic determinants of his existence. By the same token a new dimension is opened. Man enters the dimension of the noetic, in counter distinction to the somatic and psychic phenomena. Thereby, he becomes capable of taking a stand, not only toward the world but also toward himself. Man is being capable of reflecting, and even rejecting himself. He can be his own judge, the judge of his own deeds. In short, the specifically human phenomena linked with one another, self-consciousness and conscience, would not be understandable unless we interpret man in terms of being capable of detaching himself from himself, leaving the "plane" of the biological and psychological, passing into the "space" of the noological. (1964, pp. 44-45)

Whenever Frankl speaks of freedom he always insists that it be correlated with responsibility. It is freedom and responsibility, he says, that go to make up the wholeness of the human being. Responsibility is revealed by conscience, also an irreducible thing-in-itself, and it is given added clarity through analysis of death similar to that of Heidegger. Each person is responsible for the actualization of his or her own potentialities especially in the face of death which stands as the end to the future and the boundary of all possibilities.

In addition to revealing freedom and responsibility, Frankl's phenomenology also reveals to him a "world of meanings and values" which he calls the "objective correlate to the subjective phenomenon called human existence" (1961, p. 9). What he means by "objective" is that meanings and values are not just self-expressions of the individual as a Sartrean analysis would have it, but rather they are found by the individual in reality. It is the demanding force arising out of these values that serves as a foundation for objective morality and the possibility of experiencing moral imperatives. Since each person is unique in his or her existence, each experiences imperatives according to a particular situations and potentialities, but the unique imperatives remain objective for the particular individual who experiences them.

It is within a context of both the subjective and the objective that the essential dynamics (noodynamics) of existence are described:

The freedom to take a stand as emphasized above is never complete if it has not been converted and rendered into the freedom to take responsibility. The specific capacity to "will" remains empty as long as it has not been complemented by its objective counterpart, to will what I "ought." What I ought, however, is the actualization of values, the fulfillment of the concrete meaning of my personal existence. (1961, p. 9)

Within this subjective-objective framework Frankl is able to elaborate the concept which is the central element of his thought and the dynamic foundation of his logotherapy, that is, the will-to-meaning. "The will-to-meaning is the subjective side of a spiritual reality in which the meaning is the objective side" (1959b, p. 163). Unique and specific for each individual, it is the primary motivational force of existence. Existence falters if it is not lived in terms of transcendence, in terms of reaching beyond itself. Meaning cannot coincide with existence. "Meaning must be ahead of being; *meaning sets the pace of being"* (1964, p. 53).

The tension, or noodynamics, which exists between being and meaning is both inevitable and essential for personal growth. Contrary to the psychoanalytic understanding of tension, Frankl has found that: "Man does not need homeostasis at any cost, but rather a sound amount of tension such as that which is aroused by the demand quality inherent in the meaning of his existence" (1963a, p. 29).

But what are the meanings to be found in existence? What are the objective values that challenge the person and call each to responsibility? Frankl believes that although meaning is unique for each individual every one, can find meaning in a threefold way: first, through what is given to life (in terms of creative work); second, by what is taken from the world (in terms of experiencing values in nature and culture); and third, through the stand taken toward a fate one can no longer change (as, for example, with an incurable disease) (1964, p. 56).

It is this last category of meanings, what are called "attitudinal" values, which is emphasized by Frankl as being the most important. It is the attitude that the person takes to what Frankl labels "the tragic triad" of human existence, that is, suffering, guilt, and death, which is ultimately significant and decisive in human existence. This triad makes each person face existence. It keeps one "psychically alive" and challenges one to grow "richer and stronger" (1966, p. 109).

With this brief description of the person as a situated freedom who is responsible for realizing objective values—with an emphasis on the will-to-meaning—the essential elements of Frankl's existential analysis are disclosed. In addition, it need only be noted that he sees the present age as one of anxiety in which the values and meaning in life easily become confused or lost. More and more individuals are experiencing "existential frustration," a lack of meaning in their lives which is variously described as a sense of helplessness, a disregard for others, a fear of responsibility, and a sense of emptiness or futurelessness.

Religion and Traces of Transcendence

With the previous section serving as a brief background for an understanding of Frankl's basic conceptualization of the person, a closer look can now be taken at some passages in his analysis which seem to point toward the reality of religion and its legitimacy as an object of meaning.

Much of Frankl's thought is developed in reaction to the psychologism that he perceives in the work of Freud, Jung, and Adler. He is very critical of their reduction of human values and their failure to adequately come to terms with the spiritual or noological dimension in humanity. Reflecting on Freud's psychological model of the person, Frankl (1956) states:

Responsibility can only come to us from a higher court than ourselves. If we derive the ego from the id (the will from the instincts) and trace back the superego to the ego (moral obligation of the will) we gain no correct view, but rather, a caricature of man. (p. 686)

We are responsible first of all to our conscience, but this does not mean that we are just responsible to ourselves for ourselves. In his *Handbuch der Neurosenlehre und Psychotherapie* Frankl (1957) suggests that: "In the final analysis it must certainly appear questionable whether man could really be responsible before something—or whether responsibility is only possible when it is before some" (p. 694). And again, in *The Doctor and the Soul* he says more explicitly: "We can be responsible only to an entity higher than ourselves" (1966, p. xxi).

When speaking specifically of the religious person, Frankl describes that one as one who "interprets his existence not only in terms of being responsible for fulfilling his life tasks, but also as being responsible to the taskmaster" (1966, pp. 58-59). Reflecting on the religious person's experience of conscience, he observes:

Conscience has its "still small voice" and "speaks" to us—that is an undeniable psychological fact. What conscience says, however, is in every case a response. From the psychological point of view, the religious person is one who experiences not only what is spoken, but the speaker as well; that is, his hearing is sharper than the non-religious persons. In the dialogue with his conscience—in this most intimate of possible monologues—his God is his interlocutor. (p. 62)

In light of these passages on responsibility and conscience some preliminary questions can now be raised from within the framework of the existential analysis. Is his description of the religious person in any sense part of an essential phenomenology, and if so, why is the religious dimension not a part of his ontology? But if his description of the religious person is simply a description of the values that some individuals have found in their lives, on what grounds is Frankl so partial to these values? And what is the thrust, in terms of his existential analysis, of references such as "an entity higher than ourselves"?

Whatever the ultimate answer to these questions may be, it seems clear that some concept of transcendence is rooted in Frankl's thought. In a passage from *Man's Search for Meaning* he notes:

As soon as we have interpreted religion as being merely a product of psychodynamics, in the sense of unconscious motivating forces, we have missed the point and lost sight of the authentic phenomenon. Through such a misconception, the psychology of religion becomes psychology as religion, in that psychology is sometimes worshipped and made an explanation for everything. (1963*b*, p. 212)

Frankl is not just attacking reductionism here but also positing something objective in its own right.

In presenting his three types of values Frankl notes that for him the highest values are the attitudinal—especially the value of suffering. Yet even the value of suffering can be questioned in terms of transcendence. Frankl (1963*b*) asks: "Is it not conceivable that there is still another dimension possible, a world beyond man's world; a world in which the question of ultimate meaning of human suffering would find an answer?" (p. 187).

In Frankl's description of love there are demands for transcendence which also seem to be within the phenomena themselves. In *The Doctor and the Soul* he speaks of love as intuiting the essence of the other person. Frankl sees this essence as ultimately independent of existence, and this explains why it is that love can outlast the death of the beloved. Later he suggests how it is that the experience of love is possible: "Love can only be experienced *sub specie aeternitatis*. The real lover, in the moment of loving, in his surrender to that moment and to the object of his love, cannot conceive that this feeling will ever change" (Frankl, 1966, p. 146).

At the end of a moving passage in *Man's Search for Meaning* Frankl (1963*b*) describes his own love for his wife:

I did not know whether my wife was alive, and I had no means of finding out . . . , but at that moment it ceased to matter. There was no need for me to know; nothing could touch the strength of my love, my thoughts, and the image of my beloved. Had I known then that my wife was dead, I think that I would still have given myself, undisturbed by that knowledge, to the contemplation of her image, and that my mental conversation with her would have been just as vivid and just as satisfying (p. 61).

Although not explicitly asking the question of transcendence, the phenomenological descriptions of love provide the basis for the possibility of raising the question.

Having looked at religion from the perspective of the existential analysis and having seen the traces of transcendence in the phenomena of suffering and love, to complete this section we need only focus on what Frankl says explicitly of religion and God.

In keeping with the dynamics of his existential analysis Frankl understands the question of God's existence in terms of ultimate meaning. Is there an ultimate meaning to existence, especially in light of the "tragic triad," and how can this ultimate meaning be experienced by the human being? In answer to this question Frankl (1970) speaks of "supra-meaning" which supercedes "dimensionally" one's capacity as a finite being and yet is capable of being grasped in an existential act (pp. 143-48). Reflecting on this ultimate meaning he finds that:

This meaning necessarily transcends man and his world and, therefore, cannot be apprehended by merely rational processes. It is rather accessible to an act of commitment which emerges out of the depth and center of man's personality and is thus rooted in his total existence. In one word, what we have to deal with is no intellectual or rational process, but a wholly existential act which perhaps could be described by what I call "Urvertrauen zum Dasein" which in turn could be translated by "the basic trust in Being". (1962a, pp. 27-28)

We are called in our existence to decide between two alternatives, ultimate meaning or ultimate absurdity. The decision is the mode of existence which one chooses. It is a decision made in faith which seems to reveal in the one who makes it an already existing trust in God.

It would seem, however, that there is in the person more than the possibility of affirming transcendence through faith. What seems to be the ground of this possiblity is Frankl's feeling that all, at least unconsciously, are basically religious and that trust in ultimate meaning and faith in being, however dormant, are indispensable for existence. As he says, "It is my contention that man really could not move a limb unless deep down to the foundations of existence, and out of the depths of being, he is imbued by a basic trust in the ultimate meaning" (1970, pp. 150-51).

Commenting on an interesting case of the "conversion" of a long-time prisoner which had been presented for his opinion, Frankl (1959a) interprets what actually occurred as "a reversion—to be precise, a return to a connection—the return to 'religio.' This religion was subconsciously existent, although repressed" (p. 10). He explains that:

We have passed the stage of accepting repressed instinctuality alone. There also exists a subconscious spirituality, morality, and religiosity. But this religiosity was repressed—the patient had grown up in the contemporary nihilism, materialism, and naturalism. What logotherapy does is go one step beyond Freud. Did not Freud once say that the human being is not only subconsciously more immoral than he believes himself to be—but also more moral than he thinks himself to be?—and we dare to add: occasionally, *man is also more religious than he supposes himself.*

There is, then, in everyone a religiosity which is easily repressed. Much of this repression is caused by what Frankl (1970) calls the "stumbling blocks" of authoritarianism, rationalism, and anthropomorphism which try to conceptualize God (p. 149). One cannot really speak of God; to speak of God is to make being into a thing. Frankl does allow, however, for some personification of God if it is analogically understood. As he phrases it, "man cannot speak of God but he may speak to God. He may pray" (p. 146). It is through prayer, in fact, that one gives witness to faith:

One day, a few days after the liberation, I walked through the country past flowering meadows, for miles and miles, toward the market town near the camp. Larks rose to the sky and I could hear their joyous song. There was no one to be seen for miles around; there was nothing but the wide earth and sky and the larks' jubilation and the freedom of space. I stopped, looked around, and up to the sky—and then I went down on my knees. At that moment there was very little I knew of myself or of the world—I had but one sentence in mind—always the same: "I called to the Lord from my narrow prison and He answered me in the freedom of space." (1963*b*, p. 142)

As a conclusion to this section of the article some light can be thrown on the preliminary question raised in regard to Frankl's understanding of religion and transcendence.

There seem to be three aspects of his resolution of the question of the religious dimension in the human person. First, the religious dimension can only be grasped or consciously entered by an existential affirmation which some make and some do not. Second, all have an inherent religiosity but for a variety of reasons many individuals have it in a repressed or subconscious form. Third, Frankl himself is a man of faith who trusts in ultimate being.

The reason why Frankl is so partial to the values of the religious person seems to be that these values are in some sense a part of one's essential phenomenology, albeit for some unconsciously so. Why, then, is not the religious dimension a part of his dimensional ontology? There does not seem to be an adequate answer to this question. Perhaps an explanation lies in the fact that the religious dimension is not conscious in everyone or in the fact that Frankl finds nothing in the human world which gives us any ground for speaking of God. But it is ironic at best that in terms of existential analysis he seems to have precluded the existential act whereby the religious dimension can be realized.

The Role of Religion in Logotherapy

More and more, a doctor is confronted with the questions: What is life? What is suffering after all? Indeed incessantly and continually a psychiatrist is approached today by patients who confront him with human problems rather than neurotic symptoms. Some of the people who nowadays call on a psychiatrist would have seen a pastor, priest or rabbi in former days, but now they often refuse to be handed over to a clergyman, so that the doctor is confronted with philosophical questions rather than emotional conflicts. (1963*b*, p. 184)

In this section of the article the logotherapy developed by Frankl in response to "philosophical questions" is seen in its relation to religion. This relationship is of special interest because both logotherapy and religion (to some extent at least) have foundations in his dimensional ontology.

Logotherapy, conceived as a supplement to the work of Freud and Adler, is a therapy which deals primarily with neurotic self-concern and especially with noogenic neuroses, that is, with existential frustration and the experience of meaninglessness. This therapy is predicated on the existential analysis; it is a psychotherapy in spiritual terms which stresses the individual's responsibility and the meaning to be found or values to be realized in existence.

It is precisely this emphasis on the spiritual dimension that Frankl feels is missing in the psychotherapy of the first two Vienna schools. These schools, which he finds blind to values and therefore forced to ignore the will-to-meaning, approach the human person in terms of a psychic mechanism ruled by the law of cause and effect. When existential or philosophical problems arise, they can only deal with them by turning the discussion to the pathological roots from which the questions stemmed. Their inadequate conception of the person forces them into a psychologism whereby they can only analyze every act in terms of its psychic origin and on that basis decide whether or not its content is valid.

What, then, is the understanding of values given in logotherapy? To begin with, the values that a person chooses and the meanings that one finds remain the patient's own affair. The aim of the logotherapist is to confront the patient with this responsibility and to challenge the person with the values to be found in life. The therapist rests content when the patient begins to evaluate:

Existential analysis aims at nothing more and nothing less than leading men to consciousness of their responsibility. It endeavors to help people experience this element of responsibility in their existences. But to lead a person further than this point, at which he profoundly understands his existence as responsibility, is neither possible or necessary. (1966, p. 275)

Logotherapy "makes no statement about responsibility to what and for what," and therefore, it understands responsibility as a "formal ethical principle." Its exercise is in relation to creative, experiential, and especially attitudinal values but only as these values are uniquely specified by each individual.

In regard to religious values and ultimate meaning logotherapy maintains this same basic stance of neutrality. "Logotherapy does not cross the boundary between psychology and religion. But it leaves the door to religion open and it leaves it to the patient whether or not to pass the door" (1970, p. 143). The reason for this stance toward religion seems to come both from the nature of the religious affirmation and from practical considerations. True religious feeling, which arises within the patient only spontaneously as an existential act, could only be hampered by countertransference on the part of the therapist (1966, p. 276).

Furthermore, Frankl (1970) insists that "logotherapy must be available for every patient and usable in the hands of every doctor, whether his *Weltanschauung* is theistic or agnostic" (p. 143).

Frankl finds a dimensional difference between logotherapy and religion. Logotherapy is anthropology concerned with the human; religion is theology and is concerned with transcendence. Their goals are different; the former, he says, is concerned with health, the latter with salvation (1966, p. xv). The effects of religion, however, are clearly of therapeutic value. Religion gives the person a meaning in life. In the realm of ultimate meaning, in fact, Frankl (1966) feels that the psychotherapeutic value of religion is such that logotherapy has nothing to offer to the religious person (p. 271). While not a substitute for religion, logotherapy is an attempt to fill some of the same psychological needs for meaning in life; often, in fact, logotherapy leads to religious awakening. In short, religion is logotherapeutic, and logotherapy may lead to religion.

Finally, what about the question of the logotherapist's own values. Is the therapist simply applying a method, or are one's own values important in the therapeutic relationship? Frankl is not very explicit on this point. He notes, for example, in "Psychiatry and Man's Quest for Meaning" that a sound philosophy of life may be the most valuable asset for a psychiatrist to have when treating a patient in despair (1962*b*, p. 94). The function of the therapist's values, however, in a theory in which they should not influence the patient is not very clear aside from the fact while "he cannot show his patient *what* the meaning is, . . . he may well show him that there is a meaning" (1970, p. ix).

Final Observations

Frankl's dimensional ontology with its emphasis on the existential analysis compensates for the somewhat truncated view of humanity proposed by a more traditional psychoanalytic theory. With an anthropology in terms of freedom, responsibility, and meaning he has rehumanized the psychoanalytic person. In effect, he has stood Freud on his head, changing the person from an object to a subject and changing values from subjective self-expressions back to objective reality. In this upending, moreover, the fortunes of religious value have been reversed. Frankl accepts religion at face value as a real phenomenon, as in some sense objective, and as psychologically very healthy. Religion is no longer a neurosis with its origin in repressed sexuality. It is, or at least it can be, that which realizes in a unique and perhaps incomparable way our basic will-to-meaning.

In terms of his dimensional ontology, however, there does seem to be some ambiguity between the spiritual dimension and its relation to the dimension in which the transcendent is affirmed in an existential act. The spiritual dimension, characterized by the will-to-meaning, is itself part of an essential phenomenology of the person even though what is affirmed in this dimension is the result of an existential act unique to each individual. If, in fact, there is in everyone an "unconscious religiosity" and if a basic trust in ultimate meaning is a *sine qua non* of existence, it is not clear why the religious dimension is not included in the dimensional ontology—as a dimension in its own right or perhaps more properly as an essential part of the spiritual dimension.

The important issue, it seems to me, in trying to understand the place of religion in Frankl's thought is his handling of transcendence. While protesting the making of God into a thing, Frankl seems quite at home with a dimensional difference between finite and infinite, between the human world and the divine world. In addition, this difference is reflected in a distinction between meaning and supra-meaning, a distinction which in terms of the phenomenology he has been applying does not seem to make much sense. Why, as the work of Maslow (1970, 1971) might suggest, could not God be considered in terms of transpersonal values and meaning, not as an object of value, but as an objective value?

In respect to logotherapy, therefore, why could there not be a "formal religious principle" analogous to the formal ethical principle, a religious principle which would challenge as an area or kind of meaning while leaving the specification of that meaning up to the individual? And why could the therapist not point out the existence of the religious subconscious or explore the possibility of a supra-meaning? And even if transcendence is approached through an existential act, would it not seem that influence is just as likely when religion is not mentioned by the therapist as when it is?

Although there are problems with the place of religion in the theory and practice of logotherapy, these problems do not alter the fact that Frankl has made a major contribution to the humanization of psychology and psychiatry. At the same time he has provided for revealed religions an excellent framework and dynamic form for their specific content. But perhaps what is most important in his work is the task he sets himself of finding a unified and holistic concept of the human person.

References

Frankl, V. *Theorie und therapie der neurosen.* München: E. Reinhardt, 1956. Quoted in D. F. Tweedie, Jr., *Logotherapy and the Christian faith.* Grand Rapids: Baker Book House, 1965.

———. *Handbuch de neurosenlehre und psychotherapie.* Wien: Urban & Schwarzenberg, 1957. Quoted in ibid.

———. "Observations." In S. Stendal and R. Corsini (eds.), *Critical Incidents in Psychotherapy.* Englewood Cliffs, N.J.: Prentice Hall, 1959*a*.

———. "The Spiritual Dimension in Existential Analysis and Logotherapy." *Journal of Individual Psychology,* 1959*b*, *15*, 157-65.

———. "Dynamics, Existence and Values." *Journal of Existential Psychiatry,* 1961, *2*, 5-16.

———. "Logotherapy and the Challenge of Suffering." *Pastoral Psychology,* 1962*a*, *13*, 25-28.

————. "Psychiatry and Man's Quest for Meaning." *Journal of Religion and Health*, 1962*b*, *1*, 93-103.

————. "Existential Dynamics and Neurotic Escapism." *Journal of Existential Psychiatry*, 1963*a*, *4*, 27-42.

————. *Man's Search for Meaning*. New York: Washington Square Press, 1963*b*.

————. "The Philosophical Foundations of Logotherapy." In E. Straus (ed.), *Phenomenology: Pure and Applied*. Pittsburgh: Duquesne University Press, 1964, 43-59.

————. *The Doctor and the Soul*. Richard and Clara Winston, trans. New York: Alfred A. Knopf, 1966.

————. "Collective Neuroses of the Present Day." *Psychotherapy and Existentialism*. New York: Simon & Schuster, 1967, 113-31.

————. *The Will to Meaning*. New York: New American Library, 1970.

Maslow, A. *Religions, Values, and Peak Experiences*. New York: Viking Press, 1970.

————. *The Farther Reaches of Human Nature*. New York: Viking Press, 1971.

A CHRISTIAN CLIENT CONSIDERS CARL ROGERS

Joan L. Jacobs

I am an ordinary person except for two things in my life which make me feel more than ordinary. I have been a committed Christian for many years. It has been a basic, life-changing commitment. A second, far less significant, but deeply rewarding experience has been a year in therapy with a competent psychologist.

I became a Christian in 1948 at the juncture of a personal crisis, some enlightening reading in C. S. Lewis, and the renewed friendship with a Christian I had known some time before. My entrance into the Christian community surrounded me with warm friendships, helpful direction, and a settledness about my whole person that was very meaningful. Some of the problems which caused me to seek therapy early in 1973 were rooted well before 1948, but my Christian conviction, the satisfactions of a personal relationship to God, kept me functioning at a practical level during the years when I recognized needs but was unsure where to turn for deeper understanding about myself.

During the year of therapy, but not part of it, I was involved in a class designed to assist us to become more effective in a helping role with troubled people. When one person in this course, who had some previous training, complained at the outset that the content was "too Rogerian," I was introduced to Carl Rogers.

As I learned about Rogers in the class sessions, I recognized him in the therapy. It was helpful to have the opportunity to get a superficial but significant intellectual grasp of Rogers' "learnings" and at the same time to experience opening myself to the psychologist in response to his client-centered sensitivity.

All through the therapy I was very conscious of my continued commitment to the Christian faith, and at the same time I became increasingly conscious that some aspects of Carl Rogers' convictions and experience appeared to fit with both my own experience and my understanding of some Christian doctrines.

Curiosity to know Carl Rogers better led me to read *On Becoming a Person* (1961) and *Person to Person* (1967). I felt especially included in

©*Journal of Psychology and Theology*, 1975, *3*, 25-30. Used by permission of the author.

Rogers' own invitation to readership among people "who might be interested," who want to be "strengthened in their own living." He hopes his writing will be meaningful since we are all involved in human relationships (1961, p. 32).

I write comfortably about this heavy subject, Carl Rogers and Christianity and myself, even as I realize I know so little. The field of psychology is fearfully complex and the outsider can easily err as he tackles something like this. But perhaps Rogers himself is my model. He repeatedly opens himself to discussion. He will often say something like this: ". . . though the following propositions are stated firmly in order to give them clarity, I am actually advancing them as decidedly tentative hypotheses" (Rogers and Stevens, 1967, p. 16). Even though this may be because of his loyalty to the scientific approach, I am always impressed with the humility of this reservation of his both because of the depth of his experience and the feel of reality to me of much of what he says. So he himself encourages me to think about these things, and when my Christian experience draws me to different views, I share them without the embarrassment that a novice might have when confronting a man of tested wisdom and skill.

I find three places where Rogers mentions Christianity. First, there is the intriguing matter of Rogers' own personal contact with the Christian faith as he recalls his early years. He describes his parents as being determined that for their family there could be "no alcoholic beverages, no dancing, cards, or theater, very little social life" (1961, p. 5). Some might be mystified as to the context of such conviction, but many know that only a narrow, largely bygone, but significant era of Protestantism can be readily identified by such a sad twisting of the large love of God. Biblically, the relative lack of importance to God about these very things makes them all the more tragic as they have indelibly influenced thousands of lives as negative values. Rogers, however, evidently had the advantage (denied to many within the church) of parents who cared consistently and seemed, apart from the prohibitions, to be positive people. Rogers' early exposure to Christianity was put aside with his emergence into what was most assuredly a larger, more accepting and exciting world. I am reminded of the philosopher Lin Yutang, who, although he much later returned to the Christianity he rejected, said at the time that leaving the Christian faith was a "process (which) came as naturally as the weaning of a child or the dropping of a ripe apple to the ground; and when the time came for the apple to drop, I would not interfere with its dropping" (1974, p. 400).

A second reference Rogers makes to Christianity is given as he talks about personal goals and the purposes of life. He refers to those who "give themselves completely and devotedly to a cause outside of themselves such as Christianity. . . ." (1961, p. 165). But the genius of Christianity is that it is an inside cause as well. Both in our creation by God and by our "new birth" (when God is invited to enter our lives) we are bound internally with him. Of course Rogers can describe Christianity any way he wishes, but he denies his own pleasure in the scientific quest when he fails to use the definition given in the Bible, which is Christianity's handbook.

Rogers accurately records a third and more serious matter which concerns me as a Christian. He states that along with Freud and others, "Protestant Christian tradition has permeated our culture with the concept that man is basically sinful, and only by something approaching a miracle can his sinful nature be negated" (1961, p. 91). Many Christians feel a lack of worth that has come through the inaccurate teaching of the church. Too often the doctrine of "total depravity" is wrongfully interpreted to mean that each man is totally depraved rather than the entire race is touched by sin. Because our culture has its roots in Christianity, this has affected many who don't consider themselves religious or Christian. C. S. Lewis (1943) rejects this misinterpretation "on the logical ground that if our depravity were total, we should not know ourselves to be depraved" (p. 54). The core of the good news of Christianity is that men are worth so much that God became one of us in order to relate to us, in order for us to relate to him. The Bible teaches that every man is made in God's image (which incidentally is a reasonable explanation for Rogers' "commonality" of man). Further, the Bible says that though man belongs to a fallen race (which accounts for the fact that his behavior is worse than that of animals) he is still characterized in John 1:9 as being lighted by God. There is something positive at the core of every man which can respond to him. Rogers (1961) concludes from his extensive therapeutic experience "that the innermost core of man's nature . . . is positive . . ." (p. 91).

The Christian and Rogers differ again at this point in this way: the fall of man from his perfection at creation, graphically described in Genesis 3, places him in need of someone outside himself to lift him out of the unmanliness which has claimed him. This is Jesus Christ, and in his life, death, and resurrection he has made this possible. When man identifies himself with Christ, he is nearest to his beginning as a creation of God, he is at his best, which is his most human. C. S. Lewis (1943) again helps me by saying that when a man is in the place God designs for him, his "nature is fulfilled . . . . : a broken bone in the universe has been set, the anguish is over" (p. 40).

Rogers (1961) on the other hand finds that man becomes most fully himself, most "self-enhancing and other-enhancing," when he is free in the accepting and sensitive climate of therapy to work through to "an increasing trust in his own organism as a means of arriving at the most satisfying behavior in each existential situation." He finds that in the degree that individuals are open to their total experience, "doing what 'feels right'" proves to be a competent and trustworthy guide to behavior which is truly satisfying. Rogers believes that this behavior will not be anti-social, because this "experiencing" will take into account his needs as a social animal. Again, Rogers formulates this out of the consistent results of thousands of hours of counseling.

Other differences surface as I continue to read and try to digest the "feel" of Rogers. I am truly impressed with the gentle and relentless skill Rogers and his followers bring to therapy to help a client get at the core of himself, and the rich reward for both therapist and client in their unique relationship. I sympathize with Rogers' desire that his kind of accepting therapeutic climate might exist increasingly in life outside the counseling hour. It is obvious that this is a better world to the extent that this takes place. Concerned people look for a realistically possible solution for the pain of the whole world, something that will work out the total human dilemma. Yet I would despair if I thought that there is nothing else on this exploding and agonizing globe but a few hundred men and women sensitive enough and equipped enough with Rogers' skill to bring about a reduction of distress in, at most, a few thousand lives for, at best, a few years.

Then as I read Rogers describe the "organismic process" by which clients move toward true satisfaction in the sifting and sorting of all the necessary data (social demands, needs, memories rightly interpreted, perception of the moment in time during which these forces are brought to bear in decision) I listen to him, in order to make his process perfectly clear, move to the term "hypothetical person," and I begin to have faith only in this imaginary man. I have had this year of good Rogerian therapy, but even though I have emerged more free to be myself, glad I'm me, more able to relate, I feel his "organismic process" something of a burden for twenty-four-hour existential living. I am overcome by what is involved in including all the data in his kind of decision making, even though I know it is an unconscious as well as a conscious process, and even though I am no longer threatened by making a mistake. I much prefer the freedom to "live and move and be," as Paul says in Acts 17, in the love of a relational God who has promised ways (forgiveness, clear understanding, acceptance) out of the maze of guilts and other psychological and spiritual prisons.

Jesus Christ is the embodiment of this relational God, and is available to every man. How many of his critics have closely examined the historicity of the New Testament documents and then finding them reliable, have not gone on to observe the beautiful sensitivity with which Jesus approaches individuals of every kind? How much has he influenced Carl Rogers?

In another area I became increasingly aware of something missing: it is in the matter of relationships as they develop between people based on what I've "heard" Rogers say. In spite of the fact that human relationships are very important to him, he gives me this idea that people are islands. I think of the floating islands that meet and touch and move apart in Lewis' *Perelandra* (1968). There are significant meetings! Barry Stevens describes her relationship with Rogers when they finally met as a "matching," having arrived by very different paths to the same highway (Rogers and Stevens, 1967, p. xiv). And besides an unusually close "matching" like this, Rogers seems to bring to every relationship, no matter how fleeting in time, the accepting quality of himself.

The islands touch, and maybe if they are pliable enough, their shores may meet for miles but they owe each other nothing. There is no meshing, no overlap, only inevitable separation. This is a sensitive matter, because awareness of another's identity must keep us from uninvited, unwanted intrusion. I struggle for a way to express how different it is for the Christian, and I am relieved to remember the biblical concept of the "body of Christ." We believers are a body—fingers, toes, hands, feet and all that the parts mean to each other, independent yet indispensable for life and wholeness. Paul expresses this well in 1 Corinthians 12. I have experienced being part of this body in fact, and tossed the idea about for a long time without realizing how much it means to me.

Then I realize somehing else is missing and a word Rogers avoids pours over me—love. I am glad he seldom uses this word. It is so misused. All the ways we use "love" in our culture fall short of what Rogers conveys so well about caring. When the New Testament was written the word "agape" began to be used for the love of God—the Greeks had no such use for it before. You have to read the New Testament to try to understand this love. Rogers can't use this meaning. So this word "love" is both too little and too big in his context.

Another issue arises in the matter of Rogers' prohibitions against "ought" and "should." He objects to these because they are part of the "introjected values" which he says have covered up that good, positive core of man. They are not the basis of spontaneous, rewarding activity. One day at breakfast I discussed this with my husband and daughter. Finally he said, "Well, if ought/should have to do with Annie and Marilyn 'ought' to help more around the house, I think they 'ought' to be in our vocabulary." Marilyn said, "I think they shouldn't." He replied, "I think they should." Here we have Rogers' problem! We become grudging servants. The expectations come from an outside source, and the resulting behavior does not spring from *me,* but from someone else who has imposed himself on me. Ought/should can become the parents of judgments, especially when the emotions of relationships are in conflict: "I ought to love my mother, but I can't stand being around her"; or, worse, "You ought to love your mother." Then come confusing guilts. Rogers sees these things clearly.

When the "oughts" come from God, they are always with our welfare in mind. For instance, when Jesus said men ought always to pray and not to faint, he was saying something like, "If you're feeling heavy, dialogue with me will lighten your load." Or a rewarding ought/should can come from within. Once I asked a family to dinner more from "ought" than "want," but the ensuing friendship has been very rich.

For me "ought" often seems simpler than the organismic process which Rogers suggests will bring the rewarding behavior. I wake up feeling loggy. I am greeted by two laundry hampers overflowing with contributions of seven responsibly busy family members. My feelings tell me, "Nuts. Every man for himself," but I start to wash. The alternative means more hot water and soap, mutual annoyances over who didn't include what in their load, the machine running at night above my father's apartment, and I don't like "every man for himself." Perhaps this is a matter of semantics, and Rogers' "process" is the same as my "ought." Still I doubt that the hushing of ought/should (taken at its most superficial level, which is what people commonly do with an authority like Rogers) will get more of the world's work done or build relationships.

Although I have mentioned some departures from Rogers, there are many ways in which he enriches me, and if the Christian community will listen, he reminds us of things we already own but have handled carelessly. Rogers has painstakingly but unerringly come upon many of God's principles of healthy human behavior. It is interesting that while Christians willingly accept truth when it comes from the world of the physical sciences (like Einstein's theory of relativity) we are suspicious of truth when it comes from the social sciences, particularly psychology and psychotherapy. To the extent that Rogers agrees with God's description of how men ought to be, he is describing God's system and we evangelicals are poorer when we ignore this. I have learned a lot about what it means to be a Christian from this non-Christian man.

One major contribution Rogers makes to Christians is to bolster our belief in the uniqueness of individuals. I substitute the word "unique" when Rogers uses the word "worth" in connection with people. "Worth" presupposes a quality put on something by someone who can see relative values, and only God gives us worth in that sense. I think Barry Stevens is right in wanting to use the concept of "equality" instead of "worth" (Rogers and Stevens, 1967, p. 29). Without the biblically defined God, man is *worth* no more than a cat or a dog. So we find that without this understanding of worth even a great man like Albert Schweitzer was opposed to killing the rats and insects in his hospital. Rogers enters into the very real cultural battle today on the side of the uniqueness of the individual. He also insists, while struggling with all of the contradictions involved, on the ability of people to make choices. Christians who are exposed broadside to the fatalism and determinism of our day can use this help.

Probably the best known of Rogers' formulations, the one which all Christians would do well to learn thoroughly, the one which distinguishes the truly effective therapist, is a combination of three qualities of character. The first is "unconditional positive regard," which very thinly reduced is saying, "You are altogether acceptable to me just as you are."

The second is "empathy," the quality of hearing accurately what a person is saying with his voice, attitude, and body. The third is "personal congruence," an honesty within the therapist or helping person which calls him to a deep genuineness, an inner agreement with himself. Contrary to popular misconception, this honesty does not have to be expressed, but it must be experienced. The degree to which these three characteristics become an integral part of any person will be the degree to which he will be effective in helping another. They are each abundantly demonstrated in the behavior of Jesus, and having them spelled out by Rogers on the basis of their proven usefulness has been a source of satisfaction to me.

Another of Rogers' contributions is his conclusion that change does not happen until we accept ourselves for what we are. Christians have a most unrealistic inclination to deeply desire to change without accepting their humanity. In their eagerness to be better people they become impatient with themselves and others. Rogers observes that change comes about when we not only acknowledge but *accept* where we are at the moment. I have personally discovered this self-acceptance to be a source of peace during which God mysteriously brings me on. I have ceased to try to remake myself.

Rogers reminds us that change is normal, that part of living is to be in a state of process while many Christians tend to feel a need to have arrived at perfection. In this process Rogers has found that given freedom to change, characteristically people move to "an increased openness to experience." Christians are often boxed in by fear of openness, nailed shut by unbiblical and outside authority. The biblical absolutes keep us from disaster—there are very few of them. To be alive to fresh and new experiences is not unchristian.

Another way Rogers describes people in process is they become free to experience "increasingly existential living." A man becomes free to live fully in each moment. Christians tend to do a lot of living in the past and in the future. Really, the moment is all we have at hand and God does not want us to emasculate that, even though we know the future to be brighter. Paul said, ". . . for I have learned in whatever state I am to be content" (Phil. 4:11). We might sum up these ways Rogers helps Christians by saying that he reminds us not to be ashamed to function at a truly human level. God made us human.

I appreciate the fact that in writing these things I have only hinted at the philosophical implications behind them, and only touched on those things that have to do with living day to day. But that is where the needs of all men seem most demanding to them. I also appreciate the fact that Rogers is equally uncomfortable with praise and criticism, and he needs neither acclaim nor defense. I'm sure I cannot imagine the magnitude of his gifts to all of the social sciences. I do thank him for opening new doors for me in the process of living, for stimulating my thinking, and for enriching my experience as a Christian.

References

Lewis, C. S. *The Problem of Pain*. Riverside, N.J.: The Macmillan Co., 1943.
————. *Perelandra*. Riverside, N.J.: The Macmillan Co., 1968.
Rogers, C. *On Becoming a Person*. New York: Houghton Mifflin, 1961.
Rogers, C., and Stevens, B. *Person to Person: The Problem of Being Human*. Moab, Utah: Real People Press, 1967.
Yutang, L. *The Importance of Living:* New York: Putnam, 1974.

GOD AND BEHAVIOR MOD: SOME THOUGHTS CONCERNING THE RELATIONSHIPS BETWEEN BIBLICAL PRINCIPLES AND BEHAVIOR MODIFICATION

Rodger K. Bufford

My interest in this topic was first stimulated by an article in *Potomac*, April 29, 1973. The article included excerpts from an interview with Harold Cohen, Director of the Institute for Behavioral Research. With regard to behavior modification, Cohen states that there is basically nothing new in the principles that are applied. "They are just grandma's rules. It's like gravity. We are just trying to use them systematically" (Hilts, 1973). Cohen went on to say that "God was the first behaviorist with his 'thou shalts' and 'thou shalt nots.' . . . We are just trying to make it science."

While Cohen may have been more than a little flippant in his reference to God as a behavior modifier, his point can be taken seriously. Consider the history of Israel: It basically consists of a sequence of periods in which the Israelites obeyed God and received his blessings, alternating with periods in which they disobeyed and received punishment. Our purpose here is to consider various biblical principles regarding human behavior and note the similarities and contrasts between them and the findings and practices of behavioral psychology, particularly as applied in behavior modification.

Before going into our main discussion, some important distinctions must be noted. Ferster suggests that behavioral psychology includes: (1) a body of knowledge, (2) a method and philosophy of science, (3) a systematic way of looking at the psychological makeup of organisms, and (4) a set of principles useful for analysis and understanding of observed behavior (Ferster, Culbertson, and Boren, 1975). In addition, I believe, behavioral psychology involves: (5) a technology for systematically applying knowledge to solving practical problems and (6) an implicit ontology. While a comparison of behavioral approaches to biblical approaches at the level of basic assumptions (metaphysics and ontology) is an important effort, it is beyond the scope of the present article. Here we will be mainly concerned with behavioral psychology as a body of knowledge (or a set of observations) and as a technology for application of that knowledge. It will be argued that the knowledge acquired from behavioral research and the

Based in part on presentations made to the Psychology Department, Westmont College, Santa Barbara, California, and to the Western New York Regional Association of the American Scientific Affiliation. © *Journal of Psychology and Theology*, 1977, *5*, 13-22. Used by permission of the author.

technological application of that knowledge is, in large measure, consistent with a biblical world view.

We shall begin our discussion by examining principles of establishing positive behavior: the role of social influence, the emphasis on the positive, and procedures for favorably influencing one's own behavior. Next, we will focus on dealing with negative behaviors, examining the principle of substituting one behavior for another, and the use of punishment.

Establishing Positive Behavior

Social Influences

In Exodus 20, in the section which sets forth the Decalogue or Ten Commandments, the Bible reports: "I, the Lord your God, am a jealous God, visiting the iniquity of the fathers on the children . . . to the third and fourth generation of them that hate me" (v. 5). For a long time this puzzled me. Why would God do such a thing? An examination of the role of social influence on behavior suggests one manner in which this principle operates.

The Bible recognizes the importance of social influence in a number of passages. We are instructed not to associate with angry men or we might learn their ways and get into trouble (Prov. 22:24-25). Similarly, we are instructed to avoid fools so that we do not come to harm (Prov. 13:20). It is noted that those who engage in evil practices not only do so, but also encourage others to do the same (Rom. 1:32). In a positive sense we are encouraged strongly to associate with those who obey God, to develop personal relationships (fellowship) with them, and to encourage them (Heb. 3:13; 10:25). Similarly, the Bible notes that those who associate with wise men will become wise (Prov. 13:20). Clearly, the Bible recognizes that our associates are an important influence in our lives.

Psychologists, including behaviorists, also recognize the importance of social influence in our daily lives; it is particularly critical at certain ages, specifically late adolescence (Thornburg, 1973). This is true for at least two reasons: first, we tend to imitate behaviors of others around us; second, the approval of our associates is a primary mechanism of social influence on our behavior. In *Principles of Behavior Modification* (Bandura, 1969), Bandura suggests that modeling influences have three effects: (1) acquisition of new response patterns which did not previously exist in the individual's repertoire, (2) strengthening or weakening of inhibitory responses, and (3) facilitation of previously learned responses.

To elaborate, the first manner in which observing the behavior of others may influence us is that we may learn to do things that we previously did not do. A child may learn to open a door with an unusual latch by observing an adult opening the door. Second, observation of the consequences of someone else's behavior may either increase or decrease the probability that we will perform the observed behavior. Here Bandura is concerned primarily with behavior which has typically been punished in some context. To illustrate, imagine a child who enters a new classroom; he observes other children talking out of turn, wandering around the room, horseplaying, etc., and "getting away" with it. In the past, he has been punished for these activities. However, in this classroom he is likely to exhibit them also, due to the effects of observing the other children. The same process could work in reverse; the child who normally is a classroom rowdy enters a new classroom in which the teacher enforces strict discipline. He observes another child talk out of turn and be disciplined. As a result, the normally rowdy child is on his best behavior in this classroom.

The third manner in which the behavior of others may influence us is in facilitating previously learned responses. Bandura distinguishes this from inhibition/disinhibition by noting that such behaviors have typically not been followed by unpleasant consequences. Thus, what we are talking about here is a function similar to a discriminative stimulus or instruction. The individual already has some low disposition to engage in the activity in question. Observing another person performing that activity, particularly if he is rewarded for it, indicates to the observer that there is a good chance that he will be rewarded for this activity on this particular occasion. In a busy office, for example, one worker may observe another, whose desk is near a window, get up and peer out. The second worker, too, goes over to the window just in time to see the fire engines arrive to put out the fire in a building across the street. On this occasion, the second worker was reinforced for doing what the first worker did, i.e., looking out the window, by seeing the exciting events going on outside. Going to the window is something he occasionally did anyway, but on this occasion it was prompted by the action of his co-worker.

Typically, a child does the same things his parents do and often for the same reasons. After all, if the parent did not find them rewarding in some measure, he wouldn't do them either. Thus, we know, for example, that the single most important factor in determining whether the child will smoke is whether or not his parents smoke. This is just one example of the possible outworking of the principle of Exodus 20:5, visiting the iniquities of the father on the children. On the other hand, if the parent exhibits some desirable action, such as being patient, the child, too, may learn to behave in a patient manner.

In this context, the biblical principle regarding how we are to teach our children God's principles is very instructive. Teaching children God's Word is a responsibility of the parents, especially the father (Eph. 6:4). The best way this teaching can be accomplished is by teaching precept in the context of practice, interwoven in the normal fabric of daily routines. The Bible teaches that God's word is to become an integral part of our every activity; to paraphrase, we are to teach it to our children as we get up in the morning, as we drive to the grocery store, when we sit down to relax, as we go about our work, and as we prepare for bed (Deut. 6:4-9).

Let me give you an example. In teaching our own children about obedience and in attempting to convey the notion that obedience is not an arbitrary convention for the convenience of parents, we found the presence of stop signs and traffic lights very helpful. We would note that there was a stop sign at the corner. Daddy stopped the car; he was being obedient. The same was done with the red light. We went on to talk about the possible consequences of failing to be obedient: someone might run into our car and hurt us; also, a policeman might stop us and punish (discipline) Daddy. In this way we attempted to convey the message that obedience is a necessary and universal aspect of the social order. When we are disobedient, bad things happen. Similar examples were used in other aspects of daily activities as the occasion gave opportunity.

The importance of these principles has recently been emphasized in a number of behavior modification practices. For example, in my own work on a residential unit for adolescents with disordered behaviors, one of the practices found most helpful in altering undesirable behaviors was to have peers who had shown behavioral improvements use their influence on those who were deviant.

Similarly, for alcoholics, there is evidence that the events which surround their drinking activities, including social contingencies, are an important factor in excessive drinking. Thus, arranging social reinforcements to follow abstinence or moderate drinking and absence of social reinforcements following excessive drinking appears to be an important element in treatment of alcoholism (Hamburg, 1975).

Think Positive (Reinforcement)

The emphasis on the positive is clearly seen in Scripture: "Whatever is true, whatever is honorable, whatever is right, whatever is pure, whatever is lovely, whatever is of good repute, if there is any excellence and if anything worthy of praise, let your mind dwell on these things" (Phil. 4:8).

Perhaps the single most basic tenet of the behavioral approach is its emphasis on positive reinforcement. In application this frequently involves ignoring all negative behaviors while attending to and reinforcing positive behaviors. The practical value of this principle is thoroughly documented by the literature showing the desirable behavioral and emotional effects of positive reinforcement (Ferster, Culbertson, and Boren 1975).

The effect of paying attention to the positive things which people do is manifested not only in changes in the behavior of those directly involved. It also has effects on us and on those who merely observe or hear about it. First, it influences our own emotional behavior: Reacting negatively to others produces unpleasant and harmful emotional and biological changes in us; conversely, responding positively produces desirable emotional effects. For example, the teacher who is constantly nagging and scolding her students ends the day exhausted and with a splitting headache. By contrast, the teacher who devotes most of her time to encouraging and reinforcing desired student behavior is relaxed and cheerful at the end of the day.

Second, the way we deal with one individual influences the manner in which others interact with us. If we are critical and punishing, they fear and avoid us; if we are warm and encouraging, they seek us out. Failure to emphasize the positive aspects of other people's behavior can not only result in detrimental physical and emotional effects on ourselves, it can reduce our effectiveness in changing their behavior.

Furthermore, the attitudes and behavior of our children often reflect our own actions regarding this principle. We are instructed not to provoke our children to wrath (Eph. 6:4); there is no simpler way to violate this principle than to take for granted the things which they do well, while at the same time constantly nagging them regarding their shortcomings. Behavior psychology has demonstrated that both the behavioral and emotional effects of focusing a substantial amount of our attention on the desired behaviors are positive.

Much as our actions with regard to others influence our emotions and physical condition, so also the things we think about influence our attitudes, emotions, and, ultimately, our actions. I am much more likely to feel well if I am thinking about what a nice day it is than I would be if I were fretting about being ticketed for speeding while the three cars in front of me, which were going equally fast, were not stopped. Similarly, if someone approaches me with a request, I will be more likely to respond positively if I am thinking about the nice day than about the traffic ticket.

At the opposite extreme from thinking positive is gossip. The Bible very clearly teaches us not to gossip. This encouragement not to gossip takes at least three forms: first, there is the encouragement already mentioned to focus one's attention on the pleasant things (Phil. 4:8); second, there is an explicit scriptural injunction to avoid gossip (cf. Gal. 5:15); finally, there is a scriptural instruction to constructively help the person who commits an act which is offensive (Prov. 11:12; 1 Peter 2:1).

The notion that gossip has undesirable effects in a social system is presented in *Walden II* (Skinner, 1948) and in the application of Skinner's behavioral principles in the utopian community, Twin Oaks (Kinkade, 1973). At Twin Oaks it is a rule of conduct that any grievance with an individual may only be discussed with him. One may not say bad things about a person when he is not around.

The Bible teaches that one of the adverse effects of backbiting and criticism is that we may "be consumed of one another" (Gal. 5:15). Staats (1971) describes the potentially devastating effects of gossip; he notes that derogating a model results in reducing his influence on an observer. At the practical level, this suggests that if we criticize our children's teachers in front of our children we reduce their effectiveness as teachers. About whom are we most likely to gossip? Unfortunately, I suspect, it is those very people who have the potential for the most positive influence on the behavior of our children.

Self-Control

In many respects, the "self-controlled" person typifies the scriptural picture of the Christian life. We are told that those who are disciples of Jesus will be characterized by love (John 13:34-35). In the context of Scripture, we learn that love embodies patience, absence of jealousy, and endurance (1 Cor. 13:4-8). Part of the perfecting process of the Christian life is the development of patience and endurance (James 1:2-4; Rom. 5:1-5). The manifestation of the Holy Spirit includes peacefulness, even temper, and *self-control* (Gal. 5:22-23). Living a peaceful, quiet life which merits the respect of others is upheld as a goal (1 Thess. 4:10*b*-11; 1 Tim. 2:2). Finally the Christian is to exhibit temperance (or self-control) in all things (1 Cor. 10:24-27).

Self-control has been a major concern among many behaviorists. In a certain sense, the use of the term "self-control" within a behavioral framework is anomalous; Rachlin (1970) appropriately notes that the ultimate control for the behavior is still presumably environmental. However, this concept does raise an important issue, namely, that the way in which a person acts at one point in time may influence his subsequent actions. Thus, a given behavior may not only be a *response,* it may also function as an antecedent *stimulus* for a subsequent behavior or as a *consequence* of a prior behavior (technically this is referred to as *chaining*).

To the behaviorist, self-control is a procedure whereby the individual exerts control or influence over his own behavior by any of a variety of techniques such as placing himself in certain situations, performing certain activities, or thinking certain thoughts, the effect of which is to alter the probability of subsequent behavior. For example, the person might clap his hand over his mouth to keep from laughing aloud, or he might put the candy away in a cupboard to keep from eating it. A common feature has to do with *immediacy* versus *delay* of reinforcement or punishment. Choosing to be thin next week rather than to eat candy next week poses no problem. The difficulty occurs when we must choose between eating candy *now* and being thin next week; here the candy, though a small magnitude reward, may be more influential than being thin due to its immediacy (Rachlin, 1970).

The application of self-control in smoking may be illustrative. One of the things which the smoker is encouraged to do in applying self-control procedures to smoking is to write down and memorize three reasons why he should quit smoking and three bad things about smoking. He is to repeat these to himself several times a day, preferably in quiet moments. Certain times of day seem to be more effecₜive than others; thus one man found that thinking about these things while sitting on the toilet was most effective (Hilts, 1973).

In the area of weight control, a self-control procedure might focus on situations in which food is consumed. For example, it might be noted that the person makes a number of trips daily to other offices in his building. Each time he passes the snack machines and stops to purchase some goodies. By planning his trips so that he would not pass the snack area, the frequency of snacking could probably be reduced. Other recent approaches to this problem have emphasized covert behavior or thoughts rather than actions. An overweight person who enjoys eating apples might be treated in the following fashion:

The behaviorist might sit you down and ask you to imagine a large piece of pie. He would spend some time describing the marvelous aroma, the fresh apples, the still-warm flavor. He would have you imagine dipping your fork into the soft crust and lifting it to your mouth. And when you get it to your mouth, he would quickly change gears. It tastes terrible, like cardboard, he would say. It's a sloppy, gooey mess of revulsion. If the scenario is repeated often enough, apple pie no longer has the same attraction. (Hilts, 1973)

A basic problem with the self-control approach is the motivation of the individual involved: He can circumvent the whole effort by simply not co-operating in the preliminary behaviors. Similarly, the processes can be worked in reverse; it is this reversibility which is caricatured in the movie "Clockwork Orange."

Another area of application of the principles of self-control is in developing tolerance to pain, frustration, and stress. Skinner and other behaviorists note that patience can only be developed by means of a sequence of exposures to various types of stress in a gradually increasing degree of severity (Skinner, 1948). This closely parallels the manner in which the Bible describes the development of patience (James 1:2-4; Rom. 5:3-5). Furthermore, God promises us that he will not present us with stresses beyond our ability to cope (1 Cor. 10:13); this is something no behaviorist can promise.

It is interesting to note the similarity between some of these self-control techniques and the biblical concept of meditation. The Bible encourages us to meditate on God's word "day and night" (Josh. 1:8; Ps. 1:2), when we get up, when we are traveling back and forth, when we sit in our houses, and when we lie down to sleep (Deut. 6:4-9). In this fashion, our lives can be favorably influenced much as the smoker was influenced by "meditating" on three reasons to quit smoking and the three bad things about it.

A practical example of the application of the meditation principle may be taken from my own recent experience. Periodically, my wife and I have disagreements. It had been my standard operating principle that these disagreements were primarily her fault. In reading Proverbs, I came across, and memorized, two proverbs dealing with reactions to criticisms by others: "Whoever loves discipline loves knowledge, but he who hates reproof is stupid" (Prov. 12:1); "As a sparrow in its flitting, as a swallow in its flying, so a curse without cause does not alight" (Prov. 26:2). The implications are twofold: First, if I have done something amiss, then criticism serves to draw my attention to it and gives me a chance to learn to act more appropriately; second, if I find myself becoming upset by criticism, I should look for what I have done wrong—if I was in no way responsible I would probably not have become upset. Having learned and thought about these principles, it was not long before I had occasion to put them into practice. The interesting thing is that when the next dispute with my wife developed, I was promptly reminded of these principles and prompted to react in a somewhat different manner than that which had been my custom. The results were gratifying. I still often neglect to follow these principles, to my regret.

Coping with Negative Behaviors

Substituting Positive Behavior

A basic biblical principle is that simply removing undesirable behavior is not adequate (cf. Matt. 12:43-45). Rather, the Bible clearly teaches the principle of replacing undesirable behaviors with desirable behaviors. Thus, "let him who steals steal no more, but let him labor, performing with his own hands what is good in order that he may have something to share with him who has need" (Eph. 4:28); "therefore, laying aside falsehood, speak truth . . ." (Eph. 4:25); ". . . do not get drunk with wine but be filled with the Spirit" (Eph. 5:18); ". . . do not participate in the unfruitful deeds of darkness but instead even expose them" (Eph. 5:11); "not returning evil for evil nor insult for insult, but giving a blessing instead" (1 Peter 3:9); and, finally, "failure to do good is sin" (James 4:17).

Similarly, a fundamental emphasis of the behavior modification approach is that it is not enough to simply remove undesirable behaviors; rather, alternative prosocial behavior must be developed (Bandura, 1969; Ullman and Krasner, 1969). Often this is referred to as developing competing behavior (Bandura, 1969) or reinforcing an incompatible performance (Ferster, et al., 1975). One example of the application of this principle may be seen in the approach to aggression described below.

Aggression. The Bible clearly teaches that we should not routinely meet aggression with counteraggression. Rather, "whoever slaps you on your right cheek, turn to him the other one also" (Matt. 5:39). We are also told to make every effort to live peacefully with others and not to avenge ourselves (Rom. 12:17-20) and that those who live by the sword will die by the sword (Matt. 26:51-52).

Gerald Patterson, who espouses a social learning theory of aggression, points out that aggression breeds aggression. This occurs because, in the typical aggressive episode, both aggressor and complier are reinforced: the aggressor is positively reinforced because he gets what he wants; the complier is negatively reinforced because complying terminates or avoids the presentation of painful stimulation. An example of this is the "protection" racket. The mobster gets money and the businessman avoids bodily harm and/or the possibility of financial loss of greater magnitude through the burning or bombing of his business establishment. The same principle operates in an aggressive interaction between two children. Johnny wants the toy truck which Carl has; Carl refuses to give it to him. Johnny hits Carl, who drops the truck and runs back home crying; Johnny gets the truck. Next time Carl gives up the toy without resistance; both children benefit: Johnny has the toy and Carl does not get hit.

In order to prevent an aggressive system from being perpetuated, Patterson emphasizes the importance of three principles: (1) teach alternative responses; for example, cooperation, negotiation, and sharing; (2) ignore minor infractions to avoid the possibility of inadvertently reinforcing them; and (3) punish major aggressive episodes with brief aversive consequences, usually time out. A major emphasis of this approach is to *model and reinforce nonaggressive behavior*. This approach shows definite parallels with the biblical view.

The Role of Punishment

One of the problems with deviant and antisocial behavior is that it often has immediate pleasant (rewarding) effects; not uncommonly, the unpleasant effects are more delayed. The "bully" who takes toys from other childen by force immediately gets the toy he wants. Eventually the other children will not play with him, but this outcome is much less immediate. The Bible teaches that although the unpleasant consequences of such behavior may often be delayed, they are inescapable (Prov. 29:16; Rom. 6:20-23). "Sentence against evil is not executed quickly . . . but it will not be well" (Eccles. 8:11-13; see also Eccles. 12:13-14); what you sow you'll reap (Gal. 6:7-8); those who sow the wind shall reap the whirlwind (Hos. 8:7). Often the consequences of sin are received in one's own person (physically and psychologically) (Rom. 1:27). The operation of these principles is illustrated in the life of David; his sin with Bathsheba resulted in physical symptoms (Ps. 32) and in family difficulties throughout the balance of his life (2 Sam. 11–18).

Although the Bible provides no obvious link between the problem of the delayed consequences of evil and the need for punishment, biblical teaching regarding the use of punishment is extremely clear. As suggested above, God's dealing with the Jews throughout biblical history clearly includes punishment for their misdeeds. Particularly in the book of Proverbs, the Bible advocates the use of a literal *rod* in dealing with children's misbehavior (Prov. 13:24; 22:15; 23:13-14; 29:15, 17). In more general terms, we are told that "reproofs for discipline are the way of life" (Prov. 6:23). The use of punishment plays a vital role in teaching the principle that certain behaviors must be avoided for the person's own good as well as for the good of others. The alternatives are less pleasant.

The role of punishment is an area of considerable controversy in the behavioral literature. Skinner (1953) is clearly opposed to punishment, as is Ferster (Ferster, Culbertson, and Boren, 1975). However, among other behavioral psychologists, the acceptance of punishment appears to be growing. Logan and Wagner (1965) suggests that both reinforcing and punishing effects are *enhanced* by the contrast between them. Either alone is less effective. This is sometimes referred to as the "principle of the carrot and the whip." A person who simply punishes is avoided. One who only rewards finds it difficult to discourage certain undesirable behaviors which have intrinsic rewarding as well as punishing consequences.

Behaviorists such as Goldiamond have noted that the natural aversive consequences of deviant (immoral) behavior are often deferred, thus they tend to be ineffective in suppressing deviant behavior. Boren (personal communication) cites running into the street as an example of a situation in which the natural aversive consequences are so delayed they fail to negate the positive consequences without use of punishment. This has been amply illustrated by my observations of a neighborhood child. George, a two-year-old, was repeatedly warned by his parents not to go into the street. He would continue his play activities as if he had not heard. In a few minutes he was in the street, either playing in it or crossing to the other side. Dad or Mom ran after him and brought him back, scolding all the way. George giggled. A few minutes later the incident was repeated. This went on for several months. Then one day George happened to run across the street just as a car was approaching: fortunately, he was unhurt; on this occasion he was promptly spanked. It is doubtful, however, that he learned not to go into the street from one such occasion. Getting to the other side of the street, plus the fun of being chased by Mom or Dad, is probably such a powerful reinforcement that the only way to discourage such behavior is to provide consistent punishment.

Staats is a behavioral psychologist who clearly advocates the use of punishment; he says: ". . . at least in our present state of social advancement, it is impossible to raise a socially controlled child without the use of some form of aversive stimulation" (1971, p. 234). He goes on to say that: "When punishment is employed, it is suggested that it be as infrequent as possible, as slight as is *necessary to be definitely aversive,* applied immediately but of short duration, and *be paired with words so that words will later on be capable of substituting for the direct punishment"* (p. 236).

It is particularly instructive to note the parallels between biblical principles and the principles of punishment given above by Staats. The rod is definitely painful, but can be applied briefly. It is conducive to pairing punishment with words; and the frequent references to reproof imply that this should be done.

With regard to the notion that punishment be used as infrequently as possible, you will remember what was said above regarding aggression and the importance of ignoring minor infractions. Perhaps this is one significance of the instruction: "Fathers, do not provoke your children to anger" (Eph. 6:4).

The behavioral approach emphasizes that punishment is to be carried out in a matter-of-fact manner and then forgotten. One then proceeds to encourage positive behavior as if nothing bad had happened. This viewpoint parallels two biblical principles: First, wrong behavior (sin) has inevitable consequences (Rom. 6:20-23); second, that God's forgiveness is sure and immediate if we repent (John 6:37; 1 John 1:9), and He no longer deals with us in terms of our transgression (Ps. 103:3, 12; Jer. 31:34).

Conclusion

Sidman (1960) makes the observation that "data is fickle." By this he means that a set of observations has significance independent of the theoretical system which leads to collection of the data. Thus the observation that children who are frustrated tend to exhibit behavior typical of younger children may be interpreted in terms of the frustration-regression hypothesis in the psychodynamic tradition as well as interpreted in terms of extinction and a consequent increase in the probability of a previously reinforced behavior in the behavioral tradition. Given the view that the world is God's creation, the Bible is God's revelation, and the assumption that God does not contradict himself, it is reasonable to expect that all good data (i.e., reliable, accurate observations of events in the world) will be consistent with the Bible.

Behavior modification is essentially a technology; it is concerned with the application of knowledge gained in the laboratory to the alteration of behavior in the sphere of daily living. Behavior modification becomes a matter of concern for us chiefly in terms of the *means* which are employed and the *goals* toward which the technology is applied. Specifically, we must examine technological methods to determine whether they are consistent with, or violate, biblical standards for methodology. Similarly, we must ascertain whether the particular goals toward which technology is applied are consistent with biblical principles. What has been shown here is that in many points the technology growing out of the behavioral psychology can be demonstrated to be consistent with biblical teachings. In fact, the observations collected by behavioral psychologists and the technology which they have developed may contribute positively to an effective application of biblical principles in practical daily living. The question of the relationship between Scripture and behavioral psychology at the level of basic assumptions remains to be explored.

The Bible teaches us principles, but leaves it to us to work out their application. As a former pastor used to say: "The Bible doesn't tell us everything about anything: It tells us all we need to know about all we need to know." Insofar as behavioral technology is compatible with Scripture, it is useful in helping to translate biblical principles into practical applications.

References

Scripture quotations from the New American Standard Bible. Carol Stream, Ill.: Creation House, 1960.

Bandura, A. *Principles of Behavior Modification.* New York: Holt, Rinehart and Winston, 1969.

Ferster, C. B., Culbertson, S., and Boren, M. C. P. *Behavior Principles* (2nd ed.). Englewood Cliffs, N.J.: Prentice-Hall, 1975.

Hamburg, S. "Behavior Therapy in Alcoholism." *Quarterly Journal of Studies on Alcohol,* 1975, *36,* 69-87.

Hilts, P. "The Behaviorists." *Potomac,* April 29, 1973, 18.

———. "Mastering Yourself." *Potomac,* April 29, 1973, 21.

Kinkade, K. "A Walden II Experiment." New York: Morrow, 1973.

Logan, F., and Wagner, A. *Reward and Punishment.* Boston: Allyn & Bacon, 1965.

Rachlin, H. *Introduction to Modern Behaviorism.* San Francisco: W. H. Freeman, 1970.

Sidman, M. *Tactics of Scientific Research.* New York: Basic Books, 1960.

Skinner, B. F. *Walden II.* New York: The MacMillan Co., 1948.

———. *Science and Human Behavior.* New York: The MacMillan Co., 1953.

———. *Beyond Freedom and Dignity.* New York: Alfred A. Knopf, 1971.

Thornburg, H. *Child Development.* Dubuque, Ia.: W. C. Brown, 1973.

Ullmann, L., and Krasner, L. *A Psychological Approach to Abnormal Behavior.* Englewood Cliffs, N.J.: Prentice-Hall, 1969.

THE ORIGINS OF RELIGION IN THE CHILD

David Elkind

Every social institution, whether it be science, art, or religion, can be regarded as an externalized adaptation which serves both the individual and society. From the point of view of the group, social institutions provide the ground rules and regulations which make society and social progress possible. Looked at from the standpoint of the individual, social institutions afford ready-made solutions to the inevitable conflicts with social and physical reality which the individual encounters in his march through life. Social institutions, therefore, originate and evolve out of the adaptive efforts of both society and the individual. It follows that any complete account of the origins of religion must deal both with individual and social processes of adaptation.

In the present paper, I propose to treat the origins of religion solely from the perspective of the individual and not from that of society. It is not my intent, therefore, to give a comprehensive account of the origins of religion in general nor in any way to negate the central importance of social factors in the origination and historical evolution of religion. All that I hope to demonstrate is that religion has an individual as well as a social lineage and that this individual lineage can be traced to certain cognitive need capacities which emerge in the course of mental growth. To whatever extent religion derives from society's efforts to resolve the conflicts engendered by these individual need capacities, we are justified in speaking of the origins of religion in the child.

Briefly stated, the paper will describe four cognitive need capacities with respect to the age at which they first make their appearance, the problems of adaptation which they engender, and the corresponding resolutions offered by religion. A concluding section will take up the question of the uniqueness of religious adaptations from the point of view of the individual.

Emergence of Cognitive Need Capacities in the Child

In describing the mental development of the child, this presentation will lean rather heavily upon the work of the Swiss psychologist, Jean Piaget.

© *Review of Religious Research*, 1970, *12*, 25-42. Used by permission of the author.

For more than forty years Piaget has been studying the mental development of the child. He has evolved a general theory of intelligence, wherein he derives the thinking of adults from the gradual elaboration of mental abilities in the child (Flavell, 1963; Elkind, 1967). In effect, Piaget argues that each new mental capacity carries with it the need to realize itself through action and that, in the course of such realization, the individual comes into conflict with social and physical realities. The resolution of each such conflict results in structural changes which we call growth and which in turn pave the way for new conflicts and further growth in an unending dialectic.

Although Piaget's theory would seem to have rather direct implications for religious development, he has not himself, except for a few early papers (Piaget, 1923, 1930) dealt with the problem at length. It seems to me, however, that the major elements common to most religions provide comfortable solutions to some of the conflicts which Piaget's cognitive need capacities engender in the course of their realization. I must emphasize, however, that this is my way of viewing the problem and is not necessarily the way in which Piaget would deal with the issue, were he to attack it.

Before proceeding to the discussion of the cognitive need capacities themselves, it might be well to give a few concrete illustrations of the way in which their efforts at realization result in problems of adaptation. Once the child acquires language and a rudimentary understanding of causality, for example, he enters the notorious "why" stage. He soon discovers, however, that parents do not appreciate such questions, particularly when they are endlessly repeated. The child's attempts to realize his capacity for causal understanding thus bring him into conflict with the adult world. In the same way, when the child of four or five years begins to realize his emerging capacity to deal with quantitative relations, he again comes into conflict with others. His constant concern with "who has more" fails to endear him either to his parents or to his siblings. In short, every cognitive capacity is in itself a need which prompts behaviors that can create discord between the child and his social and physical milieu.

Infancy and the Search for Conservation

During the first two years of life, the human infant makes truly remarkable progress. From an uncoordinated, primarily reflex organism, he is within the course of a short two-year period transformed into an upright, talking, semi-socialized being, more advanced intellectually than the most mature animal of any species. Of the many accomplishments during this period, none is perhaps as significant or of such general importance as the discovery that objects exist when they are no longer present to the senses, that is to say, the discovery that objects are *conserved*.

To the adult, for whom the world and the self are clearly demarcated, it is hard to envision the infant's situation. The closest we can come to it is in a state of reverie or semi-consciousness when the boundaries of awareness waver and we are imbedded in the very pictures we are sensing. This is the perpetual state of the infant for whom all awareness can hardly be more than a series of blurred pictures following one another in an unpredictable sequence. Only gradually does the child begin to separate his own actions from things and to discriminate among different things, such as the human face. Even when the response to the human face occurs, usually in the second and third months of life, there is still no awareness that the face exists when it is no longer present. An infant, for example, who is smiling delightedly at an adult peering at him from the side of the crib will turn his head away immediately if the adult ducks out of sight. The infant does not cry; he behaves as if the adult drops out of existence when he disappears (Piaget, 1952).

Only toward the end of the second year and as a consequence of a series of progressive learnings and coordinations does the infant give evidence that for him objects now exist and have a permanence of their own quite independent of his immediate sensory experience. At this age, for example, the young child will search for objects, such as candy or a toy, which he saw hidden from view. This awareness of the permanence or conservation of objects comes about when the progressive coordinations of behavior give rise to internal representations or images of absent objects. It is the two-year-old's capacity to mentally represent absent objects which results in their conservation.

The construction of permanent objects is important because it is a prerequisite for all later mental activity. All of our concepts start from or involve objects in one way or another, so the recognition of their permanence is a necessary starting point for intellectual growth in general. Object permanence, however, is just the first of many such permanences or conservations which the child must construct. As his mental capacities expand, he encounters new situations which parallel, though at a higher level of abstraction, the disappearance of objects. Illusions are a case in point. A spoon in water looks bent or even broken, the moon appears to follow us when we walk, just as the sun appears to revolve around the earth. Similar problems present themselves on the social plane. The child must learn to distinguish, for example, a true invitation to stay at a friend's home from an invitation which is, in fact, a polite dismissal. In all of these cases the child has to distinguish between appearance and reality, between how things look and how they really are. Infancy thus bears witness to a new mental ability, the capacity to deal with absent objects, and to a corresponding need, *the search for conservation,* a life-long quest for permanence amidst a world of change.

One of the problems of conservation which all children eventually encounter, and to which they must all adapt, is the discovery that they and their loved ones must ultimately die. In contrast to the conservation of the object, which is first transient and only later permanent, the child begins by assuming that life is everlasting and is shocked when he finds out that it is transient. After the initial recognition, often accompanied by intense emotional outbursts, the child seeks means whereby life can be conserved, a quest which continues throughout his existence.

In many cases, the conflict between the search for conservation and the inevitability of death does not arise with its full impact until adolescence. Religion, to which the young person has already been exposed, offers a ready solution. This solution lies in the concept of God or Spirit which appears to be religion's universal answer to the problem of the conservation of life. God is the ultimate conservation since he transcends the bounds of space, time, and corporality. By accepting God, the young person participates in his immortality and hence resolves the problem of the conservation of life. Obviously, whether in any particular case the young person will accept the religious solution will be determined by a host of personal and sociocultural factors. All that I wish to emphasize here is that religion offers an immediate solution to the seemingly universal human problem posed by the search for conservation of life and the reality of death.

Early Childhood and the Search for Representation

As was true for the period of infancy, the preschool period is one of rapid mental growth and of wide-ranging intellectual accomplishments. Foremost among these is the mastery of language. With the conquest of language the child goes far beyond the representation of things by mental images. Language is a series of conventional signs which bear no physical resemblance to that which they represent. The child must now painstakingly learn to represent all of those objects which were so laboriously constructed during the first years of life. The child is not, however, limited to representing things by language, he can now also employ symbols which bear some semblance to the objects which they represent. At this stage, the child creates his own playthings and transforms pieces of wood into boats, pieces of paper into airplanes, and odd-shaped stones into animals (Piaget, 1951). It is at this stage too, that the child dons adult clothes and plays house, store, and school. All of these behaviors, the mastery of language, and engagement in symbolic play activities bear witness to a new cognitive capacity, the ability to use signs and symbols, and to a new cognitive need, *the search for representation*.

The search for representation, which makes its appearance in early childhood, like the search for conservation, continues throughout life. At each point in his development, the young person seeks to represent both the contents of his own thought and those of his physical and social environment. As his knowledge of himself and his world grows more exact, he seeks more exacting forms of representation. Not only does his vocabulary increase at an extraordinary rate, but he also begins to acquire new tools of representation, such as mathematics and the graphic arts. Yet, the more exacting the child becomes in his search for representation, the more dissatisfied he becomes with the results. One reason, to illustrate, why children usually give up drawing in about the fourth or fifth grade is their disgust with the discrepancy between what they wish to portray and what they have actually drawn. In the same way as the child matures, he gradually realizes that language is a lumbering means at best for conveying his thoughts and is hopelessly inadequate for expressing his feelings.

For the young person who has accepted God, the search for representation poses special problems. If religion provided only a concept of God and nothing else, he would be at a loss to represent the transcendent. How, after all, does one signify that which is neither spatial, temporal, nor corporeal? Religion, however, affords more than a simple God concept; it also provides representations of the transcendent. In primitive religions the representations were totems or idols; whereas in modern "revealed" religions, the transcendent finds its representation in Scripture. Here again, however, as in the case of the concept of God, the individual's acceptance of the religious solution is multi-determined and difficult to predict in the particular case. What must be stressed is that once the individual accepts the concept of God, the question of his representation is an inevitable outcome of the search for representation in general.

Childhood and the Search for Relations

The school-age period is one of less rapid intellectual growth than was true for the preceding two periods. During this epoch in the child's life he is, for the first time, exposed to formal instruction and must acquire a prescribed body of knowledge and special skills such as reading and writing. The acquisition of a prescribed body of knowledge, however, presupposes a mental system which is in part at least comparable to the mental system of adults who transmit the knowledge. Such a system does come into being at around the sixth or seventh year, the traditional "age of reason." Research on children's thinking has shown that this is in fact quite an appropriate designation of the accomplishments of this age period. It is only at about the age of six or seven, for example, that the child manifests the ability to make logical deductions (i.e., to recognize that if A is greater than B, and if B is greater than C, then A must be greater than C, even if he has not compared A and C directly); to next classes (i.e., recognize that, say, boys + girls = children, and children − boys = girls, etc.) and to seriate relations (group elements systematically so that $A>B>C>D<E<F$, etc.) (Piaget, 1952; Elkind, 1961, 1965).

One general feature of this new ability to reason in a logical manner is that the child now tries to relate phenomena in the world about him in a systematic manner. The youngster at this stage wants to know how things work, how they are put together, where they come from, and out of what they are made. Moreover, his concepts of time and space have broadened, and he can now grasp historical time and conceive of such distant places as foreign countries. It is the age period during which Robinson Crusoe has his greatest appeal, because Crusoe describes in marvelous detail all the building, planting, hunting, and fishing activities in which he engages. In a very real sense, then, the child is trying to relate things to one another with respect to time, space, causality, and origin. It seems appropriate, therefore, to speak of the new ability that surfaces at school age as *the capacity for practical reason* and of the corresponding need as *the search for relations.*

The search for relations, which makes its appearance in childhood proper, continues throughout life. As the young person matures, he seeks to relate himself to his social and physical milieu and to relate the things and events in his world to one another. While this search for relations is often gratifying, it is also on occasion disheartening. There are many events in life which cannot be related to one another in any simple, rational way. The quirks of fate and accident are of this kind and defy man's rational answer to the question, "Why did this happen to me?" So, while the quest for relations helps man to understand himself and his world better, it also makes him aware of how much he cannot know and understand.

Within the religious sphere, the young person who has accepted the concept of God and his scriptural representation is confronted with the problem of putting himself in relation to the Transcendent. Here again, in the absence of a ready-made solution, the young person might flounder and his resolution of the problem would be makeshift at best. Religion, however, affords a means whereby the individual can relate himself to the deity, for it offers the sacrament of worship. By participating in worship, the young person can relate himself to the transcendent in a direct and personal way. To be sure, the young person's acceptance of religion's answer to the problem will again be determined by a variety of factors. Indeed, some of our reserach (Elkind and Elkind, 1962; Long, Elkind, and Spilka, 1967), suggests that many young people reject the formal worship service but nonetheless engage in individual worship in the privacy of their rooms. In any case, for the adolescent who has accepted God and his scriptural representation the question of relating himself to God is an inevitable one, no matter how it is resolved.

Adolescence and the Search for Comprehension

The physical and physiological transformations so prominent in adolescence frequently obscure the equally momentous changes undergone by intelligence during the same period. As a consequence of both maturation and experience, a new mental system emerges in adolescence which enables the young person to accomplish feats of thought that far surpass the elementary reasonings of the child. One feat that makes its appearance is the capacity to introspect, to take one's thought and feelings as if they were external objects and to examine and reason about them. Still another feat is the capacity to construct ideal or contrary-to-fact situations, to conceive of utopian societies, ideal mates, and preeminent careers. Finally, in problem-solving situations the adolescent, in contrast to the child, can take all of the possible factors into account and test their possibilities in a systematic fashion (Inhelder and Piaget, 1958).

Implicit in all of these new mental accomplishments is the capacity to construct and think in terms of overriding theories which enable the young person not only to grasp relations but also to grasp the underlying reason for them. To use a biological analogy, the child is concerned with "phenotypes," whereas the adolescent focuses his attention upon the "genotypes," the underlying laws and principles which relate a variety of apparently diverse phenomena. It seems reasonable, therefore, to characterize the mental ability which emerges in adolescence as the capacity for theory construction and the corresponding need as *the search for comprehension.*

As in the case of the other need capacities we have considered, the search for comprehension persists throughout life, although it takes different forms at different stages in the life cycle. The search for comprehension is also like the other need capacities in the sense that it never meets with complete success. Whether it be in the field of science, art, history, or government, each new effort at comprehension uncovers new puzzles for the understanding. The same holds true on the personal plane. Although the adolescent, to illustrate, now has a conception of personality which enables him to understand people in depth, he still encounters human foibles and eccentricities which defy his generalizations. And, though his new-found capacity for comprehension enables him to hold a mirror to his mind, he still frequently fails to understand himself.

In the domain of religion, the problem of comprehension arises naturally to those who have accepted God, his scriptural representation, and the sacrament of worship. Many young people often seek such comprehension on their own with the result that they become bewildered and disheartened by the failure of their efforts. Religion again provides a solution. Every religion contains a body of myth, legend, and history which provides a means for comprehending God in his various aspects.

In modern religions, the resolution to the problem of comprehension is provided by theology. It may be, however, that the ferment within present-day theological discussions makes it more difficult than heretofore for the young person to accept the religious solution to the problem of comprehension. Be that as it may, for the individual who has accepted

God, his representation, and his worship, the problem of comprehension must be faced regardless of how it may be resolved.

Conclusion

I am aware that the foregoing discussion probably raises many more questions than it has answered. All that I have tried to do is to present a scheme to illustrate the extraordinary fit between certain basic cognitive need capacities and the major elements of institutional religion. It is probable that this fit is not accidental and that religion has, in part at least, evolved to provide solutions to the problems of adaptation posed by these need capacities. To the extent that this is true, then to that extent are we justified in speaking of the origins of religion in the child.

Psychologists who have concerned themselves with religious phenomena (e.g., Allport, 1960; Dunlap, 1947; James, 1902) are in general agreement with respect to one point, namely, that there are no uniquely religious psychic elements. Insofar as anyone has been able to determine, there are no drives, sentiments, emotions, or mental categories which are inherently religious. Psychic elements, it is agreed, become religious only insofar as they become associated with one or another aspect of institutional religion. Nothing which has been said so far contradicts this position, with which I am in complete agreement.

Nonetheless, the view that there are no uniquely religious psychic elements does not preclude the possibility that there may be uniquely religious *adaptations.* Adaptations, by definition, are neither innate nor acquired but are instead the products of subject (individual or society) environment interaction. Every adaptation is thus a construction which bears the stamp of both nature and nurture, yet is reducible to neither one. The same holds true for religious adaptations. The concept of God, Spirit, or more generally, the Transcendent, cannot be reduced to the search for conservation any more than it can be traced to the phenomenon of death. Contrariwise, neither the search for conservation nor the phenomenon of death is in itself religious, although it may well take part in the production of religious elements. Like a Gestalt, such as a painting or a melody, the Transcendent is greater than the sum or product of its parts.

As suggested above, once the concept of God or Spirit is accepted as the ultimate conservation, it necessarily entails genuinely religious problems for the other emerging need capacities. These problems can, in turn, be immediately resolved by the ready-made constructions afforded by institutional religion, such as Scripture, worship, and theology. From the standpoint of the individual, therefore, the concept of God or of the Transcendent lies at the very core of personal religion. At the same time, however, whether the concept of God is a personal construction or one acquired from institutional religion, it is always superordinate, transcending the particular individual or social needs as well as the phenomenal facts out of which it arose.

References

Allport, G. W. *The Individual and His Religion.* New York: The Macmillan Co., 1960.

Dunlap, K. *Religion: Its Function in Human Life.* New York: McGraw-Hill Book Co., 1947.

Elkind, D. "The Development of Quantitative Thinking." *Journal of Genetic Psychology,* 1961, *98,* 37-46.

————. "Discrimination, Seriation and Numeration of Size and Dimensional Differences in Young Children" Ibid. *104,* 275-96.

————. (ed). *Six Psychological Studies by Jean Piaget.* New York: Random House, 1967.

Elkind, D., and Elkind, S. F. "Varieties of Religious Experience in Young Adolescents." *Journal for Scientific Study of Religion,* 1962, *2,* 102-12.

Flavell, J. H. *The Development of Psychology of Jean Piaget.* New York: Van Nostrand, 1963.

Inhelder, B., and Piaget, J. *The Growth of Logical Thinking from Childhood Through Adolescence.* New York: Basic Books, 1958.

James, W. *Varieties of Religious Experience.* New York: Longmans, 1902.

Long, D., Elkind, D., and Spilka, B. "The Child's Conception of Prayer." *Journal for the Scientific Study of Religion,* 1967, *4,* 101-9.

Piaget, J. *La Psychologie et les foi religieuses.* Geneve: Labor, 1923.

————. *Immanentisme et foi religieuse.* Geneve: Robert, 1930.

————. *Play, Dreams, and Imitation in Childhood.* New York: W. W. Norton, 1951.

————. *The Child's Conception of Number.* New York: Humanities Press, 1952.

————. *The Construction of Reality in the Child.* New York: Basic Books, 1954.

SECTION
EIGHT

POPULAR CHRISTIAN PSYCHOLOGIES

This section begins with Collins' analysis of current pop Christian psychologies. It is followed by two critiques of popular Christian psychologies mentioned in Collins' article. The final article in this section is a model of counseling which the author claims is biblical and can be used with laymen in the church.

Many of us as students of psychology have been asked by a friend or relative, "So you're studying psychology! Well, what do you think of Norman Vincent Peale?" EST? or Bill Gothard? or any one of a host of current pop psychologies? While Collins has restricted his discussion to "Christian" pop psychologies, much of what he says can apply to the more general variety. The nine common elements Collins found in these popularizers are: relevance, simplicity, practicality, avoidance of the academic, communication skills, personal appeal, biblical orientation, reactionary nature, and uniqueness. Only Biblical Orientation seems not to be characteristic of the general mass of pop psychology available in our society. What is the appeal of the popularizer: social unrest, political and/or economic unrest, personal despair or all of the above. Collins maintains that one of the most consistent messages of the Christian popularizer of psychology is criticism of the church for its failure to meet the Christian's need and the offer of hope and help in the popularizer's message.

Is Collins, with his many popular writings, one of the persons he is warning us to avoid? Or is he one of the professionals like James Dobson and Bruce Narramore whom he feels are now fortunately entering this arena to clarify the confusion created by the popularizers and who are offering balanced expertise to the layman.

Jay Adams' Nouthetic Counseling is one of the popular psychologies described in the previous article by Collins. While less read in the psychological community, Adams is widely known in the pastoral counseling community. Adams claims to be biblical in his counseling theory and his extensive use of scriptural quotations gives Adams an authentic sound to many Christians.

In this article Carter has analyzed Adams' view of the nature of man, the nature of pathology, his counseling model, the process of counseling, and the counselor and his techniques. Adams has adopted the biblical Greek word *noutheteo,* which means confront or admonish, as the name and model for his theory. Adams is very critical of Freud and Rogers and psychology in general, but has borrowed much from Glasser, Mowrer, and Szasz. Adams' style of counseling is rather directive and behavioral, apparently derived from Mowrer's emphasis in the early 1960s. In keeping with Adams' request, Carter has begun his critical analysis of Adams from a biblical framework but also adds a psychological evaluation.

Though Bill Gothard and his Basic Youth Conflict Seminars have dropped out of the media, he continues to speak to over 10,000 persons in each of his biweekly seminars in various parts of the country. Gothard does not claim to have a psychology but he does claim to have discovered the biblical principles for successful living. Hence, Collins cites him as an example of a popularizer.

In this article, Carter has analyzed the structure and content of Gothard's basic seminar. There are seven principles: design, authority, responsibility, ownership, motivation, freedom (moral), and success. These principles as articulated in his seminar and in the Red Notebook (available only to those who attend) apply to all mankind. If they are followed, according to Gothard, the person will live successfully whether one is a believer or not. Carter also analyzed his view of the nature of man, the nature of pathology, and Gothard's theory of therapy and maturity. The article closes with an evaluation. Gothard seems to have the effect of polarizing people more than any of the popularizers. After being exposed to his view, the results seem to be either devotion to his teachings or repudiation of them.

Though Collins does not mention Crabb in his article on popular Christian psychologies, it is interesting to speculate on whether Crabb is a popularizer or a professional (Crabb holds a Ph.D. in psychology) who is clarifying the confusion caused by the popularizers. Crabb has begun this article by describing four approaches to relating psychology and Christianity which he calls: Separate but Equal, Tossed Salad, Nothing buttery, and Spoiling the Egyptians. These four approaches are similar in structure to the four models Carter (chapter 5) describes, but the style and tone are rather different. Crabb proceeds to describe his model of mental health and mental problems. He goes on to describe his seven-stage model of counseling and suggests that various theorists such as Adler, Rogers, and Gestalt fit into his model. It will be interesting and intellectually profitable for the reader to reflect on this model while asking the question, does Crabb's model seem similar to any other well-known theory of counseling? Also, how would Freud or Frankl or a behavior modification approach fit into Crabb's model of counseling? Does Crabb's emphasis on the church promote consensual or committed religion (Fleck, chapter 4) in the counselee?

POPULAR CHRISTIAN PSYCHOLOGIES: SOME REFLECTIONS

Gary R. Collins

The popularizing of psychology is not a recent phenomenon. For many years, magazine writers, newspaper columnists, sales managers, preach-ers, and numerous others have attempted to apply the conclusions of psychology to a variety of human problems. The advice from these popularizers has often shown considerable deviation from the established findings of scientific psychology, but thousands of people have been influenced nevertheless and have brought fame, acclaim, and sometimes fortune to these dispensers of popular self-help psychology.

It is difficult to know how much these popularizers have influenced Christians over the years. Liberal elements of the church, with their greater willingness to accept psychology, probably have, in general, been sympathetic to the popularizers whereas the theological conservatives may have been more resistant and skeptical. During the past decade, however, all of this has changed dramatically. A number of dedicated people have appeared, each of whom in different ways has combined a popular form of psychology and a biblically related religion into self-help formulae which are widely dispensed through lectures, books, and cassette recordings. Keith Miller's *A Taste of New Wine,* published in 1965, heralded the coming of the Christian popularizers, but others such as Bruce Larson, Tim LaHaye, and Bill Gothard—to mention the best known—have attracted large followings especially during the 1970s.

Currently, about fifty persons, all claiming to be Christians, have attracted attention for their psychologically oriented approaches to the problems of living. Some, like Paul Tournier, deal with a variety of topics and appeal to liberal and conservative Christians alike. Others such as Charlie Shedd or Walter Trobish attract more limited audiences and restrict their subject matter to a few basic topics such as sex or marriage. Some of the popular speaker-writers have had formal training in psychology but most have little or no training in this field and even flaunt their lack of psychological expertise.

Professional counselors often are inclined to criticize the popularizers or dismiss them as being simplistic, potentially harmful, and of no importance. It must be recognized, however, that literally thousands of people follow the teachings of these popular leaders and uncritically accept their advice on such significant issues as how to rear children, have a better marriage, cope with depression, mature spiritually, get along with people, succeed at work, or have a more satisfying sex life. The Christian popularizers must be meeting some human needs that neither the church nor the profession of psychology are meeting. It is important, therefore, that these growing popular movements be taken seriously and examined carefully. In the paragraphs which follow we will seek to consider what the popularizers all have in common, why they are attractive to people, and what their popularity means to the mental health professions both now and in the future.

The Common Elements

Although there are some exceptions, the popularizers appear to have at least nine characteristics in common. In presenting this list there has been no attempt to make value judgments. The following characteristics may or may not be good, but they give a clue as to the reasons for the popularizer's appeal.

Revelance. Each of these movements focuses on issues which are of personal concern to people: marriage, loneliness, failure, phoniness, sex, etc. Most of these issues are presented along with case histories or personal illustrations which stimulate interest and make it easy for the listener or reader to identify with the topic being discussed.

Simplicity. In general, the popularizers avoid references to theory, technical terms, or the extreme complexity of human behavior. Simple explanations are given for problem behavior, along with simple solutions. Adams (1970), for example, lists only two causes of human problems: sin and organic malfunctioning. The latter is best treated by a physician, the former by an ordained pastor who confronts the counselee with the sin in his life.[1]

Practicality. Most of the popularizers give specific advice telling people precisely what to do in order to cope with a problem. These formulae or principles of behavior often are accompanied by success stories which are used both to demonstrate that the formulae have worked with others in the past and to create the expectation that they will work again in the future. This assumption of certain success is seen clearly in LaHaye's book on depression. "Of one thing I am confident," he writes, "you do not have to be depressed . . . I am convinced that by using the formula in this book, you can avoid ever being depressed again" (1974, p. 12).

Avoidance of the academic. Although they often borrow ideas from other writers, the popularizers give appearance of being disinterested in

---

[1]In a recent book (1973), Adams lists a third cause of problems, demon activity, but he dismisses this as being of no current importance since the devil is assumed to be bound at present.

scholarly debate. They make little reference to books, journals, or other authorities, avoid numerous footnotes, often have no index in their books, and do not qualify their conclusions as would writers in more scholarly literature.[2] In general the popularizers are more concerned about people than about research, theory, theology, or academics. This person-emphasis is, of course, very appealing to audiences.

Communication skills. Each of the popularizers is a good communicator. Using simple, understandable language they present clear, explicit messages. Very often several channels of communication are used including books, speeches, pamphlets, radio broadcasts, and cassette recordings. This "multi-media" approach creates maximum exposure which in turn contributes to the popularity of the speaker and his or her message.

Personal appeal. All of the popularizers possess attractive personalities which are appealing to their followers. There are, of course, large individual differences among the popular leaders, and because of this, they do not all attract the same followers. Bill Gothard, for example, seems to be liked for his casual manner, humility, and sincerity; Keith Miller is attractive because of his honesty and open attitude; Marabell Morgan is humorous and spices her material with references to sex; Jay Adams is a dynamic and powerful speaker; Paul Tournier is a grandfatherly type of person whose deep interest in people shines through all of his writings and speeches. Each of these people is appealing in a unique way, and each has a following centering around the personality of the leader.

Biblical orientation. The popularizers differ from each other theologically and while some, like Gothard, refer to the Bible frequently, others, such as Bruce Larson, mention it less often. Nevertheless, each takes the Scriptures seriously, and all attempt to apply Christianity to life in a way that will help others. This acknowledgement of the importance of Christianity undoubtedly attracts people who would fear or otherwise avoid a strictly secular psychology.

Reactionary nature. Each of the popularizers is dissatisfied with something. Adams, for example, opposes secular psychology (1970); Miller resists phoniness in the church and static Christianity (1965, 1973); Tournier began his writing career by opposing a form of medicine which ignores the spiritual and psychological nature of man (1965); Larson resists "deadness" both in the church and in the lives of Christians (1965, 1974); and Peale, for several decades, has resisted "negative thinking" and the attitude which says "I can't" (1952, 1974). The spirit of opposition to some injustice or faulty thinking doubtless attracts followers who are equally dissatisfied and willing to join with a leader who is seeking to bring change for the better.

[2]An exception to this might be Adams, who, in his books on counseling, uses numerous footnotes (1970, 1973). When he writes for more popular audiences, however, Adams, like the other popularizers, is much less scholarly (1972).

Uniqueness. Each of the popularizers has something unique—a fresh new writing style, a new message, a new way of presenting an idea. Many of Bill Gothard's critics have noted, for example, that his principles for living are not especially new, but they are presented in a uniquely creative way and this probably accounts for much of his popularity.

The Popularizers' Appeal

Why are these popular Christian psychologies flourishing today? Most of the leaders in these movements have little or no training in psychology and some are untrained theologically. Nevertheless they attract great numbers of followers who are looking for practical advice about psychological and spiritual matters. In the absence of research in this area we can only speculate concerning the reasons for the popularity of these leaders, but probably the characteristics as listed in the above section explain part of the appeal. One might wonder, however, why so many popularizers have come into prominence within the past decade. Surely the above characteristics are not new to the 1970s. Why therefore, have the popularizers come into prominence at this time in history?

Perhaps a part of the answer lies in the current state of the society. The 1960s were years of great social unrest in America. Assassinations, riots in the streets, increases in crime, decreases in morals, turmoil in the universities, an unpopular war abroad, an apparent breakdown in the family unit, widespread dissatisfaction with the traditional church—all of this doubtless created a widespread attitude of discouragement and insecurity. The political corruption, ecological crisis, and economic problems of the 1970s have further shaken our faith in the future and made people especially receptive to anyone who brings a message of hope and confidence.

This is precisely what the popular Christian psychologies have proclaimed: the assurance of stability, hope for the future, concise practical answers to the problems of life, and a promise of success in coping with stress. This message is presented clearly, authenticated by appeals to Scripture, and supported by numerous case histories and testimonies which demonstrate that the popular psychologies do, in fact, work.

Coupled with this message of hope is a formula for action. People are urged to apply principles in a practical way—taking action at a time when to do nothing would be painful and depressing. The popularizers each imply that his solution is superior to the techniques that people have used in the past and thousands have jumped on what they perceive as a "winning bandwagon."

The enthusiasm of these followers also contributes to the leaders' popularity. People like Bill Gothard, Jay Adams, or Tim LaHaye make no apparent attempts to attract disciples, but each has a band of enthusiastic disciples who create a cult-like atmosphere around a somewhat reluctant guru. This follower devotion helps to create controversy around the leader, and the controversy attracts more people, especially those who are curious. Enthusiastic followers are also verbal in their testimonies and most willing to recommend their leader's writings and ideas to others. By word of mouth the popularity spreads.

The Popularizers' Message

It is possible, perhaps, to dismiss the popular movements as fads which will fade as quickly as they arose. But even fads must arise for some good reason. By their prevalence and widespread popularity the movements discussed in this article have demonstrated that there are human needs which are not being met elsewhere. People who flock to the Gothard and LaHaye seminars or read the books of Miller, Peale, and Trobish must have questions which are not being answered in their churches or schools. Such people want help with their marriages, child rearing, spiritual growth, or interpersonal relations, and they are turning to the popularizers for answers.

One of the clearest messages that comes from the Christian popularizers, therefore, is that the local church has failed to show people how their faith can be applied to the practical problems of life. Bill Gothard, for example, has a sincere concern for pastors and a deep respect for the local church, but the fact that his seminars exist is living proof that the local congregations have failed to provide guidance in practical Christian living.

It is difficult to place the blame for this failure. Perhaps the seminaries are at fault for teaching a dead orthodoxy which leaves the graduate proficient in Greek and Hebrew but profoundly ignorant of basic human needs and interpersonal skills. Perhaps church leaders are to blame for ignoring the ways in which Scripture speaks to the needs of individuals. Perhaps individual Christians are guilty for taking their Christianity so lightly that, like the believers in Corinth (1 Cor. 3:1-6), people today have remained spiritual babies, following after a variety of "expert" leaders who spoon-feed their followers with predigested answers that can be swallowed with no need to chew over ideas. More feasible, perhaps, is the conclusion that we are living in an age of experts when things are so complicated that people have learned to look to specialists in human behavior for help with the problems of daily living.

Why, however, are the specialists in most cases untrained in psychology? Might it be that the professionals are partially at fault for leaving the popular field to others? We have learned in graduate school that psychology is a science which is best applied in the classroom, counseling room, or laboratory. We have tended to look askance at people like Joyce Brothers who popularize psychology, but when untrained persons like Ann Landers or Tim LaHaye appear on the scene, we are also critical because their advice is simplistic and lacking in sophistication. The problem may not be so much with the popularizers who are trying to help people or with the followers who are seeking answers. The rise of the popularizers may be largely because professionals have avoided a needy area—that of helping Christians and others to cope with the stresses of the twentieth century and to live abundant and balanced lives. The popular Christian psychologies, therefore, present both the church and the professional counselor with a challenge. If we disagree with the popularizers, our task is not so much to criticize as to rise up and do a better job.

For the professional such a challenge is extremely risky. By dabbling in the popularization of psychology, the professional loses respect and prestige among his academic colleagues, and any more in this direction is almost certain to bring criticism, misunderstanding, and charges that we are oversimplifying complex human behavior. Fortunately, some professionals are moving in this direction anyhow—men like James Mallory, James Dobson, Bruce Narramore, and Quentin Hyder. The alternative is to leave the popular field to those who are psychologically untrained and unaware of the harm that they might be doing.

How does a professional influence the people who currently follow the popularizers? As a start, let me make four suggestions. First, we must earn a hearing. To do this our professional degrees help, but we must also demonstrate a deep devotion to Christ, a belief in the authority of Scripture, a sincere interest in people, and an ability to communicate on a popular level. Not everyone can meet these criteria, but they are essential prerequisites for any professional who hopes to reach the popular marketplace.

Second, we must help untrained people to evaluate the popularizers and their conclusions. As a start, we might share the following suggestions:

1. Examine the qualifications of the popularizer. Is he speaking or writing in an area for which he is qualified by training or experience?

2. Spend some time summarizing the major tenets and basic assumptions of the system.

3. Test these conclusions against the Scriptures. Is the Bible an authority or merely a springboard for the popularizer's own ideas? Does he use good hermeneutics or does he, for example, snatch verses out of context to prove a point?

4. Is the system internally consistent or weakened by contradictions?

5. How are case histories used? Are they illustrative, or does the popularizer use cases as major support for his conclusions? Remember, one can find a case history to support almost any conclusions.

6. What other basis does the popularizer use to support his conclusions? Does he appeal to logic, research facts, etc.?

7. Don't be too much inclined to agree with a whole system. Ask if the system really works as well as its advocates claim. Remember, no one is perfect.

8. Be slow to attack personalities. It's more important to evaluate and criticize ideas than to attack people whose life work is being scrutinized.

Third, we ourselves must write and speak about practical issues in a clear concise way which nevertheless does not overlook individual differences or the complexity of behavior. Our work must be consistent with the teachings of Scriptures and as psychologically sophisticated as possible. We might apply the above criteria to our own work.

Finally, we must launch our efforts on at least two fronts. First we must appeal to the layman, helping him to cope with the problems in his own life and assisting him in reaching fellow believers through a process of peer counseling. Then we must help the pastor to counsel more effectively and to deal more efficiently with the needs of his congregation. The church leader must be shown the importance of preventive psychology (using the church to prevent problems from arising in the first place or to arrest budding problems before they get worse). He must be helped to see how psychology can clarify his understanding of the Scriptures and how it can help in the practical nature of his ministry.

Recently, a pastor's wife offered the opinion that people, especially professional people, who disagree with the conclusions of Bill Gothard are simply jealous of his success. While there might be an element of truth in this analysis, it doubtless would be much more accurate to conclude that the professionals are distressed over the potential harm that can come when psychologically untrained persons dispense psychological advice on a massive scale. The popular Christian psychologies do not pose a threat so much as they present stimulus for professionals to enter a field which we have too long neglected.

References

Adams, J. E. *Competent to Counsel.* Grand Rapids: Baker Book House, 1970.

———. *Christian Living in the Home.* Grand Rapids: Baker Book House, 1972.

———. *The Christian Counselor's Manual.* Nutley, N.J.: Presbyterian & Reformed Publishing Co., 1973.

Larson, B. *Dare to Live Now.* Grand Rapids: Zondervan Publishing House, 1965.

———. *The One and Only You.* Waco: Word Books, 1974.

LaHaye, T. *How to Win over Depression.* Grand Rapids: Zondervan Publishing House, 1974.

Miller, K. *A Taste of New Wine.* Waco: Word Books, 1965.

———. *The Becomers.* Waco: Word Books, 1973.

Peale, N. V. *The Power of Positive Thinking.* New York: Prentice-Hall, 1952.

———. *You Can if You Think You Can.* Englewood Cliffs, N.J.: Prentice-Hall, 1974.

Tournier, P. *The Healing of Persons.* New York: Harper & Row, 1965.

ADAMS' THEORY
OF NOUTHETIC COUNSELING

John D. Carter

Perhaps the best place to begin describing Jay Adams' conception of Christian counseling is where he does. Adams, by his own description, was a pastor when he was approached by a man who was in obvious emotional need. Adams did not know how to respond and passed off his need with some vague generalizations. A month later the man died. Adams feels the man knew he was dying and wanted some help from his pastor, "but I had failed him" (1970, p. xi).

Later in taking classes and reading, Adams became frustrated by Freudian and Rogerian concepts which did not seem biblical to him. At this point he became acquainted with O. H. Mowrer and his book *The Crisis in Psychiatry and Religion.* In this and a later book *The New Group Therapy,* Mowrer emphasizes responsibility, confession of sin, and sinful behavior as the cause of pathology. Adams spent two months studying with Mowrer. For someone with theological and speech degrees, but with no formal training in psychology, and someone who in addition was disillusioned with Rogers and Freud, Mowrer's concepts probably appeared to parallel certain biblical concepts. Though Adams acknowledges his debt to Mowrer, he denies he is a Mowrerian (1970, p. 19; 1973, p. 19). For someone fully acquainted with Mowrer's two books mentioned above, Adams' debt to Mowrer is strongly evident, though his latest work (1973) shows Adams has moved somewhat away from Mowrer.

The remainder of the article will consist of an analysis of Adams' theory of counseling by focusing on five fundamental aspects: the nature of man, pathology, the counseling model, the counseling process, and the counselor and his techniques. The final two sections will evaluate Adams' nouthetic counseling theory from a biblical and psychological perspective.

The Nature of Man

In this section Adams' conception of man's nature will be examined first psychologically and then biblically.

An earlier version of this paper was delivered at the First Annual Convention of the Western Association of Christians for Psychological Studies, Santa Barbara, California. May 24-25, 1974. © *Journal of Psychology and Theology,* 1975, *3,* 143-55.

In keeping with his view of pathology, Adams states: "Nouthetic counseling assumes that the feelings are not the most profound level of human relationship with which one must be concerned in counseling" (1970, p. 92). He goes on to say that God describes love in attitudinal and behavioral forms in defining love as commandment keeping (John 14:15). Consequently, nouthetic counselors spend less time finding out how clients feel than they do in seeing how clients behave (Adams, 1970, p. 93). In a footnote to this statement Adams says voluntary changes in behavior are a function of intelligent decisions and affect the emotions as a result, thus reaching the whole man. He goes on to say, "People feel bad because of bad behavior; feelings flow from actions" (Adams, 1970, p. 93). The sequence is clear. God's commands deal with attitudes and behavior. The individual decides to respond consistently or nonconsistently with these commands and good or bad feelings follow accordingly. Somehow this is communicated to the whole person though what the "whole person" means to Adams is unclear since little is said about it. The psychic cause of problems does not appear to be the whole person but rather the preconditioning problem—an habitual response pattern. "The client has programed himself by his past activities to act in certain ways in response to given stimuli" (p. 149). The emphasis is clear: Behavior, actions, and habits are the most central aspects of the person for nouthetic counseling theory while inner aspects of man are not recognized.

Adams' definitions of feelings, attitudes, and behavior help clarify his view of the nature of man. "The word *feeling* refers to the perception of a bodily state as pleasant or unpleasant. . . . Visceral, muscular, galvanic or other emotional responses of the body are responses to judgments made about the environment and oneself" and basically come in two kinds: good and bad (1973, p. 112). Feelings are involuntary and may be unconscious (pp. 110-11). In reference to this definition two things should be noted: one, emotion is a bodily response and is equated with feelings: two, a faculty or process of judgment has been introduced which elicits emotional reactions but which itself is never described, interpreted or grounded in the nature of the person. In addition, the nature of feelings can be further clarified by describing what they are not. A person cannot feel inferior according to Adams because inferiority is not an emotion but a judgment, conviction, or belief. Adams maintains that Rogerians are in serious error because they reduce thoughts, beliefs, opinions, attitudes, and convictions to feelings. This, says Adams, is a serious confusion of words and meanings (pp. 112-13).

"An *attitude* is that combination of presuppositions, beliefs, convictions, and opinions that make up one's habitual stance at any given time toward a subject, person or act" (p. 115). It is an habitual pattern of thought or mind set which strongly influences behavior. Attitudes may be more easily changed than feelings and may trigger bitterness, anger, or fear. Adams' definition of attitudes is essentially cognitive while psychologists almost universally maintain that attitudes are affective (emotion or feeling) though they may have a cognitive and/or behavior component (Baron, Byrne, and Griffith, 1974, p. 165ff.).

The term *behavior* refers to the activities of the whole person which may be judged by God. "Behavior is responsible conduct" (Adams, 1970, p. 116). This view according to Adams is biblical and is a narrower definition of behavior than that of Skinner who "subsumes both attitudes (behavior of the brain) and feeling (behavior of the glands, etc.) under the word" (1973, p. 116). The overwhelming thrust of Adams' view of man's nature (at the very least his psychic functioning) is clear. Behavior is the central focus of his theory and of most fundamental significance. Attitudes are second, somewhat more interior though as habitual thought patterns they tend toward a behavioral-external focus. Feelings are the most internal and least accessible aspects of the person. They are described as following (caused by) behavior. According to Adams, this sequence is clearly the biblical ideal (p.135). However, as will be indicated in a later section, somehow the sequence becomes reversed in the person with problems or pathology. Feelings when listened to motivate sinful behavior (p. 118), but feelings are also somehow mediated by judgments as indicated above. The status of unconscious attitudes or feelings is unclear since Adams does not address the issue nor does he deal with any interior aspect of man.

Biblically Adams seems to hold a dichotomous view of man since he says that soul and spirit are used interchangeably (p. 9, n. 9). However, the image of God in man is a more central concept in nouthetic theory. The image is moral and cognitive (p. 116). In the fall the image became distorted and "a reflection of the father of lies" (1970, p. 218). Adams speaks of the Christian as *restoring* the image by eliminating disorder and confusion (1973, p. 342). The Fall, says Adams, was a fall into lost control over the environment (1970, p. 128). God calls the Christian to master his environment by his grace. "In this way he *may once again* (emphasis supplied) reflect the image of God by subduing and ruling the world about him" (p. 129). This view of the Fall either represents a suborthodox view (the image is never lost, only marred; Berkhof, 1941, pp. 203-4), or represents a looseness in terminology. In either case it is congruent with Adams' orientation in which the Christian is actively confronting the environment and the counselor is actively confronting the client. The cognitive aspect of the image would seem to be related to judgment or intellectual process which mediated feelings though this connection is never made. Adams does not systematically integrate what he says psychologically about man in terms of behavior, attitudes, judgment, and feelings to his discussion of the image of God in man. In addition the words soul, spirit, and heart which are used in the Bible to describe the interior aspects of the person almost never occur in Adams' writings.

Pathology

Adams' view of pathology can be simply described by the title of chapter 14 in *The Christian Counselor's Manual,* "Sin is the problem." Many Christian counselors and therapists will react with surprise to such an equation of sin and problems, but Adams' position is quite clear. He begins the chapter by saying, "Christian counselors should not need to be reminded that they have been called to labor in opposition to the world, the flesh and the devil. . . . Counseling therefore must be understood as a spiritual battle" (1973, p. 117). He goes on to say, "Sin, then, in all of its dimensions, clearly is the problem with which the Christian counselor must grapple" (p. 124).

The fundamental themes of sin, says Adams, are apparent in the Genesis 3 account of the Fall. The basic temptation was the satisfaction of desire rather than obedience. Satan's appeal then was the same as it is today. This can be seen by comparing "the lust of the flesh, the lust of the eye, and the pride of life" (1 John 2:16) with Genesis 3:6. According to Adams, the options are desire versus God's commandment, which reflects the conflict between two distinct things: two moralities, two religions, two ways of living. For Adams two ways of living are: "the feeling-motivated life of sin oriented towards the self" which is diametrically opposed to "commandment oriented life of holiness oriented towards God" (1973, p. 118). Living according to feeling rather than obeying God's commandments is a basic hindrance to holiness and must be dealt with by every counselor. The difference between these two patterns is further expanded by Adams in a footnote indicating they are patterns of love or lust, God's commandments, or the counselee's desire. They recognize different authorities, Bible or the self; and they have different goals, eternal joy or temporary pleasure.

The reason that feelings are so strongly tied to sin in Adams' model appears to be that he equates feeling with desire and desire is tied to actions, i.e., sinful actions (1973, p. 120). The feeling-desire-action sequence or feeling-oriented life Adams describes as hedonistic. It has become a more explicit concept in his most recent work, *The Christian Counselor's Manual.* However, Adams does recognize that God is not opposed to pleasure and good feelings, but these are always from him and are enduring (p. 120, n. 3). How God gives those permanent good feelings is not discussed. He also admits at points that not all desire is in opposition to Scripture (p. 123). In addition, Adams seems to recognize that feelings do not have to lead to sinful actions, since what he calls commandment living often occurs in *spite* of feelings. Again how this occurs is not discussed.

Nevertheless, the real thrust of Adams' whole approach is that listening to one's own feelings is detrimental. Even having any feelings at all appears to be a liability since they so easily direct the person away from God's commandments. Thus, the real cause of problems (i.e., pathology) is sin and disobedience in any case where there is no organic or chemical unbalance. He does not say that feelings are the real cause of mental illness since there is no such thing as nonorganic mental illness (pp. 9-10; 1972, p. 3ff., 1970, p. 40).

Regarding specific pathology three levels of complexity exist:

1. Presentation problems: e.g., "I'm depressed" (often presented as a *cause* when really an effect);
2. Performance problems: e.g., "I haven't been much of a wife" (often presented as an effect when really a *cause*);
3. Preconditioning problems: e.g., "I avoid responsibility whenever the going gets tough" (often presented as an effect when really the underlying *cause*) (p. 148).

Adams goes on to say that the preconditioning problem is an habitual response pattern which often clarifies the relationship between the other two and represents their roots. The relationship between behavior and feelings is as follows: Behavior occurs and a judgment of self-judgment (conscience) evaluates the behavior; feelings (good or bad) follow the judgment, and these feelings in turn lead to further behavior. The cycle can then repeat itself (1973, p. 135). Focusing, submitting to, or listening to feelings rather than responding to God's commandments is the key to pathology. The former is to side with Satan and the latter is to obey God's Word. In a footnote, hedonism appears to be equated with listening to feelings and is the closest Adams ever comes to a theory of motivation (p. 121). What motivates (1) the initial behavior, (2) the judgment of that behavior, and (3) the listening to feelings instead of responding to God is never explained.

Counseling Model

Adams (1970, p. 41) takes the Greek word *noutheteo* as his model of counseling though together in its verb and noun form it occurs only 13 times in the New Testament. The word is translated "admonish" or "warn" in the King James Version. The root meaning is "to put in mind," hence admonish, warn, advise, or counsel all touch on its meaning. Adams recognized the difficulty in finding a one-word English equivalent so he usually renders it "confront nouthetically" but occasionally "an authoritative nouthetic confrontation." Nouthetic counseling or nouthetic confrontation, the terms are used interchangeably, consists of at least three basic elements (p. 44). First, the word *noutheteo* is used in conjunction with the word *didasko,* to teach. The latter deals with the impartation of information while nouthetic implies a problem which needs to be solved. "In short, nouthetic confrontation arises out of a condition in the counselee that God wants changed" (p. 45). The second element in nouthetic confrontation is that problems are solved by verbal means. The third element in *noutheteo* is intended verbal correction. Adams summarizes these elements in his counseling by saying that the counselor makes a well-intended effort to influence the counselee, an effort which is motivated by love and which implies no thought of punishment. While Adams' basic summary of the meaning of the word *noutheteo* is correct, he shifts its meaning when he translates it and takes it into his model for counseling. The reason for this shift appears to be that Adams connects warning and admonition with the biblical framework of authority and hence he speaks of authoritative nouthetic confrontation.

There seems to be four basic characteristics in Adams' model of nouthetic counseling, each with its own weakness. First, the confrontation for Adams is inseparable from authority and appears to have crept in on the same ground. However, neither the word *noutheteo* nor its biblical context always necessitates either confrontation and/or authoritative declaration through this face-to-face interaction. For example, Colossians 3:16 reads, "Let the word of Christ dwell in you richly in all wisdom, teaching and admonishing *(noutheteo)* one another in psalms and hymns and spiritual songs with grace in your heart to the Lord." The verse as well as the context does not suggest much that could be called confrontation. However, this is of minor import.

Second, Adams merges the two basic purposes or goals of nouthetic counseling with the goals of Scripture as he sees them but gives no biblical grounds for making *noutheteo* the model for counseling. Adams links two of Paul's statements: "Whom we preach, warning (noutheteo) every man, and teaching every man in all wisdom, that we may present every man perfect in Christ Jesus" (Col. 1:28) and "All scripture is given by inspiration of God and is profitable for doctrine, for reproof, for correction, for instruction in righteousness" (2 Tim. 3:16). "Here, the same nouthetic goals that Paul had previously stated in Colossians 1:28 seem to be in view" (p. 51). Adams says the Scriptures are nouthetically oriented. "Nouthetic confrontation is, in short, confrontation with the principles and practices of Scripture." It is authoritative instruction in love (p. 54). Love as a relationship is based on the responsible observance of God's commandments. Authoritative instruction requires directive techniques which seek to reverse the sinful pattern of covering sin and hiding from God which began at the Fall (p. 55). "Instead of excuse-making or blame-shifting, nouthetic counseling advocates the assumption of responsibility and blame, the admission of guilt, the confession of sin, and the seeking of forgiveness in Christ." Thus Adams maintains that nouthetic counseling rests on the dynamics of redemption and its authority resides in the full authority of God. These two goals may be summed up as change: change toward God. Hence, preaching and counseling have the same overall goal—God's glory—and the same result—enabling men to become pure in heart (p. 70). It will be shown in the next section that counseling is closely connected with church discipline.

Third, Adams' model of counseling strongly emphasizes multiple or team counseling. "One-to-one counseling has its place. . . . However, multiple counseling is to be preferred as the rule rather than the exception" (p. 237). He goes on to suggest that as many others as are intimately involved with the problem should be involved in the counseling . Team counseling, the use of two counselors, which was the approach assumed through *Competent to Counsel* (1970, p. 204) is not to be confused with group therapy or sensitivity groups. Group therapy, as practiced by Mowrer or groups which allow for ventilation of feeling, especially anger, are unscriptural according to Adams (p. 237) and become group slander when the participants go home and talk about each other (1973, p. 269). This is simply less than an adequate representation of group therapy.

Fourth, counseling as conceived by Adams has a strong similarity to counseling in the legal sense. It is directive and advice giving; the counselor imparts information and the client listens since the counselor has the authority of God and the Scripture behind him. This similarity to legal counseling has not escaped Adams and he explicitly seems to accept the parallel in at least two places (p. 17; 1970, p. 84). Counseling in the psychological sense is not to be confused with the legal meaning of counsel. The biblical concept of psychological counseling will be described in the section on the biblical criticism of Adams.

The Process of Counseling

The first underlying ingredient in counseling for Adams appears to be that people need meaning in life. While he agrees with Frankl in this he says that Frankl and other existentialists offer nothing. The Bible gives long-term hope which can be fused into a meaningful pattern of living (p. 35). After describing ten specific problems which need hope (the list in general seems to cover everything) Adams explains how the counselor may give hope. "One way to raise hope is by taking the people seriously when they talk of sin" (p. 46). What Adams means is that the nouthetic counselor accepts the person's self-report at face value, especially the uncomplimentary aspects, i.e., in this area he does not contradict the counselee. Adams states that the reconciliation/discipline dynamic gives hope, and consists of following the three steps to reconciliation described in Matthew 18:15-17: (1) If a brother transgresses against you go to him, (2) if he won't hear this take one or two with you, and (3) if he won't hear these go to the church and it must be heard or discipline results. Adams intends for counseling to help the client learn how to do this correctly.

In addition to the basic underlying ingredients, a general sequence of the process of counseling can be outlined. Adams suggests using the Personal Data Inventory (PDI) which is listed in the appendix of *Competent to Counsel* and appear in modified form in his most recent book (1973). The PDI has a general, health, religious, personal, and family-history section consisting of eight to ten questions each. It also has several questions dealing with the present problem: What is it, what has been done about it, and what is the client's expectations in regard to it? Adams suggests that the early sessions be used to gather more data but by the sixth session the major issues ought to be known and by the eighth to tenth session the specific problem ought to be well on the way toward reaching a solution (pp. 233-34). Termination dates should be discussed and set with the counselee for specific problems. While Adams does not state the exact desirable length of counseling, it is clearly not very lengthy and there are only twelve pages (one for each session) in the homework book given to clients (1970, p. 195).

Nouthetic counseling has general and specific objectives. The general objectives are to honor God, to strengthen Christ's church, and to benefit the counselee by building him up in the faith; but if the client is an unbeliever, evangelism becomes a prerequisite to the others. The specific or the other goals should answer the question: "What in particular do I wish to do for this counselee (What at this point? What later on?)" (1973, p. 235). However, these goals may be reversed as new data forces re-evaluation. In addition to these general and specific objectives, there are three basic elements of each counseling session: (1) the transitional matters, i.e., the carry-over from the previous sessions; (2) the discovery and discussion of new material; and (3) the commitment of the counselee to new biblical beliefs, decisions and/or behavior (p. 235). As has been hinted at above and as will be described in more detail later, nouthetic counseling is very confronting, directive, and problem-centered. The nouthetic counselor focuses on *what*, not *why*. "*What* was done? *What* must be done to rectify it? *What* should future responses be?" (1970, p. 48). The *why* is already known before counseling begins: Men are born sinners. The counselor directs his attention to specific problems in terms of their level: presentation, performance, or preconditioning. However, the approach is varied according to the individual but the focus is always on specific expressed problems whether attitudinal, verbal, or behavioral.

The Counselor and His Techniques

Nouthetic counseling theory maintains that the Holy Spirit is the principle person in counseling. This is true according to Adams because nouthetic counseling is in its fullest sense simply an application of the means of sanctification (1970, p. 73). Consequently the Holy Spirit is really *the* counselor. "Ignoring the Holy Spirit or avoiding the use of the Scripture in counseling is tantamount to an act of autonomous rebellion. Christians may not counsel apart from the Holy Spirit and His Word without greviously sinning against Him and the counselee" (1973, pp. 6-7). In light of these assertions, it is not surprising when Adams says, "Actually, counseling becomes truly nouthetic only when the counselee is a Christian" (1970, p. 68). What the nouthetic counselor has to offer a nonbeliever apparently is very limited except to evangelize him. "To be true to God's commission and thus offer an adequate solution to man's need, evangelism is absolutely essential to counseling" (p. 69). In anticipation of an objection to the imposition of values and standards on the counselee, Adams says that the counselor does not impose his own standards but he seeks to impose God's standards.

Aside from the divine counselor, who should be the human counselor? "While every Christian must become a counselor to his fellow Christians, the work of counseling as a special calling is assigned particularly to the pastor" (1973, p. 9). The reason of this assertion, according to Adams, is that there are only three causes of personal problems of living specified in the Scripture: demonic activity, personal sin, and organic illness. These three are interrelated. All options are covered under these heads leaving no room for a fourth: nonorganic mental illness. This assertion of no nonorganic mental illness is absolutely central in Adams' thought and he devotes a large portion of two chapters to the topic in *The Big Umbrella* (1 and 6) and most of two chapters in *Competent to Counsel* (1 and 3). Consequently there simply is not place for the psychiatrist or a psychologist or any other professional practitioner. In his haste to eliminate the psychological practitioner, Adams seems to have eliminated man's fallen or sinful nature. The problems of living are seen to be ascribed to sinful nature, but Adams' counseling operates as if they were functions of sinful actions. Psychologically this view is consistent with Glasser (1965), Mowrer (1961, 1964), and Szasz (1960), but theologically it becomes Pelagianism. The whole of Adams' emphasis is that all man needs to do is to reorganize his bad habits by changing his mind (with the aid of the Spirit to effect this change); man's sinful nature and any of its psychological consequences are not discussed as sources of problems and neither is the New Testament's concept of *flesh* with its connections to sin. The flesh, as well as the heart, soul, and spirit, reflects the spiritual and psychological interior of man which Adams seems to avoid at every opportunity.

Congruent with his assertion that pastors are to be counselors, Adams asserts that "a good seminary education rather than medical school or a degree in clinical psychology is the most fitting background for a counselor" (1970, p. 61). More specifically Adams asserts that the Bible sets forth goodness and knowledge as the qualifications for good counselors. This is derived from Romans 15:14, "And concerning you, my brethren, I myself also am convinced that you yourselves are full of goodness, filled with all knowledge, and are able to admonish (nouthetically confront) one another" (pp. 59-60). To these two Adams adds information, attitudes, and the desire to help others, as well as skills in interpersonal relations. These latter skills are viewed as the application of wisdom (p. 62).

As has been indicated before, nouthetic counseling is directive and problem-centered. The nouthetic counselor imparts information, gives advice, and focuses on problems in a confrontive manner. The nouthetic counselor cannot "listen" or "accept" clients' sinful attitudes or verbalizations since the "acceptance of sin is sin" (p. 102). Consequently, support as conceived of by psychology or psychiatry is unacceptable. "Akin to modern concepts of love are the equally untenable ideas about support, empathy, and sympathy held by many counselors . . . yet this view as it is popularly expounded is antithetical to all that the Bible says about change" (1973, p. 154). Support is passive; therefore it is wrong for three reasons: (1) The counselor must never support sinful behavior; (2) support is harmful because it not only acknowledges but approves of the counselee's failure in handling his problems; and (3) there is no biblical evidence that the minister "stands by passively 'being' but neither *doing* nor *saying"* (1970, p. 157). Empathy is acceptable only as problem solving efforts by the counselor since then alone is it truly empathy; otherwise it is "faith without works" (1973, p. 159). These statements do not imply, according to Adams, that love is not present. The nouthetic counselor is to admonish his counselees as brothers. Admonishing is the evidence that the counselor loves since a simple biblical definition of love is: the fulfillment of God's commandments. Love is a responsible relationship to God and man (1970, p. 55).

Adams' criticism of acceptance, support, empathy, and listening, as well as other similar counselor-counselee relationship factors or techniques, would seem to be directed against the Rogerian approach. Equally heavy criticism is directed toward the psychoanalytic concept of transference. "By transference *Rogerians and other Freudians* (emphasis supplied) mean that clients frequently redirect their feelings (often negative) from one person to another (in this case to the counselor). . . . But is transference a technique that Christians may use? No." (p. 101). This approach encourages the counselee to perpetuate and multiply his sin and guilt. Positive transference is no better since it fosters fantasy and an unrealistic relationship.

If all these techiques are closed, what can the nouthetic counselor do? He may give advice and information, confront, or admonish, call for repentance, explain biblical passages and repeatedly call for or appeal to the counselee's Christian commitment. More specifically, he is to motivate the client to change by appealing to rewards and punishments, both in this life and eternally, for good and bad behavior since God does this. He may also appeal to the mercies of God in Christ or submit himself for the Lord's sake (1 Peter 2:13), for the sake of conscience toward God (1 Peter 2:19), or for the sake of righteousness (2 Peter 3:14) (1973, p. 167). In addition to these approaches there are two frequently used techniques: (1) the assignment of homework which Adams suggests should begin the first week (p. 301). The importance of homework is heavily stressed in Adams' latest book with three chapters devoted to it. This is partly true because the second half of *The Christian Counselor's Manual* is largely a how-to-do-it book. The homework begins the first session by the counselor assigning some specific task relevant to the client's problem even if it is only counting the number of times it is resisted. The difficulty of the assignments is increased as the client makes progress. The client is praised for his success, and parents or spouses are encouraged to give reward for newly learned appropriate behavior but not for the reinitiation of previously learned behavior (p. 166). (2) A second frequently used nouthetic technique is total restructuring which consists of looking at the problem from all areas of the person's life, such as social activity, friends, church-Bible-prayer-witness, work-school, physical health-sleep, marriage-sex, family-children, finances, and any other area. For example, Adams heavily stresses this approach with homosexuals. By focusing on all areas of the homosexual's life and by pressing for biblical change in each, the homosexual life will become reorganized and relapse prevented. In addition to these techniques, he recognizes and even stresses the need for a medical examination to assess any physical complications. Sleep loss and its effects are commonly a factor in problems involving perceptual distractions (e.g., schizophrenia) according to Adams (pp. 384-87).

Criticism and Evaluation: Biblical

Since Adams says, "I want to alter any or all of what I have written provided that I can be shown to be wrong biblically; I am not interested in debate which moves off non-Christian suppositions. . . . I have attempted to re-examine counseling (suggestively but not exhaustively) in a biblical manner, and I ask therefore, that my work shall be similarly criticized" (1970, p. 269). I will begin my evaluation of his views in light of the Scripture and will try to stay within Adams' framework in describing counseling. First, Adams' view of man is thoroughly sub-Christian, how can he be critical of others? Adams' view of man in a psychological sense is almost completely external and behavioral. The only thing that seemingly prevents him from being a full-fledged Skinnerian or Mowrerian is Adams' metaphysical commitment to God and the Bible. Consequently, his view of man is pushed down on the scriptural view of man much like a cookie cutter is pushed down on dough. What fits inside the cookie cutter is retained, what falls on the outside is excluded. Behavior and all externally observable qualities fall on the inside. Behavior is translated into the active effort of commandment keeping. The New Testament concepts of spirit, soul, and heart fall outside the cookie cutter, as does the flesh also, and so are conceptually and explicitly *not* included in his description of man or his problems. However, though infrequently these aspects of man do appear in his texts, they do not change Adams' behavioristic conception of man and his problems. In contrast to Adams' external behavioral orientation, Jesus focuses on the heart and makes this inner aspect fundamental. Just a few references will show how basic a concept the heart is in biblical psychology: "Out of the abundance of the heart the mouth speaks" (Matt. 12:34); a good man brings good out of his heart (Matt. 12:35); out of the heart proceed evil thoughts (Matt. 15:19); and doubt (Mark 11:23), conviction (Acts 2:37), and belief (Rom. 10:9) take place in the heart. Adultery is also not just a behavioral act but an event which can take place in the heart without external evidence (Matt. 5:28). Finally, the first and greatest commandment stresses the internal aspect of man who is to love God with all his heart, soul, and mind (Matt. 22:37).

In addition, the passive commands and exhortations of Scripture are also ignored, such as "Abide in Christ" (John 15:4); "Let the peace of Christ dwell in your hearts" (Col. 3:15); and "be anxious for nothing" (Phil. 4:6). These passive commands which focus on the inner or central aspects of human nature are apparently excluded along with heart, soul, and spirit because they are not assertive and do not lend themselves to behavioral definition. Parallel with the loss of man's inner nature goes the loss of an inner definition of sin in terms of the thoughts and intents of the heart and its deceitfulness (Jer. 17:9; Mark 7:21). Since the heart and the inner aspect of sin are dwarfed, so necessarily is the fall and the extent of the atonement. Furthermore, nouthetic counseling as a discussion of sanctification suffers since what the Christian is being sanctified from is inadequately defined. While Adams explicitly omits the heart, soul, and spirit and the inner aspects of sin (the flesh) in his conceptualization of man and pathology, they often implicitly appear in Adams' discussion of counseling. Adams' discussion of attitude is a conceptual curiosity; it is halfway between the heart and behavior. It is defined so as to include some inner aspects of man, but it does not enter into his approach to problems or pathology but like heart it has a way of creeping into his practical discussion of specific counseling problems.

The conceptual status of the inner aspect of man (heart, soul, and spirit) and the inner nature of sin (the flesh) is so fundamental that no model of man and counseling can be called biblical without it. It appears that Adams has fallen victim to the very charges he levels at others. A number of evangelicals and conservatives in the various aspects of the field of counseling, e.g., Gary Collins, James Dobson, William Hulme, Quentin

Hyder, Bruce Narramore, Clyde Narramore, and Wayne Oates are repeatedly charged with having subbiblical views. Yet Adams' strong emphasis on behavior and confrontation appears to have come directly from Mowrer and to have blinded Adams to the Scriptures' emphasis on the inner aspects of man and sin. Thus Adams is simply subscriptural, not so much for what he asserts but for what he omits and the bias that this omission introduces.

The second basic criticism of Adams from a biblical perspective is his choice of *noutheteo* and its cognate *nouthesia* as a model of counseling. A biblical rationale for the choice of this concept is never given, rather it is simply asserted as true. In terms of its centrality *noutheteo* and its cognate are infrequent. Together these words occur only thirteen times in the New Testament. While Adams links *noutheteo* to preaching and discipline, its position in the network of biblical concepts is neither basic nor central.

On the other hand, I would offer the suggestion that *parakaleo* and its cognate *paraklesis* make a much more adequate model of counseling from a biblical perspective. These words or concepts are much more central biblically. Together they are translated in the King James Version twenty-nine times as "comfort," twenty-seven times as "exhort," fourteen times as "consolation," and forty-three times as "beseech," and infrequently as "desire," "entreat," and "pray." Furthermore, and perhaps of greater import, *paraklesis* is listed as a gift to the church (Rom. 12:8). The basic meaning of these words is "to call to one side" but it has implications. It can be a request for help as an individual calls on Jesus for help, e.g., the leper (Mark 1:40) or the centurion who wanted his servant healed (Matt. 8:5). It can be the strengthening call of encouragement or exhortation as Paul frequently did, e.g., on his trip through Greece on his way to Jerusalem (Acts 20:2). It can be consolation or comfort which is received during or after a period of stress, e.g., as Christians share with other Christians the help they have received (2 Cor. 1:4; 7:6-7). The suggestion of *paraklesis* as a model of Christian counseling is a suggestion, not an assertion. Berry (1974) has also recognized the appropriateness of *paraklesis* as a model of biblical counseling. The concept is broad enough to support a variety of therapeutic techniques from crisis intervention to depth therapy, and it is a gift given to the church which is clearly different than the gift of prophet or teacher. On the other hand, *nouthesia* represents a rather narrow range of functioning which Christians are to engage in but does not have the status of a gift to the church and does not have the centrality that Adams wants to give it.

Criticism and Evaluation: Psychological and General

In the former section the nouthetic counseling model was evaluated from a biblical perspective, i.e., from the orientation Adams is seeking to maintain. In this section nouthetic counseling theory and Adams' approach will be evaluated from a psychological and external framework. First, nouthetic counseling theory has all the assets and liabilities of a confrontational behavioral-responsibility approach (e.g., Mowrer). This emphasis demands immediate verbal and behavioral change. Since inner, affective and/or unconscious processes are assumed not to exist or to be irrelevant, the observed external changes are presumed to represent the cure. Hence, Adams' therapy is in the same position as every other type of therapy rather than some presumed special superior category. His theory tells him what pathology is, what techniques to use, and what constitutes the cure.

The validity of any approach rests on its conceptual adequacy and its empirical support. A discussion of the conceptual adequacy from a biblical perspective has already been made, and additional psychological comments will be made shortly. However, it is not the intention of this article to criticize Adams from the viewpoint of any particular type of therapy since the reader can do that himself, but a comment on the empirical validity of nouthetic counseling is in order. Adams repeatedly throughout his works claims significant and rapid success in counseling. Those who are familiar with the research literature on psychotherapy and counseling and its attendant conceptual and methodological problems will be well aware of the difficulty that Adams would have in establishing that his approach produces significantly better than chance results, let alone the superiority of his therapy when compared to other therapies.

However, one of the reasons for his apparent success is its surface character. Specific verbal and behavioral responses are demanded because God has commandments and the client is a believer (Adams, 1973, p. 235). (1) These responses bring immediate change and decrease external (surface) conflict but they don't bring any deep personality change. (2) Repeated confrontation may lead the client to repress his internal problem and adopt a compulsive style of behavior coupled with denial and repression of inner tension. (3) In addition, Adams' clients may be a very self-selected group since they must endure repeated authoritative confrontation.

A second psychological criticism of Adams involves his failure to understand the psychologists he most severely criticizes, namely Rogers and Freud. Transference, for example, is described in terms of its outer manifestation without apparently understanding that in psychoanalytic theory it is related to the defenses, particularly projection. It is occurring everywhere for the patient, and the analyst is simply the person who is dealing with it without reacting to it. Furthermore, in a quotation given previously, transference as a concept is attributed to "Rogerians and other Freudians" (Adams, 1973, p.101), a clear indication of his psychological naiveté. Adams also states, "The Freudian viewpoint boils down to this, that God is to blame for the misery and ruin of man" (1970, p. 214).

Needless to say, Freud and most psychoanalysts will hardly recognize this as their position even if by God Adams is referring to religion or to the person's conception of God.

Rogers, on the other hand, does not fare any better than Freud. Rogers is accused of not truly being client-centered because he listens only to feelings and not to what a person is thinking. This reduces his interest in the client to a one-dimensional aspect. Consequently, Rogerians are not truly client-centered while nouthetic counselors are (p. 88). In addition, Adams' limited understanding of Rogers leads him to think a Rogerian (nondirective) counselor won't be able to help a client immediately threatening suicide, again indicating his clinical naiveté. Furthermore, given Adams' definition and discussion of feelings cited above, it should be evident that Adams does not understand the affective processes Rogers describes as feelings. Adams' blending of Freud and Rogers has already been alluded to in the preceding paragraph, but other therapists receive the same uninformed treatment. Rollo May is asserted to illustrate the link between Rogers and Freud because he gives a quotation from Freud against advice-giving therapy (p. 79). It appears that Adams presumes May is a Rogerian because Rogers also opposes giving advice to clients.

The reason for Adams' failure to understand various perspectives of counseling appears to be that he has never read the original authors (or at least understood them) as indicated by his failure to cite their original works. Only two references to Freud's works are cited in Adams' three major books on counseling, apart from labeling three of Freud's metapsychological works as antireligious. Rogers fares better with five references to his original works. While the author may have overlooked a reference or two to either author, Freud and Freudians and Rogers and Rogerian therapy are repeatedly described from secondary sources. Mowrer and Skinner are both less frequently and less harshly criticized, though like every other therapy not based on the Bible, they too are rejects. However, Freud's view on lay analysis can be used and is quoted to support Adams' view that medical training is not a necessity for counseling (p. 37).

The most glaring weakness of nouthetic counseling theory is that it has no theory of personality. No stages of growth or development are given. No theory of motivation or fundamental dynamic tendency of the person is articulated such as Freud's instincts (libido), Maslow's or Rogers' self-actualization, Adler's striving for superiority, or Frankl's will to meaning. Even the processes of how attitudes are formed and how behavior becomes habitual are never described. In addition, the mechanism or processes explaining the how and/or why judgments are formed, and how and/or why feelings are listened to and focused on are not given. The implication of the absence of a theory of personality is that Adams has no processes in which to ground his views of pathology and no processes to explain how therapy or counseling works. Rather Adams has a descriptive analysis of behavior, attitudes, and feeling but no explanation of pathology, and he has a description of what the counselor does and says but no explanation of why it works. If Adams had not excluded man's sinful nature, as well as his heart, soul, and spirit, he would have had some biblical concepts on which to base his personality theory, but as indicated he disregarded or ignored them. Consequently, Adams' theory of nouthetic counseling is deficient on both biblical and pyschological grounds.

References

Adams, J. *Competent to Counsel.* Grand Rapids: Baker Book House, 1970.

———. *The Big Umbrella.* Grand Rapids: Baker Book House, 1972.

———. *The Christian Counselor's Manual.* Nutley, N.J.: Presbyterian & Reformed Publishing Co., 1973.

Baron, R. A., Byrne, D., and Griffith, W. *Social Psychology.* Boston: Allyn & Bacon, 1974.

Berkhof, L. *Systematic Theology.* Grand Rapids: Eerdmanns, 1941.

Berry, C. M. "Counseling in the Medical Office." *Journal of Psychology and Theolgy,* 1974, *2,* 174-81.

Glasser, W. *Reality Therapy.* New York: Harper & Row, 1965.

Mowrer, O. H. *The Crisis in Psychiatry and Religion.* Princeton: Van Nostrand, 1961.

———. *The New Group Therapy.* Princeton: Van Nostrand, 1964.

Szasz, T. *The Myth of Mental Illness.* New York: Sell, 1960.

THE PSYCHOLOGY OF GOTHARD AND BASIC YOUTH CONFLICTS SEMINAR

John D. Carter

The popularity of Bill Gothard's Seminar on Basic Youth Conflicts ought to make sociologists, psychologists, and observers of religious movement take note. The attendance over the past years has risen steadily from a few thousand in 1968 to over 250,000 last year (1973). There were twenty-six seminars in over twenty different cities during the past year including an advance seminar for pastors and youth leaders who have already attended the Basic Seminar. The Spring 1974 Seminar in Los Angeles registered over thirty thousand in attendance at the Long Beach Arena and the three special television area hook-ups.

While the purpose of this paper is not to analyze the emergence of the seminars as a basic mass religious movement, it is interesting to speculate on whether Gothard and his seminars should be compared to Billy Graham and his rallies about twenty years ago, or to the emergence of the Jesus Movement and popular religion or to popularity of psychology among the youth. However, it is the purpose of this paper to analyze the psychological character of Gothard's thoughts and to some extent its biblical base. Therefore, this paper is conceptual in nature and focus. The difficulty of this task will probably be evident to any person in the academic or professional community who has attended the seminar. Gothard has published nothing; rather those who attend the seminar receive a red loose-leaf binder and over 160 pages of outlined notes distributed in sections throughout the week-long seminar (28 to 30 hours). The indirect quotations in this paper are from the red notebook or the author's notes taken during the Chicago, 1973 (spring); Los Angeles, 1973 (fall); or the Los Angeles, 1974 (spring) seminars. The outlines in the red notebook are elaborated verbally in each seminar, hence the seminars vary somewhat in detail since Gothard usually delivers them extemporaneously on each occasion. The outlined notes do not form an integrated or conceptual whole but rather are topical in nature, including self-image, chain of command (family), conscience, rights, freedom, success, purpose, friends,

An earlier version of this paper was delivered at First Annual Convention of the Western Association of Christians for Psychological Studies, Santa Barbara, California, May 24-25, 1974. © *Journal of Psychology and Theology*, 1975, 2, 249-59. Used by permission of the author.

dating, and commitment. Thus these notes contain a vast amount of material on a variety of topics with varying degrees of conceptual organization.

It is beyond the scope of a single paper to analyze Gothard's whole set of notes. Instead, the goal is to evaluate the nature and structure as it relates to psychology. As indicated above it is evident that Gothard's notes are topically organized rather than conceptually organized. This is not intended to be a criticism but an observation. Gothard's intention seems to be to provide practical help for the Christian layman rather than to write a theological or psychological treatise. However, the purpose of this paper is conceptual, and it consists of analyzing three basic concepts in Gothard's thought: the nature of man (success), the nature of pathology (levels of conflict), and the therapuetic procedures (success *et al*). Each of these concepts represents basic topics or sections of the notes and a relevant aspect of psychological functioning. These three topics also are the conceptual pillars or seed ideas around which most of the notes are organized. These analyses will be followed by some general psychological observations and an evaluation of the nature of Gothard's thoughts from a biblical perspective since this is the perspective he adopts and claims as support for his system. The structure of the paper allows the reader to make his own psychological evaluation.

The Nature of Man

Gothard clearly is a trichotomist though he recognizes that not all Christians hold to this position. He divides man into spirit, soul, and body. The soul is further subdivided into mind, emotions, and will. In some of Gothard's diagrams the Greek words *nous, kardia,* and *boulima* are used to describe respectively those three aspects of the soul listed above. This division of man into spirit, soul, and body is very significant since these three parts enter into his notion of both health (he calls it success) and therapy, as well as Gothard's theory of music as it relates to spiritual health and pathology. Therefore these areas will be examined as they relate to the nature of the person.

First, healthy or successful living is a result of balance—a balance of the spiritual and the physical input. Second, there are five basic steps toward becoming a whole person, i.e., to therapy: (1) be reborn in your *spirit;* (2) rebuild your *thought structure;* (3) refocus your *emotions;* (4) redirect your *goals;* and (5) reproduce your life in *others* (emphasis Gothard's). Gothard indicates that the first four of these steps involve beginning with the spirit and successively bringing the three aspects of the soul (mind, emotions, and will) into line with the spirit. In Gothard's diagrams the spirit is above the soul with its three aspects in the order indicated which are in turn above the body. The reason the last step does not involve the body or the lower nature appears to be Gothard's understanding of salvation. He maintains that salvation has three facets: (1) rebirth in the spirit which took place in the *past* and is step one above; (2) steps two through four described above occur in the *present* along with step five as a natural outgrowth of the other four; and (3) the body will be saved in the *future* when Christ returns. There is no therapeutic principle for the body other than bringing it into balance by developing the first four, i.e., developing the spirit, mind, emotions, and will. As Gothard's spirit/soul/body diagram is repeated in the red notebook to illustrate steps one through four, the body part of the diagram is relabeled flesh and/or the lower nature. This change is duly noted by Gothard, who explains that the flesh is the weaker or unregenerate human nature and not the body. However, psychologically and conceptually this shift is not accidental. The body, flesh, physical, and sensual tend to be equivalent terms for Gothard with the meaning of the latter term prevailing. Thus the body becomes equivalent to the sensual. On the other hand in several diagrams Gothard equates spirit with conscience by placing it in parentheses after spirit. In the Minister's (church) Manual Gothard does not even use spirit at all but substitutes conscience for spirit in the diagram of the person. Gothard's position appears to be a modification of Nee's (1968) position which makes conscience one of the three aspects of the human spirit's functions. Thus for Gothard the human spirit equals conscience and the body equals the flesh.

As an aside it is interesting to speculate on the origin of some of Gothard's ideas especially the division of the soul into mind, emotions, and will. Nee (1964, 1968) divides the soul into the same three parts. It is difficult to know with certainty if Gothard was influenced by Nee (or anyone else for that matter) though some of Gothard's ideas and diagrams are rather similar to Nee's diagrams. Gothard never indicates the source of his material, if any, except an occasional reference to a "psychiatrist" or "someone has said" followed by an indirect quotation which on occasions sounds not unlike Glasser or Mowrer.

In relating the three aspects of man to pathology, Gothard maintains that God's standard for the person is to have the mental, emotional, and volitional—i.e., the soul or the three psychological functions—integrated around the spirit. This in turn balances the physical, producing inner balance or success which is equivalent to moral freedom for Gothard. When the soul or the psychological function becomes integrated around the sensual or physical, the spiritual aspect of man is underdeveloped and has last place. This state of affairs (according to Gothard) corresponds to society's standards and is concupiscence from the biblical perspective (defined by Gothard as a strong abnormal sexual desire or appetite). If the guilt from concupiscence is not handled correctly a condition of reprobation will begin to develop. In this condition all standards are rejected and the spiritual aspect of man becomes stronger. Thus pathology, from the perspective of the nature of man, results from the increasing dominance of the sensual (body-flesh), as the psychic side with it, at the expense of the spiritual until the spiritual eventually ceases to function. If the model of personality as superego (conscience), ego, and id can be thought of as equivalent to the model of personality as spirit, soul, and body (sensuality) then there is a strong parallel between Gothard's and Mowrer's (1961, 1964) theory of pathology. Mowrer (1961, 1964) argues that when the ego sides with the id and they repress the superego, pathology eventually results. Though the comparison with Mowrer made here is only suggestive it will help orient the psychologically trained reader to understand the nature of Gothard's approach to pathology as it relates to the nature of personality.

In addition to the material already mentioned regarding the nature of the person, Gothard proposes a theory of music which is consonant with his trichotomus view of man. The spirit is related to the melody. If there is too much tension between the rise and fall of the melody, a craving or lack of fulfillment is created while too little tension tends to produce depression or a mood of despair. The soul is related to the harmony among the chords. If there is too much dissonance, confusion and rebellion result, i.e., there are no laws—any kind of chord can be made, but if there is too much consonance, as in some Christian music, gushy sentimentality results. The body is related to the rhythm. If there is too much repetition sensuality is stimulated and if there is too little variation in the rhythm and accent then distraction results. This theory of music is given in the seminar but not in the red notebook. Little else is said about it except that Gothard exhorts the audience to avoid strong rhythmic music (rock music) since it only stimulates sensuality. There is little more which can be said about Gothard's theory of man except possibly to elaborate on his therapeutic steps outlined above. What has been said in this section does not conceptually integrate or relate well with the material in the other section simply because Gothard does not tie his material together conceptually. Concupiscence as a pathology can be thought of as a violation of the freedom or moral freedom which is one of the seven divine principles of living.

The Nature of Pathology

Violation of divine principles is the cause of problems, i.e., pathology. For Gothard there are seven underlying divine principles of living: design, authority, responsibility, ownership, motivation, freedom (moral), and success. Excluding motivation these principles represent a loose sequential outline of the entire seminar if the dating and friendship sections can be subsumed under success as successful interpersonal relationships. A detailed summary of these principles cannot be given since Gothard does not describe them in relationship to the whole seminar or even their conceptual centrality for his system of thought.

In certain seminars the first three principles of living, especially responsibility, are described to some extent while the last five are only given one or two sentence descriptions. In other seminars all seven may only be listed in passing and they are never described as overarching principles in the red notebook. This obscures the already meager conceptual coherence of Gothard's thought. However, what is stressed is that these principles are supernatural and universal in character, i.e., they apply to Christians as well as non-Christians. The person who violates them experiences the consequences, and those who live by them will lead a satisfying life whether they realize that these are God's principles or not. This emphasis apparently refers particularly to principles of design, authority, and responsibility since the thrust of the latter five are directed to the Christian.

In addition Gothard has an explicit theory of pathology which is elaborated under the topic of design. Gothard's theory of pathology is described in terms of four levels of conflict in which each succeeding level is more fundamental than the previous one. The four levels are: (1) surface problems (problems visible to others), (2) surface causes (inner tensions), (3) root problems (basic personality conflicts), and (4) the root cause (the person's response to God). Examples of surface problems are argumentativeness, hostility, lying, stealing, self-centeredness, and sensual habits or actions. Examples of surface causes are rebellion and distrust, insecurity, worry, frustration, and nervousness. (Gothard says that when he started the seminar he had not discovered levels three and four; they were added in about 1971). There are only three root problems: bitterness, temporal values, and moral impurity. The root problems are derived from the following verses of Scripture: Hebrews 12:15-17; 1 Corinthians 10:6-13; and 1 Timothy 3:1-10. Gothard also maintains that the lists of sinful attitudes and behavior listed in Romans 1, Galatians 5, and Colossians 3 break down into these three root problems. In addition there is some sequential movement from the root problem of bitterness to temporal values to immorality in thought, action, and habit. Gothard does not elaborate on this movement. Finally there is only one ultimate root cause: a wrong response to God, i.e., resisting God's grace to assist in following the seven principles for living.

The levels of conflict are obviously a dynamic theory of pathology regardless of what one thinks of its content. First, there are surface actions with successive deeper internal levels of personality behind them. Second, functioning at each level is explained by fewer motives or attitudes at the next deeper level until there is only one root cause of pathology. While this description represents Gothard's explicit theory of pathology, there are implicit indications of pathology at other points. For example, in discussing the nature of man, spiritually abnormal or pathological conditions were indicated which bear no correspondence to the above description. However, it is both explicitly and implicitly implied throughout the seminar and the red notebook that violation of the seven principles constitutes sin (pathology). These principles of living are the divine principles represented by each area of the notebook (and each basic topic in the seminar). There is a pathology associated with each area but all of these are reducible to resisting the grace of God, though this is never fully explicated in the seminar. Thus Gothard has a general theory of pathology and specific subtheories which are integratable in principle with the general theory. These seven principles as they relate to the level of conflict constitute the closest Gothard ever comes to a conceptual skeleton (structure) for his system of thought.

Therapy, Counseling, and Maturity

Gothard does not have an explicit statement on therapy. However, the whole thrust and design of the seminar is to provide help, counseling, or therapy to those who are experiencing problems. Since there are violations of each of the seven principles of living there are also therapeutic procedures related to each. Not all of these procedures can be described in a paper of this length. Therefore, therapeutic procedures related to the principles of design, authority, and success have been selected for discussion. The principle of design is concerned primarily with the acceptance of the self. Negative attitudes toward the self are viewed by Gothard as bitterness toward God as the designer of the self. The first step to self-acceptance is to begin a new and intimate relationship with God the designer. The second is to thank him for his workmanship so far. This involves accepting God as the author of one's physical features, parents, and physical environment and that he has goals for the self that involve one's current circumstances. The third step is to cooperate with God by developing the qualities God has given us and to view the self and its future from his value system. God is trying to build character and inner attitudes. Fourth, try to reproduce Christ's character in others. Gothard supports each step with Bible verses and many illustrations. In addition he analyzes an extended example of a teenage girl who was quite depressed.

A second therapeutic procedure grows out of the authority principle. God has a divine chain of command. God, who is on top, holds the father who is depicted as a hammer, and who comes down on the mother (a chisel) who in turn is chipping away on the teenager—a diamond in the rough. Gothard repeatedly stresses the importance of recognizing one's position in this chain. Rebellion and self-direction are not options for the individual even when those who are in authority are not acting responsibly. The person is not responsible for them and their position but only for himself. He must obey those over him in all things unless they require one to sin. By sin Gothard means overt, blatant sin since he says a Christian teenager should stay home from church if his non-Christian parents tell him to do so.

In situations which appear to be sins individuals may suggest nonsinful creative alternatives to those in authority, offered in the spirit of respect and obedience. However, if and only if these alternatives are rejected may the individual refuse. Gothard says that in these situations God may be calling the individual to suffer the consequences for Christ's sake. However, Gothard seems to indicate that most individuals do not reach this point of suffering. Those in authority either see the wisdom of the creative alternatives and/or the co-operative, obedient person and thus change their requirements. The chain of command also applies to employers and employees in principle though the details are not elaborated.

If those in authority over the individual require things that are not sin, obedience is required because those in authority are God's instruments to produce God's purpose in the individual. It is hard to overstate the emphasis Gothard gives to this concept. Even single adults living away from home and supporting themselves should respect parents' wishes. Gothard gives the example of a 21-year-old girl living away from home who wanted to marry a Christian young man believing it was God's will. Gothard said she should respect her parents' judgment even though they were not Christians. Disobedience, which involves offspring resisting their parents, Gothard maintains, will be repeated when the offspring have their own children. He asserts that individuals become like those who are resisted and so the dynamics of the rebellion are recapitulated at a later date in one's own children. Thus, accepting the authority in the chain of command as God's instruments to perfect his purpose avoids the recapitulation of rebellion and allows God to shape one's character as he would. In addition Gothard appeals to the chain of command when the individual faces temptation. When faced with a sensual temptation Gothard suggests that the individual pray for those immediately higher in the chain of command and those immediately lower. The example given is a wife who is tempted because her husband is not acting in such a way as to provide an umbrella-like shield. The wife's way of coping with the temptation is not to fight the temptation or to blame the husband but to pray for her husband and her children. Gothard maintains that the wife cannot have problems unless the husband has failed in some way, because even the devil *must* follow the chain of command and could not have tempted her if the husband had not failed in some way. Not much more can be said about this therapeutic remedy for temptation since Gothard has not developed it as extensively as he has his simple obedience to the authority principle.

The third therapeutic procedure which involves successful living has already been described to some extent in the first section of the paper as part of the nature of man. Those five steps to becoming a whole person, or to use Gothard's terminology, obtaining success or "achieving inner balance," are extended by a discussion of fasting and prayer. For the

Christian the first four of the five steps essentially consisted of reading and memorizing Scripture. This is followed by praying back to God some of the scriptural content and meditating on its content. Fasting and prayer are added to these steps to increase sensitivity to God and the achievement of spiritual success. Gothard says that the concept of success in the Scripture is always connected with fasting. Gothard gives a number of reasons for fasting such as repentance for sin, seeking God's will, concern for God's work, concern for deliverance or protection, and as part of worship. A two-page outline is given for a day of fasting and prayer. Fasting is highly recommended and stressed heavily for increasing sensitivity to God. If a Christian can't fast all day then one meal is recommended. In some seminars Gothard even stressed the physiological benefit of fasting. In the red notebook the material on fasting follows immediately the five steps to inner balance described in the first section of the paper and should be thought of as the integral consequence of them; prayer and meditation are woven throughout the entire sequence.

The therapeutic procedures described thus far are essentially carried out by the individual himself. The example of Gothard's own counseling procedure given in the seminar appears to consist chiefly of engaging in some dialogue about surface problems until Gothard perceives which of the three root causes is involved. At this point Gothard asks a penetrating question or makes an observation designed to get at the root problem, or in the case of authority problems, some observation or suggestion about the chain of command. With these observations, suggestions, encouragements or similar ones from the red notebook the person goes home to work out his problems.

Gothard apparently maintains some type of counseling center at his Chicago area headquarters. The existence or nature of these facilities is not made public at the seminars. Thus, the full nature of Gothard's counseling procedures at his Chicago area center is unknown. It is reasonable to assume that they are probably longer than one session but not much longer and that any techniques are consistent with the design, authority, and success procedures described above and elaborated more fully in the seminar and the red notebook.

Criticism and Evaluation

The criticism and evaluation of the Gothard seminar must of necessity be general in light of the vast amount of concrete material. First, a general evaluative description will be made. Second, the weakness of the seminar will be described. Third, its strength will be cited. Finally, the clinical implication for various types of individuals will be noted. Criticism is perhaps too strong a word to use when seeking to evaluate Gothard. Criticism is not what a developing child or a creative artist needs when he begins a project. Gothard's project is clearly just beginning if he is attempting to develop a biblical psychology or to relate the Scripture to the full range of Christian experience. What Gothard has developed in a most basic sense is a psychology of God the Father. It is a psychology of the vertical relationship with God, a psychology of submission and obedience. It is a psychology of passive acceptance and of being the follower. If the whole seminar can be summed up in a phrase, it is: "Have the right attitude." Have the right attitude toward everything—God, self, family, conscience, rights, sensuality, friends, and all of life.

Gothard's biblical psychology has its strengths and weaknesses in terms of its basic emphasis, thrust, and focus. Because the material is so massive (over 160 outlined pages) and so concrete (as many as ten verses on some pages) there may be fragmentary or passing comments which run counter to these thrusts or focus of these themes, but the themes remain. First, there is no emphasis on human, peer, or interpersonal relationships as such. The whole of what might be called the horizontal aspect of human or Christian experience is either eclipsed by the authority (chain of command) emphasis or is simply omitted. When Gothard does describe interpersonal relationships such as enemies, family, dating, or friendship they are discussed from the viewpoint of God's design or purpose for them or their position in the chain of command. Perhaps the best example of this focus is the husband-wife relationship. The wife is always described as under her husband and over the children. Her relationship to her husband as peer, coparent, and helpmate is simply not discussed. A marriage relationship can hardly be adequate with only the authority dimension present. In addition, Gothard seems to stress and direct most of his attention to the bottom of the chain, i.e., to the wife and not the husband; to the adolescent and not the parents; and to the employee and not the employer. In fact in the seminar there is nothing said about the correct attitude and behavior of those higher in the chain. Those on the bottom are to leave those higher up to God. This one-sided emphasis is corrected in the Advanced (leadership) Seminar where a great deal of attention is directed to men, husbands, and leaders and nothing is said to women (who are not present). Presumably women have no leadership function, even as parents.

There is an even greater difficulty created by the exclusion of the relational dimension of human experience; the whole interpersonal aspect of the Christian community on fellowship *(koinonia)* and brotherly love *(phileo)* is lost. Much if not all of the biblical concept of agape-love is also ignored. Thus, the supportive, nurturant, and therapeutic aspects of the body of Christ are not mentioned, and such passages as Romans 15:1, 2 Corinthians 1:14; Galatians 6:2; 1 Thessalonians 5:14; Hebrews 12:12 are ignored. Needless to say, the base for therapy or counseling is eliminated when the interpersonal dimension is ignored. Without a therapist who supports, empathizes, or allows transference, most of the standard counseling and therapeutic approaches are not possible. The missing dimension of relationships is evident in Gothard's approach to therapy described above: rebirth, memorization, meditation, prayer, and fasting are for the most part carried out alone. At only one point was another person mentioned as a therapeutic agent. In a passing remark Gothard says that he had a friend who listened regularly to his memory work and offered spiritual suggestions. Without these sessions Gothard says he would not be where he is today. This relationship sounds like counseling or therapy, but there is nothing in Gothard's model or approach to explain why a counselor was a clinical necessity for him or why it is a clinical necessity for others.

Some of the imbalance created by ignoring the church or community aspect of Christian experience is rectified by Gothard's discussion in the Advanced Seminar of helping the widow. He also recommends that fathers relate more to their families and that they encourage their children to seek personal advice from grandparents and other relatives. However, the larger community of believers is ignored as far as fellowship *(koinonia)* is concerned and relationship to the larger family exists solely to assist individual growth. Nevertheless even with these modifications the New Testament's emphasis on love (both *agape* and *phileo*) remains absent. The omission of the interpersonal or relational dimension including love, fellowship, and any affectional human emotions constitutes a glaring omission of staggering proportions in light of their place and emphasis in the New Testament.

In addition to the absent relational dimension, the inner dimension of spontaneity, joy, and the freedom and liberty which exist in Christ is absent. Gothard's psychology of the vertical dimension stresses obedience and rule-keeping. Gothard repeatedly says throughout the seminar that there are an X number of reasons why some specific action should or should not be undertaken. In fact the Bible for Gothard appears to be a book of rules and not the revelation of a person. God seems to be an impersonal diety who articulated a vast number of principles for human beings to follow with varying degrees of consequences for disobedience. Gothard's God in a real sense is not a loving Father caring for his children, but a cosmic deity who requires human conformity to his principles. Gothard's God is the God of Mount Sinai but *not* the God of John 3:16 or 1 John 3:1. Consequently Gothard's seminar has a conformity-obedience-achievement emphasis which seems to assume the believer is a rebel who needs to be pressured into conformity. Conformity is maintained by obedience and a conscious effort at eliminating nonconformity lest rebellious behavior spontaneously emerge. Freedom is freedom to obey or do as one ought, *not* the freedom to love, serve, and enjoy God. The affective-emotional side of man which leads to joy, spontaneity, creativity, and love is dissolved into rule-keeping. Gothard's rule-keeping approach tends toward sanctification by works which Paul inveighs so strongly against in Galatians 3 and Colossians 2. The loving response of the believer to God's love is never discussed (1 John 4:19) nor the joy of Christian life as a basis for response to God (Phil. 2:1-2). Thus Gothard's system tends to have a morality of law (legalism) emphasis rather than the love-grace morality emphasis of the New Testament (1 John 3:10-11, 4:19; Gal. 3:1-3; Col. 2:20–3:4; Rom. 6:14-15).

However, Gothard's system should be commended for its strengths. It is obvious that Gothard has spent a great deal of time searching the Scripture and meditating on its implications. The wealth of the biblical material dealing with men in the red notebook will provide a rich stimulus for anyone seeking to develop a biblical psychology for years to come. In this regard several aspects of his system should be stressed. One, Gothard has a depth dynamic model of pathology in keeping with the scriptural emphasis on the heart. Two, he has a dynamic model of psychic functioning in stressing the relationship of the body, soul, and spirit. Three, Gothard stresses inner attitudes as fundamental to actions rather than the reverse which is consistent with Scripture. Four, Gothard in outlining his basic principles for living has discovered some basic biblical principles which have psychological counterparts. Five, Gothard cites a vast number of Scripture verses which have psychological implications (though at points he appears to be proof texting and exegetically weak). Six, by stressing prayer, fasting, and meditation Gothard has called attention to some dynamic biblical therapeutic processes.

Many of the potential therapeutic strengths of Gothard's dynamic and inner emphasis, however, are lost because he stressed doing, controlling, and making oneself live the Christian life. Even his focus on having the right attitudes becomes something to be done; some part of one's life needs to be controlled. The passive commands dealing with the inner life, such as "let the peace of God rule in your hearts" (Col. 3:15), "abide in me" (John 15:4), "be anxious for nothing" (Phil. 4:6), are either ignored or tend to be turned into actions. Fasting tends to become a coping mechanism to deal with certain problems or situations. Meditation tends to become a mechanism to create inner balance or spirituality. Thus the rule-keeping emphasis of the seminar tends to eclipse depth and inner and dynamic aspects and transforms the biblical therapeutics into a self-sanctification by works or doing.

I have said "tends toward a doing approach" because the rule-keeping and obedience emphasis of the vertical dimension is *overly* stressed by Gothard. However, obedience is a biblical principle. The average Christian (i.e., someone with good self-image or good ego strength) can benefit from his exposure to the seminar, as I myself have, because he is able to focus on those aspects relevant to his life and ignore the rest. Thus for the average, normal, healthy individual Gothard's seminar is like a smorgasbord where the individual can select what he needs or wants and can ignore the rest. However, persons with weak egos or depressive tendencies do not fare so well. I know of eight therapists in addition to myself who have seen people with depressive symptoms either during or shortly after the seminar. Their symptoms are obviously part of the personality and defense structure. However, the massive number of rules or principles to be followed trigger off the symptoms in individuals who were already having difficulty. On the other hand persons with obsessional tendencies probably fare much better as long as they can tie into Gothard's system and continue to expand their obsessional defenses. One of the therapists mentioned above, who has an extensive client load from a very large evangelical church, has frequently picked up clients whose obsessional defenses have failed about six months after attending the Gothard seminar.

Perhaps clinically Gothard's seminar can be summed up in Christ's words. "For whosoever hath, to him shall be given, and he shall have more abundance; but whosoever hath not, from him shall be taken away even that which he hath" (Matt. 13:12). Those Christians who are basically psychologically healthy can benefit spiritually from the seminar while many with pathological tendencies do not benefit. Also individuals who are "acting out" and need controls seem to benefit from the obedience control emphasis but underlying dynamics may not be touched. Theoretically and structurally, Gothard's psychology of God the Father, authority, obedience, and the vertical dimension needs to be balanced. Gothard needs to add the psychology of Christ, the church, and human relationships, i.e., the psychology of warmth, fellowship, and love with other believers. He also needs to add the psychology of the Spirit, the fruit of the Spirit, and abiding or walking in the Spirit, i.e., the psychology of joy, spontaneity, worship, and dynamic living. With these additions to his system Gothard could be well on his way to a biblical psychology.

References

Mowrer, O. H. *The Crisis in Psychiatry and Religion.* Princeton, N.J.: Van Nostrand, 1961.
———. *The New Group Therapy.* Princeton, N.J.: Van Nostrand, 1964.
Nee, W. *The Release of the Spirit.* Indianapolis: Sure Foundation, 1964.
———. *The Spiritual Man,* Vols. 1, 2. New York: Christian Fellowship, 1968.

BIBLICAL COUNSELING:
A BASIC VIEW

Lawrence J. Crabb, Jr.

When someone states that he will discuss a biblical approach to counseling, one has very little idea what to expect. Conferences on Christian psychology and biblical prophecy have much in common. Advocates of radically different viewpoints each claim Spirit-led support from the infallible Word. Pre-tribs, mid-tribs, and post-tribs debate the timing of the rapture while a-mils and pre-mils decide what to do with the Jews. It's reassuring to realize that God is not waiting for a unanimous vote before he acts.

Christian counselors similarly find themselves divided in their understanding of which approach to counseling is truly biblical. Christianized versions of T.A., gestalt therapy, rational-emotive therapy, psychoanalysis, and behavior modification continue to compete for the allegiance of evangelicals. For some, confusion has given way to clarity in Bill Gothard's Systematic Theology of Practical Christian Living. Others have warmly responded to the nouthetic counselors' insistence that their approach is truly biblical. How does one go about typing everything together into a package and calling it biblical?

The first step seems to be arriving at a broad position on the thorny and far-from-resolved problem of integrating psychology and Christianity. The integration is simple enough to describe. There is a body of revealed truth in propositional form to which all true evanglicals are committed as the inerrant inspired Word of God. There is another vast literature consisting of the diverse, sometimes contradictory, theories and observations which we can simply call secular psychology. Let each be symbolized by a circle. The circle of revealed truth revolves around the person and work of Jesus Christ. Secular psychology is built upon the very different presupposition of humanism, a doctrine which fervently insists that man is the central being in the universe and that his individual welfare is supreme. The question facing the integrationist is "What is the relationship between the two circles?"

Evangelicals have generally followed one of four positions. Some folks regard the two fields as *separate but equal.* If you have the flu, see a physician. If you want to design a building, talk with an architect. If you suffer from psychological disorder, consult a psychologist or psychiatrist. The most critical issue in selecting a professional to help you is competence, not religious beliefs. If your problems are spiritual, however, check with your pastor. This position can be sketched like this.

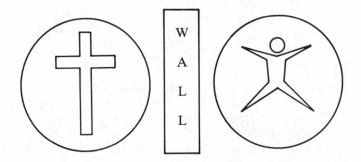

A second group tend to snatch a few relevant concepts from Scripture, mix them with helpful ideas from psychology, and serve up a tasty blend called Christian psychotherapy. The problem with this approach, which I call the *tossed salad* model, is that concepts with antagonistic presuppositions do not get along well over time. A definite tension exists which can be resolved either by discarding all but one set of presuppositions or by adopting a Hegelian view in which truth exists in the interplay between opposite positions. The latter solution, which has crept into much of our thinking, is spiritual suicide. Rather than concerning ourselves with final truth based on Scripture, we use whatever procedure seems right to us according to the pragmatic criterion "Does it work?" We assume that truth represents that synthesis of all competing ideas which seems to best fit the current situation. The absolutes of Scripture become flexible limits which can bend to accommodate our understanding of what appears most workable. Biblical epistemology however is firmly rooted in the logical law of antithesis (if A is true, Non A is false) which absolutely refuses to accept concepts which are in any way inconsistent with each other regardless of their apparent value. When we treat this law casually, the authority of Scripture is lost and man's wisdom becomes supreme. There is a way that seems right to a man, but Scripture teaches that the long-term consequence of following that is spiritual death. We must not only insist upon the authority of Scripture but we must also go to great lengths to be sure that all of our concepts come under that authority. At the very least, that means (1) that integrationists will need to be as familiar with Scripture as they are with psychology and (2) that whenever the findings of psychological research contradict Scripture, these findings will be discarded.

We might sketch the *tossed salad* model in this way.

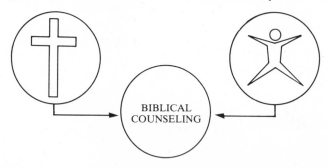

A third group has neatly solved the problem of integrating the two disciplines by eliminating one of them. Because they insist that secular psychology, with its humanistic stain, has nothing to offer, I call them *nothing butterists*. Nothing but the Word. Nothing but the Lord. Nothing but faith. This approach can be easily sketched.

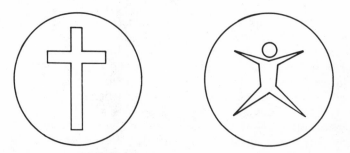

Many of our current popularizers of Christian psychology, especially those from the pastoral community, would fall into this category. I take issue with my nothing-butterist colleagues on at least two grounds: (1) their insistence that psychology has nothing to offer. I rather think that much truth has been discovered which in no way violates the truth which God has propositionally revealed. (2) For some reason, nothing butterists seem to reduce counseling to a simplistic model of "identify sin and command change." A certain gentle sensitivity to emotional pain is often lost in their unwarranted assumption that all problems reflect willful sin.

I subscribe to a fourth view of integration which I call *spoiling the Egyptians.* Leave Egypt in the strength of a redeeming God, absolutely depend upon his infinite resources, refuse any compromise with his commands but gladly accept whatever help God provokes the Egyptians to offer. Let me sketch the model this way.

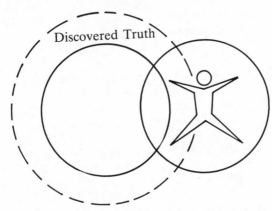

Secular psychology often stumbles onto a biblical concept, then develops it through research. Christians are free to profit from the thinking of secular psychologists but must carefully screen and reject the concepts which depend upon humanistic presuppositions and contradict Scripture. Whatever involves no departure from the character and word of God is quite acceptable as sustenance on our difficult journey to the Promised Land. As I sketch my model, you'll notice that I have spoiled a number of Egyptians, who although they are regrettably still in Egypt have helped me in my pursuit of a biblical psychology.

After choosing a position on integration, the next step in developing a biblical model is to define the limits of what can be considered biblical, or put another way, to clearly articulate the presuppositionary base upon which one intends to build. We need to agree on a few clear essentials, a form broad enough to include every possible fragment of relevant truth but narrow enough to deserve the title biblical. One conservative theologian has stated that the central presupposition of Christianity is Jesus Christ as the second person of the sovereign triune God as presented in the Bible, his infallible Word. He adds that this presupposition is ". . . the central truth of the entire system of truth and reality in the universe, the truth so

integrated with all other truth as to sustain it and be revealed in it."
Everyone who accepts this belief and is fervently committed to working
within its broad boundaries can rightly be called evangelical. Those who
reject or question this position should not, in my judgment, call themselves
evangelical.

I begin my model with the irreducible fact that an infinite personal God
really exists. He is infinite, but I am finite. I am therefore a contingent
being. He is personal and I too am personal, made in his image. So I am a
dependent personal being. As a personal being, I have certain personal
needs which must be met if I am to truly live as a person. As a contingent
being, these needs must be met outside of myself. What are these personal
needs? Paul stated that his purpose in life was Christ; to honor him, please
him, serve him. Frankl insists that our lives require a meaning beyond
ourselves. I am suggesting that our first personal need is *significance,* the
compelling necessity to see our lives as fitting into and moving toward a
logically meaningful goal.

The second essential ingredient required for effective personal living is
security, the experience of being loved unconditionally by someone whole.
Glasser stresses the need to be caringly involved with at least one other
person. Rogers builds his entire approach to counseling around this need for
genuine, unconditional, nonpossessive acceptance. Paul basked in the
thrilling knowledge of a personal God who loved him and gave himself for
him. I am proposing, without taking further time to defend it, that as a
personal being I basically need significance and security if I am to be truly
whole.

As a contingent being, I require a source of meaning and love outside of
myself. No finite point can serve as its own framework for integration. The
finite depends for its existence and character on its infinite context. I am
finite. So I turn to the infinite. If that something infinite is impersonal, then
I am in trouble. Undesigned impersonality can provide nothing but
random direction which is logically meaningless and brute impersonal
matter which is incapable of love. If there is no personal God, or if I fail to
make him the context of my life, then I can have neither significance nor
security. If the infinite however is personal then there is meaning available
in infinite design and direction. I become a truly significant being in a
meaningfully ordered universe, a being who can actually shape the course
of history by my choices. I can also enter into a relationship with a personal
God. We are two persons who can care for each other. There is therefore
love available through involvement with the infinite Person. Christians
believe that the only valid source of significance, a life full of meaning, and
security, a persevering love which accepts me at my worst, is Christ.

But our entire race has been separated from God by sin. Apart from God
we are left to our own resources to meet our needs. And so we develop
alternative strategies for finding significance and security, strategies which
will sooner or later not work. They must fail, if not now, then in hell

forever. *It is my thinking that the core of all psychopathology is the desperate but sinful attempt to meet needs apart from God, an attempt based on the satanically inspired belief that it can be done.* All of us have been programed by Satan through a false world system to believe that in order to be significant and secure, we need _____. How we have learned to finish that sentence is the basic problem. We believe a lie and we organize our lives around it. Adler calls this a guiding fiction. Perhaps we believe that our personal worth (our significance or our security) depends upon financial success, flawless behavior, great achievement, consistent praise, the absence of all criticism, a loving spouse, a closely knit family, and the like.

Some of these beliefs are more realistic and achievable than others. As long as life provides what we believe we need, we function relatively well. But life apart from God guarantees nothing. Stephan Crane tells of the man who approached the universe and said: "Sir, I exist." To which the universe responded, "However, that fact creates in me no sense of obligation."

Whenever a problem arises which we unconsciously believe is a threat to our significance or security, we consciously *evaluate* that event as terrible and consequently *feel* personally threatened. We may try another behavioral approach to overcoming this obstacle to our significance and security, and if we are successful, we feel much better. But the real problem has not been solved. We are still depending on something other than God and what he chooses to provide to meet our needs. Our modern thinking on marriage offers a classic example of depending upon something or someone other than God to meet our deepest needs. So many books teaching women how to be Christian wives are really textbooks on how to more effectively manipulate husbands. The message seems to be, "You need your husband to love you or you can never be secure; here are a few feminine tricks to seduce your husband into meeting your needs." Now I have not the slightest objections when my wife follows every bit of the advice offered in these books. I love it. But I am concerned that a central problem is remaining untouched: Spouses are regularly turning to each other to meet their personal needs. I call this a tick on a dog relationship. The problem with most such marriages is that there are two ticks and no dog.

If we cannot manipulate our environment to better provide for our needs, the natural response is to retreat into a position of safety. "If my husband cuts me down, I will establish a distance between us so that his cuts won't hurt as much." Now what is the problem here? With her conscious mind, this woman evaluates the event of her husband's criticism as terrible. This evaluation is the visible evidence of a deeply programed belief that she needs her husband's love if she is to exist as a secure worthwhile person. To rebuke her withdrawal and, in the name of Scripture, to command submissive acceptance of her husband is to suggest that she put her personal neck on the chopping block. Before she will be able to willingly and rationally move toward her husband, she will have to change her mind about what she requires to be secure.

Let me sketch my theory of mental health and psychopathology.

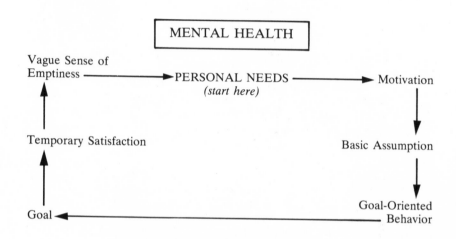

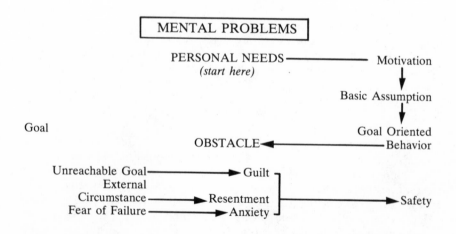

I need significance and security. I am motivated to meet my needs. I learn a basic assumption which tells me what goal I must reach in order to become significant and secure. I then engage in behavior designed to reach that goal. If my behavior is effective and I reach the goal, I feel good. But, because nothing apart from Christ truly satisfies, I sense a vague discontent and go back through the cycle again. I believe that most people today whom we would not call neurotic function in the way the sketch of mental health suggests.

If however I encounter an obstacle en route to meeting my goal, I become frustrated. Behavior therapists, reality therapists, nouthetic counselors, and others emphasize changing your behavior from inappropriate to appropriate, or from irresponsible to responsible, or from sinful to biblical. But the real problem is not the behavior. The person is headed toward a wrong goal determined by a false idea about what constitutes significance and security.

If the obstacle derives from an unreachable goal (for example, I need to be perfect in order to be loved), the person will likely come down hard on himself for failing to reach the necessary goal and feel guilty. If the obstacle is an environmental circumstance (for example, I need to win the promotion to be significant but the boss gave it to another), the likely consequence is resentment against whatever the client perceives as blocking his path to the goal. A third possible obstacle is a fear of failure, for example, "I need to have a man love me but I'm afraid to get married; my husband might reject me." In this case, the predictable psychological reaction is anxiety. Miller and Dollard's classic conflict paradigm is helpful in understanding this particular disorder.

People who fail to reach their goals and who therefore feel insignificant and insecure tend to desire protection from further hurt. I agree with Adler that most neurotic symptoms are best understood as moving the person toward safety. If I am too depressed to work, I cannot fail on the job. If I suffer from a compulsive disorder, my husband's rejection will be a response to my problem, not to me. Neurotic symptoms often have a rather complex etiology but are most easily understood by a teleological analysis of what goals the symptoms are directed toward, what is achieved through the symptoms, safety from what.

A woman once consulted me concerning severe, almost continuous headaches which apparently had an organic basis but which had plagued her for nearly two years. By studying the consequences of the headaches, it became clear that they were having at least two definite effects. First her mother was displaying a great deal of interest and concern in her because of the headaches and second, her mother was terribly inconvenienced and very worried about them. Further analysis suggested that my client's basic assumption involved the belief that she desperately needed her mother's love in order to be secure. She had encountered two obstacles en route to the goal: (1) a fear of failure which created anxiety and (2) an environmental block (her mother, who had in some ways rejected her) which produced resentment. The headaches relieved her fear of rejection by eliciting attention, and they also served as a safe expression of hostility toward her mother. To openly discuss her relationship with her mother would have been too threatening and to verbally express her anger would have risked further rejection. The symptoms therefore moved her toward a safe but costly resolution of her problems. When my client understood the reason for her headaches, we then discussed her wrong belief that she needed her mother's love in order to be secure. As she slowly began to grasp the love of the Lord, she began to initiate the break in appropriate dependency. Over a period of three months her headaches disappeared.

Paul tells us that the essential element in transformation is renewing our minds. Skinner renews circumstances. Rogers renews feelings. Glasser renews behavior. Analysts renew the personality. Christ renews minds. The basis of all transformation is to think differently, to believe differently, to change your basic assumptions. About what? Understand that your significance and security as a contingent personal being depends exclusively on your relationship to Christ.

The big problem, of course, is grasping that biblical insight in a way that really transforms us. To tell a depressed person that "Jesus loves you" usually elicits about as much interest as informing someone who is starving that a balanced diet is important for health.

How can we change the thinking of our clients and ourselves in a way that touches our deepest inward parts where it really counts? Let me illustrate. A woman consulted me concerning her habit of uncontrollably lashing out at people who in any way crossed her. How do you go about helping her? Insisting that she control her behavior in accord with biblical standards had produced nothing but frustration. She was a sincere Christian who for years had been trying to behave more graciously but experienced consistent defeat. She was at the point of wondering whether God really existed and, if he did, whether he cared about her at all.

My first concern was to communicate that I accepted her. Since my acceptance would be meaningless till she knew that I understood how she felt, I simply tried to empathize with her, to enter at least a bit into the emotional pain she felt. She began to share the hurt she experienced at the hands of her harshly rejecting mother. She then shared her deep fear of being rejected again. We discussed her present reactions to the experience of rejection, how perhaps, she was lashing out in a defensive attempt to protect herself whenever she felt threatened. At that point I began exploring her basic assumptions about what constituted security. Massive rejection as a child had taught her that rejection hurt and it hurt badly. She came to approach life with the idea, the guiding fiction, that she could not exist as a secure person in the presence of any criticism or rejection. Her central problem to my way of thinking was a false assumption, the belief that she was worthless unless she was totally loved by everyone. She believed that any rejection rendered her hopelessly insecure. Now that simply isn't true. A person's security rests on the love of Christ and his atoning work on the cross by which he can forever accept anyone who trusts in him as Savior. But because she unconsciously believed that her security rested on the absence of rejection, she evaluated any current rejection as terrible, she felt angry toward those who were stripping her of her security, and she lashed out.

She understood that the Lord loved her but had never thought through the relevance of his love to her need for personal security. She was still chained to other people, depending on their love, and furious with them for letting her down so often. When I explained to her that her security in Christ made her free from *needing* acceptance from everyone else, her response was, "Swell, now how do I stop getting mad?"

It is at this point that counseling cannot proceed without a commitment to believe what God says. Resistance often becomes a problem because the sin nature is thoroughly committed to unbelief. This particular woman however did agree that the Scripture was true and that she would co-operate in a program to make it *experientially* true in her life. I then instructed her to write on a three-by-five card the sentence "All I need to be secure is Jesus' love and I have it; therefore I have all that I need to respond in any situation as a secure woman." Whenever she felt angry, she was to picture her mind as a tape recorder and consciously thrust into the recorder a tape which played this sentence over and over. Then, and here is another critical point in therapy which often takes a while to work through, she was to deliberately choose by an act of her will to say something kind to her attacker, believing that she had all she needed within her to do so. She was to choose this behavior regardless of how she felt.

After the first week, she reported that she would say a few gracious things but only through gritted teeth. She still felt furious. After several weeks of religiously following the program, she burst into tears in my office and said, "For the first time in my life, I can really believe that Jesus loves me." Further therapy helped her come to the point where she could express her anger acceptably, without a bitter spirit, in an attempt to constructively deal with problem relationships.

The entire process of counseling can be sketched in a simple seven-stage model.

It seems to me this model lays down a broad form within which there is considerable room for freedom in technique and approach. Rogerian reflection is useful at Stage 1. Adlerian life-style analysis is helpful at Stage 2. Stage 3 can sometimes be facilitated by free association, dream analysis, and historical tracing. Cognitive restructuring, cognitive dissonance theory, and rational-emotive procedures are all appropriate at Stage 4. Gestalt techniques, straightforward moral persuasion, and contractual agreement may help in Stage 5. Behavior modification, psychoactive drugs, and hypnosis have a place in Stage 6. And Stage 7 is the sabbath—sit back and enjoy what has happened. Rest in the wonderful feelings of realized significance and security.

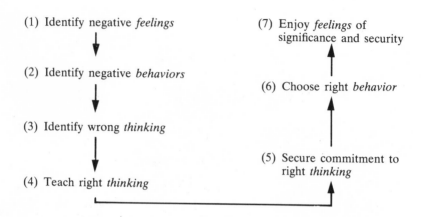

(1) Identify negative *feelings*

(2) Identify negative *behaviors*

(3) Identify wrong *thinking*

(4) Teach right *thinking*

(7) Enjoy *feelings* of significance and security

(6) Choose right *behavior*

(5) Secure commitment to right *thinking*

The Place of the Local Church in Biblical Counseling

Wouldn't it be nice if it all worked that smoothly? The truth of the matter is that counseling rarely proceeds quite so nicely. One reason why our counseling efforts so often do not really reach the final stage of enjoying the results is because we are failing to use a major God-given resource as effectively as we should. I am speaking of the local church. Let me close this paper by suggesting a few thoughts in this regard.

If we agree that a person's basic personal needs are significance and security it can be seen that the input of the local church becomes critical in promoting personal maturity. Significance comes from understanding that I belong to the God of the universe who is directing my life as a part of the most important project going on in the world today, the building of the church of Jesus Christ. I can really make a difference in my world for eternity. I can have impact. Pastors and congregations need to stop thinking of the pastor as endowed with all the gifts and responsibility to do the work of the church. Paul teaches in Ephesians that pastors are to equip the saints for the work of the ministry, so that they too can enjoy the thrilling significance of contributing to God's eternal purposes. A man in my home church was utterly miserable a year ago. His marriage was on the rocks, he felt depressed, and he was losing his grasp on God. Although he was able to keep functioning and to pretend that he was a happy Christian, he felt alone, inadequate, and hopeless. In this past year he has come to see himself as a minister, building up other people in the local body, sharing with them what he knows of the Lord by heading a small group Bible study, helping his wife develop spiritually by loving her as Christ loved the church. Today he is a vibrant, excited, whole Christian, still battling depression sometimes but growing stronger all the time.

Local churches are not only uniquely designed to provide a vehicle for meeting significant needs, they are also a natural resource for developing

Christian security. What a tragedy that in so many churches fellowship is reduced to sitting next to another believer for one hour a week, sharing a hymnbook, shaking his hand, and glibly commenting, "Nice sermon today, wasn't it." God designed local bodies to experience close, open, deep relationships. Meaningful Christian fellowship, where I share a burden and you help me, where I bring you food when you're sick, where we get together during the week to encourage one another, to discuss problems with our kids and to seek God's wisdom, where I know you'll accept me no matter what I do—meaningful Christian fellowship goes a long way toward meeting security needs.

In an effort to narrow the distressingly wide gap between the ideal and reality, I am beginning in South Florida a counselor training program to help local churches become communities where personal needs can better be met. I define three levels of counseling based on the seven-stage model I have already presented.

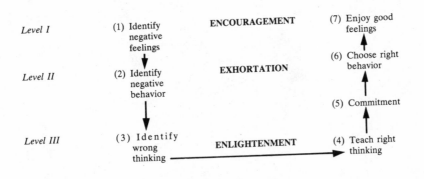

Level I   Counseling by Encouragement
Every member of the body needs to be trained in level I counseling: how to be more sensitive, how to listen, how to communicate care.

Level II   Counseling by Exhortation
A group of mature believers can be taught biblical principles for handling common problem areas and trained to help people approach difficulties biblically.

Level III   Counseling by Enlightenment
A few selected Christians in each local church could be trained in perhaps six months to a year of once a week classes to handle the deeper, more stubborn problems which don't yield to encouragement or exhortation.

Counseling people who desperately need significance and security in an environment which potentially provides both is an exciting possibility. Counseling in that setting should help us to better grasp that Jesus Christ, the second person of the sovereign, triune Godhead as revealed in the inerrant, infallible, objective Word of God, is the foundation of all counseling that is truly biblical because he alone can meet our deepest personal needs.

Adams, J., 88, 92, 144, 158, 236, 276, 377, 378, 380-82, 386-401
Adler, A., 324, 340, 400, 419, 421
Aggression, 28, 49, 61, 134, 136, 363-64
American Psychological Association (APA), 83
Allport, G., 41, 66-68, 70, 72, 73, 76, 86, 132, 145, 218, 244, 375
Anger, 127, 130, 202, 392
Anthropology, theological, 98, 99, 103, 104
Anti-Christian bias, 53
Anti-religious bias, 15
Anti-Supernatural bias, 84
Aristotelian, 15
Arminianism, 17, 108

Behavior modification, 82, 112, 116, 118-20, 254, 258, 325, 356-67, 420
Behaviorism, 15, 54, 56, 57, 82
Behavioristic orientation, 43, 54, 104, 112, 365, 366

Calvinism, 17, 49, 108
Christian Association for Psychological Studies (CAPS), 54, 92, 173
Client-centered therapy, 48, 51, 52, 348-54
Clinical Pastoral Education (CPE), 46-48
Cognitive development, 178-88, 190-98, 200-210
Cognitive theory, therapy, 228-30, 254-72
Committed religious orientation, 66, 67, 71-76, 78, 79, 184, 186, 188, 225, 226
Conscience, 32, 40, 84, 129, 213, 240, 248, 249, 332, 404, 405
Consensual religious orientation, 67, 68, 70, 72-79, 184, 186, 188
Conservation of objects, 193, 197, 369, 370
Conservative, 31-34, 39, 40, 88, 97
Constructive sorrow, 248-53
Conversion, 28, 45, 53, 179, 216-26
Counsel for Clinical Pastoral Training, 50
Counseling. See Psychotherapy

Depravity, 31
Determinism, 40, 57, 291
Diagnostic and Statistical Manual, 304
Dispensationalism, 17
Dogmatism, 218-26
Duke University, 51

Ellis, A., 42, 83, 84, 96, 254-56, 265
Erikson, E., 190
Existentialism, 105, 337-43, 350
Existentialist, 33
Extrinsic, 66-68, 70, 71, 74, 77-79, 218-26

Fear, 35-37
Forgiveness, 51, 237, 238, 243, 298-300
Frankl, V., 28, 86, 87, 325, 337-46, 378, 392, 400, 418
Freud, S., 15, 41, 44, 51, 83, 84, 88, 96, 325, 326, 327-35, 340, 350, 378, 399, 400
Freudian, 27, 43, 53, 399
Fromm, E., 83, 96, 319
Fuller School of Psychology, 51

Gestalt Psychology, 56
God, 28, 30, 41-44, 46, 73, 87, 89, 90, 97, 98, 102, 105-9, 117, 118, 123, 124, 126-31, 133-37, 140-42, 144-46, 156, 158, 161, 163, 164, 167, 169, 171-75, 208, 212-14, 241, 243, 267-71, 277, 298-300, 310, 317, 325, 328, 331-35, 341-43, 346, 349, 350, 353, 356-58, 364, 366, 371-75, 387-89, 391-93, 395-97, 400, 406-8, 410-13, 416-19, 421, 423-26
Gothard, B., 377-79, 381-84, 385, 402-13
Guilt, 21, 28, 30, 32, 46, 51, 84, 104, 166, 175, 176, 228, 229, 242, 248-53, 276, 277, 327, 351, 352, 383

Hamartiology, 100, 104-6
Healing, 40, 53, 108, 176, 243, 275, 277
Health/Healthy, 121, 122, 140, 143-46, 154, 335
Hell, 49, 50, 178
Hermeneutics, 234
Holiness, 121, 122, 140-43, 145, 146, 156
Holy Spirit, 30, 31, 33, 38, 87, 97, 98, 112, 117, 118-20, 142, 161, 162, 175, 242, 267-69, 275, 371, 375, 393, 394, 413
Homosexual behavior and condition, 296-98
Homosexuality, 281, 282, 285, 286, 287-92, 295-300, 301-15, 396; types of,, 305-6
Humanistic Psychology, 59

Identification, 69, 276, 278
Identity, 38, 240
Integration, 15-23, 29-31, 48, 49, 54, 57, 59, 60, 86, 97, 98, 114, 141, 148; models of, 18-21, 54, 55,

Integration (con't.)
81, 95, 99-111, 114, 122, 148, 158-60, 235, 243, 244
Internalization/Interiorization, 67, 69, 70, 126, 181, 182, 225, 226, 249, 252, 253, 270
Intimacy, 49, 123, 167, 171-77
Intrinsic, 66-68, 69, 71-73

James, W., 83, 375
Jesus Christ, 18, 29, 30, 38, 45, 53, 87, 97, 98, 106-9, 118, 120, 123, 126, 127, 134, 135, 137, 141, 142, 144-46, 156, 158, 161-64, 166, 167, 174, 179, 195, 196, 200-202, 204-9, 214, 216, 228, 229, 231-45, 267, 269, 270, 300, 310, 325, 350, 351, 361, 384, 391, 396, 397, 407, 408, 413, 414, 417, 418, 420-24
Journal of American Scientific Affiliation, 90
Journal of Clinical Psychology, 86
Journal of Psychology and Theology, 24, 41-43, 54, 90
Journal of Pastoral Care, 39
Jung, C., 83, 88, 96, 121, 122, 150-53, 154, 176, 324, 340

Kohlberg, L., 56, 178, 179, 200, 202, 203, 211-15

Levels of scientific inquiry, 54, 55, 56, 162; data, 17, 18, 48, 55, 58, 62, 63, 90, 141; theory, 17, 18, 48, 55, 57, 58, 63, 90, 102
Liberal, 39, 40, 49-53, 88, 97, 286
Link-Care Foundation, 52
Logotherapy, 47, 339, 343-46
Love, 28, 89

Maslow, A., 42, 62, 110, 121, 123, 131, 164, 166, 167, 169, 177, 346, 400
Maturity, 66, 86, 121-38, 148-60, 172, 179, 185, 191, 200, 302, 407-9, 424
May, R., 121, 400
Mind, 15
Mind/Body problem, 40, 95, 96
Moral development, 200-215
Morality, 32, 33, 289-93, 295, 331, 332, 338
Mowrer, O., 36, 52, 85, 96, 110, 175, 378, 386, 392, 394, 398, 399, 404, 405

Naturalism, 84
Nature of man, 21, 27, 29, 51, 85, 103, 104, 155, 159, 320-43, 386-88, 397, 403-5
Noutheteo, 390, 391, 398
Nouthetic Counseling, 41, 47, 378, 386-401

Paraklesis, 94, 398
Piaget, J., 55, 56, 178-80, 182, 184, 186, 187, 190, 191, 201-5, 207-9, 368-74
Pastoral Counseling, 38-41, 50, 51
Peer Counseling, 52
Phenomenological, 104, 105
Prayer, 48, 184
Psychoanalysis, 15, 30, 82, 327-35

Psychoanalytic Theory, 27, 48, 51, 52, 104, 148, 324, 366, 399
Psychoanalytic Therapy, 53, 229
Psychopathology, 91, 101, 103-5, 108, 142, 143, 145, 293, 387, 389, 390, 394, 397, 399, 403-7, 419, 420
Psychotherapy, 20, 46, 53, 101, 171, 228-36, 282, 301, 310-12, 318, 333, 334, 348-54, 399, 407-9, 415
Purpose in Life, 218-26

Rational-Emotive Therapy, 50
Reformation, 29
Reformed, 122, 161
Religiosity, dichotomous model of, 66-68; trichotomous model of, 66, 68-79
Religious development, 180-84
Responsibility, 27, 32, 53, 109, 110, 200, 201, 203, 299, 337-40, 344, 345, 358
Reinforcement, 116
Rogers, C., 27, 42, 51, 52, 88, 109, 110, 121, 122, 148-54, 157, 162, 164, 190, 244, 276, 324, 325, 348-54, 378, 400, 418, 422
Rogerian, 43, 52, 82, 228, 230, 276, 395, 399, 400
Rosemead Graduate School of Professional Psychology, 51

Salvation, 29, 32, 50, 52, 132, 155, 157, 158, 176
Sanctification, 32, 100, 121, 123, 142, 155, 161, 167, 168, 169, 229, 230, 254, 267-75, 393
Scientific Method, 43
Self-actualization, 62, 84, 110, 121-23, 131, 143-45, 148-49, 152-54, 156-60, 161-69, 173
Self-esteem, 247, 250, 251
Self-verbalization, 254-67
Sex, 27, 28, 61, 381, 404; the fear of, 49
Sexual dysfunction, 317-22
Sexuality, 20, 281-323
Sin, 16, 52, 53, 91, 103, 104, 108, 121, 124-38, 143, 144, 163, 171, 176, 198, 209, 232, 242, 250, 268, 270, 281, 296, 299, 350, 389, 394, 395, 397, 398, 409, 418
Sinful, 32, 292
Skinner, B. F., 42, 44, 58, 360, 362, 365, 388
Soteriology, 91, 92, 100, 104
Soul, 15, 103, 144, 397, 403-5, 412
Spilka, B., 66-68, 72-78, 184-88, 373
Spirit of man, 82, 85, 103, 117, 119, 175, 397, 403-5
Superego, 32, 405
Supernatural, 38, 46, 53, 88

Ten Commandments, 213
Tournier, P., 28, 42, 47, 275, 276, 379, 381

Values, 69, 284, 289, 353

Watson, J. B., 15
Wesleyan, 122, 161
Wundt, W., 15